C++
Explorer's Handbook

A Beginner's Guide to Mastery

By

Mike Zephalon

About Author

Mike Zephalon was born in Toronto, Canada, and developed a passion for technology and programming at an early age. His journey into the world of coding began when he was just a teenager, experimenting with simple scripts and exploring the vast possibilities of web development. Mike pursued his studies at the University of Toronto, where he majored in Computer Science. During his time at university, he became deeply interested in JavaScript, captivated by its versatility and power in building dynamic, interactive web applications.

Over the years, Mike has worked with several tech startups and companies, where he honed his skills as a front-end developer. His dedication to mastering JavaScript and its frameworks has made him a respected voice in the developer community. Through his books and tutorials, Mike aims to empower new and experienced developers alike, helping them unlock the full potential of JavaScript in their projects.

Table of Contents

1. Introduction to C++

1.1 What is C++?

C++ is a high-level, general-purpose programming language that was developed by Bjarne Stroustrup in 1985 as an extension of the C programming language. It is widely used for system/software development, game development, real-time simulations, and embedded systems. C++ is known for its efficiency, flexibility, and performance, making it a popular choice for developers who need to write high-performance applications.

C++ supports multiple programming paradigms, including procedural, object-oriented, and generic programming. This versatility allows developers to choose the best approach for their specific needs. Additionally, C++ is a compiled language, meaning that the source code is translated into machine code by a compiler before execution, which results in highly optimized and fast-running programs.

1.2 Evolution of C++

Since its inception, C++ has undergone several revisions, with each new standard introducing features that improve the language's usability, performance, and safety. The most significant updates include:

- **C++98**: The first standardized version of C++, which established the core features of the language.

- **C++11**: A major update that introduced features like auto type deduction, range-based for loops, and smart pointers.

- **C++14**: A minor update that refined and extended the features introduced in C++11.

- **C++17**: Introduced features like structured bindings, std::optional, and parallel algorithms.

- **C++20**: A significant update that added concepts, ranges, coroutines, and modules, among other features.

- **C++23**: The latest standard as of 2025, which continues to refine and expand the language with features like std::expected, std::generator, and improved support for compile-time programming.

1.3 Why Learn C++ in 2025?

In 2025, C++ remains a relevant and powerful programming language for several reasons:

- **Performance**: C++ allows for fine-grained control over system resources, making it ideal for performance-critical applications.

- **Portability**: C++ code can be compiled and run on a wide range of platforms, from embedded systems to supercomputers.

- **Community and Ecosystem**: C++ has a large and active community, with a wealth of libraries, frameworks, and tools available to developers.

- **Legacy Code**: Many existing systems and applications are written in C++, and maintaining or extending these systems requires knowledge of the language.

- **Modern Features**: With the continuous evolution of the language, C++ has adopted modern programming practices that make it easier to write safe, efficient, and maintainable code.

2. Setting Up the Development Environment

2.1 Choosing a Compiler

To write and run C++ programs, you need a compiler that translates your source code into machine code. Some popular C++ compilers in 2025 include:

- **GCC (GNU Compiler Collection)**: A widely used open-source compiler that supports multiple programming languages, including C++.

- **Clang**: A compiler that is part of the LLVM project, known for its excellent diagnostics and support for modern C++ standards.

- **Microsoft Visual C++ (MSVC)**: The C++ compiler provided by Microsoft as part of the Visual Studio IDE, commonly used for Windows development.

2.2 Integrated Development Environments (IDEs)

An IDE provides a comprehensive environment for writing, debugging, and testing code. Some popular IDEs for C++ development in 2025 include:

- **Visual Studio**: A powerful IDE from Microsoft that supports C++ development with features like IntelliSense, debugging, and profiling.

- **CLion**: A cross-platform IDE from JetBrains that offers advanced code analysis, refactoring, and debugging tools.

- **Code::Blocks**: An open-source, cross-platform IDE that is lightweight and easy to use, making it a good choice for beginners.

2.3 Installing the Tools

To get started with C++ programming, you need to install a compiler and an IDE. Here are the general steps:

1. **Install a Compiler**: Download and install a C++ compiler like GCC, Clang, or MSVC. On Linux, you can install GCC using your distribution's package manager (e.g., sudo apt-get install g++ on Ubuntu). On Windows, you can install MSVC as part of Visual Studio.

2. **Install an IDE**: Download and install an IDE like Visual Studio, CLion, or Code::Blocks. Follow the installation instructions provided by the IDE's website.

3. **Configure the IDE**: Set up the IDE to use the installed compiler. This usually involves specifying the path to the compiler in the IDE's settings.

3. Writing Your First C++ Program

3.1 Understanding the Structure of a C++ Program

A basic C++ program consists of the following components:

- **Preprocessor Directives**: These are instructions to the compiler that are processed before the actual compilation begins. The most common directive is #include, which is used to include header files.

- **Main Function**: Every C++ program must have a main function, which serves as the entry point of the program. The execution of the program starts from the main function.

- **Statements and Expressions**: These are the instructions that perform operations and control the flow of the program.

- **Comments**: Comments are used to annotate the code and are ignored by the compiler. They help make the code more readable and understandable.

3.2 Writing a Simple C++ Program

Let's write a simple C++ program that prints "Hello, World!" to the console.

```cpp
#include <iostream>  // Preprocessor directive to include the iostream library
int main() {
    // Print "Hello, World!" to the console
    std::cout << "Hello, World!" << std::endl;

    return 0;  // Indicate that the program ended successfully
}
```

3.3 Compiling and Running the Program

To compile and run the program, follow these steps:

1. **Save the Program**: Save the code in a file with a .cpp extension, such as hello.cpp.

2. **Compile the Program**: Open a terminal or command prompt and navigate to the directory where the file is saved. Use the compiler to compile the program. For example, if you're using GCC, you can compile the program with the following command:

This command tells the compiler to compile hello.cpp and create an executable file named hello.

3. **Run the Program**: After compiling, you can run the program by executing the generated executable. On Linux or macOS, you can run the program with:

On Windows, you can run the program by typing:
hello.exe

The program should output:
Hello, World!

3.4 Understanding the Code

Let's break down the code to understand each part:

- #include <iostream>: This line includes the iostream library, which provides input and output functionality. The std::cout and std::endl used in the program are part of this library.

- int main() { ... }: This is the main function where the execution of the program begins. The int before main indicates that the function returns an integer value. The return 0; statement at the end of the function indicates that the program has completed successfully.

- std::cout << "Hello, World!" << std::endl;: This line prints the text "Hello, World!" to the console. std::cout is the standard output stream, and << is the insertion operator used to send data to the output stream. std::endl is used to insert a newline character and flush the output buffer.

4. Basic Concepts in C++

4.1 Variables and Data Types

Variables are used to store data in a program. In C++, you must declare a variable with a specific data type before you can use it. Some common data types in C++ include:

- **int**: Used to store integer values.
- **float**: Used to store single-precision floating-point numbers.
- **double**: Used to store double-precision floating-point numbers.
- **char**: Used to store single characters.

- **bool**: Used to store boolean values (true or false).

Here's an example of declaring and using variables:

```cpp
#include <iostream>
int main() {
    int age = 25;  // Integer variable
    float height = 5.9f;  // Floating-point variable
    char grade = 'A';  // Character variable
    bool isStudent = true;  // Boolean variable

    std::cout << "Age: " << age << std::endl;
    std::cout << "Height: " << height << std::endl;
    std::cout << "Grade: " << grade << std::endl;
    std::cout << "Is Student: " << isStudent << std::endl;

    return 0;
}
```

4.2 Control Structures

Control structures allow you to control the flow of execution in a program. The most common control structures in C++ are:

- **if-else**: Used to make decisions based on conditions.
- **switch**: Used to select one of many code blocks to be executed.
- **for loop**: Used to iterate over a range of values.
- **while loop**: Used to repeat a block of code as long as a condition is true.
- **do-while loop**: Similar to the while loop, but the condition is evaluated after the loop body.

Here's an example of using control structures:

```cpp
#include <iostream>
int main() {
    int number = 10;

    // if-else statement
    if (number > 0) {
        std::cout << "Number is positive." << std::endl;
    } else if (number < 0) {
        std::cout << "Number is negative." << std::endl;
    } else {
        std::cout << "Number is zero." << std::endl;
    }

    // for loop
```

```
for (int i = 0; i < 5; i++) {
    std::cout << "i = " << i << std::endl;
}

// while loop
int count = 0;
while (count < 3) {
    std::cout << "Count = " << count << std::endl;
    count++;
}

return 0;
}
```

4.3 Functions

Functions are blocks of code that perform a specific task. They help in organizing code, making it more modular and reusable. In C++, a function is defined with a return type, a name, a parameter list, and a body.

Here's an example of defining and using a function:

```
#include <iostream>
// Function to add two numbers
int add(int a, int b) {
    return a + b;
}

int main() {
    int result = add(5, 3);  // Call the add function
    std::cout << "Result: " << result << std::endl;

    return 0;
}
```

4.4 Arrays and Strings

Arrays are used to store multiple values of the same type in a single variable. Strings are sequences of characters, and in C++, they can be represented using the std::string class.

Here's an example of using arrays and strings:

```
#include <iostream>
#include <string>

int main() {
```

```cpp
    // Array of integers
    int numbers[5] = {1, 2, 3, 4, 5};

    // Accessing array elements
    for (int i = 0; i < 5; i++) {
        std::cout << "numbers[" << i << "] = " << numbers[i] << std::endl;
    }

    // String
    std::string name = "John Doe";
    std::cout << "Name: " << name << std::endl;

    return 0;
}
```

4.5 Pointers and References

Pointers and references are powerful features in C++ that allow you to work with memory addresses. A pointer is a variable that stores the memory address of another variable, while a reference is an alias for an existing variable.

Here's an example of using pointers and references:

```cpp
#include <iostream>
int main() {
    int number = 42;

    // Pointer
    int* ptr = &number;  // ptr stores the address of number
    std::cout << "Value of number: " << number << std::endl;
    std::cout << "Address of number: " << ptr << std::endl;
    std::cout << "Value at address stored in ptr: " << *ptr << std::endl;

    // Reference
    int& ref = number;  // ref is a reference to number
    ref = 100;  // Changing ref changes number
    std::cout << "New value of number: " << number << std::endl;

    return 0;
}
```

5. Object-Oriented Programming in C++

5.1 Classes and Objects

C++ supports object-oriented programming (OOP), which allows you to model real-world entities as objects. A class is a blueprint for creating objects, and it defines the properties (attributes) and behaviors (methods) that the objects will have.

Here's an example of defining a class and creating objects:

```cpp
#include <iostream>
#include <string>

// Define a class
class Person {
public:
    // Attributes
    std::string name;
    int age;

    // Method
    void introduce() {
        std::cout << "Hello, my name is " << name << " and I am " << age << " years old." <<
std::endl;
    }
};

int main() {
    // Create an object of the Person class
    Person person1;
    person1.name = "Alice";
    person1.age = 30;

    // Call the introduce method
    person1.introduce();

    return 0;
}
```

5.2 Encapsulation

Encapsulation is the concept of bundling data (attributes) and methods (functions) that operate on the data into a single unit, or class. It also involves restricting access to some of the object's components, which is achieved using access specifiers like private, protected, and public.

Here's an example of encapsulation:

```cpp
#include <iostream>
#include <string>
```

```cpp
class Person {
private:
    std::string name;
    int age;

public:
    // Setter methods
    void setName(std::string n) {
        name = n;
    }

    void setAge(int a) {
        if (a > 0) {
            age = a;
        }
    }

    // Getter methods
    std::string getName() {
        return name;
    }

    int getAge() {
        return age;
    }

    void introduce() {
        std::cout << "Hello, my name is " << name << " and I am " << age << " years old." << std::endl;
    }
};

int main() {
    Person person1;
    person1.setName("Bob");
    person1.setAge(25);

    std::cout << "Name: " << person1.getName() << std::endl;
    std::cout << "Age: " << person1.getAge() << std::endl;
    person1.introduce();

    return 0;
}
```

5.3 Inheritance

Inheritance is a mechanism that allows a class to inherit properties and behaviors from another class. The class that inherits is called the derived class, and the class from which it inherits is called the base class.

Here's an example of inheritance:

```cpp
#include <iostream>
#include <string>

// Base class
class Animal {
public:
   std::string name;

   void eat() {
      std::cout << name << " is eating." << std::endl;
   }
};

// Derived class
class Dog : public Animal {
public:
   void bark() {
      std::cout << name << " is barking." << std::endl;
   }
};

int main() {
   Dog dog;
   dog.name = "Buddy";
   dog.eat();
   dog.bark();

   return 0;
}
```

5.4 Polymorphism

Polymorphism allows objects of different classes to be treated as objects of a common base class. It is typically achieved through function overriding and virtual functions.

Here's an example of polymorphism:

```cpp
#include <iostream>
#include <string>
```

```cpp
// Base class
class Animal {
public:
    virtual void makeSound() {
        std::cout << "Animal sound" << std::endl;
    }
};

// Derived class
class Dog : public Animal {
public:
    void makeSound() override {
        std::cout << "Woof!" << std::endl;
    }
};

// Derived class
class Cat : public Animal {
public:
    void makeSound() override {
        std::cout << "Meow!" << std::endl;
    }
};

int main() {
    Animal* animal1 = new Dog();
    Animal* animal2 = new Cat();

    animal1->makeSound();  // Output: Woof!
    animal2->makeSound();  // Output: Meow!

    delete animal1;
    delete animal2;

    return 0;
}
```

6. Advanced Topics in C++

6.1 Templates

Templates allow you to write generic and reusable code. They enable you to define functions and classes that operate with any data type.

Here's an example of a function template:

```cpp
#include <iostream>
// Function template
template <typename T>
T add(T a, T b) {
    return a + b;
}

int main() {
    std::cout << "Sum of integers: " << add(5, 3) << std::endl;
    std::cout << "Sum of doubles: " << add(3.5, 2.7) << std::endl;

    return 0;
}
```

6.2 Standard Template Library (STL)

The STL is a powerful library in C++ that provides a collection of template classes and functions, including containers (like vectors, lists, and maps), algorithms (like sorting and searching), and iterators.

Here's an example of using the STL:

```cpp
#include <iostream>
#include <vector>
#include <algorithm>

int main() {
    std::vector<int> numbers = {5, 2, 9, 1, 5, 6};

    // Sort the vector
    std::sort(numbers.begin(), numbers.end());

    // Print the sorted vector
    for (int num : numbers) {
        std::cout << num << " ";
    }
    std::cout << std::endl;

    return 0;
}
```

6.3 Exception Handling

Exception handling allows you to handle runtime errors gracefully. In C++, exceptions are handled using try, catch, and throw blocks.

Here's an example of exception handling:

```cpp
#include <iostream>
int divide(int a, int b) {
    if (b == 0) {
        throw "Division by zero!";
    }
    return a / b;
}

int main() {
    try {
        int result = divide(10, 0);
        std::cout << "Result: " << result << std::endl;
    } catch (const char* msg) {
        std::cerr << "Error: " << msg << std::endl;
    }

    return 0;
}
```

6.4 Lambda Expressions

Lambda expressions allow you to define anonymous functions inline. They are useful for short, throwaway functions that are used only once.

Here's an example of a lambda expression:

```cpp
#include <iostream>
#include <vector>
#include <algorithm>

int main() {
    std::vector<int> numbers = {1, 2, 3, 4, 5};

    // Use a lambda expression to print each element
    std::for_each(numbers.begin(), numbers.end(), [](int n) {
        std::cout << n << " ";
    });
    std::cout << std::endl;

    return 0;
}
```

In the following chapter, we will discuss about the evolution of computer programming languages and their evolution from machine languages.

As we know C++ is a high-level language. We'll discuss the concepts of C++, in this chapter. Moreover, you will be able to write your first program, after going through this chapter, i.e. "Hello World". Furthermore, you'll understand the concepts of Constants, Variables, Data types and some of the operators that may help you writing and understanding a C++ program.

Background of C++

C++ is considered a properly structured programming language, that's why this is so popular. C++, as you know, is a high-level language because it allows a programmer to concentrate on the problem at his hand, without worrying about the system that the program may be using. There are many languages who claim to be system or machine independent but C++ is one of the best among them.

Like many other languages, C++ is basically derived from ALGOL, which was the first language to have a structure. ALGOL was developed in the early 1960s and it made a path for structured programming and its concepts. Very first work in ALGOL was done by two scientists name as Guiseppe Jacopini and Corrado Bohm. Both of them published research in 1960 which defined a thorough idea of structured programming.

In 1967, a computer scientist named as Martin Richards designed a language designed a programming language; he named Basic Combined Programming Language aka. BCPL. In 1970, Ken Thompson developed a language, known as "B". Following him, Dennis Ritchie, in 1972, developed the concept of language "C".

Following all the concepts from the languages, ALGOL, BCPL, B and C, Bjarne Stroustrup, developed C++ in mid 1980s.

C++ Programming

Now, when you know about the background of C++, i guess, you'll be eager to write your first program. This section will let you know the basic parts of a C++ program, so that you'll be able to write your very first program.

How to write a C++ program

First of all, we need to understand, the "Global Declaration". Your program is considered a little world; a world of computer universe. So, we may start our program with global declaration.

Secondly, only one function, in your program must be named as "main". Main is the starting of the basic program, after global declaration. Main can have two kinds of code;

Declaration

Declaration is considered the data that you may use to justify or write your program or function. If you declare something in a function, it'll be known as "Local Declaration". We call them local declarations because they are read, only be the function itself.

Statements

Statements are some commands to the machine that is using the program. Statements cause the machine to perform the actions, such as adding or subtracting numbers, multiply them, taking their average etc.

Simple Program

We know that C++ allow us to make declarations and statements at the same time, but, every time, we should write a program, which should be well organized so that any other programmer or even the machine could understand it fast. This is the reason; we follow the language C's concepts of organization. The concept states that one should perform declaration first and statements second. Moreover, most of the times, one should use comments for the identification of the sections; Declarations and Statements.

A C++ program is a mixture of two components main (Main) and fun (function). In other words, function is called or used by main. Usually, we write the code for the "main", first. After that, we'll code the function and sub functions, in their order.

Moving forward, there is another concept; concept of preprocessor directives or precompiler directives. These are some statements which give instructions to a compiler or processor to execute the program in a unique pattern.

A statement which is globally used as a preprocessor directive is, "include". This statement allows the compiler to extract some data from global libraries, known as header files. Without these header files or libraries, you will not be able to write even a single program, because it'll be so complex to write the commands even for your input or output. Even, you will need an "include" command, to write your very first program. This will be used to instruct C++ that you will be in need for the input and output libraries, so that you may print your desired data to the console screen.

Hello World

Your first C++ program is going to be very straightforward. It will include just one precompiler directive and no global or local declaration would be made. It will just display a greeting to the user on a console screen. Because this program is not so complex, it will contain only two statements; first, to display a greeting, the second one would be used to terminate our program.

We will write the precompiler directive in the very beginning of our program. Precompiler directives must start with a number sign i.e. "#", in any C++ program.

The syntax for our precompile directive would be:

#include <iostream.h>

In this precompiler directive, we may write # first and there should be no space between "#" and "include". Statement "include" will include the concerned library in your program, which will be mentioned in the pointed brackets "<>".

In the following statement, "iostream" is a short form for "input output stream" and ".h" is to represent header file.

Moreover, we'll use another statement in our program which is:

using namespace std;

For understanding this statement, we have to consider a classroom with a boy and a girl; sharing the same name and class, but having different functions. So, when you will call their name, both will respond. The very same confusion can be a part of programming, as if there is a function named as "poi()" and in some other library there is another function named as "poi()", your compiler would not be able to identify your desired function. To overcome this difficulty, we usually use this statement.

Moving forward, our program's executable part would be starting with a function header, such as:
Int main (void)

For this statement, we have to understand that the "int" states that this specific function will send back an integer value to the machine or operating system.In the concerned statement, our function's name is "main" and it has no specific parameters, as we have voided the parameter list with "(void)".

Now, there are two more statements, with first, we will be able to print our desired data. And with the second, we will be able to terminate the program.
cout << "Hello world";

This statement is used to display or print the desired data, in this case "Hello World". This statement uses an operator "<<", this operator allows us to print or display data in our console. This statement contains inverted commas "". Whatever, you will be writing in these commas, will be displayed in your console.

Finally, the program will be terminated with a statement:
return 0;

This statement will simply end the program and will hand over the control to operating system again. Now, if you need to write your program, you'll need a compiler first. There are many compilers available, online and offline, to execute your code in C++. If you need to compile your code offline Turbo C++ and Dev C++ are highly recommended and if you need to compile your code online, you may search for any online C++ compiler.

Typically, the first program is known as "Hello World", but we'll change the odds. We will be writing our first program as "Hello to the world of C++!"

So, if you have a compiler now, you are all set to write your very first program. We'll start with header files and then the body of program and we will terminate it with our termination statement.

So, your first program should look something like this:

```
#include <iostream> using
namespace std;

int main()
{ cout << "Hello to the world of C++!"; return 0;
   }
```

When you'll execute this program, there will be a console screen popping up with the text:
Hello to the world of C++!

We've already written our first program so now; we will be discussing some more important concepts of programming in C++.

Constants

The concept of constants in programming is very similar to the concept of constant in Mathematics. Constants are the values or data which remains unchanged during the execution of a code or program.

In this section, we will define different types of constants in programming.

Integer Constants

First thing first, integers are stored in binary formation. You'll code integers, as you use them in your daily routine, for example you will code eight simply as 8.

The following table will show you different integers, their values in programming and their data types

Value in programming	Number	Data Type
98	+98	int
-865	-865	int
-68495L	-68495	long int
984325LU	984325	unsigned long int

Character Constants

Whenever, you'll find an integer, closed between two single apostrophes, this would be character constant.

Moreover, there is a chance that you'll find a backslash "\" between those apostrophes.

For most machines, ASCII character set is used, i.e.

ASCII Characters	Symbolic Display
Null character	"\0"
newline	'\n'
horizontal tab	'\t'
alert (bell)	'\a'
backspace	'\b'
form feed	'\f'
vertical tab	'\v'
single quote	'\''
backslash	'\\'
carriage return	'\r'

Float Constants

Float constants are stored as two parts in memory as float constants are numbers having decimal parts. The first part, they obtain in memory is significand and the second is exponent.

Float constant's default type is "double". You must write a code to specify your desired data type, i.e. "float" or "long double". We may remember that "f" or "F" is used to represent float and "l" or "L" is used to represent long double.

In the following table, some of the examples of float, double and long double are shown:

Value in Programming	Number	Data Type
.0	0.00	double
0.	0.00	double

3.0	3.0	double
5.6534	5.6534	double
-3.0f	-3.0	float
5.6534785674L	5.6534785674	long double

Boolean Constants

These constants are predefined keywords and they cannot be defined or declared by the programmer. It has two predefined constants, "True" and "False". In programming, we represent this kind of constant as "bool".

Programming Constants

In this part, we are going to understand different programming constants, and ways to write and define constants in a C++ program. Usually, there are three types of programming constants.

Defined Constants

A way to define a constant in a C++ program is to use a precompiler statement "define". Like every other precompiler directive, it starts with a "#". For example, a traditional precompiler directive for "define" would be:

#define TABLE_SIZE 150

Define directives are usually placed in the beginning of the program, so that anyone reading your program, can find them easily.

Memory Constants

Another way to code constants is by using a memory constant. These constants use a C++ type qualifier to remember that the specified data cannot be changed.

C++ programming provides us with an ability to define named constants. We just have to add type qualifier in our code, before constant. For example:

<u>Code</u>:
```
#include <iostream>
using namespace std;
#define val 50
#define floatVal 9.7
#define charVal 'K' int
main()
```

```
{
cout << "Integer Constant in our code: " << val << "\n"; cout <<
"Floating point Constant in our code: " << floatVal << "\n"; cout <<
"Character Constant in our code: "<< charVal << "\n" ; return 0;
                    }
```

Output:

In the case of this code, a console screen will pop up with the output:

Integer Constant in our code: 50

Floating point Constant in our code: 9.7

Character Constant in our code: K

Literal Constants

Literal constant is a constant which is unnamed and used to specify your desired data. As we know constant cannot be changed so we just have to code its data value in a statement.

Literal constant is the most common form of constant. Here is a table to show different kind of literal constants.

Values	Type
'C'	Character Literal
7	Numeric Literal 7
C + 8	Another Numeric Literal (8)
5.6534	Float Literal
Hello	String Literal

Data Type

A data type defines a set of operations and values that have the ability to apply on the concerned values. For example, a switch of a light bulb can be compared to a computer system as it has two different values; True as On, and False as off. Since the bulb switch contain just these two values, we can consider its size as two. There are just two operations that can be done with a bulb switch:

- We can turn it On
- We can turn it Off

In a C++ program, functions have their own unique types. Usually, a function's type is specified by the data it returns. C++ usually contains five standard data types:

- void (Void)
- Int (Integer)
- char (Character)
- bool (Boolean)
- float (Floating Point)

void (Void)

In C++, void has no operations or no functions. In simpler words, both the set of operations and the set of values are empty. It is a very useful data type in programming although it seems unusual. Typically, it is a generic data type that can represent any other standard data types.

int (Integer)

In C++, integer is a number without having a fraction part, we usually call it an integral number. Our concerned language supports three types of integers as its data types:

- short (Short Integer)
- Int (Integer)
- long (Long Integer)

C++ allows us to use an operator "size of", that may tell us the size of our data types. Whenever, we are coding in C++, we should keep this statement in mind:

sizeof (long int) => sizeof (int) => sizeof (short int)

char (Character)

We usually think of characters as the alphabet or numbers, but programming has its another definition. By this definition a character can be any number, value or symbol that can be represented by the machine or computer's alphabets.

Moreover, we have to remember that C++ usually treat characters as an integer because it uses memory as an integer i.e. between 0 to 255.

bool (Boolean - logical data in C++)

Boolean data types have two functions, True and False. Traditionally, a zero is considered as false and any non-zero part is considered as true.

float (Floating Point)

Float data type or floating point is usually a data type having a fractional part. When coding in float data type, we should always consider this statement:

sizeof (long double) => sizeof (double) => size of (float)

We may think that the data type, float and data type, integer are the same, but there are many differences as the "float" is always declared in a C++ program.

Data Types	Implementations
Void	void
Integer	Unsigned short int, unsigned int, unsigned long int, short int, int, long int
Character	char
Floating point	float, double, long double
Boolean	bool

Variables

Variable, in C++ are memory locations, having different data types, such as character or integers. Variables are manipulatable and changeable because the use a set of different operations.

Variable Initialization

By using an initializer, we can declare and initialize a variable at the very same time. Basically, initializer set up the variable's very first value. Usually, an identifier is followed by a "=" sign to first initialize and then define a variable's initial value, when the function starts. Simple syntax of initialization is:

Int count = 0

Moving forward, we have to keep in mind that whenever a variable is defined, it is not automatically initialized. The programmer should be the one to initialize any variable, when the program starts.

Variable Declaration

Every variable, in a program, must be defined and declared. In C++, we use Definition to create different objects and we use Declaration to name those objects. Whenever a programmer creates a variable, definition reserves memory for it and definition assigns it a symbolic name. Variables, when assigned, hold data that is required by the program to fulfil its task.

In C++, multiple variables of the similar types can be declared in a single statement. Many programmers use this technique but we won't be recommending this as this is not a good programming technique. This reduces the efficiency of program and the efficiency for the execution process of compiler.

How to write a C++ program

C++ have three unique features that sets it apart from most of the programming languages:

- Expressions
- Pointers
- Classes

In this chapter we will discuss the very first of these concepts, i.e. Expressions. We have already used expressions in Mathematics, but the way to use expressions is unique to "C++" and its precursor "C". The concept of expressions is tied to the concept of precedence, operators, statements and associativity.

Expressions

Expression, in a C++ program, is a sequence of operators and operands that eventually reduces to a single value. For example, 10 * 2.

In the following example, the expression reduces to 20. In C++, final value can be of any data type, other than void.

Operators

Operators are the language specific syntactical tokens that require some action to be performed. Many operators are derived from the concepts of Mathematics. For example, "Sign of Multiplication (*)" is an operator used in C++. It multiplies two numbers.

Every programming language has unique operators to perform unique operations.

Operand

For any defined operator, there may be one or more than one operand. Operand has to receive any operator's action. In above example, (10 * 2), Multiplier and Multiplicand are the operands of Multiplication.

There are no limit of operand sets and operators to form an expression. The only rule is that when program will evaluate the expression, the answer should be a single value, that may represent the expression.

Primary Expressions in a C++ Program

In C++, most initiatory kind of expressions are Primary Expressions. It contains just one operand and no operator. We have to remember that operand can be a name, parenthetical expression or a constant in Primary Expression.

Names

It is an identifier which defines a function, a variable or any other object in C++.

Constants

Another type of primary expressions are Constants. Constants are the pre recognized or declared data whose value is unchangeable during the compilation and execution of a program.

Parenthetical Expressions

Last kid of primary expression is parenthetical expression. It is a primary expression because its value is always reducible to a single value. So, the complex expression in a parenthetical expression may be bound to make it a primary expression.

Binary Expressions in C++

Binary expressions in C++ are typically formed by operand-operator-operand relation. These expressions are the most common. Any two numbers subtracted, multiplied, divider or added are written with the operator between two operands. Or may be in algebraic expressions. Most common types or binary expressions are:

Additive Expressions

First type of binary expressions is additive expressions. In this kind of expression, second operand is added to the first operand or the second operand is subtracted from the first operand. It depends upon the operator, that is used. These kinds of expressions use parallel algebraic notations for example, a + 18 and b - 90. Here are two sample programs to show such kind of expressions:

For Addition:

```
#include <iostream>
using namespace std;
int main()
{
// Declaration of integers int
    firstinteger, secondinteger, sum;
```

```cpp
// Printing input and output
    commands   cout << "Enter any
    integer: "; cin >> firstinteger;
    cout << "Enter another integer: ";
    cin >> secondinteger;
// Sum of two integers is stored in the variable
    "sum" sum = firstinteger + secondinteger;
// Printing sum of first and second integer cout << firstinteger
    << " + " <<  secondinteger << " = " << sum;    return 0;
}
```

For Subtraction:

```cpp
#include <iostream>
using namespace std; int
main()
{
// Declaration of integers int
    firstinteger, secondinteger, sub;
// Printing input and output
    commands cout << "Enter any
    integer: "; cin >> firstinteger;
    cout << "Enter another integer: ";
    cin >> secondinteger;
// Subtraction of second integer from first is stored in the variable
    "sub" sub = firstinteger - secondinteger;
// Printing the subtraction  of second integer from first integer
    cout << firstinteger << " - " <<  secondinteger << " = " <<
    sub;    return 0;
}
```

Multiplicative Expressions

This expression is known as multiplicative expression because of its first operator, i.e. Multiplication. We consider it on top, in binary expressions. Its value is calculated as the product of two operands, i.e. $5 * 2 = 10$.

In such expressions, division is a little more complex. In division if both operands are integers, the result would be the integral value of quotient. It would be expressed as an integer, i.e. $5 / 2 = 2$. Here are two sample programs to show such kind of expressions:

For Multiplication:

```cpp
#include <iostream>
using namespace std; int
main()
```

```cpp
{
// Declaration of integers int
    firstinteger, secondinteger, mul;
// Printing input and output
    commands   cout << "Enter any
    integer: "; cin >> firstinteger;
    cout << "Enter another integer: ";
    cin >> secondinteger;
// Product of two integers is stored in the variable
    "mul" mul = firstinteger * secondinteger;
// Printing sum of first and second integer cout << firstinteger
    << " * " <<  secondinteger << " = " << mul;    return 0;
}
```

For Division:

```cpp
#include <iostream>
using namespace std;
int main()
{
// Declaration of integers int
    firstinteger, secondinteger, div;
// Printing input and output
    commands cout << "Enter any
    integer: "; cin >> firstinteger;
    cout << "Enter another integer: ";
    cin >> secondinteger;
// Integral value of quotient in division of first integer and second integer is stored in the
    variable "div" div = firstinteger / secondinteger;
// Printing the subtraction  of second integer from first intege r
    cout << firstinteger << " / " <<  secondinteger << " = " <<
    div;    return 0;

}
```

Assignment Expressions

Assignment expression is an expression which usually evaluates the operands on the right side of an equation and automatically places its value to the variable on the left side. There are two types of assignment expressions:

Simple Assignment

Simple assignment is a form of assignment expressions which is present in the form of algebraic expressions such as $x = 60$, $y = n + 20$, $z = x + y$.

The thing to remember, in a simple assignment, is that the left operand should be a single variable. In such expressions, the value of the right side is evaluated and it becomes the value of the entire expression. In the following table there are some examples of simple assignment and how its value is calculated.

Expression	Value of "n"	Value of "m"	Value of Expression	Result of Expression
n = m -1	20	15	14	**14**
n = m + 20	20	15	35	**35**
n = m * 0	20	15	0	**0**

Compound Assignment

Compound assignment is considered as a shorthand writing for the simple assignment. In this case, left operand should be repeated in the right side.

To evaluate a compound assignment, machine first changes it into simple assignment and then performs the operations to identify the final result of the expression.

In the following table, it is shown that how a compound assignment is converted into a simple assignment:

Compound Assignment	Simple Assignment
n %= m	n = n % m
n /= m	n = n / m
n *= m	n = n * m
n -= m	n = n - m
n += m	n = n + m

In the following table there are some examples of compound assignment and how its value is calculated.

Expression	Value of "n"	Value of "m"	Calculation of Expression	Result of Expression

n %= m	20	15	n=(20/100)* 15	**3**
n /= m	20	15	n = 20 / 15	**1.33**
n *= m	20	15	n = 20 * 15	**300**
n -= m	20	15	n = 20 - 15	**5**
n += m	20	15	N = 20 + 15	**35**

In C++, we use compound assignments as:

For Addition:

```
#include<iostream>
using namespace std; int
main()
{ int n = 5, m = 2;
//Compound assignment expression n += m means n =
   n + m n += m; cout << n << endl; return 0;
}
```

For Subtraction:

```
#include<iostream>
using namespace std; int
main()
{ int n = 5, m = 2;
//Compound assignment expression n -= m means n
   = n - m n -= m; cout << n << endl; return 0;
}
```

For Multiplication:

```
#include<iostream>
using namespace std; int
main()
{ int n = 5, m = 2;
//Compound assignment expression n *= m means n =
   n * m n *= m; cout << n << endl; return 0;
}
```

For Division:

```
#include<iostream>
using namespace std; int
main()
{ int n = 5, m = 2;
//Compound assignment expression n /= m means n
  = n / m n /= m; cout << n << endl; return 0;
}
```

Postfix Expressions

In C++, postfix expressions operate just after the primary expression, followed by an operator.

Function call

Function call is an elementary component in structured programming. Function call is basically a postfix expression. In such expressions, operand is the function's name and it follows its operator. We have to remember that function call always has some value so it can be used in other expressions, except from void.

Postfix Increment and Postfix Decrement

Both postfix increment (n++) and postfix decrement are postfix operators. Usually every program, in C++ require the value 1 to be added in its variable. In most of the programming languages, this can be done in binary expressions.

C++, on the other hand provides its programmer an ability to code this in both binary as well as unary expressions.

In postfix increment, the variable increases its value by 1. So, "n++" is calculated as the variable "n" being increased by "1". This expression is similar as assignment expression:

n++ means that n = n + 1

On the other hand, postfix decrement (n--) also have values and results but in this case, machine reduces your variable (n) by 1 i.e. n - 1.

Postfix Expressions	Value of n (Before)	Evaluation of Expression	Value of n (After)
n--	20	20 - 1	**19**
n++	20	20 + 1	**21**

For Postfix Increment:

```cpp
#include <iostream>
using namespace std; int
main()
{ int n, a;
    cout <<"Enter any integer: ";
    cin >> n; a = n++;
    cout << "Post Increment Operation:"<<endl;
    // Value of a will not change
    cout << "a = " << a << endl;
    // Value of n will change after execution of
    a=n++; cout << "n = " << n;  return 0;
}
```

For Postfix decrement:

```cpp
#include <iostream>
using namespace std; int
main()
{ int n, a;
    cout <<"Enter any integer: ";
    cin >> n;  a = n--;
    cout << "Post Increment Operation:"<<endl;
    // Value of a will not change
    cout << "a = " << a << endl ;
    // Value of n will change after execution of
    a=n--; cout << "n = " << n; return 0;
}
```

Statements

In C++ any action performed by a program is caused by statements. It translates the executable commands into machine language. In C++ there are six kinds of statements:

- Expression statement
- Compound Statement
- Labeled Statement
- Iterative Statement
- Selection Statement
- Jump Statement

Most important among them is compound statement and expression statement. We will be discussing these two statements in this section.

Expression Statement

In C++, any expression can be turned into a statement, by placing a semicolon ";" after it. Whenever a C++ compiler sees a semicolon, it evaluates the value of expression, saves it in variable and discards it before compiling the next argument or statement. Just consider an expression statement to be:

n = 69

It means that the value of this expression is 69. The compiler will save the value 69 in the variable "n". After storing 69 in "n", compile will terminate this expression and will discard its value. Then compiler will continue to the next statement. However, the value of "n" will remain stored in "n".

Example Program:

```
#include <iostream> using namespace std;
int main() {

    // declaration statement
    int n = 69, m;
    cout << "Enter the value of m: ";
    cin >> m;
    // expression statement
    n = n + 1;
     // expression statement
    std::cout << "n = " << n << '\n';
    // return statement
    return 0;
}
```

A bit more complex statement in expression statements can be:
n = m = 69;

This statement consists of two statements. If we factorize this statement, we will see the expressions clearly **n = (m = 69);**

The compiler will assign the value 69 to "m" during the compilation process. After evaluating "m", the compiler will terminate and discard the value of "m" and then will start to calculate the value of "n". After the compiler's execution of this statement, 69 will stored in both the variables "m" and "n". Moving forward, consider a postfix expression as an expression statement, i.e.: **n++**

In this expression, the value of expression is 69. It is also the value of our variable "n", before it is increased by 1. When the compiler will execute the statement, the value of the variable "n" will be 70. But the value of the expression, i.e. 69, will be terminated.

Moreover, we have a special type of expression statement known as null expression. This expression statement has no value and no side effect and this can be very useful in some complex statements. Null expression is represented as a single semicolon.

;

Compound Statement

In C++, a compound statement is a coding unit consists of some statements or no statement. We may also call compound statement; a block. This statement allows many statements to execute as a single unit. While writing your first program, you used a compound statement, i.e. while writing the body of the function main. In C++, every program has a compound statement in it, which we call function body.

Every compound statement has some parts in it, i.e.

- Opening Brace "{"
- Declaration and Definition (Optional)
- Statement Section (Optional)
- Closing Brace "}"

As we mentioned that declaration, definition and statement section is optional, but one them must be present in your compound statement. Otherwise, there would be no need of a block.

As for your first program, the compound statement was:

```
{ // Opening Brace
        cout << "Hello to the world of C++!"; // Statement
        return 0; //  Return Statement
} // Closing Brace
```

We have to remember that, semicolon, after this statement is not needed. If you place a semicolon after the closing brace, compiler will consider it a syntax error.

Furthermore, we have to remember that we may declare and define a statement anywhere in a block but it makes the program so difficult to read and understand. Declaration and definition of a statement on the top of the block is considered a good programming technique. It allows a programmer to read, understand, rewrite and maintain a C++ program easily. We may also put comments "//" in a block to remember the statements. For example:

```
{ // Opening Brace // declaration statement int n = 69, m;
    cout << "Enter the value of m: ";
    cin >> m;
    // expression statement
    n = n + 1;
```

```cpp
    // expression statement
    std::cout << "n = " << n <<
    '\n';
    // return statement
    return 0;
} // Closing Brace
```

Conclusion: The Enduring Relevance of C++ in 2025 and beyond

As we conclude this comprehensive introduction to C++ and the process of writing C++ programs, it is evident that C++ remains one of the most powerful, versatile, and widely used programming languages in 2025. Its rich history, continuous evolution, and adaptability to modern programming paradigms have solidified its position as a cornerstone of software development. Whether you are a beginner taking your first steps into programming or an experienced developer looking to expand your skill set, C++ offers a robust foundation for building efficient, high-performance applications.

The Evolution of C++: A Language That Adapts to Change

C++ has come a long way since its inception in 1985. Over the decades, it has evolved from a simple extension of the C programming language to a sophisticated, feature-rich language that supports multiple programming paradigms, including procedural, object-oriented, and generic programming. The introduction of modern standards like C++11, C++14, C++17, C++20, and C++23 has brought significant improvements to the language, making it more expressive, safer, and easier to use.

In 2025, C++ continues to embrace modern programming practices, such as compile-time programming, concepts, ranges, and coroutines. These features enable developers to write cleaner, more maintainable, and more efficient code. The language's ability to adapt to the changing needs of the software industry ensures that it remains relevant in an era dominated by emerging technologies like artificial intelligence, machine learning, and quantum computing.

Why C++ Remains Relevant in 2025

1. Performance and Efficiency

C++ is renowned for its performance and efficiency. It provides fine-grained control over system resources, allowing developers to optimize their code for speed and memory usage. This level of control is particularly important in performance-critical applications, such as game development, real-time simulations, and embedded systems. In 2025, as the demand for high-performance computing continues to grow, C++ remains the language of choice for developers who need to push the boundaries of what is possible.

2. Portability and Cross-Platform Development

C++ is a highly portable language, meaning that code written in C++ can be compiled and run on a wide range of platforms, from embedded devices to supercomputers. This portability makes C++ an ideal choice for cross-platform development, where the same codebase can be used to target multiple operating systems and hardware architectures. In 2025, with the proliferation of IoT devices, autonomous vehicles, and edge computing, the ability to write portable code is more important than ever.

3. Legacy Code and Industry Adoption

Many existing systems and applications are written in C++, and maintaining or extending these systems requires knowledge of the language. Industries such as finance, aerospace, automotive, and gaming rely heavily on C++ for their critical systems. In 2025, as these industries continue to evolve, the demand for C++ developers remains strong. Learning C++ not only opens up opportunities to work on cutting-edge projects but also provides the skills needed to maintain and improve legacy systems.

4. Modern Features and Best Practices

The continuous evolution of C++ has introduced modern features that align with best practices in software development. Features like smart pointers, lambda expressions, and the Standard Template Library (STL) enable developers to write safer, more expressive, and more maintainable code. In 2025, these features, combined with the latest standards like C++23, empower developers to tackle complex problems with confidence and efficiency.

5. Community and Ecosystem

C++ boasts a large and active community of developers, educators, and enthusiasts. This vibrant community contributes to a wealth of resources, including libraries, frameworks, tools, and tutorials, that make it easier to learn and use C++. In 2025, the C++ ecosystem continues to thrive, with new libraries and tools being developed to support emerging technologies and programming paradigms. The strong community support ensures that C++ remains a dynamic and evolving language.

The Future of C++: Opportunities and Challenges

As we look to the future, C++ faces both opportunities and challenges. On the one hand, the language's performance, flexibility, and portability make it well-suited for emerging technologies like AI, machine learning, and quantum computing. On the other hand, the increasing complexity of software systems and the demand for higher levels of abstraction pose challenges for C++ developers.

Opportunities in Emerging Technologies

C++ is well-positioned to play a key role in the development of emerging technologies. For example:

- **Artificial Intelligence and Machine Learning**: C++ is often used in the development of high-performance AI and machine learning frameworks, such as TensorFlow and PyTorch. Its ability to handle large datasets and perform complex computations efficiently makes it an ideal choice for AI applications.

- **Quantum Computing**: As quantum computing continues to advance, C++ is being used to develop quantum algorithms and simulations. Its low-level control and performance characteristics make it a natural fit for this cutting-edge field.

- **Autonomous Vehicles and Robotics**: C++ is widely used in the development of autonomous vehicles and robotics systems, where real-time performance and reliability are critical. Its ability to interface with hardware and handle complex control systems makes it a preferred language in these domains.

Challenges in Modern Software Development

While C++ offers many advantages, it also presents challenges, particularly in the context of modern software development:

- **Complexity**: C++ is a complex language with a steep learning curve. The introduction of modern features and paradigms, while beneficial, can also make the language more difficult to master. Developers must invest time and effort to stay up-to-date with the latest standards and best practices.

- **Safety and Security**: C++ provides a high degree of control over system resources, but this control comes with the risk of errors like memory leaks, buffer overflows, and undefined behavior. Ensuring the safety and security of C++ code requires careful attention to detail and the use of modern tools and techniques.

- **Abstraction and Productivity**: As software systems become more complex, there is a growing demand for higher levels of abstraction and productivity. While C++ has made strides in this area with features like the STL and smart pointers, it still lags behind some other languages in terms of developer productivity and ease of use.

The Importance of Learning C++ in 2025

In light of these opportunities and challenges, learning C++ in 2025 is more important than ever. Whether you are a student, a professional developer, or an enthusiast, mastering C++ provides you with valuable skills that are applicable in a wide range of industries and domains. Here are some reasons why learning C++ is a worthwhile investment:

1. Career Opportunities

C++ developers are in high demand across various industries, including finance, gaming, aerospace, automotive, and more. By learning C++, you open up a wide range of career opportunities, from working on cutting-edge technologies to maintaining and improving legacy systems. The skills you gain from learning C++ are transferable to other programming languages, making you a versatile and valuable asset in the job market.

2. Understanding Low-Level Programming

C++ provides a deep understanding of low-level programming concepts, such as memory management, pointers, and system resources. This knowledge is invaluable for developing high-performance applications and understanding how software interacts with hardware. Even if you primarily work with higher-level languages, having a solid foundation in C++ can enhance your ability to write efficient and optimized code.

3. Building High-Performance Applications

If you are interested in building high-performance applications, such as games, real-time simulations, or embedded systems, C++ is the language of choice. Its performance characteristics and fine-grained control over system resources make it ideal for applications where speed and efficiency are critical.

4. Contributing to Open Source and Community Projects

The C++ community is vibrant and active, with many open-source projects and libraries that you can contribute to. By learning C++, you can become part of this community, collaborate with other developers, and contribute to the development of tools and libraries that benefit the broader software ecosystem.

5. Staying Ahead of the Curve

As technology continues to evolve, staying ahead of the curve is essential for any developer. By learning C++ and keeping up with the latest standards and features, you position yourself at the forefront of software development. This knowledge not only enhances your technical skills but also prepares you to tackle the challenges and opportunities of the future.

Final Thoughts: Embracing the Power of C++

C++ is a language that has stood the test of time. Its ability to adapt to changing technological landscapes, combined with its performance, flexibility, and portability, ensures that it remains a vital tool for developers in 2025 and beyond. Whether you are building high-performance applications, working on legacy systems, or exploring emerging technologies, C++ provides the foundation you need to succeed.

As you embark on your journey to learn C++, remember that mastery of the language requires patience, practice, and a willingness to embrace its complexities. The rewards, however, are well worth the effort. By mastering C++, you gain the skills and knowledge needed to tackle some of the most challenging and exciting problems in software development.

In conclusion, C++ is not just a programming language; it is a powerful tool that empowers developers to create innovative, efficient, and high-performance solutions. As we move forward into the future, the enduring relevance of C++ ensures that it will continue to play a pivotal role in shaping the world of technology. Whether you are a seasoned developer or a beginner, now is the perfect time to embrace the power of C++ and unlock your full potential as a programmer.

2. Getting Started with C++

Introduction

C++ is a powerful, high-performance programming language that has been widely used in software development for decades. It is an extension of the C programming language with added features such as object-oriented programming (OOP), templates, and exception handling. C++ is known for its efficiency, flexibility, and versatility, making it a popular choice for developing system software, game engines, embedded systems, and performance-critical applications.

This guide provides a detailed introduction to the basics of C++ programming, covering essential topics such as data types, control structures, functions, arrays, strings, pointers, and dynamic memory allocation. By the end of this guide, you will have a solid understanding of the foundational concepts of C++ programming, enabling you to write efficient and effective code.

2. Basics of C++ Programming

Data Types and Variables

In C++, data types define the type of data that a variable can hold. C++ supports a wide range of data types, including:

1. **Primitive Data Types**:

   - int: Stores integers (e.g., 5, -10).
   - float: Stores single-precision floating-point numbers (e.g., 3.14f).
   - double: Stores double-precision floating-point numbers (e.g., 3.14159).
   - char: Stores single characters (e.g., 'A', 'b').
   - bool: Stores boolean values (true or false).
   - void: Represents the absence of a type (used in functions and pointers).

2. **Derived Data Types**:

   - Arrays: A collection of elements of the same type.
   - Pointers: Variables that store memory addresses.
   - References: Aliases for existing variables.

3. **User-Defined Data Types**:

   - struct: A collection of variables of different types.
   - class: A blueprint for creating objects (used in OOP).
   - enum: A set of named integer constants.

Variables are used to store data in a program. They must be declared with a specific data type before use.

For example:

```
int age = 25;
float price = 99.99f;
char grade = 'A';
bool isPassed = true;
```

Constants and Literals

- **Constants**: Variables whose values cannot be changed after initialization. They are declared using the const keyword.

  ```
  const int MAX_SIZE = 100;
  const float PI = 3.14159f;
  ```

- **Literals**: Fixed values used in the code. Examples include integer literals (42), floating-point literals (3.14), character literals ('A'), and string literals ("Hello").

Operators and Expressions

Operators are symbols used to perform operations on variables and values. C++ supports the following types of operators:

1. **Arithmetic Operators**: +, -, *, /, %.
2. **Relational Operators**: ==, !=, >, <, >=, <=.
3. **Logical Operators**: &&, ||, !.
4. **Assignment Operators**: =, +=, -=, *=, /=.
5. **Bitwise Operators**: &, |, ^, ~, <<, >>.
6. **Ternary Operator**: ? : (conditional operator).

An **expression** is a combination of variables, literals, and operators that evaluates to a single value. For example:

```
int result = (a + b) * (c - d);
```

Type Conversions

Type conversion is the process of converting one data type to another. C++ supports two types of conversions:

1. **Implicit Conversion**: Automatically performed by the compiler.

   ```
   int num = 10;
   double value = num; // Implicit conversion from int to double
   ```

2. **Explicit Conversion**: Manually performed using casting operators.

```
double pi = 3.14159;
int intPi = (int)pi; // Explicit conversion from double to int
```

Input and Output (cin, cout, cerr, clog)

C++ uses the iostream library for input and output operations:

- cin: Used for input (e.g., cin >> variable;).
- cout: Used for output (e.g., cout << "Hello, World!";).
- cerr: Used for error messages (unbuffered).
- clog: Used for logging (buffered).

Example:

```
#include <iostream>
using namespace std;

int main() {
    int age;
    cout << "Enter your age: ";
    cin >> age;
    cout << "You are " << age << " years old." << endl;
    return 0;
}
```

3. Control Structures in C++

Conditional Statements

Conditional statements allow you to execute code based on specific conditions:

1. **if Statement**:

   ```
   if (condition) {
       // Code to execute if condition is true
   }
   ```

2. **else if Statement**:

   ```
   if (condition1) {
       // Code for condition1
   } else if (condition2) {
       // Code for condition2
   }
   ```

3. **switch Statement**:

```
switch (variable) {
    case value1:
        // Code for value1
        break;
    case value2:
        // Code for value2
        break;
    default:
        // Code if no case matches
}
```

Looping Statements

Loops are used to execute a block of code repeatedly:

1. **for Loop**:

```
for (int i = 0; i < 10; i++) {
    // Code to execute
}
```

2. **while Loop**:

```
while (condition) {
    // Code to execute
}
```

3. **do-while Loop**:

```
do {
    // Code to execute
} while (condition);
```

Break, Continue, and Goto Statements

- break: Exits a loop or switch statement.
- continue: Skips the current iteration of a loop.
- goto: Jumps to a labeled statement (not recommended due to readability issues).

4. Functions in C++

Function Declaration and Definition

A function is a block of code that performs a specific task. It consists of a declaration (prototype) and a definition:

```
// Declaration
int add(int a, int b);

// Definition
int add(int a, int b) {
    return a + b;
}
```

Function Overloading

Function overloading allows multiple functions with the same name but different parameters:

```
int add(int a, int b) {
    return a + b;
}

double add(double a, double b) {
    return a + b;
}
```

Default Arguments

Default arguments allow you to specify default values for function parameters:

```
void printMessage(string message = "Hello") {
    cout << message << endl;
}
```

Inline Functions

Inline functions are expanded in place to reduce function call overhead:

```
inline int square(int x) {
    return x * x;
}
```

Recursion

Recursion occurs when a function calls itself:

```
int factorial(int n) {
    if (n == 0) return 1;
    return n * factorial(n - 1);
```

}

5. Arrays, Strings, and Pointers

Single and Multidimensional Arrays

- **Single-dimensional Array**:

  int numbers[5] = {1, 2, 3, 4, 5};

- **Multidimensional Array**:

  int matrix[2][3] = {{1, 2, 3}, {4, 5, 6}};

Strings and Character Arrays

- **Character Array**:

  char name[] = "John";

- **String Class**:

  #include <string>
  string name = "John";

String Manipulation Functions

C++ provides functions for string manipulation in the <cstring> and <string> libraries:

```
#include <cstring>
char str1[] = "Hello";
char str2[] = "World";
strcat(str1, str2); // Concatenates str2 to str1
```

Pointers and Pointer Arithmetic

- **Pointers**:

  Variables that store memory addresses.
  int num = 10;
  int *ptr = # // ptr stores the address of num

- **Pointer Arithmetic**:

  int arr[] = {1, 2, 3};
  int *ptr = arr;

```
ptr++; // Moves to the next element in the array
```

Pointers to Arrays and Functions

- **Pointer to Array**:

```
int arr[] = {1, 2, 3};
int *ptr = arr;
```

- **Pointer to Function**:

```
void display() {
    cout << "Hello" << endl;
}
void (*funcPtr)() = display;
funcPtr(); // Calls the display function
```

Dynamic Memory Allocation (new, delete)

C++ allows dynamic memory allocation using new and delete:

```
int *ptr = new int; // Allocates memory for an integer
*ptr = 10;
delete ptr; // Frees the allocated memory
```

```
int *arr = new int[5]; // Allocates memory for an array
delete[] arr; // Frees the allocated array
```

Let's begin,

In the previous chapter, we covered what C++ is, its history, what it does, and what different types of compilers are and learned about C++'s uses and features and how to install C++ on a computer.

When we consider a C++ program, it tends to be characterized as an assortment of articles that convey utilizing conjuring each other's strategies. Let us currently momentarily investigate what a class, article, strategies, and moment factors mean.

Object: Objects have states and practices; for example, A canine has states—color, name, breed just as practices— swaying, yapping, eating. An item is an example of a class.

Class: A class can be characterized as a layout/plan that portrays the practices/expresses that object of its sort support.

Methods: A technique is essentially conducted. A class can contain numerous strategies. It is in scenarios where the rationales are composed, information is controlled, and every one of the activities is executed.

Instance Variables: Each article has its special arrangement of example factors. An article's state is made by the qualities allocated to these occasion factors.

Example:

#include <iostream> using namespace std; // main() is where program execution begins.
   int main() {
     cout << "Hello"; // prints Hello
   return 0;
   }

Compile And Execute C++ Program

How about we see how to save the document, gather and run the program. Kindly follow the means given below.

Open an editor and add the code as above.
As an example, save the record .cpp
In a command window, navigate to the directory where you saved the document.
Type 'g++ example.cpp' and press enter to arrange your code. If your code is error-free, the order brief will take you to the next line and generate an executable record called a.out.
Presently type 'a.out' to run your program.
You will want to see 'Hello' imprinted on the window.

Syntax:

$ g++ example.cpp
$ ./a.out Hello

Make sure you have g++ on your path and that you're running it in the same directory as example .cpp

Semicolons And Blocks

In C++, the semicolon is an assertion eliminator. That is, every individual assertion should be finished with a semicolon. It demonstrates the finish of one sensible substance.

For instance,

a = b; b = b + 1; add(a, b);

A block is a collection of logically related sentences enclosed in opening and closing braces.
{
  cout << "Hello"; // prints Hello
  return 0;
}

Identifiers

A C++ identifier is used to identify a variable, function, class, module, or any other user-defined entity. An identifier in C++ starts with a letter from A to Z, a to z, or an underscore (_), followed by zero or more letters, underscores, or numerals (0 to 9) and punctuation characters like @, $, and %. C++ is a case-sensitive programming language.

Keywords

The reserved terms in C++ are shown in the table below. These reserved terms may not be used as names for constants, variables, or other types of identifiers.

asm   else   new   this

auto enum operator throw bool explicit private true break export protected try case extern public typedef catch false register typeid

char   float   reinterpret_cast type name

class for return union const friend short unsigned const_cast goto signed using continue if size of virtual default inline static void delete int static_cast volatile do long struct wchar_t

double   mutable   switch   while
dynamic_cast namespace   template

Comments

Explanatory statements can be included in the C++ code as program comments. Anyone reading the source code will benefit from these remarks. All programming languages provide comments in some way.

Single-line and multi-line comments are supported in C++. The C++ compiler ignores all characters available inside each comment.

Comments in C++ begin with /* and conclude with */.

Example:

• /* This is a comment */

A comment can also start with //

• cout << "Hello World"; // prints Hello World

Data Types

You must utilize numerous variables to store diverse information while developing a program in any language. Variables are just reserved memory regions where values can be stored. This implies that when you make a variable, you set aside some memory for it.

You could want to save data of different data types, such as character, wide character, integer, floating-point, double floating point, boolean, and so on. The operating allocating memory determines what can be kept in reserved memory regarding the variable's data type.

Primitive Built-In Types

C++ provides a wide range of built-in and user-defined data types to programmers. Seven fundamental C++ data types are listed in the table below.

Type	Keyword
Boolean	bool
Character char Integer	int
Floating point	float
Double floating-point	double
Valueless	void
Wide character	wchar_t

One or more of these types of modifiers can be used to modify any of the fundamental kinds.

- signed

- unsigned

- short

- long

The table below shows the type of variable, the amount of memory needed to store the value in memory, and the highest and lowest values saved in such variables.

Type	Typical Bit Width	Typical Range
char	1 byte	−127 to 127 or 0 to 255
unsigned char	1 byte	0 to 255
signed char	1 byte	−127 to 127
int	4 bytes	−2,147,483,648 to 2,147,483,647
unsigned int	4 bytes	0 to 4,294,967,295
signed int	4 bytes	−2,147,483,648 to 2,147,483,647
short int	2 bytes	−32,768 to 32,767

Type		
unsigned short int	2 bytes	0 to 65,535
signed short int	2 bytes	−32,768 to 32,767

Type	Typical Bit Width	Typical Range
long int	8 bytes signed	−2,147,483,648 to 2,147,483,647 same
long int	8 bytes	as long int 0 to 4,294,967,295
unsigned long int	8 bytes	− (2^63) to (2^63)-1
long long int	8 bytes	0 to 18,446,744,073,709,551,615
unsigned long long int	8 bytes	
float	4 bytes double 8 bytes	
long double	12 bytes wchar_t	
	2 or 4 bytes	One wide character

Example:

```
#include <iostream> using
namespace std; int main() {
   cout << "The Size of char: " << sizeof(char) << endl;   cout << "The Size of int: " <<
sizeof(int) << endl;
   cout << "The Size of short int: " << sizeof(short int) << endl;   return 0; }
```

Output:

The Size of char: 1
The Size of int: 4
The size of short int: 2

Variable Types

A variable is a kind of named stockpiling that our projects might get to. In C++, every factor has a sort that determines the memory size and format, the scope of qualities that might be put away inside that memory, and the arrangement of tasks that can be applied to the variable.

Letters, numbers, and the highlight character would all be able to be utilized in a variable's name. Either a letter or a highlight should be utilized as the primary person. Since C++ is case-delicate, upper and lowercase characters are unique.

Sr. NoDescription and Type

1   **bool**
    True or false is stored in this variable.
2   **char**
    A   single octet is usually used (one byte). This is a type that is made up of integers.
3   **int**

The machine's most natural size of integer.

4 **float**

A floating-point value with single precision.

5 **double**

A floating-point value with double precision.

6 **void**

The absence of type is represented by this symbol.

7 **wchar_t**

A type with a large number of characters.

Variable Declaration

A variable announcement guarantees the compiler that there is just a single variable of the predefined type and name, permitting the compiler to keep gathering without knowing the entirety of the variable's subtleties. A variable statement possibly has significance when the program is incorporated; the compiler requires a simple variable definition when the program is connected.

When utilizing a few documents, a variable assertion is helpful because you might announce your variable in one of the records that will be accessible when the application is connected. You might pronounce a variable anyplace by utilizing the extern watchword.

Example:

#include <iostream> using namespace std;

// Variable declaration: extern int x, y; extern int z; extern float a;

int main () {
  // Variable definition:
  int x, y;   int z;   float a;

  // actual initialization   x = 20;   y = 10;   z = x + y;   cout << c << endl;

  return 0; }

Output:

30

Lvalues and Rvalues Are Two Distinct Sorts of Qualities

In C++, there are two sorts of articulations. A lvalue is a sort of significant worth. "Lvalue" articulations are articulations that allude to a memory area. A lvalue can be found on either the left or right half of a task.

The word rvalue alludes to information esteem that is put away in memory at a particular area. A value is an articulation that can't have a worth given to it; in this manner, it can just happen on the right half of a task, not the left.

A scope is a section of the program where variables may be declared, and there are three areas where variables can be expressed in general:

1. Local variables are found within a function or a block.

2. Formal parameters are located in the specification of function parameters.

3. Global variables are variables that exist outside of all functions.

Local Variables

Local factors are factors that are characterized inside a capacity or square. They must be used by explanations that are incorporated inside that capacity or code block.

Example:

#include <iostream> using namespace std;

int main () {   // Local variable declaration: int x, y;   int z;

  // actual initialization   x = 20;   y = 10;   z = x + y;   cout << c;

  return 0; }

Global Level Variables

Global factors are characterized toward the start of the program, outside of any capacities. The worth of the worldwide elements will stay consistent during the existence of your program.

Any capacity approaches a global variable. That is when a global variable is pronounced, it is accessible for use all through the entire program.

Example:

#include <iostream> using namespace std;

// Global variable declaration: int g;

int main () {
  // Local variable declaration: int x, y;
  // actual initialization   x = 20;   y = 10;   z = x + y;   cout << a;

  return 0; }

Initializing Local and Global Variables

When you declare a local variable, the system does not automatically initialize it; you must do it yourself. When you declare global variables like follows, the system will automatically initialize them:

Data Type	Initializer
int	0
char	'\0'
float	0
double	0
pointer	NULL

Constants

Constants, often known as literals, are fixed values that the program cannot change.

Constants are split into Integer Numerals, Floating Point Numerals, Characters, Strings, and Boolean Values and can be of any fundamental data kinds.

Integer Literals: A whole number strict is a decimal, octal, or hexadecimal steady. A prefix determines the basis or radix of a number: 0x or 0X for hexadecimal, 0 for octal, and none for decimal.

A number exacting can be given a suffix that is a combination of U and L, which stands for unsigned and lengthy. It is possible to promote or promote the postfix, and it can appear in any grouping.

Example:

- 212   // Legal

- 215u   // Legal

- 0xFeeL   // Legal

Floating-point: A number part, a decimal point, a partial part, and a type part make up a gliding point exacting. Floating-point literals can be addressed in decimal or unique structure.

You should incorporate the decimal point, the example, or both while addressing in decimal structure and the whole number piece, the partial part, or both while addressing in remarkable structure. e or E presents the marked example.

3.14159   // Legal

.e55   // Illegal: missing integer or fraction

314159E-5L   // Legal

210f   // Illegal: no decimal or exponent

510E   // Illegal: incomplete exponent

Boolean Literals

Boolean Literals are a sort of Boolean rationale.

There are two Boolean literals in C++, the two of which are essential for the standard jargon.

- True is addressed with a worth of valid.

- False is a worth that addresses False.

You ought not to take the worth of tangible equivalent to 1 and bogus equivalent to 0 into thought.

Literals of Characters

Single statements are utilized to exemplify character literals on the off chance that the exacting beginnings with the letter L (capitalized just), it is a comprehensive person strict (e.g. L'x') that ought to be saved in a variable of type wchar t. Something else, it's simply a restricted person strict (like 'x') that might be kept in a burn type variable.

Escape Sequence	Meaning
\\	\ character
\'	' character
\"	" character
\?	? character
\a	Alert or bell
\b	Backspace
\f	Form feed
\n	Newline
\r	Carriage return
\t	Horizontal tab
\v	Vertical tab
\ooo	Octal number of one to three digits
\xhh. . .	Hexadecimal number of one or more digits

Example:

```
#include <iostream> using namespace std; int main() {
   cout << "Hello\tHello\n\n";    return 0; }
```

Output:

Hello   Hello

Literals in a String

Double quotes are utilized to typify string literals. Plain characters, get away from groupings, and all-inclusive characters are among the characters in a string similar to character literals.

String literals can be utilized to partition an extended line into various lines, and whitespace can isolate them.

Example:

"Hello, ABC"

"Hello, \

ABC"

Modifier

C++ permits the char, int, and double data types to have modifiers going before them. A modifier is utilized to adjust the importance of the base sort to ensure that it all the more definitively fits the requirements of different circumstances.

The information type modifiers are recorded here

- signed
- unsigned
- long
- short

The modifiers marked, unsigned, long, and short can be applied to whole number base sorts. Furthermore, kept and unsigned can be applied to roast, and long can be applied to double.

The modifiers marked and unsigned can likewise be utilized as the prefix too long or short modifiers.

C++ permits shorthand documentation for proclaiming unsigned, short, or whole long numbers. You can just utilize the word unsigned, short, or long, without int. It consequently suggests int. For instance, the accompanying two assertions both pronounce unsigned number factors.

Qualifiers Types

Sr. NoQualifier & Meaning

1   **const**
    Objects of type const cannot be changed while your application is running.

2   **volatile**

The modifier volatile informs the compiler that a variable's value can be altered in ways not explicitly indicated in the program.

3   **restrict**
Initially, a pointer qualified by restricting is the only way to access the object it references to. Only C99 introduces the determined type qualifier.

Storage Classes

In a C++ application, a storage class specifies the scope and lifespan of variables and functions. These specifiers come before the type they're changing, and they're put before the type they're changing. The storage classes mentioned here can be utilized in C++ applications.

- **auto:** For all local variables, the auto storage class is the default storage class.

  Example:

  { int x;   auto int month; }

- **register:** The register storage class is used to create local variables that should be kept in a register rather than RAM. The variable's maximum length is equal to the register size; therefore it can't be used with the unary '&' operator.

  Example:

  {
    register int m; }

- **static:** The static storage class tells the compiler to keep a local variable alive for the duration of the program instead of creating and deleting it every time it enters and exits scope. As a result of making local variables static, their values are preserved between function calls.

  Example: static int count = 5;

- **extern:** The extern storage class is utilized to give a reference to a worldwide variable that is shared by all application documents. At the point when you use "extern", the variable can't be initialized since everything it does is allude the variable name to a formerly determined capacity address.

  At the point when you have a few documents and you pronounce a worldwide variable or capacity that will be utilized in different records also, you'll use extern to offer a reference to the predefined variable or capacity in another form. Just said, extern is utilized in one more code to characterize a worldwide variable or ability.

  Example: extern int c;
- **mutable:** The Modifiable Storage Class is a kind of capacity that can be changed.

Just class objects are influenced by the impermanent specifier, which will be tended to later in this exercise. It permits an item part to supersede the const part member. That is, a const member capacity can alter a mutable part.

Operators

A symbol that instructs the compiler to do certain mathematical or logical operations is known as an operator. C++ has a large number of built-in operators, including the following:

- Arithmetic Operators

- Relational Operators

- Logical Operators

- Bitwise Operators

- Assignment Operators

- Misc Operators

Arithmetic Operators

Operator	Description	Example
+	Adds two operands	C + D
−	Subtracts second operand from the first	C - D
*	Multiplies both operands	C * D
/	Divides numerator by de-numerator	D / C
%	Modulus Operator and the remainder of after an integer division	D % C
++	Increment operator increases integer value by one	C++
--	Decrement operator decreases integer value by one	C--

Relational Operators

Operator	Description	Example
==	Condition is set to true if the values of two operands are equal.	(C == D) is not true.

!=	Checks whether the values of two operands are equal; if they aren't, Condition returns true.	(C != D) is true.
>	Checks whether the left operand's value is greater than the right operand's value; if it is, Condition is true.	(C > D) is not true.
<	Checks whether the left operand's value is smaller than the right operand's value; if it is, Condition is true.	(C < D) is true.
>=	If the left operand's value is larger than or equal to the right operand's value, then Condition is true.	(C >= D) is not true.
<=	The Condition is true if the left operand's value is less than or equal to the right operand's value.	(C <= D) is true.

Logical Operators

Operator	Description	Example
&&	The logical AND operator is what it's called. The condition becomes true when both operands are non-zero.	(C && D) is false.
||	The logical OR operator is what it's called. Condition is true if one of the two operands is non-zero.	(C || D) is true.
!	It's known as the Logical NOT Operator. Its operand's logical state is reversed when it is used. The Logical NOT operator returns false if a condition is true.	!(C && D) is true.

Bitwise Operators

p	q	p & q	p | q	p ^ q
0	0	0	0	0
0	1	0	1	1
1	1	1	1	0
1	0	0	1	1

Assignment Operators

Operator	Description	Example
=	The assignment operator is simple. Values from the right side operands are assigned to the left side operand.	A = C + D will assign value of C + D into A
+=	Using the assignment operator AND, The right operand is added to the left operand, and the result is assigned to the left operand.	A += C is equivalent to A = A + C
-=	AND (subtract AND) (assignment) (subtract AND) (a The right operand is subtracted from the left operand, and the result is assigned to the left operand.	A -= C is equivalent to A = A - C
*=	The multiply AND assignment operator adds the right and left operands together and assigns the result to the left operand.	C *= A is equivalent to C = C * A
/=	Divide AND assignment operator: It divides the left operand with the right operand and assigns the result to the left operand.	A /= C is equivalent to A = A / C
%=	The assignment operator AND the modulus, uses two operands to calculate the modulus and assigns the result to the left operand.	A %= C is equivalent to A = A % C
<<=	Left shift AND assignment operator.	A <<= 2 is same as A = A << 2
>>=	Right shift AND assignment operator.	A >>= 2 is same as A = A >> 2
&=	Bitwise AND assignment operator.	A &= 2 is same as A = A & 2
^=	Bitwise exclusive OR and assignment operator.	A ^= 2 is same as A = A ^ 2

	Bitwise inclusive OR and assignment operator.	A |= 2 is same as A = A | 2
|=		

Misc Operators

Sr. No Operator and Description

1 sizeof

The sizeof operation returns the variable's size. For instance, sizeof(a), where an is an integer, returns 4.

2 Condition? X : Y

(?) is a conditional operator. If Condition is true, the value of X is returned; otherwise, the value of Y is returned.

3 ,

A sequence of operations is done when the comma operator is used. The value of the whole comma expression is the value of the comma-separated list's last expression.

4 . (dot) and -> (arrow)

Individual members of classes, structures, and unions are referenced using member operators.

5 Cast

Casting operations change the data type of a variable.
Int(2.2000) would, for example, yield 2.

6 &

The address of a variable is returned by the pointer operator. For example, &a; will return the variable's real address.

7 *

A variable is pointed to by the pointer operator *. For example, *var; refers to the variable var.

Operators Precedence

The request in which terms in an expression are gathered is dictated by operator precedence. This affects how a word is judged. Certain administrators take need over others: the duplication administrator, for instance, outweighs the expansion administrator.

Category	Operator	Associativity
Postfix	() [] ->. ++ - -	Left to right
Unary	+ - ! ~ ++ - - (type)* & sizeof	Right to left
Multiplicative	* / %	Left to right

Additive	+ –	Left to right
Shift	<< >>	Left to right
Relational	< <= > >=	Left to right
Equality	== !=	Left to right
Bitwise AND	&	Left to right
Bitwise XOR	^	Left to right
Bitwise OR	|	Left to right
Logical AND	&&	Left to right
Logical OR	||	Left to right
Conditional	?:	Right to left
Assignment	= += -= *= /= %=>>= <<= &= ^= |=	Right to left
Comma	,	Left to right

Loop In C++

You could find yourself in a situation where you need to run a code block many times. Statements are usually executed in the following order: the first statement in a function is executed first, followed by the second, and so on.

Programming languages offer a variety of control structures, allowing for more complicated execution paths.

Sr. No Loop Type & Description

1   **while loop**
    While a given condition is true, it repeats a statement or a set of assertions. Before performing the loop body, it checks the condition.

2   **for loop**
    The code that controls the loop variable is abbreviated by executing a sequence of instructions numerous times.

3   **do...while loop**
    It's similar to a 'while' statement, except it checks the condition at the conclusion of the loop body.

4   **nested loops**
    One or more loops can be used within another 'while,' 'for,' or 'do.. while loop.

Control Statements for Loops

Control statements in loops alter the execution sequence. All automated objects generated in scope are deleted when execution exits that scope.

Sr. NoControl Statement and Description

1   **break statement**
     The loop or switch statement is terminated, and execution is transferred to the statement immediately after the loop or switch.

2   **continue statement**
     It forces the loop to skip the rest of its body and retest its state immediately before repeating.

3   **goto statement**
     Control is passed to the labeled statement. However, using a goto statement in your program is not recommended.

Infinite Loop

A loop becomes infinite if a condition never becomes false. The for loop is commonly used for this. Because none of the three expressions that make up the 'for' loop are required, you may create an endless loop by leaving the conditional expression empty.

Example:

```
#include <iostream> using namespace std; int main () {   for( ; ; ) {
    printf("Loop will forever run. \n");
  }    return 0;
}
```

Decision-Making Statements

The software engineer should portray at most minuscule one Condition that the program will assess or test, just as an articulation or explanations that will be executed if the condition is valid. Alternatively, further proclamations will be achieved if the condition is false.

Sr. NoStatement & Description

1   if statement
 A   Boolean expression is followed by one or more statements in an if statement.

2   if...else statement
     When the Boolean expression is false, a 'if' statement might be followed by an optional 'else' statement.

3   switch statement
 A   switch statement allows a variable to be compared against a list of values for equality.

4   nested if statements

One if or else if statement can be used inside another if or else if statement.

5   nested switch statements
One 'switch' statement can be used inside another 'switch' statement.

Conditional Operator?

Syntax:

Exp1? Exp2 : Exp3;

Expressions Exp1, Exp2, and Exp3 are used. Take note of the colon's use and location. The value of a? expression is calculated in the following way: Exp1 is evaluated. If this is the case, Exp2 is evaluated, and the value of the entire? Expression is determined. If Exp1 is false, Exp3 is considered, and its value is used as the expression's value.

Example:

```
#include <iostream> using namespace std;

int main () {
   // Local variable declaration:    int a, b = 20;

   a = (b < 20)?  30 : 50;   cout << "The value of a: " << a << endl;

   return 0; }
```

Output:

The value of a: 50

Functions In C++

A function is a group of statements that cooperate to perform a task. Every C++ program has at least one function, main (), and even the simplest program can have many functions specified.

You may break your code into different functions. It's up to you how you split your code into separate functions, but logically; each function should be doing a specific purpose.

The name, return type, and parameters of a function are all specified in a function declaration. A function definition defines the body of the function.

Function Defining

```
return_type function_name( parameter
list ) {
   body of the function }
```

A function definition in C++ is made up of two parts: a function header and a function body.

- **Return Type:** As its return type, a function can return a value. The data type of the value returned by the function is specified by the return type. Some functions perform as expected but do not return a value. In this case, the return type is referred to as void.

- **Function Name:** This is the function's actual name. The function signature is made up of the function name and the argument list.

- **Parameters:** A placeholder is what a parameter is. When you call a capacity, you send a value to the contention. This value is referred to by the actual parameter or argument. The boundary list refers to the kind, request, and a number of capacity boundaries. Parameters are optional; they might be present in a capacity.

- **Function Body:** The function body is made up of a series of explanations that show how the capability works.

Example:

```
int maxi(int number1, int number2) {
  // local variable declaration
  int result;
  if (number1 > number2)      result = number1;    else
    result = number2;

  return result; }
```

Declarations of Functions

A function declaration gives the compiler the name of the function and how to invoke it.

Syntax:

return_type function_name(parameter list);

Making a Function Call

When you create a C++ function, you must define what the function must perform. You must call or invoke a function before you may utilize it.

When a program calls a function, control is passed from the calling program to the called function. A function performs a defined job and then returns program control to the main program when its return statement is executed or its function-ending closing brace is reached.

Arguments for Functions

On the off chance that a capacity will use arguments, it needs to characterize factors that will take the values of the arguments. These factors are known as the function's formal parameters.

The formal parameters are produced when the capacity is entered and erased when left, very much like any nearby factors inside the function.

Sr. NoCall Type and Description

1 **Call by Value**
   This technique replicates an argument's real value into the function's formal parameter. Changes to the parameter inside the function have no effect on the argument in this situation.

2 **Call by Pointer**
   The address of an argument is copied into the formal parameter using this approach. The address is utilized within the function to retrieve the actual parameter used in the call. This implies that changes to the parameter have an impact on the argument.

3 **Call by Reference**
   This method copies the reference of an argument into the formal parameter. Inside the function, the reference is used to access the actual argument used in the call. This means that changes made to the parameter affect the argument.

Parameters Default Values

You might give a default worth to every one of the last contentions when you characterize a capacity. If the comparing parameters are left clear while conjuring the capacity, this worth will be used.

This is accomplished by assigning value to the parameters in the capacity definition utilizing the task administrator. When the capacity is called without an incentive for that contention, the default offered some benefit is used; in any case, if a worth is determined, the default esteem is overlooked, and the passed estimation has utilized all things considered.

Example:
#include <iostream> using namespace std;

int sum(int x, int y = 10) {   int result;   result = x + y;

  return (result);
} int main () {
   // local variable declaration: int x = 50;   int y = 100;   int result;

   // calling a function to add the values.   result = sum(x, y);
   cout << "Total value :" << Result << endl;

   // calling a function again as follows.   result = sum(a);
   cout << "Total value :" << Result << endl;

```
return 0; }
```

Output:

Total value: 150
Total value: 60

Numbers In C++

We utilize crude information types like int, short, long, buoy, and twofold when working with Numbers. While talking about C++ Data Types, the number information types, their possible qualities, and number reaches were clarified.

Numbers Defining

- i = 1000;
- l = 1000000;
- f = 230.47;

Math Operations

C++ contains a large number of mathematical operations that may be applied to a variety of integers.

Sr. NoFunction and Purpose

1 **double cos(double);**
This method returns the cosine of an angle (as a double).

2 **double sin(double);**
This method returns the sine from an angle (as a double).

3 **double tan(double);**
This function takes an angle (as a double) and returns the tangent.

4 **double log(double);**
This function accepts an integer and returns the number's natural logarithm.

5 **double pow(double, double);**
The first is a number you'd want to increase, and the second is the amount of power you'd like to gain.

6 **double hypot(double, double);**
The hypotenuse length will be returned if you provide this function the length of two sides of a right triangle.

Sr. NoFunction and Purpose

7   **double sqrt(double);**
This function takes an integer and returns the square root.

8   **int abs(int);**
The absolute value of an integer supplied to this method is returned.

9   **double fabs(double);**
The absolute value of any decimal number provided to this method is returned.

10   **double floor(double);**
Finds the smallest or largest integer that is less than or equal to the input.

Example:

#include <iostream> #include <cmath> using namespace std;

```
int main () {
   // number definition:   short  s = 10;   long  l = 100000;   float  f = 20.47;

   // mathematical operations;   cout << "sin(d) :" << sin(d) << endl;   cout << "abs(i)  :" << abs(i)
<< endl;   return 0; }
```

Arrays

In C++, an array is a data structure that stores a fixed-size sequential collection of objects of the same type in fixed size sequential order. Although an array is used to store data, it is often more convenient to think of it as a collection of similar-type variables.

Rather than defining individual variables like number0, number1,..., and number49, you declare a single array variable called numbers and use numbers[0], numbers[1],..., numbers[49] to represent individual variables.

Syntax: type arrayName [arraySize];

Sr. NoDescription

1   **Multidimensional arrays**
Multidimensional arrays are supported in C++. The two-dimensional array is the most basic type of multidimensional array.

2   **Pointer to an array**

Simply giving the array name without any index will create a reference to the first member of the array.

3 **Passing arrays to functions**
By supplying the array's name without an index, you can send a reference to the method.

4 **Return array from functions**
A function in C++ can return an array.

Strings

There are two different sorts of string representations.

1. The character string is in C style.

2. Standard C++ introduces the string class type.

Character String

The character string was concocted in the C programming language is as yet upheld in C++. This string is a one-dimensional cluster of characters, with the invalid person '0' toward the end. An invalid-ended string, then again, incorporates the characters that make up the string, trailed by null.

char a[5] = {'H', 'e', 'l', 'l', 'o'};

Example:
#include <iostream> using namespace std; int main () {
    char a[5] = {'H', 'e', 'l', 'l', 'o',};
    cout << "Message: ";   cout << a << endl;   return 0; }

Output:

Message: Hello

Null-terminated string manipulation functions include:

Sr. NoFunction
1 **strcpy(s1, s2);**
String s2 is copied into string s1.

2 **strcat(s1, s2);**
String s2 is appended to the end of string s1.

3 **strlen(s1);**
The length of string s1 is returned.

4 **strcmp(s1, s2);**

If s1 and s2 are equal, returns 0; less than 0 if s1s2; larger than 0 if s1>s2.

Sr. NoFunction

5   **strchr(s1, ch);**
The first occurrence of the character ch in string s1 is returned as a pointer.

6   **strstr(s1, s2);**
A pointer is returned for the first occurrence of string s2 in string s1.

String Class

The library includes a string class type that supports all of the operations listed above and a lot more.

Example:

#include <iostream> #include <string> using namespace std; int main () {

  string str1 = "Hello";   string str2;   int len;

  // copy str1 into str2   Str2 = str1;
  cout << "str2 : " << str2 << endl;   return 0; }

Output:

Str2: Hello

Pointers

C++ pointers are easy to understand and use, and while some C++ tasks are simpler with them, others, such as dynamic memory allocation, cannot be done without them.

A pointer is a variable whose value is the location of another variable. Before using a pointer, just like any other variable or consistent, it should be pronounced.

Syntax: type *var-name;

The asterisk bullet you used to proclaim a pointer is likewise the asterisk you use to duplicate.

float *fp;   // pointer to a float char *ch   // pointer to character

Sr. No Description

1   **Null Pointers**
Null pointer, a constant with a zero-value defined in various standard libraries, is supported in C++.

2   **Pointer Arithmetic**
    On pointers, the arithmetic operators ++, --, +, and - can be utilized.

3   **Pointers vs. Arrays**
    Pointers and arrays have a very close relationship.

4   **Array of Pointers**
    Arrays can be used to hold many pointers.

5   **Pointer to Pointer**
    You can have a pointer on a pointer in C++, and so on.

Sr. NoDescription

6   **Passing Pointers to Functions**
    Passing an argument by reference or by address allows the called function to modify the supplied
    argument in the calling code.

7   **Return Pointer from Functions**
    A function in C++ can return a pointer to a local variable, a static variable, or dynamically
    allocated memory.

Date And Time

The C++ standard library lacks a suitable data type; therefore, it inherits the structs and methods for
handling dates and times from C. To access date and time-related functions and structures in your
C++ application, you must include the ctime> header file.

The four time-related types are clock t, time t, size t, and tm. To express the system time and date as
an integer, use the clock t, size t, and time t types.

Example:

struct tm {   int tm_mon;   int tm_year;   int tm_wday;   int
tm_yday; }

Sr. No Function

1   **time_t time(time_t *time);**
    This returns the system's current calendar time as a number of seconds since January 1, 1970. If
    the system does not have any time, a value of.1 is returned.

2   **char *ctime(const time_t *time);**
    This function produces a string of the form day month year hours:minutes:seconds year\n\0.

Sr. No Function

3   **struct tm *localtime(const time_t *time);**
This gives you a pointer to the tm structure, which is used to indicate local time.

4   **clock_t clock(void);**
This gives you a rough estimate of how long the calling application has been running. If the time is unavailable, a value of.1 is returned.

5   **char * asctime (const struct tm * time);**
This returns a reference to a string containing the data contained in the structure pointed to by time, which has been transformed to the form: date (day, month) seconds: minutes: hours: minutes: hours: minutes: minutes:
minutes: minutes: minutes year\n\0.

6   **struct tm *gmtime(const time_t *time);**
This returns a tm structure with a reference to the time.
Coordinated Universal Time (UTC), which is basically Greenwich Mean Time, is used to indicate the time (GMT).

7   **time_t mktime(struct tm *time);**
The calendar-time equivalent of the time in the structure referenced to by time is returned.

8   **double difftime (time_t time2, time_t time1);**
The difference in seconds between time1 and time2 is calculated using this function.

9   **size_t strftime();**
This function allows you to format the date and time in a specified way.

Basic Input/Output

Input/Output occurs in streams, which are byte-by-byte successions. The progression of bytes from a gadget like a console, a circle drive, or an organization association with principal memory is known as info, while the progression of bytes from fundamental memory to a gadget, for example, a presentation screen, a printer, a plate drive, or an organization association is known as yield.

Sr. NoHeader File and Function

1   **<iostream>**
The cin, cout, cerr, and clog objects are defined in this file, and they correspond to the standard input stream, standard output stream, un-buffered standard error stream, and buffered standard error stream, respectively.

2   **<iomanip>**

This file declares services like setw and set precision that are helpful for conducting formatted I/O using so-called parameterized stream manipulators.

3   **<fstream>**
This file defines user-controlled file processing services.

Data Structures

Data structures are a huge and unavoidable element of any programming project. Cells, the tiniest unit of life, are just as reliant on us humans for a variety of biological processes. The basic unit of programming known as "data" underpins the whole C++ program. The implementation of data structures allows us to conduct data operations such as data representation, storage, organization, and many others in a meaningful way.

An information type is just an assortment of comparable information with a similar name. Comparable information types have comparable properties and act comparatively, like taking up a similar measure of PC memory and serving a similar capacity.

There are two significant kinds of information:

1. **Primitive data type:** These information types are otherwise called crude information types. These are pre-characterized information types that give the C++ compiler a particular significance. For example, int, coast, singe, string, double, etc.

2. **Non-primitive data type:** These information types are comprised of crude information types. Since they are not pre-characterized by the C++ compiler, they are at times known as client characterized information types. Arrays, structures, unions, classes, linked lists, enumeration, etc., are models.

Data Structures of Various Types

The usage of C++ data structures allows a programmer to mix different data types in a group and process them as a single unit, making things easier and more understandable.

In C++, data structures are divided into three categories.

1. **Simple:** In C++, these data structures are usually made up of primitive data types like int, float, double, string, and char.

2. **Compound:** These sorts of data structures can be created by merging simple data structures. It is further divided into two categories:
   - **Linear data structure:** A data structure is considered to be linear if its elements are arranged in a logical order.
   - **Non-linear data structure:** Multilevel data structures are non-linear data structures.

3. **Static and Dynamic:** Static data structures have a constant size and structure connected with some specified memory locations that are fixed at compilation time. For instance, consider arrays.

Data Structures Operations

- **Insertion:** Inserting a new data element into the data structure is referred to as this operation.
- **Deletion:** In the data structure, delete or remove an existing data element.
- **Traversal:** Process and display all data pieces in the data structure using traversal.
- **Searching:** Look through the data structure for a certain data element.
- **Sorting:** Sort the data items in the data structure in ascending or descending order, or in any other logically sequential order.
- **Merging:** It is the process of combining similar data pieces from two or more data structures to create a new data structure.

Conclusion: Mastering the Basics of C++ Programming (2025)

C++ is a versatile and powerful programming language that has stood the test of time. Since its inception in the 1980s, it has evolved into one of the most widely used languages for system programming, game development, embedded systems, and performance-critical applications. Its ability to combine low-level memory manipulation with high-level abstractions makes it a favorite among developers who seek both efficiency and flexibility. This guide has provided a comprehensive introduction to the foundational concepts of C++ programming, equipping you with the knowledge to write efficient, structured, and maintainable code.

As we conclude this exploration of C++ basics, let's reflect on the key concepts covered and their significance in the broader context of programming and software development.

The Importance of Understanding the Basics

The topics covered in this guide—data types, control structures, functions, arrays, strings, pointers, and dynamic memory allocation—are the building blocks of C++ programming. Mastering these fundamentals is crucial for several reasons:

1. **Foundation for Advanced Concepts**: Understanding the basics is essential for tackling more advanced topics such as object-oriented programming (OOP), templates, exception handling, and the Standard Template Library (STL). Without a solid grasp of these fundamentals, it becomes challenging to write efficient and scalable code.

2. **Efficient Problem Solving**: Programming is fundamentally about solving problems. A strong understanding of data types, control structures, and functions enables you to break down complex problems into smaller, manageable components and implement effective solutions.

3. **Code Optimization**: Knowledge of pointers, memory management, and type conversions allows you to write optimized code that minimizes resource usage and maximizes performance. This is particularly important in applications where efficiency is critical, such as game engines or embedded systems.

4. **Debugging and Maintenance**: Understanding how variables, functions, and memory work under the hood makes it easier to debug and maintain code. For example, knowing how pointers and memory allocation work can help you identify and fix memory leaks or segmentation faults.

5. **Versatility Across Domains**: C++ is used in a wide range of domains, from operating systems and compilers to video games and financial systems. A strong grasp of the basics ensures that you can adapt to different programming challenges and domains.

Recap of Key Concepts

1. Data Types and Variables

Data types define the kind of data a variable can hold, such as integers, floating-point numbers, characters, or boolean values. Variables are used to store and manipulate data in a program. Understanding data types is essential for writing programs that handle different kinds of data efficiently.

2. Constants and Literals

Constants are variables whose values cannot be changed after initialization, while literals are fixed values used directly in the code. Constants provide a way to define values that remain unchanged throughout the program, improving readability and maintainability.

3. Operators and Expressions

Operators are symbols used to perform operations on variables and values, such as arithmetic, relational, logical, and bitwise operations. Expressions combine variables, literals, and operators to produce a single value. Mastering operators and expressions are key to implementing logic and calculations in your programs.

4. Type Conversions

Type conversions allow you to convert data from one type to another, either implicitly (automatically) or explicitly (manually). Understanding type conversions is important for avoiding errors and ensuring that your program behaves as expected.

5. Input and Output

C++ provides the iostream library for handling input and output operations. The cin and cout objects are used for reading input and displaying output, respectively. Proper input/output handling is essential for creating interactive programs.

6. Control Structures

Control structures, such as conditional statements (if, else if, switch) and looping statements (for, while, do-while), allow you to control the flow of your program. These structures are fundamental for implementing logic and repeating tasks.

7. Functions

Functions are blocks of code that perform specific tasks. They help in organizing code, improving reusability, and reducing redundancy. Concepts like function overloading, default arguments, inline functions, and recursion further enhance the power and flexibility of functions.

8. Arrays, Strings, and Pointers

Arrays allow you to store collections of data, while strings are used to handle text. Pointers are variables that store memory addresses, enabling direct manipulation of memory. Understanding these concepts is crucial for working with data structures and optimizing performance.

9. Dynamic Memory Allocation

Dynamic memory allocation allows you to allocate and deallocate memory at runtime using new and delete. This is particularly useful for managing memory in programs that require flexibility in memory usage.

The Road Ahead

While this guide has covered the basics of C++ programming, there is still much more to explore. As you continue your journey with C++, consider diving into the following advanced topics:

1. **Object-Oriented Programming (OOP)**:

    o   Learn about classes, objects, inheritance, polymorphism, and encapsulation. OOP is a paradigm that allows you to model real-world entities and relationships in your code.

2. **Templates**:

    o   Templates enable you to write generic and reusable code. They are the foundation of the Standard Template Library (STL), which provides a rich set of data structures and algorithms.

3. **Exception Handling**:

    o   Exception handling allows you to manage errors and unexpected situations in your code gracefully. It is essential for writing robust and reliable programs.

4. **Standard Template Library (STL)**:
    o   The STL provides a collection of template classes and functions for common data structures (e.g., vectors, lists, maps) and algorithms (e.g., sorting, searching). Mastering the STL can significantly boost your productivity.

5. **File Handling**:

   o   Learn how to read from and write to files using C++ file streams. File handling is essential for working with persistent data.

6. **Multithreading and Concurrency**:

   o   Explore how to write multithreaded programs to take advantage of modern multicore processors. Concurrency is crucial for developing high-performance applications.

7. **Advanced Pointers and Memory Management**:

   o   Dive deeper into topics like smart pointers, memory pools, and custom allocators to gain finer control over memory management.

8. **Design Patterns**:

   o   Study common design patterns such as Singleton, Factory, Observer, and Strategy. Design patterns provide proven solutions to recurring problems in software design.

Best Practices for C++ Programming

As you continue to develop your skills, keep the following best practices in mind:

1. **Write Readable Code**:

   o   Use meaningful variable and function names. Follow consistent indentation and formatting conventions. Write comments to explain complex logic.

2. **Avoid Raw Pointers When Possible**:

   o   Prefer smart pointers (std::unique_ptr, std::shared_ptr) over raw pointers to manage memory safely and avoid memory leaks.

3. **Use the STL**:

   o   Leverage the power of the Standard Template Library to avoid reinventing the wheel. The STL provides efficient and well-tested implementations of common data structures and algorithms.

4. **Test Your Code**:

   o   Write unit tests to verify the correctness of your code. Use debugging tools to identify and fix issues.

5. **Optimize Judiciously**:

    o Focus on writing clear and correct code first. Optimize only when necessary and based on performance profiling.

6. **Stay Updated**:

    o C++ is an evolving language. Stay informed about new features and standards (e.g., C++20, C++23) to take advantage of the latest advancements.

The Future of C++

As of 2025, C++ continues to evolve with new standards and features that enhance its capabilities. The language remains a top choice for developers working on performance-critical applications, and its integration with modern tools and frameworks ensures its relevance in the ever-changing landscape of software development.

Whether you are building the next generation of video games, developing embedded systems for IoT devices, or working on high-frequency trading platforms, C++ provides the tools and flexibility you need to succeed. By mastering the basics and continuing to explore advanced topics, you can unlock the full potential of this powerful language.

Final Thoughts

Learning C++ is a rewarding journey that opens doors to a wide range of opportunities in software development. While the language can be challenging at times, its depth and versatility make it a valuable skill for any programmer. As you continue to practice and build projects, you will gain confidence and proficiency in using C++ to solve real-world problems.

Remember, programming is not just about writing code—it's about thinking critically, solving problems, and creating solutions that make a difference. With the foundational knowledge you've gained from this guide, you are well on your way to becoming a skilled C++ programmer. Keep learning, experimenting, and pushing the boundaries of what you can achieve with C++. The future of software development is in your hands—happy coding!

3. Object-Oriented Programming (OOP)

Introduction

Object-Oriented Programming (OOP) is a programming paradigm that organizes software design around data, or objects, rather than functions and logic. C++ is one of the most popular programming languages that supports OOP, offering a robust set of features to implement OOP concepts effectively.

1. Classes and Objects

Classes

A **class** in C++ is a user-defined data type that serves as a blueprint for creating objects. It encapsulates data (attributes) and functions (methods) that operate on the data. Classes are the foundation of OOP in C++.

```
class Car {
public:
  // Attributes (data members)
  string brand;
  string model;
  int year;

  // Methods (member functions)
  void start() {
    cout << "Starting the car..." << endl;
  }

  void stop() {
    cout << "Stopping the car..." << endl;
  }
};
```

Objects

An **object** is an instance of a class. It represents a real-world entity and can access the data members and member functions of the class.

```
int main() {
  Car myCar; // Creating an object of the Car class
  myCar.brand = "Toyota";
  myCar.model = "Corolla";
  myCar.year = 2025;
```

```
    myCar.start(); // Calling a method
    myCar.stop();
    return 0;
}
```

2. Constructors and Destructors

Constructors

A **constructor** is a special member function that is automatically called when an object is created. It is used to initialize the object's data members.

- **Default Constructor**: Takes no arguments.
- **Parameterized Constructor**: Takes arguments to initialize the object.
- **Copy Constructor**: Initializes an object using another object of the same class.

```
class Car {
public:
    string brand;
    string model;
    int year;

    // Default Constructor
    Car() {
        brand = "Unknown";
        model = "Unknown";
        year = 0;
    }

    // Parameterized Constructor
    Car(string b, string m, int y) {
        brand = b;
        model = m;
        year = y;
    }

    // Copy Constructor
    Car(const Car &obj) {
        brand = obj.brand;
        model = obj.model;
        year = obj.year;
    }
};
```

Destructors

A **destructor** is a special member function that is automatically called when an object goes out of scope or is explicitly deleted. It is used to release resources allocated to the object.

```
class Car {
public:
   ~Car() {
      cout << "Car object destroyed." << endl;
   }
};
```

3. Encapsulation and Data Hiding

Encapsulation

Encapsulation is the bundling of data and methods that operate on the data into a single unit (class). It restricts direct access to some of the object's components, which is a way of preventing unintended interference and misuse of data.

Data Hiding

Data hiding is achieved using access specifiers:

- **Private**: Members are accessible only within the class.
- **Protected**: Members are accessible within the class and derived classes.
- **Public**: Members are accessible from outside the class.

```
class Car {
private:
   string brand; // Private data member

public:
   void setBrand(string b) {
      brand = b; // Accessible within the class
   }

   string getBrand() {
      return brand; // Accessible within the class
   }
};
```

4. Inheritance

Inheritance is a mechanism that allows a class (derived class) to inherit properties and behavior (methods) from another class (base class). C++ supports several types of inheritance:

Single Inheritance

A derived class inherits from a single base class.

```cpp
class Vehicle {
public:
  void start() {
    cout << "Vehicle started." << endl;
  }
};

class Car : public Vehicle {
public:
  void drive() {
    cout << "Car is driving." << endl;
  }
};
```

Multiple Inheritance

A derived class inherits from multiple base classes.

```cpp
class Engine {
public:
  void startEngine() {
    cout << "Engine started." << endl;
  }
};

class Wheels {
public:
  void rotateWheels() {
    cout << "Wheels rotating." << endl;
  }
};

class Car : public Engine, public Wheels {
public:
  void drive() {
    startEngine();
    rotateWheels();
    cout << "Car is driving." << endl;
  }
};
```

Multilevel Inheritance

A derived class inherits from another derived class.

```cpp
class Vehicle {
public:
   void start() {
      cout << "Vehicle started." << endl;
   }
};

class Car : public Vehicle {
public:
   void drive() {
      cout << "Car is driving." << endl;
   }
};

class SportsCar : public Car {
public:
   void race() {
      cout << "Sports car is racing." << endl;
   }
};
```

Hierarchical Inheritance

Multiple derived classes inherit from a single base class.

```cpp
class Vehicle {
public:
   void start() {
      cout << "Vehicle started." << endl;
   }
};

class Car : public Vehicle {
public:
   void drive() {
      cout << "Car is driving." << endl;
   }
};

class Bike : public Vehicle {
public:
   void ride() {
```

```
        cout << "Bike is riding." << endl;
    }
};
```

Hybrid Inheritance

A combination of multiple and hierarchical inheritance.

```
class Vehicle {
public:
    void start() {
        cout << "Vehicle started." << endl;
    }
};

class Engine {
public:
    void startEngine() {
        cout << "Engine started." << endl;
    }
};

class Car : public Vehicle, public Engine {
public:
    void drive() {
        start();
        startEngine();
        cout << "Car is driving." << endl;
    }
};

class SportsCar : public Car {
public:
    void race() {
        cout << "Sports car is racing." << endl;
    }
};
```

5. Polymorphism

Polymorphism allows objects of different classes to be treated as objects of a common base class. It can be achieved through **compile-time polymorphism** (function overloading, operator overloading) and **run-time polymorphism** (virtual functions).

Compile-Time Polymorphism

- **Function Overloading**: Multiple functions with the same name but different parameters.
- **Operator Overloading**: Defining custom behavior for operators.

```cpp
class Math {
public:
    int add(int a, int b) {
        return a + b;
    }

    double add(double a, double b) {
        return a + b;
    }
};
```

Run-Time Polymorphism

- **Virtual Functions**: Functions in the base class that can be overridden in derived classes.
- **VTables**: A mechanism used by C++ to support dynamic dispatch of virtual functions.

```cpp
class Animal {
public:
    virtual void sound() {
        cout << "Animal sound" << endl;
    }
};

class Dog : public Animal {
public:
    void sound() override {
        cout << "Bark" << endl;
    }
};

int main() {
    Animal *animal = new Dog();
    animal->sound(); // Output: Bark
    return 0;
}
```

6. Abstract Classes and Interfaces

Abstract Classes

An abstract class is a class that cannot be instantiated and is meant to be a base class for other classes. It contains at least one pure virtual function.

```cpp
class Shape {
public:
    virtual void draw() = 0; // Pure virtual function
};

class Circle : public Shape {
public:
    void draw() override {
        cout << "Drawing a circle." << endl;
    }
};
```

Interfaces

In C++, interfaces are implemented using abstract classes with only pure virtual functions.

```cpp
class Drawable {
public:
    virtual void draw() = 0;
};

class Circle : public Drawable {
public:
    void draw() override {
        cout << "Drawing a circle." << endl;
    }
};
```

7. Operator Overloading and Function Overloading

Operator Overloading

Operator overloading allows you to define custom behavior for operators when used with user-defined types.

```cpp
class Complex {
public:
    int real, imag;

    Complex(int r = 0, int i = 0) : real(r), imag(i) {}

    Complex operator + (const Complex &obj) {
        Complex res;
        res.real = real + obj.real;
        res.imag = imag + obj.imag;
```

```
      return res;
   }
};
```

Function Overloading

Function overloading allows you to define multiple functions with the same name but different parameters.

```
class Math {
public:
   int add(int a, int b) {
      return a + b;
   }

   double add(double a, double b) {
      return a + b;
   }
};
```

8. Virtual Functions and VTables

Virtual Functions

Virtual functions allow derived classes to override the behavior of a function defined in the base class. They enable run-time polymorphism.

```
class Animal {
public:
   virtual void sound() {
      cout << "Animal sound" << endl;
   }
};

class Dog : public Animal {
public:
   void sound() override {
      cout << "Bark" << endl;
   }
};
```

VTables

A **VTable** (Virtual Table) is a mechanism used by C++ to support dynamic dispatch of virtual functions. Each class with virtual functions has a VTable, which is an array of function pointers pointing to the most derived implementation of the virtual functions.

```cpp
class Animal {
public:
    virtual void sound() {
        cout << "Animal sound" << endl;
    }
};

class Dog : public Animal {
public:
    void sound() override {
        cout << "Bark" << endl;
    }
};

int main() {
    Animal *animal = new Dog();
    animal->sound(); // Output: Bark
    return 0;
}
```

OBJECT ORIENTED

Classes and Objects in C++

The fundamental goal of C++ programming is to introduce object orientation to the C programming language, and classes, also known as user-defined types, are the key element of C++ that allows object-oriented programming.

A class specifies an object's form by combining data representation and methods for changing that data into a single package. Members of a class are the data and methods that make up the class.

Class Definitions in C++

When you define a class, you're essentially defining a data type's blueprint. This doesn't specify any data, but it does define what the class name implies, that is, what a class object will be made up of and what actions can be done on it.

The keyword class is used to start a class definition, followed by the class name, and lastly the class body, which is enclosed by a pair of curly brackets. A semicolon or a series of declarations must come after a class definition. For example, we used the term class to define the Box data type:

Example:

class B { public: double length;   double breadth;   double height; };

The access characteristics of the members of the class that follows it are determined by the keyword public. Anywhere inside the scope of the class object, a public member can be accessed from outside the class. You may also make a class's members secret or protected, which we'll cover in a later section.

C++ Objects

A class serves as the blueprint for things; thus, an object is essentially produced from one. Objects of a class are declared in the same way as variables of fundamental types are declared. The following statements declare two Car objects:

Car Car1;
Car Car2;

Members Having Access to Data

The direct member access operator may be used to access the public data members of a class's objects (.). To clarify matters, consider the following example:

```
#include <iostream> using namespace std;
class box {   public:     double length;     double breadth;     double height; };
int main() {   box box1;   box box2;   double volume = 0.3;
  // specification   box1.height = 3.0;   box1.length = 4.0;   box1.breadth = 7.0;
  // specification   box2.height = 20.0;   box2.length = 21.0;   box2.breadth = 14.0;
  // volume
   volume = box1.height * box1.length * box1.breadth;
   cout << "The Volume of box1: " << volume <<endl;
  // volume of box 2
   volume = box2.height * box2.length * box2.breadth;
   cout << "The Volume of box2: " << volume
<<endl;   return 0; }
```

Output:
The Volume of box1: 84
The Volume of box2: 5880

It's crucial to know that the direct member access operator cannot access private or protected members (.). We'll discover how to gain access to secret and protected users.

Detail on Classes and Objects

So far, you've learned the fundamentals of C++ Classes and Objects. There are a few more fascinating ideas linked to C++ Classes and Objects that we'll go over in the following sub-sections:

Sr. No Description

1   **Functions of Class Members:**
     A member function of a class is a function that, like any other variable, has its definition or prototype within the class declaration.

2   **Modifiers for Class Access:**
     A class member can be made public, private, or protected. Members are presumed to be private by default.

3   **Constructor and Destructor:**
     A class function is a specific function in a class that is called when a new object of that class is created. A destructor is a specific function that is run when an object is created and then destroyed.

Sr. No Description

4   **Copy Constructor:**
The copy function is a function that produces an object by initialising it using a previously generated object of the same class.

5   **Friend Functions:**
  A friend function has full access to a class's private and protected members.

6   **Inline Functions:**
In the case of an inline function, the compiler tries to extend the code in the body of the function rather than calling it.

7   **this Pointer:**
Every object has a unique pointer that refers to the actual object.

8   **Pointer:**
  A class pointer is created in the same manner as a structure pointer is created. In reality, a class is nothing more than a structure containing functions.

9   **Static Members:**
  A class's data and function members can both be declared static.

Inheritance

The idea of inheritance is one of the most essential in object-oriented programming. Inheritance enables us to define a class in terms of another class, which simplifies application development and maintenance. This also allows for the reuse of code functionality and a quick implementation time. Instead of developing entirely new data members and member methods when establishing a class, the programmer can specify that the new class should inherit the members of an existing class. The current class is known as the base class, while the new class is known as the derived class. Inheritance is a connection that is implemented.

Base and Derived Classes

A class can be derived from several base classes, allowing it to inherit data and functionalities from various sources.

To provide the base class for a derived class, we utilize a class derivation list. A class derivation list takes the form and names one or more base classes. **class derivedclass: access-specifier baseclass** Where base-class is the name of a previously created class and access-specifier is one of public, protected, or private.

It is private by default if the access-specifier is not used.

Example:
```
#include <iostream> using namespace std;
// Class-Base class shape {    public:
    void setWidth(int w) {         wd = w;       }
    void setHeight(int h) {        hg = h;       }
  protected:     int wd;      int hg; };
// Derived-class class rect: public shape {     public:
    int getArea() {          return (wd * hg);
    }
};
int main(void) {    rect r;
  r.setWidth(5);
  r.setHeight(7);
  // Print
  cout << "The Total area: " << r.getArea() << endl;
  return 0; }
```

Output:
The Total area: 35

Inheritance and Access Control

A derived class has access to all of its base class's nonprivate members. As a result, any base-class elements that should not be available to derived class member functions should be made private in the base class.

The different access kinds can be summarized in the following fashion based on who has access to them:

Access	public	protected	private
Same class	yes	yes	yes
Derived classes	yes	yes	no
Outside classes	yes	no	no

With the exclusions listed below, a derived class inherits all base class methods.

- The base class's constructors, destructors, and copy constructors.
- The base class's operators are overloaded.
- The base class's friend functions.

Types

When creating a class from a base class, the base class can be inherited in one of three ways: public, protected, or private inheritance. As previously stated, the access-specifier specifies the type of inheritance.

Protected and private inheritance is rarely utilized, while public inheritance is. The following principles apply when utilizing various types of inheritance:

- **Public class:** When a class is derived from a public base class, the base class's public members become public members of the derived class, and the base class's protected members become protected members of the derived class. The private members of a base class are never directly available from a derived class, although they can be accessed via calls to the base class's public and protected members.

- **Protected Inheritance:** When a derived class inherits from a protected base class, the base class's public and protected members become protected members of the derived class.

- **Private Inheritance:** When a derived class is derived from a private base class, the base class's public and protected members become private members of the derived class.

Multiple Inheritance

A C++ class can inherit members from multiple classes, and the expanded syntax is as follows:

class derivedclass: access baseC, access baseD.

Where access is one of **public, protected,** or **private** and would be given for every base class and they will be separated by comma as shown above. Let us try the following example

Example:
```
#include <iostream> using namespace std;
// Base class class shape {    public:     void setWidth(int w) {        wd = w;     }
    void setHeight(int h)
{
    hg = h;
    }
  protected:     int wd;     int hg; };
// Base class class paintcost {    public:       int getCost(int ar) {        return ar * 30;
    } };
```

```cpp
// Derived class class Rect: public shape, public
paintcost {   public:      int getArea() {        return (wd * hg);
    }
};
int main(void) {
  Rect r;   int ar;
 r.setWidth(7);
 r.setHeight(8);    ar = r.getArea();
 // Print the area    cout << "The Total area: " << r.getArea() << endl;
 // Print the total cost   cout << "The Total paint cost:" << r.getCost(ar) << endl;
 return 0; }
```

Output:
The Total area: 56
The Total paint cost:1680

Overloading

Function overloading and operator overloading are terms used in C++ to describe the ability to specify several definitions for a function name or an operator in the same scope.

An overloaded declaration is one that has the same name as a previously declared declaration in the same scope, but both declarations have distinct parameters and clearly different definitions.

The compiler determines which definition to apply when you call an overloaded function or operator by comparing the argument types you used to invoke the function or operator to the parameter types supplied in the definitions.

Overloading Function

In C++, function overloading means that the same function name can have several definitions in the same scope. The kinds and/or the number of arguments in the argument list must be different in each function declaration. Overloading function declarations that differ only in return type is not possible.

Example:
```cpp
#include <iostream> using namespace std;
class printd {   public:      void print(int j) {
     cout << "Printing int: " << j
<< endl;
    }
   void print(double  h) {       cout << "Printing float: " << h << endl;
    }
   void print(char* b) {
     cout << "Printing character: " << b << endl;
    }
};
```

```
int main(void) {    printd pd;
    // Call print    pd.print(4);
    // Call print    pd.print(400.223);
    // Call print    pd.print("Hello ");
    return 0;
}
```

Output:
Printing int: 4
Printing float: 400.223
Printing character: Hello

Overloading Operators

In C++, you may redefine or overload most of the built-in operators. As a result, a programmer may also utilize operators with user-defined types.

Overloaded operators are functions with unique names, consisting of the keyword "operator" followed by the symbol for the operator to be defined. An overloaded operator, like any other function, has a return type and an argument list.

Syntax: box operator+(const box&);

defines the addition operator, which may be used to combine two Box instances and yields the resultant Box object The majority of overloaded operators may be classified as non-member functions or class member functions. If we create the above function as a non-member function of a class, we must provide two arguments for each operand, as shown below:

Syntax: box operator+(const box&, const box&);

The following example uses a member function to demonstrate the idea of operator overloading. The object that will call this operator can be accessed using this operator as explained below: An object is passed as an argument whose properties will be accessed using this object, and the object that will call this operator can be accessed using this operator as explained below:

Example:
```
#include <iostream> using namespace std;
class box {    public:      double getVolume(void) {          return leng * bread * heig;
    }
    void setLength( double len ) {         leng = len;
    }
    void setBreadth( double bre ) {        bread = bre;
    }
    void setHeight( double hei ) {         heig = hei;      }
       // Overload + operator to add two Box objects.      box operator+(const box& b) {        box boxx;
```

```
        boxx.leng = this->leng + b.leng;        boxx.bread  = this->bread +
b.bread;        boxx.heig = this->heig + b.heig;        return boxx;        }
  private:
     double leng;        double bread;        double heig; };
// Main function int main() {    box box1;    box box2;    box box3;    double volume = 0.0;
  // specification    box1.setLength(8.0);    box1.setBreadth(4.0);    box1.setHeight(6.0);
  // specification    box2.setLength(11.0);    box2.setBreadth(14.0);    box2.setHeight(12.0);
  // volume    volume = box1.getVolume();    cout << "Volume of box1 : " << volume <<endl;
  // volume    volume = box2.getVolume();    cout << "Volume of box2 : " << volume <<endl;
  // Add two object as follows:    box3 = box1 + box2;
  // volume    volume = box3.getVolume();    cout << "Volume of box3 : " << volume <<endl;
  return 0; }
```

Output:
Volume of box1: 192
Volume of box2: 1848
Volume of box3: 6156

Polymorphism

Polymorphism refers to the fact that something exists in several forms. Polymorphism usually happens when there is a hierarchy of classes that are connected through inheritance.

Polymorphism in C++ refers to the fact that depending on the kind of object that calls a member function, a different function is performed.

Consider the following scenario, in which a base class is derived from two additional classes:

Example:
```
#include <iostream> using namespace std; class shape {    protected:        int wd, hg;
  public:
     Shape( int w = 0, int h = 0){        width = w;        height = h;
     }     int ar() {
        cout << "The Parent class area
:" <<endl;        return 0;
     }
};
class rectangle: public shape {    public:        rectangle( int w = 0, int h = 0):Shape(w, h) { }
     int ar () {
        cout << "The Rectangle class area :" <<endl;
        return (wd * hg);
     }
};
class triangle: public shape {    public:
     triangle( int w = 0, int h =
0):shape(w, h) { }
```

```
int ar () {
    cout << "The Triangle class area :" <<endl;
    return (wd * hg / 2);
} };
```
// Main function int main() {   shape *sh;   rectangle rc(10,7);   triangle tr(10,5);
  // store the address of Rectangle   sh = &rc;
  // call rectangle area.   sh->ar();
  // store the address of Triangle   sh = &tr;
  // call triangle area.   sh->ar();
  return 0; }

Output:
The Parent class area :
The Parent class area :

Data Abstraction

Data abstraction refers to simply exposing important information to the outer world while hiding background details, i.e. to represent the needed information in a programme without displaying the intricacies.

Data abstraction is a programming approach in which the interface and implementation are separated.
Take, for example, a television, which you can turn on and off, change the channel, adjust the volume, and add external components such as speakers, DVD players, but you have no idea how it receives signals over the air or through a cable, how it translates them, and finally displays them on the screen.

As a result, we can argue that a television clearly isolates its internal implementation from its exterior interface, allowing you to interact with its interfaces such as the power button, channel changer, and volume control without knowing anything about its internals.

Classes in C++ enable a high level of data abstraction. They expose enough public methods to the outside world to allow them to experiment with the object's functionality and change object data, i.e. state, without having to know how the class is built inside.

Your application, for example, can call the sort() method without knowing what algorithm the function uses to sort the input data. In reality, the actual implementation of the sorting feature may change between library releases, but your function call will still work as long as the interface remains the same.

Example:
```
#include <iostream> using namespace std;
int main() {    cout << "Hello " <<endl;    return 0;
}
```

You don't need to know how cout displays text on the user's screen in this case. You just need to understand the public interface; the underlying implementation of 'cout' can be changed at any time.

Data Abstraction's Advantages

Data abstraction has two major advantages.

1.   Inadvertent user-level mistakes that might damage the object's state are shielded from class internals.

2.   Without requiring changes to user-level code, the class implementation may develop over time in response to new needs or problem reports.

The class author is able to alter the data by defining data members only in the private part of the class. If the implementation changes, all that has to be done is look at the class code to determine what impact the change could have. Any function that directly accesses the data members of the previous representation may be broken if the data is public.

Data abstraction may be seen in any C++ program that implements a class with public and private members.

Example:
```
#include <iostream> using namespace std;
class Add {    public:     // constructor     Add(int a = 0) {       t = a;
    }
    // interface to outside world     void addNumb(int num) {      t += num;     }
    int getTotal() {        return t;      };
  private:
    // hidden data      int t; };
int main() {    Add ad;
  ad.addNumb(10);    ad.addNumb(20);    ad.addNumb(30);    cout << "Total: " << ad.getTotal()
<<endl;    return 0; }
```

Output:
Total: 60

Encapsulation

The following two essential components are present in all C++ programs:

Functions are the parts of a program that perform actions, and they are termed program statements. Program data is the program's information that is influenced by the program's functions.

Encapsulation is a notion in Object Oriented Programming that ties together data and the functions that change it, keeping both protected from outside intervention and misuse. The essential OOP idea of data hiding was born from data encapsulation.

Data abstraction is a technique for exposing only the interfaces and hiding the implementation details from the user, whereas data encapsulation is a strategy for packaging data and the functions that utilize it.

Encapsulation and data hiding are supported in C++ via the use of classes, which are user-defined types. We've previously seen that a class can have members who are secret, protected, or public. All items declared in a class are private by default.

Example:
```
class box {   public:
    double getVol(void) {        return len * bread * heig;      }
  private:
    double len;
    double bread;      double heig; };
```

The length, width, and height variables are all private. This implies that they can only be accessible by other Box class members and not by any other component of your application. This is one method of encapsulation.

You must define sections of a class after the public keyword to make them public (i.e., available to other parts of your program). All other functions in your application can access any variables or functions declared after the public specifier.

By making one class a buddy of another, the implementation details are exposed and encapsulation is lost. The ideal situation is to keep as many of each class's information hidden from other classes as possible.

Example:
```
#include <iostream> using namespace std;
class Add {   public:
    // constructor      Add(int a = 0) {         total = a;
    }
    // interface      void addNum(int numb) {        total += numb;
    }
    // interface      int getTotal() {        return total;      };
  private:
    // hidden data      int total; };
int main() {   Add ad;
  ad.addNum(20);    ad.addNum(30);    ad.addNum(10);      cout << "Total: " << ad.getTotal()
<<endl;    return 0; }
```

Output:
Total: 60

The total of the numbers in the above class is returned. The public members addNum and getTotal are the class's external interfaces, and a user must be familiar with them in order to utilize it. The private member total is hidden from the rest of the world, yet it is required for the class to function properly.

Interfaces

An interface specifies a C++ class's behavior or capabilities without committing to a specific implementation of that class.

Abstract classes are used to implement C++ interfaces. These abstract classes should not be confused with data abstraction, which is a notion that separates implementation details from related data.

A class becomes abstract when at least one of its functions is declared as a pure virtual function. The expression "= 0" in the declaration of a pure virtual function is as follows:

Example:
```
class box {   public:
    // virtual function      virtual double getVol() = 0;
  private:     double len;    // Box Length     double bread;    // Box Breadth     double heig;     //
Box Height };
```

An abstract class (also known as an ABC) is used to provide a suitable foundation class from which further classes can be derived. Abstract classes are solely used as a user interface and cannot be utilized to create objects. A compilation error occurs when an object of an abstract class is attempted to be instantiated.

As a result, if an ABC subclass has to be created, it must implement each of the virtual functions, implying that it supports the ABC's interface. Compilation errors occur when a derived class fails to override a pure virtual function before attempting to create instances of that class.

Example:
```
#include <iostream> using namespace std;
// Base class class shape {   public:
    // pure virtual function      virtual int getAr() = 0;      void setWidth(int wd) {        wid = wd;
    }
    void setHeight(int hg) {       hei = hg;
    }
  protected:     int wid;    int hei; };
// Derived class class rectangle: public shape {   public:    int getAr() {        return (wid * hei);
    }
};
class triangle: public shape {   public:    int getAr() {        return (wid * hei)/2;
    }
};
int main(void) {    rectangle rect;    triangle  tri;
```

```
rect.setWidth(6);    rect.setHeight(4);
// Print
 cout << "The Total Rectangle area: " << rect.getAr() << endl;
tri.setWidth(5);    tri.setHeight(7);
// Print
 cout << "The Total Triangle area: " << tri.getAr() << endl;
return 0; }
```

Output:
The Total Rectangle area: 24
The Total Triangle area: 17

How To Work with File Taking Care of In C++?

Following pointers will be canvassed:

- Opening a File
- Keeping in touch with a File
- Perusing from a File
- Close a File

Document Handling in C++

Documents are utilized to store information in a capacity gadget for all time. Document taking care of gives a component to store the yield of a program in a record and to perform the different procedures on it.

A stream is a deliberation that addresses a gadget on which activities of information and yield are performed. A stream can be addressed as a source or objective of characters of endless length relying upon its use.

In C++ we have a bunch of record-taking care techniques. These incorporate ifstream, ofstream, and fstream. These classes are gotten from fstrembase and the relating iostream class. These classes, intended to deal with the circle documents, are proclaimed in fstream, and hence we should incorporate fstream, and subsequently, we should remember this record for any program that utilizations records.

In C++, documents are primarily managed by utilizing three classes fstream, ifstream, ofstream.

- **ofstream:** This Stream class means the yield document stream and is applied to make records for composing data to records

- **ifstream:** This Stream class connotes the information document stream and is applied for perusing data from records

- **fstream:** This Stream class can be utilized for both peruse and compose from/to documents.

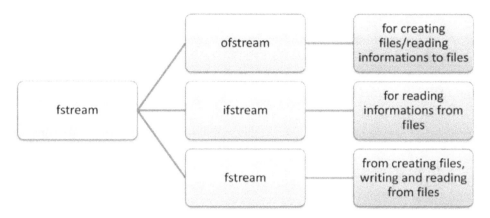

In C ++, documents are primarily managed by utilizing three classes

Source Code:

```
/* File Handling with C++ using ifstream & ofstream */
/* To write the Content */
/* Read the content*/

#include <iostream>
#include <fstream>
using namespace std;
// Driver Code int main() {
   // Creation of ofstream class object   ofstream fout;   string line;
    // by default ios::out mode, automatically deletes
    // the content of file. To append the content, open in ios:app   // fout.open("sample.txt", ios::app)
fout.open("sample1.txt");
   // Execute a loop If file successfully opened
  while (fout) {
     // Read a Line from standard input    getline(cin, line);
     // Press -1 to exit    if (line == "-1")             break;
     // Write line in file    fout << This is a line << endl;
   }
   // Close the File   fout.close();
    // Creation of ifstream class object to read the file
   ifstream fin;
   // by default open mode = ios::in mode   fin.open("sample1.txt");
    // Execute a loop until EOF (End of
File)   while (fin) {
     // Read a Line from File    getline(fin, line);
     // Print line in Console    cout << line << endl;
   }
   // Close the file   fin.close();
```

```
   return 0;
}
```

All the over three classes are gotten from fstreambase and the comparing iostream class and they are planned explicitly to oversee circle documents.

C++ gives us the accompanying tasks in File Handling:

- **Making a record:** open()
- **Understanding information:** read()
- **Composing new information:** write()
- **Shutting a document:** close()

File Handling in C++

- **Opening a File:** The principal action done on an item of one of these types is, for the most part, to connect it to a real document.

We can open a document utilizing any of the accompanying strategies:

- First is bypassing the document name in the constructor at the hour of item creation.
- Second is utilizing the open() work.

To open a record:

open()

Syntax:
void open(const char* file_ name,ios::openmode mode);

Modes	Description
in	The file is opened for reading.
out	Opens the file that will be written to.
binary	The file is opened in binary mode.
app	Opens the file and, at the end, appends all of the outputs.
ate	The file is opened, and the control is moved to the end of the file.
trunc	The data in the existing file is deleted. no create If the file already exists, it will be opened.
noreplace	If the file does not already exist, it is opened.

Syntax:

fstream new_file;

new_file.open("newfile.txt", ios::out);

In the above model, new_file is an object of type fstream, as we probably are aware fstream is a class, so we need to make an object of this class to utilize its part capacities. So we make the new_file article and call open() work. Here we use the mode that permits us to open the document to write in it.

Default Open Modes:

ifstream ios::in ofstream ios::out fstream ios::in | ios::out

Syntax:
ofstream new_file;
new_file.open("new_file.txt", ios::out | ios::app);

Here, input mode and attach mode are consolidated, which addresses the document is opened for composing and adding the yields toward the end.

When the program ends, the memory is eradicated, opens up the memory allotted, and shuts the opened documents.

It is smarter to utilize the nearby() capacity to close the opened documents after the utilization of the record.

Utilizing a stream inclusion administrator

*   **<<:** Using stream extraction administrator, we may assemble data into a document.
*   **>>:** We can read data from a record with relative ease.

An example of how to use the open() method to open/create a file is as follows:

```
#include<iostream>
#include <fstream> using namespace std; int main()
{
fstream new_file;
new_file.open("new_file",ios::out);
if(!new_file)
{
cout<<"creation failed";
} else {
cout<<"New file created"; new_file.close(); // Step 4: Closing
file } return 0; }
```

Output: New file created

• **Writing to a File Source Code:**

```
#include <iostream> #include <fstream> using namespace std; int main()
{ fstream new_file; new_file.open("new_file_write. txt",ios::out); if(!new_file)
{
cout<<"File creation failed";
} else {
cout<<"New file created"; new_file<<"Learning";    //Writing to file
new_file.close();
} return 0; }
```

Output:

New file created

```
*new_file_write - Notepad          —    □    ×

File   Edit   Format   View   Help
Learning
```

•   **Reading from a File**

```
#include <iostream> #include <fstream> using namespace std; int main()
{ fstream new_file; new_file.open("new_file_write. txt",ios::in); if(!new_file) cout<<"No such file";
} else { char ch; while (!new_file.eof()) { new_file >>ch; cout << ch; }
new_file.close(); return 0; }
```

•   **Close a File:** It is just finished with the assistance of close() work.

Syntax:
File Pointer.close()

Source Code:
```
#include <iostream> #include <fstream> using namespace std; int main()
{
fstream new_file; new_file.open("new_file.
txt",ios::out); new_file.close(); return 0; }
```

Output:
The file gets closed.

The Most Effective Method to Implement Data Abstraction In C++

Information Abstraction is showing fundamental data to the client yet concealing the foundation subtleties.

Abstraction in C++

Think about a model: An individual uses a cell phone except if he is from an IT or ECE foundation, he knows nothing other than what catches to press. This is a legitimate illustration of Data Abstraction.

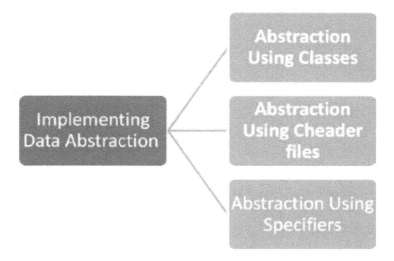

There are three different ways of executing Data Abstraction in C++:

•   Abstraction Using Classes
•   Abstraction utilizing header documents
•   Abstraction Using Specifiers
• **Private:** Abstraction in C++:

At the point when information part or part works are made private, it must be gotten to inside the class and nobody outside the class can get to it.

•   **Public:** Abstraction in C++: When information part or part works are disclosed, it very well may be gotten to by everybody.

•   **Protected:** Abstraction in C++: A secured Access Specifier is an uncommon sort of access specifier. When information part or part works are made secure, it also works to private and tends to be gotten to individuals from the class.

Kinds of Abstraction

There are two sorts of Abstraction:

1.   Data Abstraction

2.   Control Abstraction

Benefits of Abstraction

•   No one but you can make changes to your information or work, and nobody else can.
•   It makes the application secure by not permitting any other individual to see the foundation subtleties.
•   Expands reusability of the code.
•   Keeps away from duplication of your code.

Source Code:

```
#include<iostream> using namespace std; class test
{
private: int x; public: test(int a)
{ x =a; } int get()
{ return x;
}
}; int main()
{ test a(5);
cout<<"Number is: "<<a.get(); return 0; }
```

Output:
Number is: 5

How To Implement Copy Constructor in C++?

Understanding Constructors has been a riddle for some. This article will assist you with demystifying the idea of Copy Constructor in C++. Following pointers will be canvassed in this article:

•   Copy Constructor
•   Shallow Copy Constructor
•   Deep Copy Constructor

A Copy Constructor is a Constructor which introduces an object of a class utilizing one more object of a similar class.

We have the keyword const because we need to make the worth steady and ensure that it isn't altered in the code. Like a default constructor, a duplicate constructor is likewise given by the compiler. This is called Default Copy Constructor. Copy constructors can be made private. We can't duplicate the objects of the class when we make the duplicate constructor private.

Source Code:

```
#include<iostream> using namespace std; class test1 { private: int a; public:
test(int a1)
{ a = a1; }
```

```
test1(const test1 &c2)
{ x = c2.a; } int getB()
{ return a;
}
};
int main()
{
test c1(6); // Normal constructor is
called here
test c2 = c1; // Copy constructor is called here cout << "c1.a = " << c1.getB(); cout << "nc2.x = " <<
c2.getB(); return 0; }
```

Output:
c1.a = 6 c2.a = 6

Data Hiding

Data hiding is a platform developed for hiding internal object information, such as data members, in object-oriented programming. Data hiding ensures confined information admittance to class individuals and keeps up with object uprightness. In this blog, we will see how information concealing functions in C++.

- Encapsulation
- Abstraction
- Data Hiding

Encapsulation, abstraction & data hiding is firmly identified with one another. At the point when we talk about any C++ program, it comprises of two major components:

- Program explanations
- Program information

Encapsulation

Encapsulation ties the information and capacities together, which keeps the two safes from the outside impedance.

Information epitome prompted statement stowing away.

Source Code:
```
#include<iostream> using namespace std; class Encap {     private:
    // data hidden from outside world
    int number;    public:
    // function to set value of
    // variable a     void set(int x)
    {
```

```
        number =x;
      }
      // function to return value of
      // variable a        int get()
      {
        return number;
      } };
// main function
int main()
{
   Encap object;    object.set(3);    cout<<object.get();    return 0; }
```

Output:
3

Abstraction

Data Abstraction is an instrument of concealing the execution from the client and uncovering the interface.

Source Code:
```
#include <iostream> using namespace std; class Abstraction {     private:
      int number1, number2;    public:        void set(int x, int y)
      {          number1 = x;        number2 = y;
      }
      void display()
      {
        cout<<"number1 = " <<number1
<< endl;
```

```
        cout<<"number2 = " << number2 << endl;
    }
}; int main()
{
    Abstraction obj;    obj.set(20, 50);    obj.display();    return 0; }
```

Output:
number1 = 20 number2 = 50

Data Hiding

Data Hiding is a course of joining information and capacities into a solitary unit. The philosophy behind statement stowing away is to cover information inside a class, to keep its immediate access from outside the class. It assists software engineers in making classes with unique informational indexes and capacities, keeping away from extra infiltration from other program classes.

Talking about Data Hiding and information embodiment, information concealing shrouds class information parts, though information epitome shrouds class information parts and private strategies. Presently you likewise need to know the entrance specifier for understanding information stowing away.

Private, public, and protected are three kinds of security/access specifiers accessible inside a class. Generally, the information inside a class is private and the capacities are public. The information is covered up with the goal that it will be protected from unintentional control.

Private individuals/techniques must be gotten to by strategies characterized as a component of the class. Information is regularly characterized as private to keep direct external access from different classes. Private individuals can be gotten to by individuals from the class.

Public individuals/techniques can be gotten to from any place in the program. Class techniques are generally open, which is utilized to control the information present in the class. When in doubt, information ought not to be proclaimed publicly. Public individuals can be gotten to by individuals and objects of the class.

Protected members are private inside a class and are accessible for private access in the determined class.

Source Code:
```
#include<iostream> using namespace std; class Base1 {
    int number;  //by default private    public:
    void read();    void print(); };
void Base1 :: read(){    cout<<"Enter value"<<endl; cin>>number;
}
void Base1 :: print(){    cout<<"Value is "<<number<<endl;
} int main(){
```

Base1 object;   object.read();   object.print();   return 0; }

Output:
Enter value 5
Value is 5

In C++, How Do You Implement Constructors and Destructors?

C++ can undoubtedly be one of the main programming languages, on the off chance that you ask the current programming world. One of the many explanations behind it is the provisions it offers. This article will talk about one such element that is the constructor and destructor in C++.

- Constructor
- Default Constructor
- Parameterized Constructor
- Copy Constructor
- Destructor
- Virtual Destructor

Constructors and Destructors in C++

Constructor

A Constructor is a part capacity of a class. It is mostly used to introduce the objects of the class. It has a similar name as the class. The function Object is naturally referred to when an object is created. It's a unique kind of component capacity for a class.

The distinction between Constructor and other Member Functions:

1. The Constructor has a similar name as the class name.
2. The Constructor is considered when an object of the class is made.
3. A Constructor doesn't have a bring type back.
4. When a constructor isn't indicated, the compiler produces a default constructor that sits idle.
5. There are three kinds of constructors:
    i.   Default Constructor
    ii.   Parameterized Constructor
    iii. Copy constructor

A constructor can likewise be characterized in the private segment of a class. Default Constructor
A default constructor is a sort of constructor that doesn't take any contention and has no parameters.

Source Code:
```
#include <iostream> using namespace std; class test { public: int y, z; test()
{ y = 8; z = 11; }
}; int main()
{ test a;
```

cout <<"the sum is: "<< a.y+a.z; return 1; }

Output:
19

Parameterized Constructor

The passing of parameters to the constructor is conceivable. This is done to introduce the worth of utilizing these passed boundaries. This kind of constructor is known as a Parameterized constructor. The constructor is characterized as follows:

```
test(int x2)
{ x = x2;
}
```

There is a parameter that is passed to the constructor. The worth is passed when the article is made in principle work as displayed beneath.

test c(20);

Inside the fundamental capacity, we make an object of class test and pass the worth of the variable.

Source Code:
```
include <iostream> using namespace std; class test { public: int a; test(int a1)
{ a = a1; } int getB()
{ return a;
}
}; int main()
{ test c(20);
cout << "b.a = " << b.getB(); return 0; }
```

Output:
b.a = 20

Copy Constructor

A Copy Constructor is a Constructor which introduces an object of a class utilizing one more object of a similar class.

Source Code:
```
#include<iostream> using namespace std; class test1 { private: int a; public:
test(int a1)
{ a = a1; }
test(const test &c2)
{ x = c2.x; } int getB()
{ return a;
```

```
}
}; int main()
{
test c1(5); // Normal constructor is
called here
test c2 = c1; // Copy constructor is called here cout << "c1.a = " << c1.getB(); cout << "nc2.a = " <<
tc2.getB(); return 0; }
```

Output:
c1.x = 5 c2.x = 5

Destructor

Destructors are one more sort of part work that is answerable for obliterating or erasing the item. It opens up space involved by the item after it is at this point not required. A Destructor is called naturally when the article is out of extension and as of now not required. A Destructor has the name same as the class name, however, the lone distinction is that the name is gone before by a tile ~.

Syntax:
~test1

There must be just a single Destructor in a class. A Destructor has no return type and no boundaries. On the off chance that we do indicate a destructor in class, the compiler makes a default destructor. The default destructor works fine except if memory is progressively dispensed or the pointer is proclaimed in the class. The Destructor is called when:

- Function closes
- Program close
- A delete operator is called in the program.
- Block that contains the local variable finishes

Source Code:
```
#include <iostream> using namespace std; class test1 { public: int a, b; test1()
{ a = 5; b = 10; }
~test1(){ }
}; int main()
{ test x;
cout <<"the sum is: "<< x.a+x.b; return 1; }
```

Output:
15

Virtual Destructor

The lone variety to the destructor is making the destructor virtual. This is done when we have an inheritance. During inheritance, the typical destructor acts vaguely. To fix this issue, the base class destructor must be announced as virtual.

```
class base1 { public: base1()
{ cout<<"Base Constructor n"; } virtual ~base1()
{ cout<<"Base Destructor"; }
};
```

Basic Input/Output in C++

The C++ standard libraries offer a wide range of input/output capabilities, as we'll explore in the next chapters. This chapter will cover the most fundamental and often used I/O operations in C++ programming.

I/O in C++ happens in streams, which are byte sequences. The flow of bytes from a device such as a keyboard, a disc drive, or a network connection to main memory is known as input, while the flow of bytes from main memory to a device such as a display screen, a printer, a disc drive, or a network connection is known as output.

Header Files for the I/O Library

The following header files are required for a C++ program:

Sr. No Header File & Function
1   **<iostream>**
The cin, cout, cerr, and clog objects are defined in this file, and they correspond to the standard input stream, standard output stream, un-buffered standard error stream, and buffered standard error stream, respectively.

Sr. No Header File & Function

2   **<iomanip>**
This file specifies services that may be used to conduct formatted I/O using parameterized stream manipulators like setw and setprecision.

3   **<fstream>**
This file defines user-controlled file processing services.

(cout) The Standard Output Stream

The ostream class is represented by the predefined object cout. The standard output device, which is generally the display screen, is said to be "attached to" the cout object. As demonstrated in the following example, the cout is combined with the stream insertion operator, which is represented as two less than signs.

Example:
```
#include <iostream> using namespace std; int main() {
```

```
    char str[] = "Hi everyone";    cout << "The value of str: " << str << endl;
}
```

When the preceding code is built and run, the following result is obtained:

The value of str: Hi Everyone

In addition, the C++ compiler identifies the data type of the variable to be printed and chooses the proper stream insertion operator to show the value. To produce data items of built-in types integer, float, double, strings, and pointer values, the operator is overloaded.

As demonstrated above, the insertion operator can be used many times in a single statement, while endl is used to add a new line at the end of the line.

(cin) The Standard Input Stream

The istream class is represented by the predefined object cin. The conventional input device, which is generally the keyboard, is associated with the cin object. As demonstrated in the following example, the cin is used in conjunction with the stream extraction operator, which is represented as >>, which is two greater than signs.

Example:
```
#include <iostream> using namespace std; int main() {    char n[30];    cout << "Enter your name: ";
cin >> n;
    cout << "Your name: " << n << endl;
}
```

When you compile and run the code above, it will request you for a name. To see the following result, you enter a value and then press enter.

Enter your name: cp
Your name: cp

The C++ compiler additionally identifies the data type of the input value and uses the appropriate stream extraction operation to extract and store the value in the variables.

(cerr) The Standard Error Stream

The ostream class has a preset object called cerr. The cerr object is claimed to be attached to the standard error device, which is also a display screen, but the object cerr is unbuffered, and each stream insertion causes cerr's output to show instantly.

As illustrated in the following example, the cerr can also be used with the stream insertion operator.

Example:

```
#include <iostream> using namespace std; int main() {    char str[] = "Un-able to read";    cerr <<
"Error: " << str << endl;
}
```

When the given code is built and run, the following result is obtained:

Error: Un-able to read

(clog) The Standard Log Stream

The ostream class has a preset object called clog. The standard error device, which is also a display
screen, is associated with the clog object, which is buffered. This implies that each addition to clog
may result in the output being kept in a buffer until the buffer is full or flushed.

As illustrated in the following example, the clog may also be used with the stream insertion operator.

Example:
```
#include <iostream> using namespace std; int main() {    char str[] = "Un-able to read";    clog <<
"Error: " << str << endl;
}
```

When the preceding code is built and run, the following is the result:

Error: Un-able to read

With these short examples, you wouldn't be able to see the difference between cout, cerr, and clog,
but the distinction becomes evident when developing and executing large programs. So, while
displaying error messages, cerr stream should be utilized, and when displaying other log messages,
clog should be used.

C++ Data Structures

Structure is a user-defined data type that enables you to combine data items of different types.
C/C++ arrays allow you to construct variables that mix many data items of the same kind, while
structure is another user-defined data type that allows you to combine data items of other kinds.

Structures are used to represent a record. For example, let's say you want to keep track of your
library books.

You may wish to keep note of the following characteristics for each book.

- Title
- Author
- Subject
- Book-id

Structure Defining

The struct statement is used to define a structure. The struct command creates a new data type for your application with many members. The struct statement has the following format:

Syntax:
struct [struc tag] {   member definition;
    ....   member definition; };

Each member definition is a regular variable definition, such as int c float d; or any other acceptable variable definition, and the structure tag is optional. You can specify one or more structure variables before the last semicolon at the conclusion of the structure declaration, although this is optional.

Here's how you'd go about declaring the Book structure:

Example:
struct books {   char title[70];   char author[60];   char subject[90];   int book_id; } book;

Using the Member to Access Structure Members

The member access operator is used to access any member of a structure (.). The member access operator is a period between the name of the structure variable and the name of the structure member we want to access. The struct keyword is used to define variables of the structure type. The following is an example of how to use structure:

Example:

```
#include <iostream> #include <cstring> using namespace std;
struct books {    char title[70];    char author[60];    char subject[90];    int  book_id; };
int main() {
    struct books book1;       //
Declare Book1 of type Book
    struct books book2;       // Declare Book2 of type Book    // specification of book 1    strcpy(
book1.title, " C++
Programming");    strcpy( book1.author, "Chandi ");    strcpy( book1.subject, "C++ ");
book1.book_id = 64407;    // book 2 specification    strcpy( book2.title, " Billi");    strcpy(
book2.author, "hakita");    strcpy( book2.subject, "Tele");    book2.book_id = 64700;
    // Print    cout << "Booktitle : " << book1. title <<endl;
    cout << "Bookauthor : " << book1. author <<endl;
    cout << "Booksubject : " << book1. subject <<endl;
    cout << "Bookid : " << book1.book_id <<endl;
    // Print    cout << "Booktitle : " << book2. title <<endl;
    cout << "Bookauthor : " << book2. author <<endl;
    cout << "Booksubject : " << book2. subject <<endl;
    cout << "Bookid : " << book2.book_id
<<endl;    return 0;
```

}

Output:
Booktitle : C++ Programming
Bookauthor : Chandi
Booksubject : C++
Bookid : 64407
Booktitle : Billi
Bookauthor : hakita
Booksubject : Tele
Bookid : 64700

Structures as Function Arguments

A structure can be passed as a function parameter like any other variable or pointer can. Structure variables are accessible in the same way as variables in the previous example:

```cpp
#include <iostream> #include <cstring>
using namespace std;
void printbook( struct books book );
struct books {   char title[70];   char author[60];   char subject[90];   int  book_id; };
int main() {
   struct books book1;       // Declare
Book1 of type Book     struct books book2;       // Declare
Book2 of type Book
   // specification of book 1    strcpy( book1.title, " C++ Programming");    strcpy( book1.author,
"Chandi ");    strcpy( book1.subject, "C++ ");    book1.book_id = 64407;
   // book 2 specification    strcpy( book2.title, " Billi");    strcpy( book2.author, "hakita");    strcpy(
book2.subject, "Tele");    book2.book_id = 64700;
   // Print book1 info    printbook( book1 );
   // Print book2 info    printbook( book2 );
   return 0;
}
void printbook( struct books book ) {     cout << "Booktitle : " << book.title
<<endl;    cout << "Bookauthor : " << book.author
<<endl;    cout << "Booksubject : " << book.subject
<<endl;    cout << "Bookid : " << book.book_id <<endl;
}
```

Output:
Booktitle : C++ Programming
Bookauthor : Chandi
Booksubject : C++
Bookid : 64407
Booktitle : Billi
Bookauthor : hakita

Booksubject : Tele
Bookid : 64700

This chapter covers the fundamentals of C++ syntax, as well as how to compile and run programs. What is the fundamental terminology of C++, such as semicolons, blocks, and keywords, and comments. We also learn about various sorts of data and variables and how to use several examples to illustrate types. Furthermore, what are Constants and Modifiers and their many types, as well as storage class, operators, and the various types of Loop and Decision statements.

We also touched upon topics such as what is a function in C++, and how do you declare one? What are arguments and what are Numbers, Arrays, Strings, and Pointers? Finally, using various words and examples, we learn how to take care of Files in C++.

Conclusion: The Power and Future of Object-Oriented Programming (OOP)

Object-Oriented Programming (OOP) has been a cornerstone of software development for decades, and its relevance continues to grow as software systems become increasingly complex and interconnected. C++, with its robust support for OOP principles, remains one of the most powerful and widely used programming languages in the world. As we look ahead to 2025 and beyond, the principles of OOP in C++ will continue to play a critical role in shaping the future of software engineering. This conclusion provides a comprehensive overview of the importance of OOP in C++, its advantages, challenges, and its future trajectory.

1. The Importance of OOP in C++

Modularity and Reusability

One of the most significant advantages of OOP is its ability to break down complex systems into smaller, manageable, and reusable components called **classes**. By encapsulating data and behavior within classes, developers can create modular code that is easier to understand, maintain, and extend. This modularity is particularly important in large-scale software projects, where teams of developers work on different parts of the system simultaneously.

For example, in a car manufacturing simulation, classes like Engine, Wheels, and Car can be developed independently and reused across different projects. This reusability not only saves time but also ensures consistency and reduces the likelihood of errors.

Abstraction and Simplification

OOP allows developers to model real-world entities and their interactions in a way that is intuitive and easy to understand. **Abstraction** enables programmers to focus on the essential features of an object while hiding unnecessary details. This simplification is particularly useful when dealing with complex systems, as it allows developers to work at a higher level of abstraction without worrying about low-level implementation details.

For instance, a Bank Account class can abstract away the complexities of account management, such as balance calculation and transaction logging, allowing developers to focus on higher-level business logic.

Encapsulation and Data Hiding

Encapsulation is a fundamental principle of OOP that ensures data integrity and security by restricting direct access to an object's internal state. By using access specifiers like private and protected, developers can control how data is accessed and modified, preventing unintended interference and misuse.

For example, in a Person class, sensitive data like social Security Number can be marked as private, ensuring that it can only be accessed or modified through controlled methods like getSSN() and setSSN().

Inheritance and Code Reusability

Inheritance allows developers to create new classes based on existing ones, inheriting their attributes and behaviors. This promotes code reuse and reduces redundancy, as common functionality can be defined in a base class and shared across multiple derived classes.

For example, in a game development scenario, a base class Character can define common attributes like health and speed, while derived classes like Player and Enemy can add specialized behaviors.

Polymorphism and Flexibility

Polymorphism enables objects of different classes to be treated as objects of a common base class, providing flexibility and extensibility. This allows developers to write code that can work with a wide range of objects without knowing their specific types at compile time.

For example, in a drawing application, a Shape base class can define a virtual draw() method, which can be overridden by derived classes like Circle and Rectangle. This allows the application to draw any shape without knowing its exact type.

2. Advantages of OOP in C++

Performance and Efficiency

C++ is known for its performance and efficiency, making it an ideal choice for resource-intensive applications like game development, real-time systems, and high-frequency trading. OOP in C++ allows developers to write high-performance code while maintaining the benefits of modularity, reusability, and abstraction.

Compatibility with C

C++ is backward-compatible with C, allowing developers to integrate OOP features into existing C codebases. This makes it easier to modernize legacy systems and take advantage of OOP principles without rewriting the entire codebase.

Rich Standard Library

C++ provides a rich standard library that includes support for data structures, algorithms, and input/output operations. This library, combined with OOP principles, enables developers to build complex applications quickly and efficiently.

Community and Ecosystem

C++ has a large and active community of developers, as well as a vast ecosystem of libraries, frameworks, and tools. This makes it easier for developers to find solutions to common problems, share knowledge, and collaborate on projects.

3. Challenges of OOP in C++

Complexity

While OOP provides many benefits, it can also introduce complexity, especially in large-scale projects. Managing class hierarchies, ensuring proper encapsulation, and avoiding issues like diamond inheritance can be challenging.

Performance Overhead

OOP features like virtual functions and dynamic polymorphism can introduce performance overhead, especially in performance-critical applications. Developers need to carefully balance the benefits of OOP with the need for performance.

Learning Curve

C++ is a complex language with a steep learning curve, especially for developers new to OOP. Understanding concepts like templates, memory management, and operator overloading requires time and effort.

4. The Future of OOP in C++

Integration with Modern Technologies

As technology continues to evolve, C++ and OOP will play a critical role in emerging fields like artificial intelligence, machine learning, and the Internet of Things (IoT). C++'s performance and efficiency make it well-suited for these domains, while OOP principles provide the structure and organization needed to build complex systems.

Improved Tooling and Libraries

The C++ ecosystem is constantly evolving, with new libraries, frameworks, and tools being developed to simplify OOP and improve productivity. For example, modern C++ standards like C++20 and C++23 introduce new features like concepts, ranges, and coroutines, which make it easier to write clean, efficient, and maintainable code.

Emphasis on Safety and Security

As software systems become more interconnected and critical to everyday life, there is a growing emphasis on safety and security. OOP principles like encapsulation and data hiding will play a key role in building secure systems, while new language features and tools will help developers identify and mitigate potential vulnerabilities.

Cross-Platform Development

With the rise of cross-platform development frameworks like Qt and Unreal Engine, C++ and OOP will continue to be a popular choice for building applications that run on multiple platforms, including desktop, mobile, and embedded systems.

Education and Training

As the demand for skilled C++ developers continues to grow, there will be an increased focus on education and training. Universities, online courses, and coding bootcamps will play a critical role in equipping the next generation of developers with the skills needed to succeed in the world of OOP and C++.

5. Best Practices for OOP in C++

To maximize the benefits of OOP in C++, developers should follow these best practices:

Use Encapsulation Wisely

Encapsulate data and behavior within classes, and use access specifiers to control access to internal state. This ensures data integrity and prevents unintended interference.

Favor Composition Over Inheritance

While inheritance is a powerful tool, it can lead to complex and fragile class hierarchies. In many cases, composition (using objects of other classes as members) is a better alternative.

Leverage Polymorphism

Use polymorphism to write flexible and extensible code. Virtual functions and interfaces allow you to write code that can work with a wide range of objects without knowing their specific types.

Follow the SOLID Principles

The SOLID principles (Single Responsibility, Open/Closed, Liskov Substitution, Interface Segregation, and Dependency Inversion) provide guidelines for designing robust and maintainable OOP systems.

Use Modern C++ Features

Take advantage of modern C++ features like smart pointers, lambdas, and move semantics to write clean, efficient, and safe code.

6. Final Thoughts

Object-Oriented Programming in C++ is a powerful paradigm that has stood the test of time. Its principles of modularity, abstraction, encapsulation, inheritance, and polymorphism provide the foundation for building complex, scalable, and maintainable software systems. As we look ahead to 2025 and beyond, the importance of OOP in C++ will only continue to grow, driven by the demands of modern technology and the need for secure, efficient, and cross-platform solutions.

By mastering OOP concepts and best practices, developers can unlock the full potential of C++ and build software that meets the challenges of the future. Whether you're developing games, real-time systems, or AI applications, OOP in C++ provides the tools and techniques you need to succeed in the ever-evolving world of software development.

4. C++ Standard Template Library (STL), Standard Library, and Advanced Topics

Introduction

C++ is a powerful, high-performance programming language that has evolved significantly since its inception in the 1980s. One of the key reasons for its enduring popularity is its rich standard library, which includes the Standard Template Library (STL) and the C++ Standard Library. These libraries provide a wide range of functionalities that enable developers to write efficient, reusable, and maintainable code. As of 2025, the C++ Standard Library and STL have continued to evolve, incorporating new features and optimizations that align with modern programming paradigms and hardware advancements.

This document provides a detailed introduction to the C++ Standard Template Library (STL), the C++ Standard Library, and advanced topics related to their usage in 2025. We will explore the core components of these libraries, their evolution, and how they can be leveraged to build robust and efficient applications.

1. C++ Standard Template Library (STL)

The Standard Template Library (STL) is a subset of the C++ Standard Library that provides a collection of template classes and functions for common data structures and algorithms. The STL is designed to be generic, meaning that its components can be used with any data type, provided that the type meets certain requirements. The STL is divided into four main components:

1.1 Containers

Containers are data structures that store collections of objects. The STL provides a variety of container types, each optimized for specific use cases. The main categories of containers are:

- **Sequence Containers**: These store elements in a linear sequence. Examples include:

    o   std::vector: A dynamic array that provides fast random access and dynamic resizing.
    o   std::list: A doubly linked list that allows efficient insertion and deletion at any position.
    o   std::deque: A double-ended queue that supports fast insertion and deletion at both ends.

- **Associative Containers**: These store elements in a sorted order, allowing for fast lookup based on keys. Examples include:

    o   std::set: A collection of unique elements sorted by their values.
    o   std::map: A collection of key-value pairs sorted by keys.
    o   std::multiset and std::multimap: Variants that allow duplicate keys.

- **Unordered Associative Containers**: These store elements in a hash-based structure, providing fast average-time complexity for lookups. Examples include:

  - std::unordered_set: A collection of unique elements with no specific order.
  - std::unordered_map: A collection of key-value pairs with no specific order.

- **Container Adaptors**: These are specialized containers that provide a specific interface for common use cases. Examples include:

  - std::stack: A last-in, first-out (LIFO) data structure.
  - std::queue: A first-in, first-out (FIFO) data structure.
  - std::priority_queue: A queue where elements are ordered by priority.

1.2 Iterators

Iterators are objects that enable traversal of containers. They provide a unified interface for accessing elements in a container, regardless of the container's underlying implementation. The STL defines several types of iterators, including:

- **Input Iterators**: Allow reading elements in a forward direction.
- **Output Iterators**: Allow writing elements in a forward direction.
- **Forward Iterators**: Combine input and output iterators, allowing both reading and writing.
- **Bidirectional Iterators**: Extend forward iterators by allowing traversal in both directions.
- **Random Access Iterators**: Provide the most functionality, allowing direct access to any element in the container.

Iterators are a key feature of the STL, enabling algorithms to operate on containers without needing to know their internal structure.

1.3 Algorithms

The STL provides a rich set of algorithms that operate on containers through iterators. These algorithms are designed to be generic and can be used with any container that meets the necessary requirements. Some of the most commonly used algorithms include:

- **Sorting and Searching**: std::sort, std::binary_search, std::lower_bound, etc.
- **Modifying Operations**: std::copy, std::fill, std::transform, etc.
- **Non-Modifying Operations**: std::find, std::count, std::for_each, etc.
- **Numeric Operations**: std::accumulate, std::inner_product, etc.

The algorithms in the STL are highly optimized and provide a consistent interface, making it easy to write efficient and reusable code.

1.4 Functors and Lambdas

Functors (function objects) and lambdas are used to define custom behavior for algorithms and other STL components. A functor is an object that can be called like a function, while a lambda is an anonymous function defined inline. Both functors and lambdas are widely used in the STL to provide flexibility and customization.

For example, the std::sort algorithm can be customized by passing a lambda as a comparator:

```
std::vector<int> v = {5, 3, 1, 4, 2};
std::sort(v.begin(), v.end(), [](int a, int b) { return a > b; });
```

2. C++ Standard Library

The C++ Standard Library is a broader collection of libraries that includes the STL as well as additional components for input/output, strings, concurrency, and more. As of 2025, the C++ Standard Library has continued to expand, incorporating new features and improvements from the latest C++ standards (C++20, C++23, and beyond).

2.1 Input/Output (I/O) Library

The I/O library provides facilities for performing input and output operations. Key components include:

- **Streams**: std::cin, std::cout, std::ifstream, std::ofstream, etc.
- **Formatting**: Manipulators like std::setw, std::setprecision, and std::hex.
- **File I/O**: Classes for reading from and writing to files.

2.2 Strings

The std::string class provides a powerful and flexible way to handle text. It supports operations like concatenation, substring extraction, and searching. In recent years, improvements have been made to support Unicode and other advanced string manipulation features.

2.3 Concurrency

Modern C++ includes robust support for concurrent programming. Key features include:

- **Threads**: The std::thread class allows creating and managing threads.
- **Mutexes and Locks**: std::mutex, std::lock_guard, and std::unique_lock for synchronization.
- **Atomic Operations**: std::atomic for lock-free programming.
- **Futures and Promises**: std::future and std::promise for asynchronous programming.

2.4 Smart Pointers

Smart pointers are used to manage dynamic memory automatically, reducing the risk of memory leaks.

The C++ Standard Library provides three types of smart pointers:

- std::unique_ptr: Represents exclusive ownership of a resource.
- std::shared_ptr: Allows shared ownership of a resource.
- std::weak_ptr: A non-owning reference to a resource managed by std::shared_ptr.

2.5 Utilities

The Standard Library includes a variety of utility classes and functions, such as:

- std::pair and std::tuple: For grouping multiple values.
- std::optional: For representing optional values.
- std::variant and std::any: For type-safe unions and dynamic typing.

3. Advanced Topics (2025)

As of 2025, several advanced topics have gained prominence in the C++ community, driven by the evolution of the language and the demands of modern software development.

3.1 Concepts and Constraints

Concepts, introduced in C++20, allow developers to specify requirements for template parameters. This improves code readability and error messages. For example:

```
template<typename T>
requires std::integral<T>
T add(T a, T b) {
    return a + b;
}
```

3.2 Ranges

The Ranges library, also introduced in C++20, provides a more expressive way to work with sequences of elements. It simplifies code by allowing operations on entire ranges rather than individual iterators.

For example:

```
std::vector<int> v = {1, 2, 3, 4, 5};
auto even = v | std::views::filter([](int x) { return x % 2 == 0; });
```

3.3 Coroutines

Coroutines, introduced in C++20, enable asynchronous programming with a more intuitive syntax. They are particularly useful for tasks like networking and file I/O.

3.4 Modules

Modules, introduced in C++20, provide a modern alternative to header files. They improve compilation times and reduce dependency issues.

3.5 Parallel Algorithms

The C++ Standard Library now includes parallel versions of many algorithms, allowing developers to take advantage of multi-core processors.

For example:

```
std::vector<int> v = {5, 3, 1, 4, 2};
std::sort(std::execution::par, v.begin(), v.end());
```

Reflection and Metaprogramming

Reflection, expected in future C++ standards, will allow programs to inspect and manipulate their own structure. This will enable more advanced metaprogramming techniques.

Introduction to the STL

The C++ Standard Template Library (STL) is a powerful and versatile collection of template classes and functions that provide essential data structures and algorithms. It's a fundamental part of C++ and simplifies many common programming tasks. In this section, we'll introduce you to the basics of the STL and its key components.

What Is the STL?

The STL is a library that extends the C++ language by providing generic classes and functions. It's generic in the sense that it allows you to write code that works with different data types without sacrificing type safety. The STL includes various containers, algorithms, and iterators that you can use to create efficient and flexible C++ programs.

Key Components of the STL

The STL is divided into several key components:

1. **Containers:** Containers are data structures that store and manage collections of objects. Common container types include vectors, lists, queues, stacks, and maps. Each container type has unique characteristics and is suitable for specific use cases.

2. **Algorithms:** Algorithms are a set of functions that perform various operations on data stored in containers. These operations include searching, sorting, manipulating, and more. Algorithms are designed to work with different container types, making them highly reusable.

3. **Iterators:** Iterators are objects that allow you to traverse the elements of a container sequentially. They provide a uniform way to access and manipulate container elements, regardless of the container type.

4. **Function Objects (Functors):** Function objects, also known as functors, are objects that can be called like functions. They are often used in conjunction with algorithms to customize their behavior.

Benefits of Using the STL

The STL offers several advantages:

- **Productivity:** It simplifies common programming tasks by providing well-designed containers and algorithms, reducing the need to reinvent the wheel.

- **Efficiency:** STL containers and algorithms are highly optimized, resulting in efficient code.

- **Type Safety:** Generic programming in the STL maintains type safety, preventing runtime errors.

- **Reusability:** The generic nature of the STL components allows you to reuse code across different projects and scenarios.

Example: Using an STL Vector

Let's look at a simple example of using an STL vector, a dynamic array-like container, to store and manipulate integers:

```
#include <iostream>

#include <vector>
int main() {
// Create an empty vector of
integers std::vector<int>
numbers; // Add elements to the
vector numbers.push_back(10);
numbers.push_back(20);
numbers.push_back(30);
// Iterate through the vector and print its
elements for (const int& num : numbers) {
std::cout << num << " ";
} return 0;
}
```

In this example, we include the necessary headers, create a vector of integers, add elements to it, and iterate through the vector using an iterator. The STL provides us with a simple and efficient way to work with collections of data.

Containers in STL (Vectors, Lists, Maps, etc.)

The C++ Standard Template Library (STL) offers a variety of container classes, each designed for specific use cases and requirements. These containers are ready-made data structures that can store and manage collections of objects.

In this section, we'll explore some of the most commonly used container classes in the STL.

Vector

A vector is a dynamic array that can grow or shrink in size. It provides efficient random access to elements and is a versatile container for storing a sequence of elements. Vectors automatically handle memory management.

```cpp
#include <iostream>
#include <vector>
int main() {
// Create a vector of integers std::vector<int>
numbers; // Add elements to the vector
numbers.push_back(10); numbers.push_back(20);
numbers.push_back(30); // Access elements by
index std::cout << "First element: " << numbers[0]
<< std::endl;
// Iterate through the vector for
(const int& num : numbers) {
std::cout << num << " ";
} return 0;
}
```

List

A list is a doubly-linked list that provides efficient insertions and deletions at both ends of the list. It's suitable when you need frequent insertions or removals without the need for random access.

```cpp
#include <iostream>
#include <list> int
main() {
// Create a list of strings
std::list<std::string> names; // Add
elements to the list
names.push_back("Alice");
names.push_back("Bob");
names.push_back("Charlie"); //
Iterate through the list for (const
std::string& name : names) {
std::cout << name << " ";
} return 0;
```

}

Map

A map is an associative container that stores key-value pairs. It provides efficient lookups based on keys. Each key in a map is unique.

```cpp
#include <iostream>
#include <map>
int main() {
// Create a map of ages
std::map<std::string, int>
ageMap; // Add key-value pairs
to the map ageMap["Alice"] =
25; ageMap["Bob"] = 30;
ageMap["Charlie"] = 22; //
Access values by key std::cout
<< "Alice's age: " <<
ageMap["Alice"] << std::endl;
// Iterate through the map for (const auto& pair : ageMap) {
std::cout << pair.first << ": " << pair.second << " years old" <<
std::endl;
} return 0;
}
```

Set

A set is an associative container that stores unique elements in sorted order. It's useful when you need to maintain a collection of unique values.

```cpp
#include <iostream>
#include <set> int
main() {
// Create a set of integers std::set<int> uniqueNumbers; //
Add elements to the set uniqueNumbers.insert(10);
uniqueNumbers.insert(20); uniqueNumbers.insert(10);  //
Duplicate element, won't be added
// Iterate through the set for (const
int& num : uniqueNumbers) {
std::cout << num << " ";
} return 0;
}
```

These are just a few examples of the container classes available in the STL. Each container class has its own advantages and use cases, allowing you to choose the most suitable one for your specific programming needs. In the following sections, we'll dive deeper into each container class and explore their functionalities and operations.

Iterators and Algorithms

Iterators and algorithms are integral components of the C++ Standard Template Library (STL). They allow you to work with containers in a generic and efficient manner, making your code more reusable and expressive. In this section, we'll explore iterators and common algorithms used in the STL.

Iterators

An iterator is an object that provides a way to access and manipulate the elements of a container sequentially. It acts as a pointer to elements within a container and allows you to traverse the container's contents. There are several types of iterators in the STL, each with specific capabilities:

- **begin():** Returns an iterator pointing to the first element of the container.

- **end():** Returns an iterator pointing to one position past the last element of the container.

- **rbegin():** Returns a reverse iterator pointing to the last element of the container (useful for reverse traversal).

- **rend():** Returns a reverse iterator pointing to one position before the first element (useful for reverse traversal).

Here's an example of using iterators to iterate through a vector:

```
#include <iostream> #include <vector> int main() { std::vector<int>
numbers = {1, 2, 3, 4, 5}; // Using iterators to access elements for
(std::vector<int>::iterator it = numbers.begin(); it != numbers.end();
++it) { std::cout << *it << " ";
} return 0;
}
```

In this example, we use the begin() and end() functions to obtain iterators that define the range of elements in the vector.

Algorithms

The STL provides a rich set of algorithms that operate on containers. These algorithms perform various operations such as searching, sorting, and manipulation on container elements. Algorithms take advantage of iterators to work with containers, making them generic and versatile.

Here's an example of using the std::find algorithm to search for an element in a vector:

```cpp
#include <iostream>
#include <vector> #include <algorithm> int main() {
std::vector<int> numbers = {1, 2, 3, 4, 5}; int target = 3;

// Using std::find algorithm to search for the target element
std::vector<int>::iterator it = std::find(numbers.begin(), numbers.end(), target);
if (it != numbers.end()) { std::cout << "Element found at position: " <<
std::distance(numbers.begin(), it) << std::endl;
} else { std::cout << "Element not found."
<< std::endl;
} return 0;
}
```

In this example, we include the <algorithm> header to access the std::find algorithm. The algorithm takes a range defined by iterators and searches for a specific element, returning an iterator pointing to the found element or the end() iterator if the element is not found.

Benefits of Iterators and Algorithms

Iterators and algorithms offer several advantages:

- **Generic Programming:** They allow you to write code that works with various containers, promoting code reuse and maintainability.

- **Efficiency:** STL algorithms are highly optimized, leading to efficient code.

- **Expressiveness:** Code using iterators and algorithms is often more expressive and readable.

By mastering iterators and algorithms, you can harness the full power of the STL and write efficient and maintainable C++ code. In the following sections, we'll dive deeper into specific algorithms and their applications.

Generic Programming with Templates

Templates are a fundamental feature of the C++ programming language that enable generic programming. They allow you to write code that can work with different data types while maintaining type safety and code efficiency. In this section, we'll explore C++ templates and their applications.

Function Templates

A function template is a blueprint for generating functions. It allows you to define a generic function that can operate on various data types without writing separate functions for each type. Here's an example of a simple function template that swaps two values:

```cpp
#include <iostream>
```

```cpp
// Function template for swapping two
values template <typename T> void
swap(T& a, T& b) { T temp = a; a = b; b
= temp; }
int main() { int x = 5, y = 10; std::cout << "Before swap: x
= " << x << ", y = " << y << std::endl;
// Using the swap function template swap(x, y); std::cout
<< "After swap: x = " << x << ", y = " << y << std::endl;
return 0;
}
```

In this example, the swap function template works with any data type that supports assignment.

Class Templates

Class templates are similar to function templates but allow you to define generic classes. They are commonly used for container classes in the STL. Here's an example of a simple generic stack class template:

```cpp
#include <iostream>

#include <vector>
// Class template for a generic
stack template <typename T>
class Stack { public:
void push(const T& value) {
elements.push_back(value);
}
T pop() { if (elements.empty()) { throw
std::out_of_range("Stack is empty.");
}
T top = elements.back();
elements.pop_back();
return top; } bool
empty() const { return
elements.empty();
} private:
std::vector<T> elements;
};
int main() { Stack<int>
intStack; intStack.push(10);
intStack.push(20);
intStack.push(30); while
(!intStack.empty()) { std::cout
<< intStack.pop() << " ";
} return 0;
```

}

In this example, the Stack class template can be instantiated with different data types, allowing you to create stacks of integers, strings, or any other type.

Template Specialization

Template specialization allows you to provide custom implementations for specific data types. For example, you might want to implement a different behavior for a specific data type while keeping the generic behavior for others.

Here's a template specialization example for printing a message for integers:

```
#include <iostream> // Generic template
template <typename T> void printMessage(const
T& value) { std::cout << "Generic Message: " <<
value << std::endl;
}
// Template specialization for integers template <> void
printMessage<int>(const int& value) { std::cout <<
"Special Message for Integers: " << value << std::endl; }

int main() { int x = 5; double y = 3.14;
printMessage(x); // Special Message for
Integers: 5 printMessage(y); // Generic
Message: 3.14 return 0;
}
```

In this example, we specialize the printMessage template for integers, providing a different message. Templates are a powerful tool in C++ that enable code reusability and flexibility. They are extensively used in the STL to create generic containers and algorithms that can work with various data types. Understanding and effectively using templates is crucial for mastering C++ programming.

Custom Template Classes

In C++, you can create custom template classes to implement data structures or algorithms that work with different data types in a generic way. This section explores the creation and usage of custom template classes, providing you with the flexibility to design your own generic components.

Creating a Custom Template Class

To create a custom template class, you use the template keyword followed by the template parameters within angle brackets (<>). Here's a basic example of a custom template class for a generic stack:

```cpp
#include <iostream>
#include <vector>

// Custom template class for a generic
stack template <typename T> class
Stack { public:
// Constructor

Stack() {}
// Push a value onto the stack
void push(const T& value) {
elements.push_back(value);
}
// Pop a value from the stack T pop() { if
(elements.empty()) { throw
std::out_of_range("Stack is empty.");
}
T top = elements.back();
elements.pop_back(); return top; }
// Check if the stack is
empty bool empty() const {
return elements.empty(); }
private: std::vector<T>
elements; }; int main() {
// Create a stack for integers
Stack<int> intStack;
intStack.push(10);
intStack.push(20);
intStack.push(30); while
(!intStack.empty()) { std::cout
<< intStack.pop() << " "; }
std::cout << std::endl;
// Create a stack for strings
Stack<std::string> stringStack;
stringStack.push("Hello");
stringStack.push("World");
while (!stringStack.empty()) {
std::cout << stringStack.pop()
<< " ";

}
std::cout << std::endl;
return 0;
}
```

In this example, the Stack class is a template class that can be instantiated with different data types. You can create Stack objects for integers, strings, or any other type you need.

Template Class Specialization

Just like function templates, you can specialize template classes to provide custom implementations for specific data types. Here's an example of a specialized template class for complex numbers:

```cpp
#include <iostream>
#include <complex>

// Custom template class for complex
numbers template <typename T> class
ComplexCalculator { public:
// Constructor

ComplexCalculator() {} // Add two complex numbers
std::complex<T> add(const std::complex<T>& a, const
std::complex<T>& b) { return a + b;
}
};
// Template class specialization for
double template <> class
ComplexCalculator<double> { public:

// Constructor

ComplexCalculator() {}
// Add two complex numbers (specialized implementation) std::complex<double>
add(const std::complex<double>& a, const std::complex<double>& b) {
std::complex<double> result; result.real(a.real() + b.real()); result.imag(a.imag() +
b.imag()); return result;
}
}; int main()
{
// Create a complex calculator for generic types
ComplexCalculator<std::complex<float>>
floatCalculator; std::complex<float> a(1.0f, 2.0f);
std::complex<float> b(2.0f, 3.0f);
std::complex<float> result = floatCalculator.add(a,
b); std::cout << "Result (float): " << result <<
std::endl;
// Create a complex calculator specialized for doubles
ComplexCalculator<double> doubleCalculator;
std::complex<double> x(1.0, 2.0); std::complex<double>
y(2.0, 3.0); std::complex<double> specializedResult =
```

doubleCalculator.add(x, y); std::cout << "Result (double): "
<< specializedResult << std::endl; **return** 0;

}

In this example, we specialize the ComplexCalculator template class to provide a different implementation for double data types.

Custom template classes offer a powerful way to create flexible and generic components in C++, allowing your code to adapt to different data types seamlessly. They are widely used for designing data structures, algorithms, and libraries that need to work with various types of data. Understanding and utilizing custom template classes can significantly enhance your C++ programming capabilities.

Understanding Exceptions

In C++, exceptions provide a mechanism to handle runtime errors or exceptional conditions gracefully. Exceptions allow you to write code that can respond to error situations without abruptly terminating the program. In this section, we'll explore the concept of exceptions in C++ and how to use them effectively.

What Are Exceptions?

An exception is an unexpected or error condition that occurs during the execution of a program. These conditions can include situations like division by zero, accessing an out-of-bounds array element, or encountering a file that doesn't exist.

When an exceptional condition occurs, C++ allows you to throw an exception using the throw keyword. This throws an exception object that represents the error condition. The program then looks for code that can catch and handle the exception using try-catch blocks.

Throwing Exceptions

You can throw an exception in your code using the throw statement. The throw statement is followed by an exception object, which can be of any data type, but it's commonly an instance of a standard exception class or a user-defined exception class.

Here's an example of throwing a standard exception:

```
#include <iostream>
#include <stdexcept>
int divide(int a, int b) { if (b == 0) {
throw std::runtime_error("Division by
zero.");
}
return a / b; }
```

```
int main() { try { int result = divide(10,
0); std::cout << "Result: " << result <<
std::endl;
} catch (const std::runtime_error& e) {
std::cerr << "Exception caught: " << e.what() << std::endl;
} return 0;
}
```

In this example, the divide function throws a std::runtime_error exception when attempting to divide by zero. The try-catch block in the main function catches the exception and prints an error message.

Catching Exceptions

To catch exceptions, you use try-catch blocks. The code that may throw exceptions is enclosed within the try block, and you specify one or more catch blocks to handle different types of exceptions.

```
try {

// Code that may throw exceptions

} catch (const SomeExceptionType& e) {
// Handle the exception

} catch (const AnotherExceptionType& e) {
// Handle another type of exception

} catch (...) {
// Handle all other exceptions

}
```

In the example above, the catch blocks can catch exceptions of specific types, and there's a catch-all block that can handle any other exceptions that weren't caught by the previous catch blocks.

Exception Safety

Exception safety is a critical aspect of writing robust C++ code. It ensures that your code behaves predictably and consistently, even in the presence of exceptions. There are three levels of exception safety:

1. **No-Throw Guarantee**: Functions that provide this level of safety never throw exceptions. They are considered completely safe to use in any context.

2. **Basic Guarantee**: Functions guarantee that no resources will leak, but the program state might be inconsistent. This level of safety is suitable for functions that need to release resources (e.g.,

memory) but don't need to maintain a consistent state.

3. **Strong Guarantee**: Functions guarantee that the program state will remain unchanged if an exception occurs.

This is the highest level of exception safety and is suitable for operations that must leave the program in a consistent state.

Understanding and applying exception safety principles is essential to writing robust and reliable C++ code that can gracefully handle exceptional conditions.

Try-Catch Blocks in C++

In C++, try-catch blocks are essential constructs for handling exceptions. These blocks allow you to enclose code that may throw exceptions within a try block and specify how to handle those exceptions in one or more catch blocks. This provides a structured way to deal with errors and maintain program integrity even in the presence of exceptions.

Basic Syntax

The basic syntax of a try-catch block in C++ is as follows:

try {

// Code that may throw exceptions

} **catch** (const ExceptionType1& e1) {
// Handle ExceptionType1

} **catch** (const ExceptionType2& e2) {
// Handle ExceptionType2

} **catch** (...) {
// Handle all other exceptions

}

Here's a breakdown of how try-catch blocks work:

• The try block contains the code that may throw exceptions.

• Each catch block specifies the type of exception it can catch (e.g., ExceptionType1, ExceptionType2), followed byan exception object (e.g., e1, e2) that holds information about the thrown exception.

- The ellipsis (...) catch block is optional and can catch any unhandled exceptions. It's typically used as a catch-all block at the end.

Handling Specific Exceptions

In practice, you often want to handle different types of exceptions differently. For example:

try {

// Code that may throw exceptions

} **catch** (const std::runtime_error& e) {
// Handle runtime errors

} **catch** (const std::logic_error& e) {
// Handle logic errors

} **catch** (const std::exception& e) {
// Handle other exceptions derived from std::exception

}

In this example, the first catch block handles std::runtime_error, the second catch block handles std::logic_error, and the third catch block handles any other exceptions derived from std::exception.

Catching by Reference

It's important to catch exceptions by reference (e.g., const ExceptionType&) rather than by value. Catching by reference avoids unnecessary copying of the exception object and ensures you have access to the original exception information.

Catch-All Block

The catch-all block with the ellipsis (...) can be used to catch exceptions of any type that weren't caught by the preceding catch blocks. However, it's generally recommended to catch specific exceptions whenever possible and use the catch-all block as a last resort.

Nested Try-Catch Blocks

You can also nest try-catch blocks to handle exceptions at different levels of your code. For example:

try {

// Outer try block
try {

// Inner try block

// Code that may throw exceptions

```
} catch (const ExceptionType1& e1) {
// Handle ExceptionType1 at the inner level

}
} catch (const ExceptionType2& e2) {
// Handle ExceptionType2 at the outer level

}
```

In this case, if an exception of ExceptionType1 is thrown in the inner try block, it's caught by the inner catch block.

If ExceptionType2 is thrown, it's caught by the outer catch block.

Rethrowing Exceptions

Sometimes, you may want to catch an exception, perform some processing, and then rethrow the same exception or a different one. You can rethrow an exception using the throw statement within a catch block:

```
try {

// Code that may throw exceptions

} catch (const ExceptionType& e) {
// Handle the exception

// Rethrow the same or a different exception
throw AnotherException("Something went
wrong.");
}
```

Rethrowing exceptions can be useful when you need to add additional context to an exception or convert one exception type into another.

Try-catch blocks are a fundamental tool for handling exceptions in C++. They provide a structured and effective way to manage errors and ensure your programs can gracefully recover from exceptional conditions.

Custom Exceptions

In C++, you have the flexibility to define your own custom exceptions to handle specific error conditions in your code. Custom exceptions allow you to create exception classes tailored to your application's needs, making your error handling more meaningful and organized.

Creating Custom Exception Classes

To create a custom exception class, you typically derive it from the standard exception classes provided by the C++ Standard Library, such as std::exception. Here's a basic example of how to create a custom exception class:

```cpp
#include <iostream> #include
<exception> class MyException :
public std::exception { public:
MyException(const char* message) :
m_message(message) {} const char* what() const
noexcept override { return m_message.c_str();
} private:
std::string m_message;
}; int main()
{ try {
// Some code that may throw MyException
throw MyException("Custom exception
message");
} catch (const MyException& e) { std::cerr << "Caught
MyException: " << e.what() << std::endl;
} catch (const std::exception& e) { std::cerr << "Caught a
standard exception: " << e.what() << std::endl; } return 0;
}
```

In this example, we define a custom exception class MyException that inherits from std::exception. We provide a constructor that accepts a message and implement the what() function to return the error message.

Throwing Custom Exceptions

To throw a custom exception, you simply use the throw statement with an instance of your custom exception class:

```cpp
throw MyException("Something went wrong.");
```

This throws an instance of MyException with the specified error message.

Catching Custom Exceptions

You can catch custom exceptions just like you catch standard exceptions, using a catch block:

```
try {

// Code that may throw custom exceptions

} catch (const MyException& e) {
// Handle MyException

}
```

By catching custom exceptions at an appropriate level in your code, you can implement specialized error handling logic for different exceptional conditions.

When to Use Custom Exceptions

Custom exceptions are particularly useful when your application encounters specific errors that require unique handling. By creating custom exception classes, you can add context and information to the error messages, making it easier to diagnose and resolve issues.

However, it's essential to strike a balance between using custom exceptions and standard exceptions. Reserve custom exceptions for situations where they genuinely add value, and use standard exceptions for common error conditions.

Custom exceptions enhance the clarity and maintainability of your code's error handling, making it easier to understand and maintain your software as it evolves.

Exception Safety and Resource Management

Exception safety is a crucial aspect of C++ programming that focuses on ensuring that your program remains in a consistent and stable state, even when exceptions are thrown. Proper exception handling and resource management are essential for building robust and reliable C++ applications.

Three Levels of Exception Safety

C++ defines three levels of exception safety, each indicating a higher degree of reliability in the presence of exceptions:

1. **No-Throw Guarantee (Strong Exception Safety):** Code that provides a strong exception safety guarantee ensures that no resources are leaked and that the program's state remains unchanged if an exception occurs.

   This level of safety is the most robust but may be challenging to achieve in all cases.

2. **Basic Exception Safety:** Basic exception safety guarantees that no resources are leaked when an exception is thrown. However, the program's state may be partially modified, and some invariants may be temporarily broken. The goal is to leave the program in a state where it can be safely

continued or safely terminated.

3. **No Guarantee (No-Throw):** At this level, there are no specific guarantees about the program's state or resource management in the presence of exceptions. Code that offers no exception safety guarantees should be used sparingly, especially in critical sections of your application.

RAII (Resource Acquisition Is Initialization)

A fundamental concept in achieving strong exception safety is RAII (Resource Acquisition Is Initialization). RAII ties the lifetime of resources (such as memory, file handles, and locks) to the lifetime of objects. When an object representing a resource is created, it acquires the resource, and when it's destroyed (e.g., when it goes out of scope), it releases the resource.

Here's an example of RAII using C++'s std::unique_ptr for managing dynamic memory:

```
#include <memory> void exampleFunction() {
std::unique_ptr<int> dynamicInt =
std::make_unique<int>(42);
// dynamicInt automatically releases the memory when it goes out of scope

// No explicit 'delete' or memory management needed

}
```

RAII ensures that even if an exception is thrown within example Function, the std::unique_ptr will be destructed properly, releasing any allocated memory.

Best Practices for Exception Safety

To achieve exception safety in your C++ code, follow these best practices:

- Use RAII principles for resource management.

- Prefer using standard library containers and algorithms that offer strong exception safety guarantees.

- Design your functions and classes with exception safety in mind.

- Use appropriate exception types to convey the nature of errors.

- Catch exceptions at the appropriate level in your code and handle or propagate them as needed.

- Test your code thoroughly with different exception scenarios to ensure it behaves as expected.

Exception safety is a complex topic, and achieving the desired level of safety often requires careful design and testing. However, it's a critical aspect of writing reliable and robust C++ applications, particularly in environments where failures must be gracefully handled.

Best Practices in Error Handling

Error handling is a vital part of writing robust and reliable C++ programs. Properly managing errors ensures that your software gracefully handles unexpected situations and provides meaningful feedback to users. In this section, we'll discuss some best practices for effective error handling in C++.

1. Use Exception Handling

C++ provides a robust exception handling mechanism that allows you to handle errors gracefully. Instead of returning error codes or using global error variables, use C++ exceptions to propagate and handle errors. This approach promotes cleaner and more maintainable code.

```
try {

// Code that may throw exceptions

// ...

} catch (const std::exception& e) {
// Handle the exception std::cerr << "An error
occurred: " << e.what() << std::endl;
}
```

2. Define Custom Exception Classes

Create custom exception classes for different error scenarios in your application. This helps you distinguish between different types of errors and provides more informative error messages.

```
class FileOpenError : public std::runtime_error {
public:
FileOpenError(const std::string& filename)
: std::runtime_error("Failed to open file: " + filename) {}
};
```

3. Use RAII for Resource Management

As mentioned in the previous section, RAII (Resource Acquisition Is Initialization) is a powerful technique for resource management. It ensures that resources are automatically released when the corresponding objects go out of scope.

```
std::ifstream
file("example.txt"); if
(!file.is_open()) {
```

```
throw FileOpenError("example.txt");
}
// 'file' will be automatically closed when it goes out of scope
```

4. Propagate or Handle Exceptions Appropriately

Decide whether to propagate exceptions to higher levels of your code or handle them locally based on the situation. Handling exceptions at the right level of abstraction is crucial. Don't catch exceptions too early if they can be handled more effectively at a higher level.

5. Provide Clear Error Messages

When throwing exceptions or reporting errors, provide clear and informative error messages. This helps developers understand the nature of the error and facilitates debugging and troubleshooting.

6. Avoid Swallowing Exceptions

Avoid catching exceptions and silently ignoring them, as this can lead to hard-to-detect bugs. If you catch an exception and can't handle it properly, consider rethrowing it or logging it for later analysis.

```
try {

// ...

} catch (const SomeException&
e) { // Log the exception and
rethrow it logError(e); throw;
}
```

7. Test Error Scenarios

Thoroughly test your code with different error scenarios to ensure that it behaves correctly when exceptions are thrown. Use unit tests, integration tests, and edge-case testing to cover various error paths.

8. Document Error Handling

Clearly document error-handling strategies and conventions in your codebase. This makes it easier for developers to understand how errors are handled and promotes consistency across the project.

9. Consider Using Standard Library Utilities

The C++ Standard Library provides utilities for error handling, such as std::error_code and std::error_condition, which are useful for handling system-level errors. Familiarize yourself with these tools when working on system level programming.

Effective error handling is an integral part of writing high-quality C++ code. By following these best practices, you can make your code more robust, maintainable, and user-friendly.

C++ Standard Library and Advanced Topics

Input/Output Stream Classes

In C++, input and output operations are an essential part of software development. C++ provides a powerful and flexible mechanism for input and output using the C++ Standard Library's Input/Output (I/O) stream classes. These classes are the foundation for handling data streams in C++ programs, allowing you to interact with various data sources and destinations, such as files, console input and output, and even custom data structures.

Streams and Stream Classes

In C++, streams are a high-level abstraction that represents the flow of data between a program and a device or data source. Streams can be thought of as channels through which data flows, and C++ provides two primary stream classes: istream for input and ostream for output. These classes are further specialized into ifstream and ofstream for file-based I/O.

- **istream**: This class is used for reading input from various sources. The cin object, which represents standard input (usually the keyboard), is an instance of istream. You can use istream objects to read data into your program from sources like the keyboard or files.

- **ostream**: This class is used for writing output to various destinations. The cout object, which represents standard output (usually the console), is an instance of ostream. You can use ostream objects to write data from your program to destinations like the console or files.

Stream Extraction and Insertion Operators

C++ stream classes provide two fundamental operators for input and output: >> (extraction operator) and << (insertion operator). These operators allow you to perform formatted input and output operations on data.

- **Extraction Operator (>>)**: This operator is used to extract (read) data from an input stream. For example, you can use >> to read data from the keyboard into variables or from a file into program variables.

int age; cin >> age; // Reads an integer from
standard input

- **Insertion Operator (<<)**: This operator is used to insert (write) data into an output stream. For example, you can use << to display the value of variables on the console or write data to a file.

int number = 42;

cout << "The answer is: " << number << endl; // Outputs "The answer is: 42" to the console

Stream States and Error Handling

Streams can be in various states depending on their operations and the data they interact with. Common stream states include:

- **Good**: The stream is in a good state and ready for I/O operations.

- **Eof (End-of-File)**: The stream has reached the end of the file (input) or is at the end of the file (output).

- **Fail**: An operation has failed due to incorrect data or an incompatible operation.

- **Bad**: The stream is in a bad state due to severe errors.

You can use stream member functions like good(), eof(), fail(), and bad() to check and handle stream states.

File Input and Output

One of the most common uses of C++ streams is for reading from and writing to files. To work with files, you can use the ifstream and ofstream classes, which are derived from istream and ostream, respectively.

```cpp
#include <iostream>
#include <fstream> int main() {
std::ifstream inputFile("input.txt"); if (!inputFile) {
std::cerr << "Failed to open input.txt" << std::endl; return 1;
}
int value; while (inputFile >> value) {
std::cout << "Read: " << value <<
std::endl;
}
inputFile.close(); // Close the input file
std::ofstream outputFile("output.txt"); if
(!outputFile) { std::cerr << "Failed to open
output.txt" << std::endl; return 1;
}
outputFile << "Hello, File!" << std::endl;
outputFile.close(); // Close the output file
return 0;
}
```

In this example, we open an input file ("input.txt") for reading and an output file ("output.txt") for writing. We use the >> operator to read integers from the input file and the << operator to write a string to the output file.

Working with Dates and Time

Handling dates and time is a common requirement in many software applications, and C++ provides the <chrono> library in the Standard Library to assist with these tasks. The <chrono> library allows you to work with time durations, time points, and clocks in a platform-independent manner.

Time Durations

A time duration represents a span of time, such as seconds, milliseconds, or hours. C++ defines several duration types, including std::chrono::seconds, std::chrono::milliseconds, and std::chrono::hours, among others. These types are used to represent specific units of time.

You can create a time duration using literals, making it easy to specify durations in your code:

```
#include <iostream>
#include <chrono>
int main() {
// Create a duration of 5 seconds std::chrono::seconds duration =
5s; // Output the duration in seconds std::cout << "Duration: "
<< duration.count() << " seconds" << std::endl; return 0;
}
```

In this example, we create a std::chrono::seconds duration of 5 seconds using the 5s literal and then output its value in seconds.

Time Points

A time point represents a specific point in time, often referred to as a timestamp. C++ provides std::chrono::time_point to work with time points. Time points are typically based on a clock, such as the system clock or a high-resolution clock.

```
#include <iostream>
#include <chrono>
int main() {
// Get the current time point using the system clock

std::chrono::system_clock::time_point now = std::chrono::system_clock::now();
// Output the current time point as a timestamp std::time_t
timestamp = std::chrono::system_clock::to_time_t(now);
std::cout << "Current timestamp: " <<
std::ctime(&timestamp); return 0;
}
```

In this example, we use std::chrono::system_clock::now() to obtain the current time point, and then we convert it to a std::time_t value and print it as a human-readable timestamp using std::ctime().

Clocks

Clocks are the underlying mechanisms that provide time information. C++ defines several clock types, including std::chrono::system_clock, std::chrono::steady_clock, and std::chrono::high_resolution_clock. Each clock type has its characteristics, such as whether it can be adjusted (system clock) or whether it guarantees a steady tick rate (steady clock).

```
#include <iostream>
#include <chrono>
int main() {
// Use the steady clock to measure time
duration auto start =
std::chrono::steady_clock::now(); //
Simulate a time-consuming operation for
(int i = 0; i < 1000000; ++i) {
// Do some work

} auto end = std::chrono::steady_clock::now(); auto duration =
std::chrono::duration_cast<std::chrono::milliseconds>(end - start);
std::cout << "Time elapsed: " << duration.count() << " milliseconds" <<
std::endl; return 0;
}
```

In this code, we use std::chrono::steady_clock to measure the time duration of a simulated time-consuming operation. We calculate the elapsed time in milliseconds and display it.

Custom Time Units

You can define custom time units by using the std::chrono::duration template. This allows you to work with time in units that make sense for your application, whether it's microseconds or days.

```
#include <iostream>
#include <chrono>
int main() {
// Define a custom time unit for microseconds using
microseconds = std::chrono::duration<long long,
std::micro>;
// Create a duration of 500 microseconds microseconds
duration(500); // Output the duration std::cout << "Duration: " <<
duration.count() << " microseconds" << std::endl; return 0;
}
```

In this example, we define a custom time unit called microseconds and create a duration of 500 microseconds. This allows you to work with time at a very fine granularity.

Regular Expressions in C++

Regular expressions, often abbreviated as "regex" or "regexp," are a powerful tool for pattern matching and text manipulation. They are widely used in various programming languages, including C++, to search, validate, and manipulate strings based on specific patterns. C++ provides support for regular expressions through the <regex> header, which allows you to work with regex patterns and perform various string operations.

Creating a Regular Expression Object

In C++, you create a regular expression using the std::regex class. Here's how you can create a simple regex object to match an email address pattern:

```
#include <iostream>
#include <regex> int main() {
std::string text = "Emails: john@example.com, alice@gmail.com,
bob@company.org"; std::regex pattern("[a-zA-Z0-9._%+-]+@[a-zA-Z0-9.-
]+\\.[a-zA-Z]{2,}"); std::smatch matches; if (std::regex_search(text,
matches, pattern)) { for (const auto& match : matches) { std::cout <<
"Match: " << match << std::endl;
}
} return 0;
}
```

In this example, we create a std::regex object named pattern to match email addresses. We then use std::regex_search to find and print all email addresses in the given text.

Basic Regex Patterns

Regex patterns consist of characters and metacharacters that define the search criteria. Here are some common metacharacters and their meanings:

- .: Matches any single character except a newline.

- *: Matches zero or more occurrences of the preceding character or group.

- +: Matches one or more occurrences of the preceding character or group.

- ?: Matches zero or one occurrence of the preceding character or group.

- []: Defines a character class, such as [aeiou] to match any vowel.

- (): Groups characters or sub patterns together.

Regex Flags

You can specify flags when creating a regex object to control the matching behavior. Common flags include:

- std::regex_constants::icase: Perform case-insensitive matching.

- std::regex_constants::multiline: Treat the input text as a multiline string.

- std::regex_constants::grep: Use grep-style regex syntax.

std::regex pattern("pattern", std::regex_constants::icase);

Regex Match Results

When you search for matches using std::regex_search, the match results are stored in a std::smatch object. You can iterate over the matches and access the matched substrings using the smatch object.

```
std::smatch matches; if
(std::regex_search(text, matches, pattern))
{ for (const auto& match : matches) {
std::cout << "Match: " << match <<
std::endl;
}
}
```

Regex Replace

C++ also provides a way to replace matched substrings using std::regex_replace. Here's an example that replaces all occurrences of "apple" with "orange" in a text:

```
std::string text = "I have an apple and another apple.";
std::regex pattern("apple"); std::string result =
std::regex_replace(text, pattern, "orange"); std::cout
<< result << std::endl;
```

This code will output: "I have an orange and another orange."

Advanced C++ Features (Smart Pointers, Move Semantics, etc.)

In this section, we will explore some advanced features of C++ that enhance code efficiency, maintainability, and resource management. These features include smart pointers, move semantics, and other modern C++ techniques.

Smart Pointers

Smart pointers are a key feature introduced in modern C++ to manage dynamic memory more safely and efficiently. They automatically release memory when it's no longer needed, helping prevent memory leaks. C++ provides three types of smart pointers:

1. **std::unique_ptr**: This pointer represents exclusive ownership of an object. When the unique_ptr goes out of scope, it automatically deletes the associated object. Here's an example:

```
#include <memory>
int main() { std::unique_ptr<int> ptr = std::make_unique<int>(42); // When ptr goes out of scope,
the int is automatically deleted.
return 0;

}
```

2. **std::shared_ptr**: This pointer represents shared ownership of an object. Multiple shared_ptr instances can share ownership, and the object is deleted when the last shared_ptr referring to it is destroyed. This helps in scenarios where you need shared ownership.

```
#include <memory>
int main() { std::shared_ptr<int> ptr1 = std::make_shared<int>(42); std::shared_ptr<int> ptr2 = ptr1;
// Shared ownership.
return 0; // The int is deleted when both ptr1 and ptr2 go out of scope.
}
```

3. **std::weak_ptr**: This pointer provides a way to break circular references that might occur with std::shared_ptr.

It doesn't increase the reference count but can be converted to a std::shared_ptr when needed.

```
#include <memory>
int main() {

std::shared_ptr<int> ptr1 = std::make_shared<int>(42);

std::weak_ptr<int> ptr2 = ptr1; // Weak reference.

std::shared_ptr<int> ptr3 = ptr2.lock(); // Convert to shared_ptr when needed.

return 0;

}
```

Smart pointers are an essential tool for resource management in modern C++ and help eliminate many common programming errors related to manual memory management.

Move Semantics

Move semantics is another feature that significantly improves the efficiency of C++ programs, especially when dealing with large objects. It allows you to transfer ownership of resources (such as memory) from one object to another without unnecessary copying.

In C++, you can implement move semantics by defining move constructors and move assignment operators for your classes. Here's a basic example:

```cpp
class MyString {
public:
MyString(std::string str) : data(std::move(str)) {} // Move
constructor private:
std::string data;
}; int main() { std::string text =
"Hello, World!";
MyString myStr = std::move(text); // Move the string to
myStr return 0;
}
```

In this example, std::move is used to cast text to an rvalue reference, allowing the move constructor of MyString to efficiently take ownership of the string data.

Other Advanced Features

Apart from smart pointers and move semantics, modern C++ also includes various other advanced features like lambda expressions, type inference (using auto), range-based for loops, and more. These features enhance code readability and productivity, making C++ a powerful language for software development.

In the next section, we will focus on best practices for efficient C++ coding, including optimizing code for performance and maintaining high-quality code.

Best Practices for Efficient C++ Coding

Efficient coding practices are crucial for writing high-performance and maintainable C++ programs. In this section, we'll discuss best practices and guidelines that can help you write efficient and robust C++ code.

1. Use the Standard Library

Leverage the C++ Standard Library whenever possible. It provides a wealth of data structures and algorithms that are well-tested and optimized. Using library functions not only saves development time but often results in faster and more reliable code.

```cpp
#include <vector>
```

```cpp
#include <algorithm> int main() {
std::vector<int> numbers = {3, 1, 4, 1, 5, 9, 2, 6, 5, 3, 5}; // Sort the vector using a standard
algorithm.
std::sort(numbers.begin(), numbers.end());
return 0;
}
```

2. Avoid Raw Pointers

Prefer smart pointers (std::unique_ptr, std::shared_ptr, std::weak_ptr) and container classes over raw pointers. Smart pointers handle resource management automatically and reduce the risk of memory leaks.

```cpp
#include <memory>
int main() { std::unique_ptr<int> ptr =
std::make_unique<int>(42); return 0; // ptr automatically
deletes the int when it goes out of scope.
}
```

3. Use References

Pass function arguments by reference or const reference when possible. This avoids unnecessary copying of objects and improves performance.

```cpp
void modifyVector(std::vector<int>& vec) {
// Modify the vector directly.

}
int main() { std::vector<int>
numbers = {1, 2, 3};
modifyVector(numbers); return
0;
}
```

4. Avoid Global Variables

Minimize the use of global variables, as they can lead to code that is hard to understand and maintain. Instead, prefer encapsulation and pass necessary data as function arguments.

5. Optimize Data Structures

Choose the appropriate data structure for your needs. Use std::vector for dynamic arrays, std::map or std::unordered_map for key-value pairs, and std::set or std::unordered_set for unique values.

6. Profile and Benchmark Your Code

Profiling tools help identify performance bottlenecks in your code. Use profiling tools to find areas where optimization can yield the most significant improvements.

7. Optimize Loops

Efficient loops are crucial for performance. Minimize work done inside loops, precompute loop conditions, and use appropriate algorithms and data structures.

```
for (int i = 0; i < vec.size(); ++i) {
// Not efficient, as it recalculates vec.size() in each iteration.

}
```

8. Use const Correctness

Apply const correctness to your code. Use const for variables that should not be modified, and mark member functions as const when they don't modify the object's state.

9. Keep Code Clean and Readable

Follow coding standards, use meaningful variable names, and include comments where necessary. Well-organized and readable code is easier to maintain and debug.

10. Regularly Review and Refactor Code

Periodically review your codebase for improvements. Refactor code to remove redundancy, improve clarity, and apply design patterns when appropriate.

Efficient C++ coding is a continuous learning process. Stay up-to-date with C++ standards and best practices to write code that is not only efficient but also maintainable and robust.

Conclusion: The Evolution and Impact of the C++ Standard Template Library (STL), Standard Library, and Advanced Topics

The C++ programming language has stood the test of time, evolving over decades to remain one of the most powerful and versatile languages in the software development industry. A significant contributor to its success is the **C++ Standard Template Library (STL)** and the broader **C++ Standard Library**, which provide developers with a rich set of tools for building efficient, reusable, and maintainable code.

As of 2025, these libraries have continued to grow and adapt, incorporating modern programming paradigms, hardware advancements, and the needs of contemporary software development. This conclusion delves into the significance of these libraries, their evolution, and the advanced topics that have emerged, shaping the future of C++ programming.

The Enduring Significance of the STL and Standard Library

The **Standard Template Library (STL)** and the **C++ Standard Library** are cornerstones of C++ programming. They provide a comprehensive set of tools that abstract complex operations, allowing developers to focus on solving problems rather than reinventing the wheel. The STL, in particular, revolutionized C++ programming by introducing generic programming through templates, enabling code that is both reusable and type-safe.

1. Generic Programming with the STL

The STL's design philosophy is rooted in **generic programming**, which emphasizes writing code that works with any data type. This is achieved through the use of **templates**, which allow algorithms and data structures to operate independently of the underlying data types. For example, a single std::sort algorithm can sort a std::vector<int>, a std::list<std::string>, or any other container that meets the necessary requirements. This level of abstraction has made the STL a powerful tool for developers, reducing code duplication and improving maintainability.

2. Standardization and Portability

The C++ Standard Library, including the STL, is part of the **ISO C++ Standard**, ensuring that it is available on all compliant C++ implementations. This standardization guarantees that code written using these libraries is portable across different platforms and compilers, a critical feature for modern software development. Whether you are developing for Windows, Linux, macOS, or embedded systems, the Standard Library provides a consistent and reliable foundation.

3. Performance and Efficiency

One of the hallmarks of the STL and Standard Library is their focus on **performance**. The algorithms and data structures provided by these libraries are highly optimized, often outperforming custom implementations. For example, std::vector provides constant-time access to elements and efficient dynamic resizing, while std::unordered_map offers average constant-time complexity for lookups. These performance characteristics make the STL and Standard Library ideal for high-performance applications, such as game development, scientific computing, and real-time systems.

The Evolution of the STL and Standard Library (2025)

As of 2025, the C++ Standard Library and STL have continued to evolve, driven by the needs of modern software development and the advancements in the C++ language itself. The introduction of new standards, such as **C++20** and **C++23**, has brought significant improvements and new features to these libraries.

1. C++20: A Major Milestone

The **C++20** standard marked a significant milestone in the evolution of the STL and Standard Library. It introduced several groundbreaking features that have reshaped how developers write C++

code:

- **Concepts and Constraints**: Concepts allow developers to specify requirements for template parameters, improving code readability and error messages. For example, a function that requires an integral type can now explicitly state this requirement using concepts:

```
template<typename T>
requires std::integral<T>
T add(T a, T b) {
   return a + b;
}
```

- **Ranges**: The Ranges library provides a more expressive way to work with sequences of elements. It simplifies code by allowing operations on entire ranges rather than individual iterators. For example:

```
std::vector<int> v = {1, 2, 3, 4, 5};
auto even = v | std::views::filter([](int x) { return x % 2 == 0; });
```

- **Coroutines**: Coroutines enable asynchronous programming with a more intuitive syntax, making it easier to write code for tasks like networking and file I/O.

- **Modules**: Modules provide a modern alternative to header files, improving compilation times and reducing dependency issues.

2. C++23 and Beyond

The **C++23** standard and subsequent updates have continued to build on the foundation laid by C++20.

Key advancements include:

- **Parallel Algorithms**: The Standard Library now includes parallel versions of many algorithms, allowing developers to take advantage of multi-core processors. For example:

```
std::vector<int> v = {5, 3, 1, 4, 2};
std::sort(std::execution::par, v.begin(), v.end());
```

- **Reflection and Metaprogramming**: Reflection, expected in future C++ standards, will allow programs to inspect and manipulate their own structure. This will enable more advanced metaprogramming techniques, further enhancing the flexibility and power of the language.

- **Improved Unicode Support**: As global software development continues to grow, the Standard Library has improved its support for Unicode and other advanced string manipulation features, making it easier to develop applications for international audiences.

Advanced Topics Shaping the Future of C++ (2025)

As of 2025, several advanced topics have gained prominence in the C++ community, driven by the evolution of the language and the demands of modern software development.

1. Concurrency and Parallelism

With the increasing prevalence of multi-core processors, **concurrency** and **parallelism** have become critical aspects of software development. The C++ Standard Library provides robust support for concurrent programming, including:

- **Threads**: The std::thread class allows creating and managing threads.
- **Mutexes and Locks**: std::mutex, std::lock_guard, and std::unique_lock for synchronization.
- **Atomic Operations**: std::atomic for lock-free programming.
- **Futures and Promises**: std::future and std::promise for asynchronous programming.

These tools enable developers to write efficient and scalable concurrent applications, from real-time systems to distributed computing platforms.

2. Smart Pointers and Memory Management

Memory management is a critical aspect of C++ programming, and the Standard Library provides powerful tools to simplify this task. **Smart pointers**, such as std::unique_ptr, std::shared_ptr, and std::weak_ptr, automate memory management, reducing the risk of memory leaks and dangling pointers. These tools have become indispensable for modern C++ development, enabling safer and more reliable code.

3. Functional Programming

The C++ Standard Library has embraced **functional programming** paradigms, providing tools like **lambdas** and **functors** that enable developers to write more expressive and concise code. For example, lambdas can be used to define custom behavior for algorithms:

```
std::vector<int> v = {5, 3, 1, 4, 2};
std::sort(v.begin(), v.end(), [](int a, int b) { return a > b; });
```

4. Modern C++ Design Patterns

The evolution of the STL and Standard Library has also influenced the adoption of modern design patterns in C++. Patterns like **RAII (Resource Acquisition Is Initialization)**, **dependency injection**, and **type erasure** are now more accessible and easier to implement, thanks to the tools provided by the Standard Library.

The Future of C++ Programming

As we look to the future, the C++ Standard Library and STL will continue to play a central role in the evolution of the language. The ongoing development of new standards, such as **C++26** and beyond, will likely bring even more advanced features and optimizations, further enhancing the power and flexibility of C++.

1. Integration with Modern Hardware

As hardware continues to evolve, the Standard Library will need to adapt to support new architectures and paradigms, such as **quantum computing**, **AI accelerators**, and **heterogeneous computing**. This will require ongoing collaboration between the C++ standards committee and hardware manufacturers.

2. Enhanced Developer Tools

The future of C++ will also see improvements in developer tools, such as **debuggers**, **static analyzers**, and **IDEs**, to better support the advanced features of the language. These tools will make it easier for developers to write, debug, and optimize C++ code.

3. Community and Ecosystem Growth

The C++ community has grown significantly in recent years, driven by the language's continued relevance and the availability of high-quality resources. As the ecosystem expands, we can expect to see more libraries, frameworks, and tools that build on the foundation provided by the STL and Standard Library.

Final Thoughts

The **C++ Standard Template Library (STL)** and **C++ Standard Library** are foundational tools that have shaped the way developers write C++ code. As of 2025, these libraries have continued to evolve, incorporating new features and optimizations that align with modern programming paradigms and hardware advancements. By mastering these libraries and staying up-to-date with advanced topics, developers can write efficient, maintainable, and scalable C++ code.

Whether you are working on high-performance systems, embedded devices, or large-scale applications, the STL and Standard Library provide the tools you need to succeed. As the C++ language continues to evolve, these libraries will remain at the heart of C++ programming, enabling developers to tackle the challenges of tomorrow with confidence and creativity.

5. Exception Handling and File Handling in C++

Introduction

C++ is a powerful, high-performance programming language that provides robust mechanisms for exception handling and file handling. These features are essential for building reliable and efficient applications. In this detailed introduction, we will explore the concepts of exception handling and file handling in C++, focusing on their implementation, best practices, and use cases.

1. Exception Handling in C++

Exception handling is a mechanism that allows a program to handle runtime errors gracefully. It ensures that the program does not crash unexpectedly and provides a way to recover from errors. C++ provides three keywords for exception handling: try, catch, and throw. Additionally, C++ supports standard exceptions and allows developers to create custom exception classes.

1.1 Try, Catch, and Throw

Try Block

The try block is used to enclose code that might throw an exception. If an exception occurs within the try block, the program transfers control to the corresponding catch block.

```
try {
    // Code that might throw an exception
    if (errorCondition) {
        throw exception;
    }
}
```

Catch Block

The catch block is used to handle exceptions thrown by the try block. It specifies the type of exception it can handle and contains the code to manage the exception.

```
catch (ExceptionType& e) {
    // Handle the exception
    std::cerr << "Exception caught: " << e.what() << std::endl;
}
```

Throw Statement

The throw statement is used to raise an exception. It can throw any data type, but it is common to throw objects of exception classes.

throw std::runtime_error("An error occurred!");

Example

```
#include <iostream>
#include <stdexcept>
int main() {
    try {
        int age;
        std::cout << "Enter your age: ";
        std::cin >> age;
        if (age < 0) {
            throw std::invalid_argument("Age cannot be negative!");
        }
        std::cout << "Your age is: " << age << std::endl;
    } catch (const std::invalid_argument& e) {
        std::cerr << "Error: " << e.what() << std::endl;
    }
    return 0;
}
```

1.2 Standard Exceptions

C++ provides a set of standard exception classes defined in the <stdexcept> header. These classes are derived from the base class std::exception and are used to represent common types of errors.

Common Standard Exceptions

- std::runtime_error: For runtime errors.
- std::logic_error: For logical errors in the program.
- std::invalid_argument: For invalid arguments.
- std::out_of_range: For out-of-range access.
- std::bad_alloc: For memory allocation failures.

Example

```
#include <iostream>
#include <stdexcept>
int main() {
    try {
        int* arr = new int[1000000000000]; // May throw std::bad_alloc
    } catch (const std::bad_alloc& e) {
        std::cerr << "Memory allocation failed: " << e.what() << std::endl;
```

```
    }
    return 0;
}
```

1.3 Custom Exception Handling

C++ allows developers to create custom exception classes by inheriting from the standard exception classes. This is useful for defining application-specific exceptions.

Example

```
#include <iostream>
#include <stdexcept>
class MyCustomException : public std::exception {
public:
    const char* what() const noexcept override {
        return "Custom exception occurred!";
    }
};

int main() {
    try {
        throw MyCustomException();
    } catch (const MyCustomException& e) {
        std::cerr << e.what() << std::endl;
    }
    return 0;
}
```

1.4 Exception Propagation

Exception propagation refers to the process of passing an exception from a function to its caller. If an exception is not caught in a function, it propagates up the call stack until it is caught or the program terminates.

Example

```
#include <iostream>
#include <stdexcept>
void functionThatThrows() {
    throw std::runtime_error("Error in functionThatThrows!");
}

int main() {
    try {
        functionThatThrows();
```

```
  } catch (const std::runtime_error& e) {
    std::cerr << "Caught exception: " << e.what() << std::endl;
  }
  return 0;
}
```

2. File Handling in C++

File handling is a critical aspect of programming that allows applications to read from and write to files. C++ provides several classes for file handling, including ifstream, ofstream, and fstream. These classes are part of the <fstream> header and support both text and binary file operations.

2.1 File Input and Output Streams

C++ uses streams to handle file operations. The three main classes are:

- ifstream: For reading from files.
- ofstream: For writing to files.
- fstream: For both reading and writing.

Example: Writing to a File

```
#include <iostream>
#include <fstream>
int main() {
  std::ofstream outFile("example.txt");
  if (outFile.is_open()) {
    outFile << "Hello, World!" << std::endl;
    outFile.close();
  } else {
    std::cerr << "Unable to open file!" << std::endl;
  }
  return 0;
}
```

Example: Reading from a File

```
#include <iostream>
#include <fstream>
#include <string>
int main() {
  std::ifstream inFile("example.txt");
  std::string line;
  if (inFile.is_open()) {
    while (std::getline(inFile, line)) {
      std::cout << line << std::endl;
```

```
        }
        inFile.close();
    } else {
        std::cerr << "Unable to open file!" << std::endl;
    }
    return 0;
}
```

2.2 Text and Binary Files

C++ supports two types of files:

- **Text Files**: Store data in human-readable format.
- **Binary Files**: Store data in binary format, which is more efficient for large datasets.

Example: Writing to a Binary File

```
#include <iostream>
#include <fstream>
int main() {
    int data = 12345;
    std::ofstream outFile("example.bin", std::ios::binary);
    if (outFile.is_open()) {
        outFile.write(reinterpret_cast<char*>(&data), sizeof(data));
        outFile.close();
    } else {
        std::cerr << "Unable to open file!" << std::endl;
    }
    return 0;
}
```

Example: Reading from a Binary File

```
#include <iostream>
#include <fstream>
int main() {
    int data;
    std::ifstream inFile("example.bin", std::ios::binary);
    if (inFile.is_open()) {
        inFile.read(reinterpret_cast<char*>(&data), sizeof(data));
        std::cout << "Data: " << data << std::endl;
        inFile.close();
    } else {
        std::cerr << "Unable to open file!" << std::endl;
    }
    return 0;
```

}

2.3 Reading/Writing Data from Files

C++ provides various methods for reading and writing data, including:

- getline(): For reading strings.
- read() and write(): For binary data.
- << and >>: For formatted input/output.

Example: Reading and Writing Structured Data

```cpp
#include <iostream>
#include <fstream>

struct Person {
    std::string name;
    int age;
};

int main() {
    Person p = {"John Doe", 30};

    // Write to file
    std::ofstream outFile("person.dat", std::ios::binary);
    if (outFile.is_open()) {
        outFile.write(reinterpret_cast<char*>(&p), sizeof(p));
        outFile.close();
    }

    // Read from file
    Person p2;
    std::ifstream inFile("person.dat", std::ios::binary);
    if (inFile.is_open()) {
        inFile.read(reinterpret_cast<char*>(&p2), sizeof(p2));
        std::cout << "Name: " << p2.name << ", Age: " << p2.age << std::endl;
        inFile.close();
    }
    return 0;
}
```

2.4 File Operations (Seek, Tell, Close)

C++ provides methods to manipulate the file pointer and perform operations like seeking and telling.

Seek and Tell

- seekg(): Moves the input file pointer.
- seekp(): Moves the output file pointer.
- tellg(): Returns the current position of the input file pointer.
- tellp(): Returns the current position of the output file pointer.

Example: Using Seek and Tell

```
#include <iostream>
#include <fstream>
int main() {
    std::fstream file("example.txt", std::ios::in | std::ios::out);
    if (file.is_open()) {
        file << "Hello, World!";
        std::streampos pos = file.tellp(); // Get current position
        file.seekp(0); // Move to the beginning
        file << "Hi";
        file.close();
    }
    return 0;
}
```

Close

The close() method is used to close a file after operations are complete. It is good practice to close files explicitly to free resources.

Exception Handling: Dealing with Errors Gracefully

The Need for Exception Handling

In the ideal world, our C++ programs would execute flawlessly, every line of code working harmoniously like a well-conducted orchestra. However, the reality of software development is often far from perfect. Errors, unexpected inputs, or resource failures can throw a wrench into the works, causing our programs to stumble and crash.

This is where exception handling comes to the rescue. It's a mechanism that allows you to gracefully handle these unexpected events, preventing your program from coming to a screeching halt and providing a way to recover or report the error.

Limitations of Traditional Error Handling

In the past, error handling in C++ often relied on returning error codes from functions or using global error flags.

While these approaches work in simple scenarios, they become cumbersome and error-prone as programs grow in complexity.

Here's why traditional error handling can fall short:

1. **Cluttered Code:** Error handling code often gets intertwined with the main logic of your program, making it difficult to read and maintain. You end up with a maze of if-else statements or switch cases scattered throughout your code, obscuring the core functionality.

2. **Missed Errors:** It's easy for error codes to get lost in the shuffle, especially when multiple functions are involved. A function might return an error code, but the calling function might forget to check it, leading to undetected errors that can cause havoc later in the program.

3. **Limited Information:** Error codes often provide limited information about the nature of the error. This can make debugging a frustrating guessing game.

Exception Handling to the Rescue

Exception handling in C++ offers a more elegant and robust way to deal with errors. Instead of relying on error codes or flags, you can "throw" an exception when an error occurs. This exception is an object that encapsulates information about the error, such as an error message or an error code.

The exception then propagates up the call stack until it's caught by a catch block. This catches block can handle the error appropriately, such as logging the error, displaying a user-friendly message, or attempting to recover from the error.

Benefits of Exception Handling

- **Clean Code:** Exception handling code is separated from the main logic, making your code more readable and easier to maintain.

- **Guaranteed Error Handling:** Exceptions cannot be ignored. If an exception is thrown, it must be caught somewhere, ensuring that errors are not overlooked.

- **Rich Error Information:** Exception objects can carry detailed information about the error, aiding in debugging.

- **Flexibility:** You can define your own custom exception types to represent specific errors in your application.

Example: Division by Zero

```
#include <iostream>
#include <stdexcept> // For std::runtime_error
double divide(double a, double b) {     if (b == 0) {
```

```
        throw std::runtime_error("Error: Division by zero.");
    }
    return a / b;
}
int main() {    try {
        double result = divide(10, 0);
    } catch (const std::runtime_error& e) {
std::cerr << e.what() << std::endl; // Output: Error: Division by zero.
    }
    return 0;
}
```

In this example, the divide function throws a std::runtime_error exception if the divisor is zero. The main function wraps the call to divide in a try block and catches the exception in a catch block, printing the error message to the console.

By embracing exception handling in C++, you can write more robust and reliable code that can gracefully handle unexpected situations. This powerful mechanism allows you to separate error-handling code from the normal program flow, making your code cleaner, more maintainable, and easier to understand.

Exceptions in C++

In the world of C++, exceptions are objects that act like distress signals. They are thrown (raised) when something unexpected happens during program execution – an error, an invalid input, or a resource failure. Like a flare shooting into the sky, an exception interrupts the normal flow of your program and alerts you to the issue at hand.

The try-throw-catch Mechanism

C++ provides a structured way to handle exceptions using the following keywords:

1. **try :** The try block is the starting point. It encloses the section of code that you suspect might throw an exception. It's like saying, "Keep an eye out for trouble in this area."

2. **throw :** The throw statement is used within the try block to signal that an exception has occurred. You throw an exception object, which can carry information about the error (like an error message or code). This is like lighting the flare.

3. **catch :** The catch block(s) follow the try block and act as the cleanup crew. Each catch block specifies a particular type of exception it can handle. When an exception is thrown, the program searches for a matching catch block. If found, the code within that block is executed to handle the error. This is like the rescue team responding to the flare.

Built-in Exception Types

The C++ Standard Library provides several built-in exception classes to represent common error scenarios:

- **std::runtime_error :** Used for errors that occur during program execution, such as division by zero, invalid arguments, or range errors.

- **std::logic_error :** Used for errors that result from logical flaws in your code, such as invalid input or incorrect assumptions.

- **std::out_of_range :** A specific type of logic_error that indicates accessing an element outside the valid range of a container.

Examples
Throwing and Catching std::runtime_error:

```
#include <iostream>
#include <stdexcept>
double divide(double a, double b) {    if (b == 0) {
    throw std::runtime_error("Error: Division by zero."); // Throwing an exception
  }
  return a / b;
}
int main() {
  try { // try block starts here
double result = divide(10, 0);
    std::cout << "Result: " << result << std::endl; // This line won't execute if an exception
is thrown
  } catch (const std::runtime_error& e) { // catch block starts here        std::cerr << e.what()
<< std::endl; // Output: Error: Division by zero.
  }
  return 0;
}
```

Throwing and Catching std::out_of_range:

```
#include <iostream>
#include <stdexcept> #include <vector>
int main() {
  std::vector<int> data = {1, 2, 3};
```

```
    try {
        int value = data.at(5); // This will throw an out_of_range exception
    } catch (const std::out_of_range& e) {        std::cerr << e.what() << std::endl; // Output:
vector::_M_range_check: __n (which is 5) >= this->size() (which is 3)
    }     return 0;
}
```

In this example, the std::out_of_range exception is thrown because we try to access element at index 5 in the vector with only 3 elements.

Key Points:

- Exceptions are objects that signal errors or exceptional conditions.
- The try block contains code that might throw an exception.
- The throw statement is used to throw an exception.
- The catch block handles a specific type of exception.

By understanding exceptions and the try-throw-catch mechanism, you'll be equipped to handle errors gracefully and write more robust C++ code. We'll explore this further in the subsequent sections.

Throwing Exceptions

When your C++ code encounters an error or exceptional situation, it's time to raise the alarm. This is where the throw statement comes in. It's like yelling "Fire!" to alert everyone that something's wrong and needs attention.

How to Throw an Exception

The syntax for throwing an exception is simple:

throw exceptionObject;

Where exceptionObject is an object of an exception class. This object is like a package that carries information about the error.

Exception Objects: The Information Carriers

Exception objects typically belong to classes that derive from the std::exception base class. This hierarchy allows for different types of exceptions to be categorized and handled appropriately.

Here's how you can create and throw a std::runtime_error exception:

#include <stdexcept>

```
#include <string>
// ...inside a function if (/* error condition */) {
    std::string errorMessage = "Invalid input value!";    throw std::runtime_error(errorMessage);
}
```

In this example:

1. We include the <stdexcept> header to access the std::runtime_error class.
2. We create a string errorMessage to describe the error.
3. We construct a std::runtime_error object, passing the errorMessage to its constructor.
4. We use the throw keyword to throw this exception object.

Information in Exception Objects

Exception objects can store various types of information:

- **Error Message:** A human-readable string describing the error.
- **Error Code:** A numerical code that can be used for programmatic error handling.
- **Other Relevant Data:** Depending on the specific exception class, you might be able to store additional information, such as file names, line numbers, or even stack traces.

Retrieving Information from Exception Objects

The what() member function is a common way to retrieve the error message stored in an exception object.

```
try {
    // ... code that might throw an exception ...
} catch (const std::exception& e) {
    std::cerr << "Exception caught: " << e.what() << std::endl; // Print the error message
}
```

Types of Built-in Exceptions

- **std::runtime_error :** Base class for exceptions that can be detected only at runtime (e.g., division by zero, out-of-range access).

- **std::logic_error :** Base class for exceptions that arise from logical errors in your code (e.g., invalid arguments, domain errors).

- **std::exception :** The root of the exception hierarchy, providing a common interface for all exceptions.

Key Points to Remember

- The throw statement is used to raise an exception.
- Exception objects carry information about the error.
- The what() member function can be used to retrieve the error message.
- Use the appropriate exception type to categorize your errors and make your code more informative.

By understanding how to throw exceptions effectively, you equip your C++ programs with the ability to signal errors and communicate valuable information to the parts of your code that are responsible for handling those errors.

Catching Exceptions

Throwing exceptions is like sending out a distress signal. Catching exceptions is the act of responding to that signal and taking appropriate action. In C++, you catch exceptions using catch blocks that immediately follow a try block.

The try-catch Block Structure

```
try {
    // Code that might throw an exception
} catch (ExceptionType1& e1) {
    // Code to handle ExceptionType1
} catch (ExceptionType2& e2) {
    // Code to handle ExceptionType2
} // ... more catch blocks
catch (...) { // Catch-all block (optional)    // Code to handle any other exception
}
```

Let's break it down:

1. **try Block:** This is where you place the code that you suspect might throw an exception. It's like putting up a safety net around a potentially dangerous area.

2. **catch Blocks:** These blocks follow the try block and are responsible for handling specific types of exceptions. Each catch block specifies the type of exception it can handle.

3. **Exception Object:** When an exception is thrown, the program searches for a catch block that matches the type of the exception object. If a matching block is found, the exception object is passed to that block as an argument.

4. **Catch-All Block (Optional):** The catch(...) block (with ellipsis) is a special catch block that can handle any type of exception. It's typically used as a last resort to catch unexpected errors.

How the Right catch Block is Chosen

The compiler checks the catch blocks in the order they appear. The first catch block whose exception type matches (or is a base class of) the thrown exception type is executed.

Examples

Catching std::runtime_error :

```
try {
    int result = divide(10, 0); // Throws
std::runtime_error
    } catch (const std::runtime_error& e) {
std::cerr << "Runtime error: " << e.what() << std::endl; }
```

Catching std::out_of_range :

```
try {
    std::vector<int> data = {1, 2, 3};
    int value = data.at(5); // Throws std::out_of_range
} catch (const std::out_of_range& e) {
    std::cerr << "Out of range error: " << e.what() << std::endl; }
```

Multiple Catch Blocks:

```
try {
    // Code that might throw different exceptions
} catch (const std::runtime_error& e) {
    // Handle runtime_error
} catch (const std::logic_error& e) {
    // Handle logic_error
} catch (const std::exception& e) {
    // Handle any other std::exception derived exception
} catch (...) { // Catch-all block
    std::cerr << "Unknown exception caught!" << std::endl; }
```

In this example, multiple catch blocks handle different types of exceptions, providing specific error handling for each case. Note that the order of catch blocks is important, as a derived class exception (like std::runtime_error) would be caught by the base class (std::exception) if the order was reversed.

By mastering the art of catching exceptions, you'll be able to create more robust and reliable C++ programs that can gracefully handle errors and unexpected situations. This is a crucial step towards building software that is not only functional but also user-friendly and resilient.

Exception Hierarchy

Imagine a library with books arranged by genre and subgenre. This classification makes it easier to find the type of book you're looking for. Similarly, C++ exceptions are organized in a hierarchical structure, making it easier to categorize and handle different types of errors.

The Exception Class Family Tree

At the root of the C++ exception hierarchy is the std::exception class. This class provides a common interface for all exceptions, offering a what() method to retrieve an error message.

From this base class, two main branches emerge:

1. **std::runtime_error :** Represents errors that are typically detected during program execution (runtime).

   Examples include:

   ○   std::range_error : Thrown when you try to access an element outside the valid range of a container. ○   std::overflow_error : Thrown when a numerical calculation exceeds the limits of a data type.

   ○   std::underflow_error : Thrown when a numerical calculation results in a value too small to be represented.

2. **std::logic_error :** Represents errors that arise from flaws in the program's logic or invalid input.

   Examples include:

   ○   std::invalid_argument : Thrown when a function receives an argument of the wrong type or value.

   ○   std::domain_error : Thrown when a mathematical function is applied to an argument outside its valid domain (e.g., taking the square root of a negative number).

   ○   std::length_error : Thrown when an attempt is made to create an object that would exceed its maximum allowable size.

This hierarchical structure extends further, with specialized exception classes derived from these base classes to represent more specific types of errors.

Advantages of a Hierarchical Exception Structure

1. **Organization:** The hierarchy provides a logical way to group related exceptions. This makes your code more organized and easier to understand.

2. **General Catch Blocks:** You can catch a broad range of related errors with a single catch block. For example, a catch (const std::runtime_error& e) block will catch any exception derived from std::runtime_error.

3. **Flexibility:** You can define your own custom exception classes that inherit from the standard exception classes, tailoring the hierarchy to your application's specific needs.

Example: Catching a Range Error

```
#include <iostream> #include <vector>
int main() {     std::vector<int> data = {1, 2, 3};
   try {
       std::cout << data.at(5) << std::endl; // Throws
std::out_of_range
   } catch (const std::exception& e) {      // Catches any exception derived from std::exception
std::cerr << "Exception: " << e.what() << std::endl;
   }     return 0;
}
```

In this example, the catch block can handle a std::out_of_range exception because std::out_of_range is derived from std::exception.

By understanding the exception hierarchy, you can design a well-structured and effective error-handling strategy for your C++ programs. This will make your code more robust, maintainable, and easier to debug.

Multiple Catch Blocks

In the real world, emergencies come in various forms: a small fire, a major earthquake, or even a medical emergency. Similarly, your C++ programs might encounter different types of exceptions. Multiple catch blocks allow you to tailor your response to each specific exception type, ensuring that you handle errors gracefully and appropriately.

The Art of Ordering Catch Blocks

Think of your catch blocks as a series of filters, each designed to catch a particular type of exception. The key is to arrange them in order from the most specific to the most general. Why? Because of how C++ resolves which catch block to execute.

When an exception is thrown, the program starts at the first catch block and checks if the exception type matches. If it does, the code within that block is executed. If not, it moves on to the next catch block, and so on. The first matching catch block wins the race.

Example: Multiple Catch Blocks

```
#include <iostream>
#include <vector> #include <stdexcept>
void processInput(int index, std::vector<int>& data) {
   if (index < 0 || index >= data.size()) {
      throw std::out_of_range("Index out of bounds");
   }
   // ... process data[index] ...
}
int main() {    std::vector<int> data = {1, 2, 3};
   try {
      processInput(5, data);  // Potentially throws std::out_of_range       // ... other code that might
throw different exceptions ...
   } catch (const std::out_of_range& e) {
      std::cerr << "Range Error: " << e.what() << std::endl;
   } catch (const std::exception& e) {       std::cerr << "General Exception: " << e.what() <<
std::endl;
   }
   // ... continue with the rest of the program ...
}
```

In this example:

1. The process Input function checks if the index is valid. If not, it throws a std::out_of_range exception.

2. The main function has two catch blocks. The first one specifically handles std::out_of_range exceptions. The second one is a more general std::exception catch block, which can handle any other standard exceptions derived from std::exception.

If process Input throws a std::out_of_range exception, the first catch block will be executed. However, if another type of exception (e.g., std::runtime_error) is thrown from within the try block, the second catch block will handle it.

Why Ordering Matters

If you reverse the order of the catch blocks, the code wouldn't work as intended. Since std::out_of_range derives from std::exception , the general std::exception block would catch it first, and the specific std::out_of_range block would never be reached.

The Catch-All Block

Imagine you're juggling several balls in the air. You're focused on catching each one as it falls, but what if an unexpected gust of wind sends a ball flying off course? You need a safety net to prevent it from crashing to the ground. In C++ exception handling, the catch(...) block acts as that safety net, ready to catch any unexpected errors that might arise.

Syntax

The catch-all block is declared using an ellipsis (...) in place of a specific exception type:

try {

   // Code that might throw exceptions

} catch (const std::exception& e) {

   // Handle specific std::exception derived exceptions

} catch (...) { // Catch-all block

   std::cerr << "Unknown exception caught!" << std::endl;   // ... additional error handling or logging ...

}

How It Works

The catch-all block is a wildcard. It will catch any exception that isn't caught by a more specific catch block. This includes:

- **Standard Exceptions:** Any exception derived from the std::exception class that wasn't explicitly caught by a previous catch block.

- **Non-Standard Exceptions:** Exceptions thrown by libraries or external code that don't derive from std::exception.

- **Unexpected Errors:** Errors that you didn't anticipate or haven't written specific handlers for.

Role as a Safety Net

The catch-all block serves as a safety net, ensuring that no exception goes unhandled. Without it, an uncaught exception would terminate your program abruptly. The catch-all block allows you to:

- **Log the Error:** Record details about the unexpected exception, such as its type and error message.

- **Graceful Shutdown:** Perform necessary cleanup tasks before ending the program.

- **Notify the User:** Display an error message to the user, providing information about what went wrong.

Important Considerations

- **Last Resort:** The catch-all block should be your last line of defense. It's generally better to catch specific exceptions whenever possible, as this allows for more targeted and informative error handling.

- **Unknown Errors:** Since the catch-all block can catch any type of exception, you might not have detailed information about the error. This can make debugging more challenging.

- **Overuse:** Relying too heavily on the catch-all block can mask underlying issues in your code. It's important to strive for comprehensive exception handling where you anticipate and catch specific exceptions.

Stack Unwinding and Exception Safety

When an exception is thrown in C++, the program's execution doesn't simply jump to the nearest catch block. Instead, it undergoes a carefully orchestrated process called stack unwinding. This process ensures that resources are properly cleaned up and that your program can gracefully recover (or exit) from the error.

Understanding Stack Unwinding

1. **Exception Propagation:** When an exception is thrown, the program starts searching for a matching catch block. It begins in the current function and moves up the call stack, one function at a time.

2. **Destruction of Local Objects:** As the stack is unwound, the destructors of any local objects (created within the functions on the call stack) are automatically called. This is crucial for releasing resources like memory, files, and network connections that those objects might be holding.

3. **Exception Handling:** Once a matching catch block is found, the exception is handled, and the program can resume execution (if possible) or exit gracefully.

Example: Stack Unwinding in Action

```
void functionC() {    // ... some code ...
    throw std::runtime_error("Error in functionC"); }
void functionB() {    // ... some code ...
    functionC();
    // ... more code (won't be executed if exception is thrown) ...
}
```

```
void functionA() {     // ... some code ...
   functionB();
   // ... more code (won't be executed if exception is thrown) ...
}
int main() {    try {
      functionA();
   } catch (const std::runtime_error& e) {        std::cerr << e.what() << std::endl;
   }
   return 0;
}
```

In this example:

1. If an exception is thrown in functionC() , it will not be caught there.
2. The stack will unwind, functionC() will terminate and so will functionB() .
3. The exception will be caught in the catch block in main().

Exception Safety: Leaving No Mess Behind

Exception safety is the concept of ensuring that your code behaves predictably and leaves resources in a consistent state even if an exception occurs. This is crucial for preventing crashes, data corruption, and other undesirable consequences.

There are several levels of exception safety:

- **No Safety:** If an exception is thrown, the program might leak resources or leave objects in an invalid state.

- **Basic Guarantee:** If an exception is thrown, no resources are leaked, but objects might be left in an unspecified but valid state.

- **Strong Guarantee:** If an exception is thrown, the program state is rolled back to the state before the exception occurred, as if the operation had never happened.

- **Nothrow Guarantee:** The operation is guaranteed not to throw an exception.

Best Practices for Exception Safety

- **RAII (Resource Acquisition Is Initialization):** Use smart pointers and other RAII techniques to ensure automatic resource cleanup in destructors.

- **Transaction-Like Semantics:** If possible, design your operations so that they either complete successfully or leave the objects in their original state if an exception occurs.

- **Minimal State Changes:** Avoid making unnecessary changes to object states before you're sure an operation will succeed.

- **Exception-Safe Functions:** Ensure that functions you call within a try block are themselves exception-safe.

By understanding stack unwinding and striving for exception safety, you'll be able to write more robust C++ code that can handle errors gracefully and recover from unexpected situations. Your programs will be more reliable, predictable, and less prone to crashes or data corruption.

Best Practices for Exception Handling

Exception handling is a powerful tool in C++, but like any tool, it's most effective when used with precision and care. By following these best practices, you can harness the benefits of exceptions while avoiding common pitfalls and writing robust, reliable code.

Throw Exceptions for Exceptional Situations:

Exceptions are designed for exceptional circumstances, not for everyday control flow. Avoid using exceptions to handle routine errors that can be reasonably expected and handled within the normal flow of your program. Reserve exceptions for truly unexpected or unrecoverable events, such as:

- **Resource Failures:** Inability to open a file, network connection errors, or out-of-memory conditions.

- **Invalid Input:** User input that violates your program's assumptions or requirements.

- **Logic Errors:** Situations where your code encounters an internal inconsistency or impossible state.

Catch Specific Exceptions:

When catching exceptions, strive to be as specific as possible. Avoid using the catch-all block (catch(...)) unless absolutely necessary. By catching specific exceptions, you can provide targeted error handling and give more informative feedback to the user or log more detailed error messages.

```
// Good practice
try {
  // ...
} catch (const std::out_of_range& e) {
   std::cerr << "Error: Out of range access. " << e.what() << std::endl;
} catch (const std::runtime_error& e) {
   std::cerr << "Runtime Error: " << e.what() << std::endl; }
// Bad practice (catch-all) catch (...) {
```

```
    std::cerr << "Something went wrong!" << std::endl; // Not very helpful
}
```

Provide Informative Messages:

When you throw an exception, include a clear and descriptive error message that explains what went wrong. This makes debugging much easier and helps users understand the issue.

```
if (age < 0) {
    throw std::invalid_argument("Age cannot be negative."); // Informative message
}
```

Clean Up Resources (RAII):

If your objects acquire resources (memory, files, locks, etc.), ensure that their destructors properly release those resources, even if an exception is thrown. This is best achieved using the Resource Acquisition Is Initialization (RAII) idiom.

```
class File { public:
    File(const std::string& filename) {
        // ... (open file) ...
    }
    ~File() { // Destructor        // ... (close file) ...
    }
};
```

In this example, the file is guaranteed to be closed when the File object is destroyed, whether due to normal program flow or an exception.

Think About Exception Safety:

Design your functions to be exception-safe. This means they should:

No Leaks: Not leak resources if an exception is thrown.
Data Consistency: Leave objects in a valid state after an exception.
Atomicity: Either complete the entire operation successfully or roll back any changes made if an exception occurs.

By following these best practices, you can harness the power of exceptions to create more robust and reliable C++ programs. Remember, exceptions are not just for catching errors; they're a tool for designing elegant and maintainable error-handling strategies that make your code more resilient to unexpected events.

When (and when not) to Use Exceptions

Exceptions are a valuable tool in your C++ error-handling arsenal, but they're not always the best choice for every situation. Let's explore scenarios where exceptions shine and when alternative error-handling mechanisms might be more suitable.

When to Use Exceptions

Exceptional Situations: Exceptions are designed for truly exceptional, unexpected events that disrupt the normal flow of your program. This includes:

○ **System Errors:** Resource allocation failures, file system errors, network connection problems.
○ **Invalid Input:** Unexpected user input that violates your program's assumptions.
○ **Logic Errors:** Internal inconsistencies or impossible states within your code.

Unrecoverable Errors: If an error occurs that your program cannot reasonably recover from, throwing an exception is an appropriate way to signal that something has gone critically wrong. This allows the calling code (or the user) to handle the error in the most appropriate manner, such as logging the error, terminating the program gracefully, or displaying an error message.

Complex Error Handling: When error handling logic is complex and involves multiple layers of function calls, exceptions can provide a cleaner and more maintainable way to propagate errors up the call stack. Instead of passing error codes or flags through multiple function returns, you can throw an exception and let it bubble up until it's caught at an appropriate level.

Library Design: If you're designing a library, using exceptions can provide a consistent way to report errors to the library's users. This allows users to catch and handle exceptions in a way that's integrated with their own error-handling strategies.

When Not to Use Exceptions

1. **Expected Errors:** For errors that can be reasonably expected and handled within the normal flow of your program, returning error codes or using optional values might be a better choice. For example, a function that searches for an item in a list might return a nullptr if the item isn't found.

2. **Performance-Critical Code:** Exception handling can introduce some overhead, so in extremely performance-critical sections of your code, you might want to avoid using exceptions and opt for alternative error-handling mechanisms that have minimal impact on execution speed.

3. **Simple Interfaces:** If you're designing a simple interface or API, returning error codes or using optional values might be more straightforward for users to understand and handle.

Example: Optional Values (C++17 and later)

```
#include <iostream>
#include <optional> // For std::optional
```

```cpp
std::optional<int> findElement(const std::vector<int>& data, int target) {     for (int i = 0; i <
data.size(); i++) {          if (data[i] == target) {
        return i; // Return the index wrapped in an optional
    }
  }
  return std::nullopt; // Element not found
}
```

In this example, findElement returns the index of the target element if found or std::nullopt if not. The caller can then check if the optional has a value before using it.

Choosing the Right Approach

The best error handling strategy depends on the specific context, the nature of the error, and the performance requirements of your code. Consider the following factors:

- **Severity of the Error:** Is it a recoverable error or a critical failure?
- **Expectedness:** Is the error a common occurrence or a rare exception?
- **Performance Impact:** Is the code performance-critical?
- **Ease of Use:** Which approach is easier for you and other developers to understand and maintain?

By carefully weighing these factors, you can choose the most appropriate error handling mechanism for each situation, ensuring that your C++ programs are not only functional but also robust, reliable, and easy to maintain.

File Input/Output (I/O): Working with Data on Disk

The Importance of File I/O

Imagine trying to use a calculator that forgets all your calculations as soon as you turn it off. It would be frustrating, to say the least! Similarly, computer programs need a way to store data persistently, beyond the temporary confines of their memory. This is where file input/output (I/O) comes into play.

Files as Persistent Storage

Files are like external hard drives for your programs. They allow you to store data on your computer's disk (or other storage media) in a way that persists even after your program terminates. This persistent storage is essential for most real-world applications, as it enables them to:

- **Save and Load Data:** Programs can save their state, user preferences, configuration settings, or other important data to files and then load it back later when the program restarts.

- **Process Large Datasets:** Files can store massive amounts of data that would be impractical to keep entirely in memory. Programs can read from and write to files in chunks, processing the data efficiently.

- **Exchange Data:** Files provide a common format for exchanging data between different programs or systems. For example, you might save a report as a CSV file that can be opened in a spreadsheet program.

Common Use Cases for File I/O

File I/O is ubiquitous in modern software applications. Here are just a few examples:

- **Text Editors and Word Processors:** Save and load documents.
- **Image and Video Editors:** Read and write image/video files.
- **Web Browsers:** Cache web pages and store downloaded files.
- **Databases:** Store and retrieve structured data.
- **Games:** Save game progress and load saved games.
- **Logging Systems:** Record events and errors for analysis.
- **Configuration Files:** Store settings and preferences.
- **Data Analysis and Scientific Computing:** Read and write large datasets for processing and visualization.

In essence, file I/O is the bridge between your program's internal world and the external world of data storage. It allows your programs to interact with the wider world, saving and loading information, processing large datasets, and exchanging data with other systems.

By mastering file I/O in C++, you'll be equipped to build real-world applications that can store data persistently, interact with users, and integrate with other software tools. In the following sections, we'll delve into the specifics of how file I/O works in C++, exploring the different file stream classes, modes of operation, and best practices for error handling.

File Streams in C++

Think of a file stream in C++ as a pipe that connects your program to a file on your computer's disk. This pipe allows data to flow in and out of the file, enabling you to read from or write to it. C++ provides a set of classes that act as these pipes, making file input/output (I/O) a breeze.

The File Stream Family

The core file stream classes in C++ are:

- **std::ofstream (Output File Stream):** This class is used for writing data to files. It's like a one-way pipe that sends data from your program out to the file.

- **std::ifstream (Input File Stream):** This class is designed for reading data from files. It's like a one-way pipe that brings data from the file into your program.

- **std::fstream (File Stream):** This class is a combination of ofstream and ifstream . It can be used for both reading and writing to files, providing a two-way communication channel.

Inheritance Hierarchy: A Family Affair

The file stream classes inherit from a common ancestor, the std::ios class. This base class provides fundamental functionality for working with streams, including error handling, formatting, and buffer management.

```
std::ios
  |
  +-- std::fstream
      /        \
     /          \
std::ifstream   std::ofstream
```

The std::fstream class, in turn, inherits from std::iostream , which provides additional functionality for input and output operations on character streams.

Using File Streams

To use a file stream, you typically create an object of the appropriate class and then associate it with a file using the open() method. Once the file is open, you can read from it or write to it using the familiar >> (extraction) and << (insertion) operators, respectively.

```cpp
#include <iostream>
#include <fstream> // For file streams
#include <string>
int main() {
    // Writing to a file    std::ofstream outFile("output.txt"); // Create an ofstream object and open the file "output.txt"
    if (outFile.is_open()) { // Check if file was successfully opened.
        outFile << "Hello, file!\n";      outFile << 42 << std::endl;        outFile.close(); // Close the file
    } else {
        std::cerr << "Unable to open file for writing." << std::endl;
    }
    // Reading from a file
    std::ifstream inFile("input.txt"); // Create an ifstream object and open the file "input.txt"
std::string line;    if (inFile.is_open()) {
        while (std::getline(inFile, line)) { // Read line by line from the file            std::cout << line << std::endl;
```

```
    }
    inFile.close();
} else {
    std::cerr << "Unable to open file for reading." << std::endl;
}

    return 0;
}
```

In this example:

We used std::ofstream to create an output file called "output.txt" and write "Hello, file!" and the number 42 to the file.

We then used std::ifstream to open the same file ("output.txt") in read mode and printed the contents back to the console.

By understanding file streams and the hierarchy of classes that represent them, you'll be well-equipped to read from and write to files in your C++ programs.

Opening and Closing Files

In the previous section, you were introduced to file streams as the channels through which your C++ program communicates with files on your disk. Now, let's dive deeper into the mechanics of opening and closing files, the essential first and last steps in any file I/O operation.

Opening a File: The open() Method

To establish a connection between your file stream object and a physical file, you use the open() method. This method takes the file's name (as a string) as its main argument, and optionally, you can specify a mode that determines how the file will be opened and accessed.

```
std::ofstream outfile("data.txt");  // Creates an ofstream object and opens "data.txt" for writing
std::ifstream infile("data.txt");   // Creates an ifstream object and opens "data.txt" for reading
```

If the file does not exist, in case of std::ifstream , it will raise an error. Whereas, in case of std::ofstream , a new file will be created.

File Opening Modes

C++ provides several file opening modes, specified using constants from the std::ios class:

- std::ios::in : Open the file for reading (default for ifstream).
- std::ios::out : Open the file for writing (default for ofstream).
- std::ios::app : Open the file for appending (adding new content at the end).

- std::ios::ate : Open the file and move the output position to the end (used with std::ios::out or std::ios::in).
- std::ios::trunc : Truncate (discard existing content) if the file already exists (used with std::ios::out).
- std::ios::binary : Open the file in binary mode (essential for non-text files).

You can combine multiple modes using the bitwise OR operator (|).

For example:

std::fstream file("data.txt", std::ios::in | std::ios::out | std::ios::app); // Open for reading, writing, and appending.

Verifying Success with is_open()

After calling open() , it's crucial to check if the file was opened successfully. The is_open() method of the file stream object returns true if the file is open and false otherwise.

```
std::ifstream infile("nonexistent_file.txt");
if (infile.is_open()) {
    // File opened successfully
} else {
    std::cerr << "Error: Unable to open file" << std::endl;
}
```

This code tries to open a file "nonexistent_file.txt" which most likely will not exist. In that case, it will print an error message.

Closing a File: The close() Method

When you're finished working with a file, always remember to close it using the close() method. This releases the file handle and any associated system resources, ensuring that other programs can access the file and preventing potential data corruption.

```
outfile.close();
infile.close();
```

Why Closing Files Matters

Failing to close files can lead to:

- **Resource Leaks:** Your program will hold onto system resources (file handles) unnecessarily, potentially limiting the number of files other programs can open.

- **Data Corruption:** In some cases, data might not be written to the disk until the file is closed. If your program crashes before closing the file, data could be lost.

Writing to Files

In the previous section, you learned how to open a file for writing using std::ofstream . Now, let's explore how to actually put data into that file, turning it into a digital canvas for your information. C++ makes this process remarkably simple by leveraging the familiar << operator (the insertion operator) that you've already used for outputting to the console.

Writing with the Insertion Operator (<<)

With an ofstream object, you can use the << operator to write various types of data directly to a file.

```
#include <iostream>
#include <fstream> #include <string>
int main() {
    std::ofstream outfile("output.txt");    if (outFile.is_open()) {        outFile << "Hello, file!" <<
std::endl;   // Writing a string        outFile << 42 << std::endl;            // Writing an integer
outFile << 3.14159 << std::endl;        // Writing a double       outFile << true << std::endl;
// Writing a boolean
        std::string message = "This is a string.";        outFile << message << std::endl;        // Writing
a string variable
        // ... (You can write other data types as well)
    } else {
        std::cerr << "Unable to open file for writing." << std::endl;
    }

    outfile.close();    return 0;
}
```

In this example, we write various data types (a string, integer, floating-point number, boolean value, and a string variable) to the file named output.txt.

Formatting Output: Manipulators to the Rescue

You can control the format of your output in the file using manipulators, which are special objects that modify the behavior of the output stream. Some common manipulators include:

std::endl : Inserts a newline character and flushes the output buffer, ensuring the data is written to the file immediately.

std::setw(width) : Sets the width of the next output field.

std::left , std::right , std::internal : Control text alignment within the output field.

std::setprecision(precision) : Sets the number of decimal places for floating-point numbers.

std::fixed , std::scientific : Control the format of floating-point numbers.

#include <iomanip> // For std::setw and std::setprecision

// ... (inside the if (outfile.is_open()) block) ...

outFile << "Formatted output:" << std::endl;

outFile << std::setw(10) << std::left << "Name" << std::setw(5) << std::right << "Age" << std::endl;
outFile << std::setw(10) << std::left << "Alice" << std::setw(5) << std::right << 30 << std::endl;
outFile << std::fixed << std::setprecision(2); // Format floating-point numbers outFile << "Pi: " << 3.14159 << std::endl;   // Output: Pi: 3.14

In this case we added a header file iomanip . This header file provides the functionality for std::setw and std::setprecision that we used in the example.

Writing Objects to Files

You can also write custom objects to files, but it requires defining how the object should be represented in the file. This is often done using a technique called serialization, which involves converting the object's data into a format suitable for storage. We'll delve into object serialization in more detail later in the book.

Reading from Files

In the previous section, you learned how to write data to files using the insertion operator (<<). Now, let's explore how to retrieve that data back into your C++ program, unlocking the information stored in files. The extraction operator (>>), your trusty companion for reading input from the console, comes to the rescue again, this time working in conjunction with an ifstream object.

Reading with the Extraction Operator (>>)

With an ifstream object, you can use the >> operator to read various data types from a file. It works similarly to reading input from the keyboard, but instead of waiting for user input, it extracts data directly from the file.

```
#include <iostream>
#include <fstream> #include <string>
int main() {
    std::ifstream infile("input.txt");    if (infile.is_open()) {        int num;        double price;        std::string word;
        infile >> num;        // Read an integer        infile >> price;        // Read a double
        infile >> word;        // Read a string (up to the next whitespace)
        std::cout << num << std::endl;        std::cout << price << std::endl;        std::cout << word << std::endl;
        // ... (You can read more data as needed)
```

```
  } else {
    std::cerr << "Unable to open file for reading." << std::endl;
  }
  infile.close();
  return 0;
}
```

In this example, the code attempts to read an integer (num), a double (price), and a string (word) from a file named input.txt . If the file is opened successfully, the extracted values will be printed to the console.

Reading Line by Line: std::getline()

If you need to read an entire line of text from a file (including spaces), the std::getline() function is your friend. It reads characters from the input stream until it encounters a newline character ('\n').

```
std::string line;
while (std::getline(infile, line)) {
    std::cout << line << std::endl;
}
```

In this example, the while loop continues as long as std::getline() successfully reads a line from the file. Each line is then printed to the console.

Handling End-of-File (EOF): The eof() Method

When you reach the end of the file, std::getline() (and other extraction operations) will fail. You can use the eof() method to check if you've reached the end of the file:

```
if (infile.eof()) {
    std::cout << "End of file reached." << std::endl;
}
```

Alternative Ways to Check for EOF:

- **while (infile >> num)**: This loop continues as long as input operations are successful. It will stop if we reach the end of file or if there is an error in reading the file.

- **while (!infile.fail())**: This loop continues as long as there are no errors in reading the file (e.g., wrong type of data encountered). It will stop if we reach the end of file or if there is an error.

- **while (infile)**: This loop continues as long as the stream is in a good state, meaning it hasn't encountered the end of file or an error. This condition is equivalent to !inFile.fail() .

Error Handling in File I/O

File input/output (I/O) operations are not always smooth sailing. You might encounter choppy waters in the form of errors like:

File Not Found: The file you're trying to open doesn't exist.
Permission Issues: You don't have the necessary permissions to read or write the file.
Disk Full: The storage device is full and can't accommodate your data.
Read/Write Errors: A hardware failure or other issue prevents the data from being read or written correctly.

These are just a few of the many things that can go wrong. Without proper error handling, your program could crash, produce incorrect results, or leave files in an inconsistent state.

Why Error Handling is Crucial

Robust error handling is essential for building reliable and user-friendly C++ applications. It allows your program to:

- **Detect Errors:** Identify when something goes wrong during file operations.
- **Recover (If Possible):** Attempt to recover from the error or take alternative actions.
- **Inform the User:** Provide clear and informative error messages to the user.
- **Log Errors:** Record error details for later analysis and debugging.
- **Prevent Crashes:** Gracefully handle errors instead of abruptly terminating the program.

Detecting Errors

C++ file streams provide several mechanisms for detecting errors:

The is_open() Method: Always check if a file was opened successfully using is_open() . If it returns false, the file couldn't be opened.

Error State Flags: File stream objects have internal flags that indicate different error states:

○   eof() : Returns true if the end of the file has been reached.
○   fail() : Returns true if a non-fatal error occurred (e.g., trying to read a string when a number is expected).
○   bad() : Returns true if a more serious error occurred (e.g., a disk failure).

Exceptions (Advanced): C++ file streams can also throw exceptions when errors occur. We'll discuss exception handling in more detail in a later section.

Example: Error Handling with Error State Flags

```cpp
#include <iostream>
#include <fstream> #include <string>
int main() {
    std::ifstream infile("data.txt");
    if (!infile.is_open()) { //Check if file was successfully opened.
        std::cerr << "Error: Unable to open file" << std::endl;        return 1; // Indicate failure    }
    int num;
    while (infile >> num) { // Read until an error or end-of-file
        // ... (process num)
    }
    if (infile.eof()) {
        std::cout << "End of file reached." << std::endl;
    } else if (infile.fail()) {
        std::cerr << "Error reading data from file." << std::endl;
    } else if (infile.bad()) {
        std::cerr << "Fatal error occurred while reading file." << std::endl;
    }
    infile.close();
    return 0;
}
```

In this example:

- We use is_open() and eof() to check for the file opening and end of file errors.
- We use fail() to check if a non-fatal error occurred while reading. This often means the file might be in the wrong format.
- Finally, we check if the state is bad() , which indicates a fatal error while reading the file.

Example: Error Handling with Exceptions

```cpp
try {
    std::ifstream infile("data.txt");    infile.exceptions(std::ifstream::failbit | std::ifstream::badbit); //
Enable exceptions
    // ... (read from file) ...
} catch (const std::ifstream::failure& e) {
    std::cerr << "Exception: " << e.what() << std::endl;
}
```

In this example, we enable exceptions for the failbit and badbit error states. If either of these errors occurs, an std::ifstream::failure exception is thrown, which we catch and handle.

By incorporating error handling into your file I/O operations, you ensure that your programs can gracefully handle unexpected issues, providing a more robust and user-friendly experience.

Binary Files vs. Text Files

In the realm of file I/O, the distinction between binary files and text files is fundamental. Each format serves a specific purpose and requires different handling in your C++ programs.

Binary Files: The Raw Data Powerhouse

Binary files are the rawest form of data storage. They treat a file as a sequence of bytes, with no interpretation or translation of the contents. This makes them ideal for storing:

- **Non-Textual Data:** Images, audio, video, executable programs, and other types of data that aren't meant to be human-readable.

- **Serialized Objects:** Complex data structures or objects that have been converted into a byte stream for storage.

Key Characteristics of Binary Files:

- **No Newline Conversion:** Binary files don't interpret newline characters (\n) as line breaks. Each byte is treated as-is.

- **Platform Independence:** Binary files are generally platform-independent, meaning a binary file created on one system can often be read on another system without modification.

Text Files: The Human-Readable Choice

Text files store data in a human-readable format, typically using character encodings like ASCII or UTF-8. They are best suited for:

- **Structured Data:** Comma-separated values (CSV), tab-delimited files, configuration files, log files, and other data that can be easily viewed and edited in a text editor.

- **Source Code:** Your C++ programs themselves are stored in text files.

Key Characteristics of Text Files:

- **Newline Conversion:** Text files interpret newline characters (\n) as line breaks, making them easy to view and edit in a text editor.

- **Platform Dependence:** Newline characters might be represented differently on different operating systems (e.g., \r\n on Windows, \n on macOS and Linux), which can cause issues when transferring text files between platforms.

Opening and Working with Binary Files

To open a file in binary mode, you need to include the std::ios::binary flag when you open the file stream.

std::ofstream outfile("data.bin", std::ios::binary); // Open in binary mode

When reading or writing binary files, you typically work with the raw bytes of data directly. For example, you might use read() and write() member functions to read or write blocks of bytes.

char buffer[1024];
infile.read(buffer, sizeof(buffer)); // Read up to 1024 bytes

Choosing Between Binary and Text

The choice between binary and text files depends on the nature of your data and how you intend to use it.

- **Binary:** Use for non-textual data, serialized objects, or when you need maximum performance or control over the data format.

- **Text:** Use for structured data that needs to be human-readable and easily editable.

By understanding the distinction between binary and text files and how to handle them in C++, you'll be equipped to choose the right format for your data and ensure that your programs can read and write files seamlessly, regardless of their content or purpose.

Practical Examples

Let's dive into some practical examples that illustrate the power of file I/O in C++.

1. Reading a CSV File and Storing Data in a Vector of Structs

#include <iostream>
#include <fstream>
#include <sstream>
#include <string> #include <vector>

```cpp
struct Product {    std::string name;    double price;    int quantity;
};
int main() {
    std::ifstream file("products.csv");
    if (!file.is_open()) {
        std::cerr << "Error opening file." << std::endl;    return 1;
    }
    std::vector<Product> products;
    std::string line;
    while (std::getline(file, line)) {    std::stringstream ss(line);    Product p;
        std::getline(ss, p.name, ',');    ss >> p.price;
        ss.ignore(); // Ignore the comma
        ss >> p.quantity;    products.push_back(p);
    }
    file.close();
    // Display the products    for (const Product& p : products) {
        std::cout << p.name << " - $" << p.price << " (" << p.quantity << " in stock)" << std::endl;
    }
    return 0;
}
```

Explanation:

- We define a Product struct to hold product data.
- We open the CSV file and read it line by line.
- We use std::stringstream to parse each line and extract the name, price, and quantity.
- The extracted data is stored in Product structs, which are then added to the products vector.
- Finally, we print the product information.

2. Writing a Log File

```cpp
#include <iostream>
#include <fstream>
#include <ctime> // For time-related functions
void logEvent(const std::string& message) {    std::ofstream logFile("log.txt", std::ios::app); // Open in append mode
    std::time_t now = std::time(nullptr); // Get current time    char* timeStr = std::ctime(&now);
    logFile << timeStr << " - " << message << std::endl; // Add timestamp to message
logFile.close();
```

```
}
int main() {
    // ... your program logic ...    logEvent("Program started.");    // ... more logic ...
logEvent("Error encountered.");    // ... more logic ...
    logEvent("Program finished.");
    return 0;
}
```

Explanation:

- We define a logEvent function that takes a message and appends it to a log file (log.txt) along with a timestamp.

- In the main function, we call logEvent at various points to record program events.

3. Serializing Objects (Simplified Example):

```cpp
#include <iostream>
#include <fstream> #include <string>
class Person { public:      std::string name;
    int age; };
int main() {
    Person person = {"Alice", 30};
    // Write the object to a binary file
    std::ofstream outfile("person.bin", std::ios::binary);
outfile.write(reinterpret_cast<char*>(&person), sizeof(Person));      outfile.close();
    // Read the object from the binary file      Person loadedPerson;
    std::ifstream infile("person.bin", std::ios::binary);
    infile.read(reinterpret_cast<char*>(&loadedPerson), sizeof(Person));      infile.close();
    std::cout << loadedPerson.name << " " << loadedPerson.age << std::endl; // Output: Alice 30
}
```

Note: Serialization of complex objects often requires more sophisticated libraries like Boost.Serialization or Cereal.

4. Reading Configuration Settings from a Text File

```cpp
#include <iostream>
#include <fstream>
#include <string> #include <map>
```

```
int main() {
    std::map<std::string, std::string> settings;    std::ifstream configFile("config.txt");
    std::string key, value;
    while (configFile >> key >> value) {
        settings[key] = value;    }
    configFile.close();
    // Access settings
    std::cout << "Server address: " << settings["server_address"] << std::endl;    std::cout << "Port: "
<< settings["port"] << std::endl;
}
```

Explanation:

- We use a std::map to store key-value pairs representing configuration settings.
- We read the configuration file (config.txt), extracting keys and values, and store them in the map.
- Later, we access the settings using their keys.

These examples demonstrate just a few of the ways you can leverage file I/O in your C++ programs. The possibilities are vast, and by mastering these techniques, you'll be able to create applications that can interact with the outside world and store data for future use.

Conclusion: Exception Handling and File Handling in C++

C++ is a versatile and powerful programming language that has stood the test of time, evolving to meet the demands of modern software development. Among its many features, **exception handling** and **file handling** are two critical aspects that enable developers to build robust, reliable, and efficient applications.

These features are essential for managing runtime errors, ensuring data persistence, and enabling seamless interaction with external resources. As we look ahead to 2025, the importance of these concepts remains undiminished, and their proper implementation continues to be a hallmark of high-quality software.

In this detailed conclusion, we will summarize the key aspects of exception handling and file handling in C++, explore their significance in modern programming, discuss best practices, and highlight their relevance in the context of emerging technologies and trends.

1. Exception Handling in C++: A Recap

Exception handling is a mechanism that allows programs to detect and respond to runtime errors gracefully. It prevents applications from crashing unexpectedly and provides a structured way to manage errors. The core components of exception handling in C++ are the try, catch, and throw keywords, which work together to identify, raise, and handle exceptions.

1.1 Key Concepts in Exception Handling

- **Try Block**: Encloses code that may throw an exception.
- **Catch Block**: Handles exceptions thrown by the try block.
- **Throw Statement**: Raises an exception when an error occurs.
- **Standard Exceptions**: Predefined exception classes like std::runtime_error and std::invalid_argument.
- **Custom Exceptions**: User-defined exception classes for application-specific errors.
- **Exception Propagation**: The process of passing exceptions up the call stack until they are handled.

1.2 Importance of Exception Handling

Exception handling is crucial for several reasons:

- **Error Management**: It provides a structured way to handle errors, making code more maintainable and readable.
- **Program Stability**: It prevents applications from crashing due to unexpected errors, improving user experience.
- **Resource Management**: It ensures that resources like memory and file handles are properly released, even in the event of an error.
- **Debugging**: It helps developers identify and fix issues by providing detailed error messages.

1.3 Best Practices for Exception Handling

To maximize the effectiveness of exception handling, developers should follow these best practices:

- **Use Standard Exceptions**: Leverage the standard exception classes provided by C++ for common error types.
- **Create Custom Exceptions**: Define custom exception classes for application-specific errors.
- **Catch Exceptions by Reference**: Use catch (const std::exception& e) to avoid slicing and improve performance.
- **Avoid Overusing Exceptions**: Use exceptions for exceptional conditions, not for regular control flow.
- **Clean Up Resources**: Use RAII (Resource Acquisition Is Initialization) to ensure resources are released properly.

1.4 Exception Handling in Modern C++

As C++ evolves, exception handling continues to improve. Features like **noexcept specifiers** and **smart pointers** have made it easier to write exception-safe code. In 2025, exception handling remains a cornerstone of reliable software development, especially in domains like finance, healthcare, and aerospace, where errors can have severe consequences.

2. File Handling in C++: A Recap

File handling is the process of reading from and writing to files, enabling applications to store and retrieve data persistently. C++ provides a rich set of classes and functions for file handling, including ifstream, ofstream, and fstream. These classes support both text and binary file operations, making C++ a versatile language for working with files.

2.1 Key Concepts in File Handling

- **File Streams**: Classes like ifstream, ofstream, and fstream for file operations.
- **Text and Binary Files**: Two types of files supported by C++.
- **Reading and Writing Data**: Methods like read(), write(), getline(), and <</>> operators.
- **File Operations**: Functions like seekg(), tellg(), seekp(), and tellp() for manipulating file pointers.
- **File Closing**: The close() method for releasing file resources.

2.2 Importance of File Handling

File handling is essential for many applications, including:

- **Data Persistence**: Storing data in files allows applications to retain information between sessions.

- **Data Exchange**: Files are a common medium for exchanging data between applications.

- **Configuration Management**: Storing configuration settings in files makes applications more flexible and user-friendly.

- **Logging**: Writing logs to files helps developers monitor and debug applications.

2.3 Best Practices for File Handling

To ensure efficient and reliable file handling, developers should follow these best practices:

- **Check File Open Status**: Always verify that a file has been successfully opened before performing operations.

- **Use RAII**: Leverage RAII principles to ensure files are closed automatically when they go out of scope.

- **Handle Binary Files Carefully**: Use reinterpret_cast and ensure proper alignment when working with binary data.

- **Avoid Hardcoding File Paths**: Use relative paths or configuration files to make applications more portable.

- **Optimize File Operations**: Minimize the number of read/write operations and use buffering for better performance.

2.4 File Handling in Modern C++

In 2025, file handling in C++ continues to benefit from advancements in the language and its ecosystem. Features like **filesystem library** (introduced in C++17) provide a modern and portable way to work with files and directories. Additionally, the growing adoption of **cloud storage** and **distributed systems** has expanded the scope of file handling, requiring developers to integrate file operations with network protocols and APIs.

3. The Role of Exception Handling and File Handling in Modern Software Development

As software systems become more complex and interconnected, the importance of exception handling and file handling has only grown. These features play a critical role in ensuring the reliability, security, and performance of modern applications.

3.1 Reliability and Robustness

Exception handling and file handling are essential for building reliable software. By anticipating and managing errors, developers can create applications that are resilient to unexpected conditions. Similarly, proper file handling ensures that data is stored and retrieved accurately, even in the face of hardware failures or other issues.

3.2 Security

Security is a top priority in modern software development. Exception handling helps prevent vulnerabilities like crashes and memory leaks, which can be exploited by attackers. File handling, when done correctly, ensures that sensitive data is stored securely and accessed only by authorized users.

3.3 Performance

Efficient file handling is critical for performance, especially in applications that process large datasets or require real-time data access. By optimizing file operations and using techniques like buffering, developers can minimize latency and improve throughput.

3.4 Integration with Emerging Technologies

As new technologies like **artificial intelligence**, **blockchain**, and **edge computing** gain traction, exception handling and file handling will continue to play a vital role. For example:

- **AI and Machine Learning**: Handling large datasets and managing errors during model training.
- **Blockchain**: Storing and retrieving transaction data securely.
- **Edge Computing**: Managing files and handling errors in distributed environments.

4. Future Trends and Challenges

Looking ahead to 2025 and beyond, several trends and challenges will shape the future of exception handling and file handling in C++.

4.1 Trends

- **Increased Use of Standard Libraries**: The growing adoption of standard libraries like <filesystem> and <exception> will simplify file and error handling.

- **Cross-Platform Development**: The demand for cross-platform applications will drive the need for portable file handling solutions.

- **Cloud Integration**: File handling will increasingly involve integration with cloud storage services like AWS S3 and Google Cloud Storage.

- **Real-Time Systems**: Exception handling will become more critical in real-time systems, where errors must be detected and resolved quickly.

4.2 Challenges

- **Complexity**: As applications become more complex, managing exceptions and files will require greater care and expertise.

- **Security Risks**: Improper file handling can lead to security vulnerabilities like data breaches and unauthorized access.

- **Performance Bottlenecks**: Inefficient file operations can become a bottleneck in high-performance applications.

- **Compatibility**: Ensuring compatibility across different platforms and file systems can be challenging.

5. Final Thoughts

Exception handling and file handling are foundational concepts in C++ that have stood the test of time. They are essential for building reliable, secure, and efficient applications, and their importance will only grow as software systems become more complex and interconnected. By mastering these concepts and following best practices, developers can create software that meets the demands of modern users and businesses.

As we move into 2025, the continued evolution of C++ and its ecosystem will provide new opportunities and challenges for exception handling and file handling. By staying informed about emerging trends and technologies, developers can ensure that their skills remain relevant and their applications remain robust in an ever-changing landscape.

In conclusion, exception handling and file handling are not just technical features of C++—they are essential tools for building software that is reliable, secure, and performant. Whether you are developing a small utility or a large-scale enterprise application, these concepts will remain at the heart of your work, enabling you to create software that stands the test of time.

6. Data Structures and Algorithms in C++

Introduction

Data structures and algorithms are the backbone of computer science, enabling efficient data organization, storage, and retrieval. In C++, these concepts are implemented using a combination of object-oriented programming (OOP) and procedural techniques. This guide provides a detailed introduction to key data structures and algorithms in C++, including linked lists, stacks, queues, trees, graphs, sorting algorithms, and hash tables. By the end of this guide, you will have a solid understanding of these concepts and their practical implementations in C++.

1. Linked Lists

A linked list is a linear data structure where each element (called a node) contains data and a pointer to the next node. Linked lists are dynamic in nature, allowing efficient insertion and deletion operations.

1.1 Singly Linked List

- **Structure**: Each node contains data and a pointer to the next node.

- **Operations**:

    o **Insertion**: At the beginning, end, or a specific position.
    o **Deletion**: Remove a node by value or position.
    o **Traversal**: Access each node sequentially.

- **Advantages**: Dynamic size, efficient insertion/deletion.
- **Disadvantages**: No random access, extra memory for pointers.

```cpp
struct Node {
    int data;
    Node* next;
};

class SinglyLinkedList {
private:
    Node* head;
public:
    SinglyLinkedList() : head(nullptr) {}
    void insert(int data);
    void deleteNode(int data);
    void display();
};
```

1.2 Doubly Linked List

- **Structure**: Each node contains data, a pointer to the next node, and a pointer to the previous node.
- **Operations**: Similar to singly linked lists but with bidirectional traversal.
- **Advantages**: Can traverse in both directions.
- **Disadvantages**: Requires more memory for the additional pointer.

```
struct Node {
   int data;
   Node* next;
   Node* prev;
};

class DoublyLinkedList {
private:
   Node* head;
public:
   DoublyLinkedList() : head(nullptr) {}
   void insert(int data);
   void deleteNode(int data);
   void display();
};
```

1.3 Circular Linked List

- **Structure**: The last node points back to the first node, forming a loop.
- **Operations**: Similar to singly/doubly linked lists but with circular traversal.
- **Advantages**: Useful for circular data representation.
- **Disadvantages**: Risk of infinite loops if not handled carefully.

```
class CircularLinkedList {
private:
   Node* head;
public:
   CircularLinkedList() : head(nullptr) {}
   void insert(int data);
   void deleteNode(int data);
   void display();
};
```

2. Stacks and Queues

2.1 Stacks

- **LIFO Principle**: Last In, First Out.

- **Operations**:

   - **Push**: Add an element to the top.
   - **Pop**: Remove the top element.
   - **Peek**: Access the top element without removing it.

- **Applications**: Function call stack, expression evaluation, undo operations.

```cpp
class Stack {
private:
    int* arr;
    int top;
    int capacity;
public:
    Stack(int size) : capacity(size), top(-1) {
        arr = new int[capacity];
    }
    void push(int data);
    void pop();
    int peek();
    bool isEmpty();
};
```

2.2 Queues

- **FIFO Principle**: First In, First Out.

- **Operations**:

   - **Enqueue**: Add an element to the rear.
   - **Dequeue**: Remove an element from the front.
   - **Front**: Access the front element.

- **Applications**: Task scheduling, print spooling, BFS.

```cpp
class Queue {
private:
    int* arr;
    int front, rear, capacity;
public:
    Queue(int size) : capacity(size), front(0), rear(-1) {
        arr = new int[capacity];
    }
    void enqueue(int data);
```

```
    void dequeue();
    int getFront();
    bool isEmpty();
};
```

3. Trees and Binary Search Trees (BST)

3.1 Trees

- **Hierarchical Structure**: Consists of nodes with a parent-child relationship.
- **Terminology**: Root, leaf, depth, height, subtree.
- **Types**: Binary trees, N-ary trees, balanced trees.

3.2 Binary Search Trees (BST)

- **Properties**:

    o Left subtree contains nodes with values less than the root.
    o Right subtree contains nodes with values greater than the root.
    o No duplicate nodes.

- **Operations**:

    o **Insertion**: Add a node while maintaining BST properties.
    o **Deletion**: Remove a node and adjust the tree.
    o **Search**: Find a node with a specific value.
    o **Traversal**: In-order, pre-order, post-order.

```
struct TreeNode {
    int data;
    TreeNode* left;
    TreeNode* right;
};

class BST {
private:
    TreeNode* root;
    TreeNode* insert(TreeNode* node, int data);
    TreeNode* deleteNode(TreeNode* node, int data);
    TreeNode* search(TreeNode* node, int data);
    void inorder(TreeNode* node);
public:
    BST() : root(nullptr) {}
    void insert(int data);
    void deleteNode(int data);
    bool search(int data);
```

```
    void display();
};
```

4. Graphs and Graph Traversal

4.1 Graphs

- **Non-linear Structure**: Consists of vertices (nodes) and edges (connections).

- **Types**:

    o **Directed**: Edges have a direction.
    o **Undirected**: Edges have no direction.
    o **Weighted**: Edges have weights.

4.2 Graph Traversal

- **Depth-First Search (DFS)**:

    o Explores as far as possible along each branch before backtracking.
    o Uses a stack (recursion or explicit stack).

- **Breadth-First Search (BFS)**:

    o Explores all neighbors at the present depth before moving deeper.
    o Uses a queue.

```cpp
class Graph {
private:
    int V; // Number of vertices
    vector<vector<int>> adj; // Adjacency list
    void DFSUtil(int v, vector<bool>& visited);
    void BFSUtil(int v, vector<bool>& visited);
public:
    Graph(int V);
    void addEdge(int u, int v);
    void DFS(int start);
    void BFS(int start);
};
```

5. Sorting Algorithms

5.1 QuickSort

- **Divide and Conquer**: Picks a pivot and partitions the array.
- **Time Complexity**: $O(n \log n)$ average, $O(n^2)$ worst case.

- **Space Complexity**: O(log n).

```
int partition(int arr[], int low, int high) {
    int pivot = arr[high];
    int i = low - 1;
    for (int j = low; j < high; j++) {
        if (arr[j] < pivot) {
            i++;
            swap(arr[i], arr[j]);
        }
    }
    swap(arr[i + 1], arr[high]);
    return i + 1;
}

void quickSort(int arr[], int low, int high) {
    if (low < high) {
        int pi = partition(arr, low, high);
        quickSort(arr, low, pi - 1);
        quickSort(arr, pi + 1, high);
    }
}
```

5.2 MergeSort

- **Divide and Conquer**: Divides the array into halves, sorts them, and merges.
- **Time Complexity**: O(n log n).
- **Space Complexity**: O(n).

```
void merge(int arr[], int l, int m, int r) {
    int n1 = m - l + 1;
    int n2 = r - m;
    int L[n1], R[n2];
    for (int i = 0; i < n1; i++) L[i] = arr[l + i];
    for (int i = 0; i < n2; i++) R[i] = arr[m + 1 + i];
    int i = 0, j = 0, k = l;
    while (i < n1 && j < n2) {
        if (L[i] <= R[j]) arr[k++] = L[i++];
        else arr[k++] = R[j++];
    }
    while (i < n1) arr[k++] = L[i++];
    while (j < n2) arr[k++] = R[j++];
}

void mergeSort(int arr[], int l, int r) {
    if (l < r) {
```

```
      int m = 1 + (r - 1) / 2;
      mergeSort(arr, l, m);
      mergeSort(arr, m + 1, r);
      merge(arr, l, m, r);
   }
}
```

5.3 HeapSort

- **Heap Data Structure**: Uses a binary heap to sort elements.
- **Time Complexity**: O(n log n).
- **Space Complexity**: O(1).

```
void heapify(int arr[], int n, int i) {
   int largest = i;
   int l = 2 * i + 1;
   int r = 2 * i + 2;
   if (l < n && arr[l] > arr[largest]) largest = l;
   if (r < n && arr[r] > arr[largest]) largest = r;
   if (largest != i) {
      swap(arr[i], arr[largest]);
      heapify(arr, n, largest);
   }
}

void heapSort(int arr[], int n) {
   for (int i = n / 2 - 1; i >= 0; i--) heapify(arr, n, i);
   for (int i = n - 1; i > 0; i--) {
      swap(arr[0], arr[i]);
      heapify(arr, i, 0);
   }
}
```

6. Hash Tables and Hashing Techniques

6.1 Hash Tables

- **Key-Value Storage**: Uses a hash function to map keys to indices in an array.

- **Collision Handling**:

   o **Chaining**: Store multiple elements in the same bucket using linked lists.
   o **Open Addressing**: Find the next available slot using probing.

6.2 Hashing Techniques

- **Division Method**: hash(key) = key % table_size.
- **Multiplication Method**: hash(key) = floor(table_size * (key * A % 1)).
- **Universal Hashing**: Randomly choose a hash function from a family of functions.

```cpp
class HashTable {
private:
    int tableSize;
    vector<list<pair<int, int>>> table;
    int hash(int key);
public:
    HashTable(int size) : tableSize(size), table(size) {}
    void insert(int key, int value);
    int search(int key);
    void remove(int key);
};
```

Data Structures in C++

C++ allows you to use different variables and structures, such as arrays and lists. We have looked at these in brief in the first book. This chapter introduces the different ways you can use these data structures to perform different activities in C++. You can use arrays to define different variables or combine different elements across the program or code into one variable, as long as they fall into the same category.

A structure, however, allows you to combine different variables and data types. You can use a structure to define or represent records. Let us assume you want to track the books on your bookshelf. You can use a structure to track various attributes of every book on your shelf, such as:

Book ID
Book title
Genre
Author

The Struct Statement

You need to use the struct statement to define a structure in your code. This statement allows you to develop or define a new data type for your code. You can also define the number of elements or members in the code.

The syntax of this statement is as follows:

```cpp
struct [structure tag] { member definition; member definition;
...
member definition;
} [one or more structure variables];
```

It is not mandatory to use the structure tag when you use the statement. When you define a member in the structure, you can use the variable definition method we discussed in the previous book. For instance, you can use the method int i to define an integer variable. The section before the semicolon in the struct syntax is also optional, but this is where you define the structure variables you want to use.

Continuing with the example above, let us look at how you can define a book structure.

```
struct Books { int book_id; char book_title[50]; char genre[50]; char author[100];
} book;
```

How to Access Members

Once you define the structure, you can access it using a full stop, which is also called the member access operator. This operator is used as a period or break between the structure member and the variable name. Make sure to enter the variable name you want to access. You can define the variable of the entire structure using the struct keyword.

Let us look at an example of how you can use structures:

```
#include <iostream>
#include <cstring> using namespace std; struct Books { int book_id; char book_title[50]; char genre[50]; char author[100];
}; int main() {
struct Books Book1; // This is where you declare the variable Book1 in the Book structure
struct Books Book2; // This is where you declare the variable Book2 in the Book structure
// Let us now look at how you can specify the details of the first variable
Book1.book_id = 120000;
strcpy( Book1.book_title, "Harry Potter and the Philosopher's Stone");
strcpy( Book1.genre, "Fiction");
strcpy( Book1.author, "JK Rowling");
// Let us now look at how you can specify the details of the second variable
Book2.book_id = 130000;
strcpy( Book2.book_title, "Harry Potter and the Chamber of Secrets");
strcpy( Book2.genre, "Fiction"); strcpy( Book2.author, "JK Rowling");
// The next statements are to print the details of the first and second variables in the structure
cout << "Book 1 id: " << Book1.book_id <<endl; cout << "Book 1 title: " << Book1.book_title
<<endl; cout << "Book 1 genre: " << Book1.genre <<endl; cout << "Book 1 author: " <<
Book1.author <<endl; cout << "Book 2 id: " << Book2.book_id <<endl; cout << "Book 2 title: " <<
Book2.book_title <<endl; cout << "Book 2 genre: " << Book2.genre <<endl; cout << "Book 2
author: " << Book2.author <<endl; return 0;
}
```

The code above will give you the following output:

Book 1 id: 120000

Book 1 title: Harry Potter and the Philosopher's Stone
Book 1 genre: Fiction
Book 1 author: JK Rowling
Book 2 id: 130000
Book 2 title: Harry Potter and the Chamber of Secrets
Book 2 genre: Fiction
Book 2 author: JK Rowling

Using Structures as Arguments

You can use structures as arguments in a function similar to how you pass a pointer or variable as part of the function. You need to access the variables in the structure in the same way as we did in the example above.

```
#include <iostream>
#include <cstring> using namespace std;
void printBook( struct Books book );
struct Books { int book_id; char book_title[50]; char genre[50]; char author[100];
}; int main() {
struct Books Book1; // This is where you declare the variable Book1 in the Book structure
struct Books Book2; // This is where you declare the variable Book2 in the Book structure
// Let us now look at how you can specify the details of the first variable
Book1.book_id = 120000;
strcpy( Book1.book_title, "Harry Potter and the Philosopher's Stone");
strcpy( Book1.genre, "Fiction");
strcpy( Book1.author, "JK Rowling");
// Let us now look at how you can specify the details of the second variable
Book2.book_id = 130000;
strcpy( Book2.book_title, "Harry Potter and the Chamber of Secrets");
strcpy( Book2.genre, "Fiction");
strcpy( Book2.author, "JK Rowling");
// The next statements are to print the details of the first and second variables in the structure
printBook( Book1 );
printBook( Book2 );
return 0;
}
void printBook(struct Books book ) {
cout << "Book id: " << book.book_id <<endl;
cout << "Book title: " << book.book_title <<endl;
cout << "Book genre: " << book.genre <<endl;
cout << "Book author: " << book.author<<endl;
}
```

When you compile the code written above, you receive the following output:

Book 1 id: 120000

Book 1 title: Harry Potter and the Philosopher's Stone
Book 1 genre: Fiction
Book 1 author: JK Rowling
Book 2 id: 130000
Book 2 title: Harry Potter and the Chamber of Secrets
Book 2 genre: Fiction
Book 2 author: JK Rowling

Using Pointers

You can also refer to structures using pointers, and you can use a pointer similar to how you would define a pointer for regular variables.

struct Books *struct_pointer;

When you use the above statement, you can use the pointer variable defined to store the address of the variables in the structure.

struct_pointer = &Book1;

You can also use a pointer to access one or members of the structure. To do this, you need to use the -> operator:

struct_pointer->title;

Let us rewrite the example above to indicate a member or the entire structure using a pointer.

```
#include <iostream>
#include <cstring> using namespace std;
void printBook( struct Books *book );
struct Books { int book_id; char book_title[50];
char genre[50]; char author[100];
}; int main() {
struct Books Book1; // This is where you declare the variable Book1 in the Book structure
struct Books Book2; // This is where you declare the variable Book2 in the Book structure
// Let us now look at how you can specify the details of the first variable
Book1.book_id = 120000;
strcpy( Book1.book_title, "Harry Potter and the Philosopher's Stone");
strcpy( Book1.genre, "Fiction"); strcpy( Book1.author, "JK Rowling");
// Let us now look at how you can specify the details of the second variable
Book2.book_id = 130000;
strcpy( Book2.book_title, "Harry Potter and the Chamber of Secrets");
strcpy( Book2.genre, "Fiction");
strcpy( Book2.author, "JK Rowling");
```

```
// The next statements are to print the details of the first and second variables in the structure
printBook( Book1 );
printBook( Book2 );
return 0;
}
// We will now use a function to accept a structure pointer as its parameter.
void printBook( struct Books *book ) {
cout << "Book id: " << book->book_id <<endl;
cout << "Book title: " << book->book_title <<endl;
cout << "Book genre: " << book->genre<<endl;
cout << "Book author: " << book->author <<endl;
}
```

When you write the above code, you obtain the following output:

```
Book id: 120000
Book title: Harry Potter and the Philosopher's Stone
Book genre: Fiction
Book author: JK Rowling
Book id: 130000
Book title: Harry Potter and the Chamber of Secrets
Book genre: Fiction
Book author: JK Rowling
```

Typedef Keyword

If the above methods are a little tricky for you, you can use an alias type to define a structure.

For instance,

```
typedef struct { int book_id;
char book_title[50];
char genre[50];
char author[100];
}
Books;
```

This is an easier syntax to use since you can directly define all the variables in the structure without using the keyword 'struct.'

```
Books Book1, Book2;
```

You do not have to use a typedef key only to define a structure. It can also be used to define regular variables.

typedef long int *pint32; pint32 x, y, z;

The type long ints point to the variables x, y and z.

Searching Algorithms

A searching algorithm is designed to look for an element or print the same element from the program's data structures or variables. There are numerous algorithms you can use to search for elements in the structures. The algorithms are classified into the following categories:

Interval search: An interval search is one where the algorithm will look for the element in a sorted structure. These algorithms are better to use when compared to the next category since the structure is broken down and divided into parts before the element is identified in the structure—for example, binary search.

Sequential search: In these types of algorithms, the compiler moves from one element to the next to look for the element in the data structure. An example of this algorithm is linear search.
Let us look at how these search algorithms work in C++.

Linear Search

Let us understand how the search algorithm works in C++ using an example. Consider a problem where you have an array 'arr[]' with n elements; how would you look for the value 'x' in the arr[]?

Input : arr[] = {10, 20, 80, 30, 60, 50,
110, 100, 130, 170} x = 110;

Output: 6

Element x is present at index 6

Input : arr[] = {10, 20, 80, 30, 60, 50,
110, 100, 130, 170} x = 175;

Output: -1

Element x is not present in arr[].

The simplest way to perform a linear search is as follows:

Begin at the end of the array and compare the element you are looking for against each array element.
If the element matches one of the elements in your array, return the index
If the element does not match, move to the next element
If the element is not present in the array, return -1.

// C++ code to linearly search x in arr[].

If x is present then return its location, otherwise return -1

```cpp
#include <iostream> using namespace std;
int search(int arr[], int n, int x)
{
int i;
for (i = 0; i < n; i++) if (arr[i] == x) return i;
return -1;
}
// Driver code int main(void) {
int arr[] = { 2, 3, 4, 10, 40 }; int x = 10;
int n = sizeof(arr) / sizeof(arr[0]);
// Function call
int result = search(arr, n, x);
(result == -1)
? cout << "Element is not present in array"
: cout << "Element is present at index " << result; return 0;
}
```

Binary Search

As mentioned earlier, a binary search is based on the interval search algorithm, where you look for an element in a sorted array. When compared to a linear search algorithm, a binary search algorithm has a higher time complexity.

A binary search uses the whole array as the interval when the search starts. It then breaks the interval into parts to look for the search element. It divides the array into half and looks for the element in the array's lower and upper sections. Depending on where the element lies, the algorithm will break the interval into a smaller section to look for it. It continues to do this until it finds the element.

A binary search aims to use the existing information in the array after it sorts the elements. This reduces the time complexity of the algorithm to O (log n). In a binary search, half the elements are not considered after making one comparison.
Sort the array.
Compare the search element x with the element in the middle of the array.
If x is less than the middle element, ignore the right section of the array since x can only lie in the left section of the array.
We then perform the same functions with the left section of the array.
If x is greater than the middle element in Step 3, we consider the array's right section.
We will now look at two ways to implement the binary search algorithm: recursive and iterative.

Before that, let us understand the time complexity of the binary search algorithm. You can calculate the time complexity of an algorithm using the following formula: $T(n) = T(n/2) + c$

You can remove the recurrence by using a master or recurrence tree method.

Recursive Implementation

```cpp
// C++ program to implement recursive Binary Search
#include <bits/stdc++.h> using namespace std;
// a recursive binary search function. It returns
// location of x in given array arr[l..r] is present,
// otherwise -1
int binarySearch(int arr[], int l, int r, int x)
{
if (r >= l) { int mid = l + (r - l) / 2;
// If the element is present at the middle
// itself if (arr[mid] == x) return mid;
// If element is smaller than mid, then // it can only be present in left subarray if (arr[mid] > x)
return binarySearch(arr, l, mid - 1, x);
// Else the element can only be present
// in right subarray
return binarySearch(arr, mid + 1, r, x);
}
// We reach here when element is not
// present in array
return -1; }
int main(void)
{
int arr[] = { 2, 3, 4, 10, 40 }; int x = 10; int n = sizeof(arr) / sizeof(arr[0]); int result =
binarySearch(arr, 0, n - 1, x);
(result == -1) ? cout << "Element is not present in array"
: cout << "Element is present at index " << result;
return 0;
}
```

The output of the code is:
Element is present at index 3

Iterative Implementation

```cpp
// C++ program to implement recursive Binary Search
#include <bits/stdc++.h> using namespace std;
// a iterative binary search function. It returns
// location of x in given array arr[l..r] if present, // otherwise -1
int binarySearch(int arr[], int l, int r, int x)
{
while (l <= r) { int m = l + (r - l) / 2;
// Check if x is present at mid if (arr[m] == x) return m;
// If x greater, ignore left half if (arr[m] < x) l = m + 1;
```

```
// If x is smaller, ignore right half
else r = m - 1;
}
// if we reach here, then element was
// not present
return -1; }
int main(void)
{
int arr[] = { 2, 3, 4, 10, 40 }; int x = 10; int n = sizeof(arr) / sizeof(arr[0]); int result =
binarySearch(arr, 0, n - 1, x);
(result == -1) ? cout << "Element is not present in array"
: cout << "Element is present at index " << result;
return 0;
}
```

The output of the code is:
Element is present at index 3

Jump Search

The jump search algorithm is similar to the binary search algorithm in the sense that it looks for the search element in a sorted array. This algorithm's objective is to search for the search element from fewer elements in the array. The compiler can jump ahead by skipping a few elements or jumping ahead by a few steps.

Let us understand this better using an example. Suppose you have an array with n elements in it, and you need to jump between the elements by m fixed steps. If you want to look for the search element in the array, you begin to look at the following indices a[0], a[m], a[2m], ….. a[km]. When you find the interval where the element may be, the linear search algorithm kicks in.

Consider the following array: (0, 1, 1, 2, 3, 5, 8, 13, 21, 34, 55, 89, 144, 233, 377, 610). The length of this array is 16. Let us now look for element 55 in the array. The block size is 4, which means the compiler will jump four elements each time.

Step 1: The compiler moves from index 0 to 3.
Step 2: The compiler moves from 4 to 8.
Step 3: The compiler jumps from 9 to 12.
Step 4: The element in position 12 is larger than 55, so we go back to the previous step.
Step 5: The linear search algorithm kicks in and looks for the index of the element.

Optimal Block Size

When you use the jump search algorithm, you need to choose the right block size, so there are no issues in the algorithm. In the worst-case scenario, you need to perform n/m jumps. If the element the compiler last checked was greater than the search element, you need to perform m-1 comparisons when the linear search algorithm kicks in. Therefore, in the worst-case scenario, the number of jumps should be ((n/m) + m-1). This function's value will be minimum if the value of the element 'm' is square root n.

The step size, therefore, should be m = √n.

```cpp
// C++ program to implement Jump Search
#include <bits/stdc++.h> using namespace std;
int jumpSearch(int arr[], int x, int n)
{
// Finding block size to be jumped int step = sqrt(n);
// Finding the block where element is // present (if it is present) int prev = 0;
while (arr[min(step, n)-1] < x)
{
prev = step; step += sqrt(n); if (prev >= n)
return -1;
}
// Doing a linear search for x in block // beginning with prev. while (arr[prev] < x)
{ prev++;
// If we reached next block or end of // array, element is not present.
if (prev == min(step, n))
return -1;
}
// If element is found
if (arr[prev] == x) return prev;
return -1;
}
// Driver program to test function int main()
{
int arr[] = { 0, 1, 1, 2, 3, 5, 8, 13, 21,
34, 55, 89, 144, 233, 377, 610 };
int x = 55;
int n = sizeof(arr) / sizeof(arr[0]);
// Find the index of 'x' using Jump Search int index = jumpSearch(arr, x, n);
// Print the index where 'x' is located
cout << "\nNumber " << x << " is at index " << index; return 0;
}
```

The output of this code:
Number 55 is at index 10

Some important points to note about this algorithm are:

This algorithm only works when an array is sorted. Since the optimal length the compiler should jump is √ n, the time complexity of this algorithm is O (√ n). This means the time complexity of this algorithm is between the binary search and linear search algorithms.

The jump search algorithm is not as good as the binary search algorithm, but it is better than the binary search algorithm since the compiler only needs to move once back through the array. If the binary search algorithm is too expensive, you should use the jump search algorithm.

Sorting Algorithms

You use sorting algorithms when you want to arrange a list or array of elements based on the comparison operator you want to include. This comparison operator will be used to decide how the elements will be sorted in the data structure where you want to arrange the elements. Let us look at some common sorting algorithms.

Bubble Sort

The bubble sort algorithm is one of the simplest algorithms used in C++, and it works by swapping the elements adjacent to each other in the array in case they are not in the right order.

Consider the following example:

First Pass

(5 1 4 2 8) –> (1 5 4 2 8): In this step, the algorithm will compare the elements in the array and swap the numbers 1 and 5.

(1 5 4 2 8) –> (1 4 5 2 8): In this step, the numbers 4 and 5 are swapped since the number 5 is greater than 4.

(1 4 5 2 8) –> (1 4 2 5 8): In this step, the numbers 5 and 2 are swapped.

(1 4 2 5 8) –> (1 4 2 5 8): In the last step, the elements are ordered, so there is no more swapping necessary.

Second Pass

(1 4 2 5 8) –> (1 4 2 5 8)
(1 4 2 5 8) –> (1 2 4 5 8): In this step, the numbers 4 and 2 are swapped since the number 4 is greater than 2.

(1 2 4 5 8) –> (1 2 4 5 8)
(1 2 4 5 8) –> (1 2 4 5 8)

The array is already sorted, but since the compiler is not aware that the algorithm is complete, it will complete another round on the array and check if any elements need to be swapped.

Third Pass

(1 2 4 5 8) –> (1 2 4 5 8)

(1 2 4 5 8) –> (1 2 4 5 8)
(1 2 4 5 8) –> (1 2 4 5 8)
(1 2 4 5 8) –> (1 2 4 5 8)

Consider the following implementations of the bubble sort algorithm:

```cpp
// C++ program for implementation of Bubble sort
#include <bits/stdc++.h> using namespace std;
void swap(int *xp, int *yp)
{ int temp = *xp; *xp = *yp;
*yp = temp;
}
// a function to implement bubble sort
void bubbleSort(int arr[], int n)
{
int i, j;
for (i = 0; i < n-1; i++)
// Last i elements are already in place
for (j = 0; j < n-i-1; j++) if (arr[j] > arr[j+1]) swap(&arr[j], &arr[j+1]);
}
/* Function to print an array */
void printArray(int arr[], int size)
{
int i;
for (i = 0; i < size; i++) cout << arr[i] << " ";
cout << endl;
}
// Driver code
int main()
{
int arr[] = {64, 34, 25, 12, 22, 11, 90}; int n = sizeof(arr)/sizeof(arr[0]); bubbleSort(arr, n);
cout<<"Sorted array: \n"; printArray(arr, n); return 0;
}
```

The output of this code is:

Sorted array:
11 12 22 25 34 64 90

We can optimize the implementation of this sorting algorithm. The above code runs more number of times than necessary, although the array is sorted. You cannot stop the optimization since the inner loop does not perform any swaps.

```cpp
// Optimized implementation of Bubble sort
#include <stdio.h>
void swap(int *xp, int *yp)
```

```c
{ int temp = *xp; *xp = *yp;
*yp = temp;
}
// An optimized version of Bubble Sort
void bubbleSort(int arr[], int n)
{
int i, j;
bool swapped;
for (i = 0; i < n-1; i++)
{ swapped = false;
for (j = 0; j < n-i-1; j++)
{
if (arr[j] > arr[j+1])
{ swap(&arr[j], &arr[j+1]); swapped = true;
}
}
// IF no two elements were swapped by inner loop, then break if (swapped == false)
break;
}
}
/* Function to print an array */
void printArray(int arr[], int size)
{
int i;
for (i=0; i < size; i++) printf("%d ", arr[i]);
printf("n");
}
// Driver program to test above functions int main()
{
int arr[] = {64, 34, 25, 12, 22, 11, 90}; int n = sizeof(arr)/sizeof(arr[0]); bubbleSort(arr, n);
printf("Sorted array: \n");
printArray(arr, n);
return 0;
}
```

The output of the above code is:

Sorted array:
11 12 22 25 34 64 90

Selection Sort

Using the selection sort algorithm, you can sort the elements in the array by looking at the smallest element in the array in ascending order. The compiler will only perform this sorting algorithm in the part of the array with unsorted elements.

The algorithm divides the array into two arrays:

The section of the array with sorted elements
The section of the array which does not have any sorted elements
When the selection sort algorithm iterates, the element which is the smallest in the array from the unsorted section of the array. This element is then moved to the sorted section of the array.

Consider the following section:

arr[] = 64 25 12 22 11

```
// Find the minimum element in arr[0...4]
// and place it at the beginning 11 25 12 22 64
// Find the minimum element in arr[1...4]
// and place it at the beginning of arr[1...4] 11 12 25 22 64
// Find the minimum element in arr[2...4]
// and place it at the beginning of arr[2...4] 11 12 22 25 64
// Find the minimum element in arr[3...4]
// and place it at beginning of arr[3...4]
```

11 12 22 25 64

Let us write down the above example in the form of a program:

```cpp
// C++ program for implementation of selection sort
#include <bits/stdc++.h> using namespace std;
void swap(int *xp, int *yp)
{ int temp = *xp; *xp = *yp;
*yp = temp;
}
void selectionSort(int arr[], int n)
{
int i, j, min_idx;
// One by one move boundary of unsorted subarray
for (i = 0; i < n-1; i++)
{
// Find the minimum element in unsorted array min_idx = i; for (j = i+1; j < n; j++) if (arr[j] <
arr[min_idx]) min_idx = j;
// Swap the found minimum element with the first element swap(&arr[min_idx], &arr[i]);
}
}
/* Function to print an array */
void printArray(int arr[], int size)
{
int i;
for (i=0; i < size; i++) cout << arr[i] << " ";
```

```
cout << endl;
}
// Driver program to test above functions int main()
{
int arr[] = {64, 25, 12, 22, 11};
int n = sizeof(arr)/sizeof(arr[0]);
selectionSort(arr, n);
cout << "Sorted array: \n";
printArray(arr, n);
return 0;
}
```

The output of the program is:

Sorted array:
11 12 22 25 64

Insertion Sort

The insertion sort algorithm is a simple and straightforward algorithm that works in the same way you would sort or arrange playing cards. In this algorithm, the array is split into two parts – sorted and unsorted arrays. The values in the unsorted array will then be sorted and moved into the right positions.

Let us understand this algorithm better by considering how it works when the compiler tries to sort the elements in the ascending order:

Create an array with n elements.
Iterate from the first element in the array to the nth element in the array.
Compare every element in the array with its predecessor.
If the element is smaller than the predecessor, you should compare it to the other elements before the predecessor. Move the elements around to ensure there is enough space for the element which is swapped

Consider the following example:
The array is 12, 11, 13, 5, 6
12, 11, 13, 5, 6

We will add a loop where the iterative element 'i' is assigned the value 1. Since there are only 5 elements in the array, the value of 'i' can be incremented until 4.

i = 1. Since element 11 is smaller than 12, the number 12 is moved after element 11.
11, 12, 13, 5, 6

i = 2. The number 13 will stay in its position since the first three elements are sorted.

11, 12, 13, 5, 6

i = 3. The number 5 will move to the start of the array since it is the smallest number when compared to the other elements in the array. The other elements will be moved ahead.
5, 11, 12, 13, 6

i = 4. The number 6 will move next to 5 since it is smaller than all the other elements in the array.
5, 6, 11, 12, 13

Let us write the above example in C++.

```cpp
// C++ program for insertion sort
#include <bits/stdc++.h> using namespace std;
/* Function to sort an array using insertion sort*/
void insertionSort(int arr[], int n)
{
int i, key, j;
for (i = 1; i < n; i++)
{
key = arr[i]; j = i - 1;
/* Move elements of arr[0..i-1], that are greater than key, to one position ahead of their current position */
while (j >= 0 && arr[j] > key)
{
arr[j + 1] = arr[j];
j = j - 1;
}
arr[j + 1] = key;
}
}
// a utility function to print an array of size n void printArray(int arr[], int n)
{
int i;
for (i = 0; i < n; i++) cout << arr[i] << " ";
cout << endl;
}
/* Driver code */
int main()
{
int arr[] = { 12, 11, 13, 5, 6 }; int n = sizeof(arr) / sizeof(arr[0]);
insertionSort(arr, n); printArray(arr, n);
return 0;
}
```

Quicksort

The quicksort algorithm is a divide and conquer algorithm. In this algorithm, the compiler picks an element in the array as the pivot and divides the elements in the array based on that pivot. There are different ways to implement the quick sort algorithm in C++.

The algorithm can choose the first element in the array as the pivot.
The algorithm can choose the last element as the pivot (we will look at this in detail in the section below)
Choose any element in the array as the pivot.
Choose the median of the elements in the array and pick that as the pivot.
One of the most important processes in a quick sort algorithm is the partition() function. This function's target is to take an element from the array as the pivot and put it in the right position. The elements in the array which are smaller than the pivot will be moved to one side of the array while the others will move to the other section of the pivot.

Consider the following pseudo-code for this algorithm:

```
/* low  --> Starting index,  high  --> Ending index */ quickSort(arr[], low, high)
{
if (low < high)
{
/* pi is partitioning index, arr[pi] is now at right place */
pi = partition(arr, low, high);
quickSort(arr, low, pi - 1);  // Before pi
quickSort(arr, pi + 1, high); // After pi
}
}
```

Understanding the Partition Algorithm

```
/* low  --> Starting index,  high  --> Ending index */ quickSort(arr[], low, high)
{ if (low < high)
{
/* pi is partitioning index, arr[pi] is now at right place */ pi = partition(arr, low, high);
quickSort(arr, low, pi - 1);  // Before pi
quickSort(arr, pi + 1, high); // After pi
}
}
```

The pseudo code for the partition algorithm is:

```
/* low  --> Starting index,  high  --> Ending index */ quickSort(arr[], low, high)
{
if (low < high)
{
/* pi is partitioning index, arr[pi] is now at right place */
pi = partition(arr, low, high);
```

```
quickSort(arr, low, pi - 1);  // Before pi
quickSort(arr, pi + 1, high); // After pi
}
}
```

/* This function takes last element as pivot, places the pivot element at its correct position in sorted array, and places all smaller (smaller than pivot) to left of pivot and all greater elements to right of pivot */

```
partition (arr[], low, high)
{
// pivot (Element to be placed at right position) pivot = arr[high];
i = (low - 1)  // Index of smaller element
for (j = low; j <= high- 1; j++)
{
// If current element is smaller than the pivot
if (arr[j] < pivot)
{
i++;    // increment index of smaller element swap arr[i] and arr[j]
}
}
swap arr[i + 1] and arr[high])
return (i + 1)
}
```

Let us look at the illustration of this function:

arr[] = {10, 80, 30, 90, 40, 50, 70}
Indexes: 0 1 2 3 4 5 6
low = 0, high = 6, pivot = arr[h] = 70
Initialize index of smaller element, i = -1
Traverse elements from j = low to high-1
j = 0 : Since arr[j] <= pivot, do i++ and swap(arr[i], arr[j]) i = 0
arr[] = {10, 80, 30, 90, 40, 50, 70} // No change as i and j // are same
j = 1 : Since arr[j] > pivot, do nothing // No change in i and arr[]
j = 2 : Since arr[j] <= pivot, do i++ and swap(arr[i], arr[j]) i = 1 arr[] = {10, 30, 80, 90, 40, 50, 70} // We swap 80 and 30
j = 3 : Since arr[j] > pivot, do nothing // No change in i and arr[]
j = 4 : Since arr[j] <= pivot, do i++ and swap(arr[i], arr[j]) i = 2 arr[] = {10, 30, 40, 90, 80, 50, 70} // 80 and 40 Swapped j = 5 : Since arr[j] <= pivot, do i++ and swap arr[i] with arr[j] i = 3 arr[] = {10, 30, 40, 50, 80, 90, 70} // 90 and 50 Swapped

We come out of loop because j is now equal to high-1. Finally, we place pivot at correct position by swapping arr[i+1] and arr[high] (or pivot)
arr[] = {10, 30, 40, 50, 70, 90, 80} // 80 and 70 Swapped Now 70 is at its correct place. All elements smaller than 70 are before it and all elements greater than 70 are after it.

Let us look at how to implement this algorithm in C++:

```cpp
/* C++ implementation of QuickSort */
#include <bits/stdc++.h> using namespace std;
// a utility function to swap two elements void swap(int* a, int* b)
{
int t = *a; *a = *b;
*b = t;
}
```

/* This function takes last element as pivot, places the pivot element at its correct position in sorted array, and places all smaller (smaller than pivot) to left of pivot and all greater elements to right of pivot */

```cpp
int partition (int arr[], int low, int high)
{
int pivot = arr[high]; // pivot int i = (low - 1); // Index of smaller element
for (int j = low; j <= high - 1; j++)
{
// If current element is smaller than the pivot
if (arr[j] < pivot)
{ i++; // increment index of smaller element swap(&arr[i], &arr[j]);
}
}
swap(&arr[i + 1], &arr[high]);
return (i + 1);
}
```

```cpp
/* The main function that implements QuickSort
arr[] --> Array to be sorted, low --> Starting index, high --> Ending index */

void quickSort(int arr[], int low, int high)
{
if (low < high)
{

/* pi is partitioning index, arr[p] is now at right place */

int pi = partition(arr, low, high);
// Separately sort elements before // partition and after partition quickSort(arr, low, pi - 1);
quickSort(arr, pi + 1, high);
}
}
/* Function to print an array */
void printArray(int arr[], int size)
{
```

```
int i; for (i = 0; i < size; i++) cout << arr[i] << " ";
cout << endl;
}
// Driver Code int main()
{
int arr[] = {10, 7, 8, 9, 1, 5}; int n = sizeof(arr) / sizeof(arr[0]); quickSort(arr, 0, n - 1); cout <<
"Sorted array: \n"; printArray(arr, n);
return 0;
}
```

Tips to Optimize Code in C++

When you write code in C++ or any other programming language, your main objective should be to write code that works correctly. Once you accomplish this, you need to change the code to improve the following:

The security of the code
The quantity of memory used while running the code
Performance of the code

This chapter gives you a brief idea of the areas to consider if you want to improve the performance of your code. Some points to keep in mind are:

You can use numerous techniques to improve the performance of your code. This method, however, can lead to the creation of a larger file.

If you choose to optimize multiple areas in your code at the same time, it may lead to some conflict between the areas of your code. For instance, you may not be able to optimize both the performance of the code and memory use. You need to strike a balance between the two.

You may always need to optimize your code, and this process is never-ending. The code you write is never fully optimized. There is always room to improve some parts of your code if you want the code to run better.

You can use different tricks to improve the performance of the code. While you do this, you should ensure that you do not forget about some coding standards. Therefore, do not use cheap tricks to make the code work better.

Using the Appropriate Algorithm to Optimize Code

Before you write any code, you need to sit down and understand the task. You then need to develop the right algorithm to use to optimize the code. We are going to understand how the algorithm affects your code using a simple example. In the program, we are going to use a two-dimensional segment to identify the maximum value and, for this, we will take two whole numbers. In the first code, we will not look at the program's performance. We will then look at a few methods to use to improve the performance of the code.

Consider the following parameters used in the code: both numbers should lie between the interval [-100, 100]. The maximum value is calculated using the function: $(x * x + y * y) / (y * y + b)$.

There are two variables used in this function – x and y. We are also using a constant 'b' which is a user-defined value. The value of this constant should always be greater than zero but less than 1000.

In the example below, we do not use the pow() function from the math.h library.

```
#include <iostream>
#define LEFT_MARGINE_FOR_X -100.0
#define RIGHT_MARGINE_FOR_X 100.0
#define LEFT_MARGINE_FOR_Y -100.0 #define RIGHT_MARGINE_FOR_Y 100.0 using
namespace std;
int
main(void)
{
//Get the constant value
cout<<"Enter the constant value b>0"<<endl; cout<<"b->"; double dB; cin>>dB; if(dB<=0)   return
EXIT_FAILURE; if(dB>1000) return EXIT_FAILURE;
//This is the potential maximum value of the function
//and all other values could be bigger or smaller
double dMaximumValue = (LEFT_MARGINE_FOR_X*LEFT_MARGINE_FOR_X+LEFT_MAR
(LEFT_MARGINE_FOR_Y*LEFT_MARGINE_FOR_Y+dB);
double dMaximumX = LEFT_MARGINE_FOR_X; double dMaximumY =
LEFT_MARGINE_FOR_Y; for(double dX=LEFT_MARGINE_FOR_X;
dX<=RIGHT_MARGINE_FOR_X; dX+=1.0) for(double dY=LEFT_MARGINE_FOR_Y;
dY<=RIGHT_MARGINE_FOR_Y; dY+=1.0) if(
dMaximumValue<((dX*dX+dY*dY)/(dY*dY+dB)))
{ dMaximumValue=((dX*dX+dY*dY)/(dY*dY+dB));
dMaximumX=dX; dMaximumY=dY;
} cout<<"Maximum value of the function is="<<
dMaximumValue<<endl; cout<<endl<<endl;
cout<<"Value for x="<<dMaximumX<<endl
<<"Value for y="<<dMaximumY<<endl; return EXIT_SUCCESS;
}
```

Look at the code carefully. You notice that the function and value dX * dX is run by the process too many times, and the value is stored multiple times in the memory. This is a waste of CPU time and memory. What do you think we could do to improve the speed of the code? An alternative to writing the operation multiple times in the code is to declare a variable and assign this function to it. Let us define a variable d, which stores the value of the function dX * dX. You can use the variable 'd' everywhere in the code where you need to use the calculation. You can optimize other sections of the above code as well. Try to spot those areas.

The next area we need to look at is how general the lines of code are. You need to see whether the program runs as fast as you want it to. If you want to increase the speed of the algorithm, you need to tweak some functions based on the size of your input.

What does this mean?

You can improve the speed of the code you have written using multiple algorithms instead of only one algorithm. When you use two algorithms, you can instruct the compiler to switch between the algorithms based on a condition.

Optimizing Code

When you write code, every element in your code uses some space in the memory. It is important to understand how each word in your code uses memory to reduce consumption or usage. Let us consider a simple example where we try to swap the values in two variables in the memory. You can do this using numerous sorting algorithms. To understand this better, let us take a real-world example – you have two people sitting in two different chairs. You introduce a third or temporary chair to hold one of the individuals when they want to swap chairs.

Consider the following code:

```
int nFirstOne =1, nSecondOne=2;
int nTemp = nFirstOne; nFirstOne = nSecondOne;
nSecondOne = nTemp;
```

This code is easy to use, but when you create a temporary variable in your code, the compiler will assign some space in the memory for this object. You can avoid wasting memory space by avoiding the usage of a temporary variable in the code.

```
int nFirstOne = 3, nSecondOne = 7;
nFirstOne += nSecondOne;
nSecondOne = nFirstOne ? nSecondOne;
nFirstOne -= nSecondOne;
```

You may need to swap large values in the memory to a different section. How would you do this? The easiest way to do this is to use pointers. Instead of copying the same value across the memory, use a pointer to obtain the address of the value in the memory. You can then change their address instead of moving the value from one location to the next in the memory.

You may wonder how you can determine if your code is faster or how you can calculate this. When you finish writing your code, the system will translate it into a language it understands using the assembler. It will then translate this into machine code, which it quickly interprets. Every operation you write in the code takes place in the processor. It may also take place in the graphic card or mathematical coprocessor.

One operation can take place in one clock cycle, or it may take a few. For this reason, it is easier for the computer to multiply numbers compared to division. This could be the case because of the optimization the computer performs. You can also leave the task of optimization to the compiler in some cases.

If you want to learn more about how fast your code is, you should know the architecture of the computer you are using.

The code can be faster because of one of the following reasons:

The program runs in the cache memory
The mathematical coprocessor processes sections of the code
A branch predictor was used correctly by the compiler

Let us now consider the following numbers: $O(n)$, $O(\log(n) *n)$, $n*n$, $n!$. When you use this type of code, the program's speed depends on the number you key into the system. Let us assume you enter $n = 10$. The program may take 't' amount of time to run and compile. What do you think will happen when you enter $n = 100$? The program may take 10 times longer to run. It is important to understand the limits a small number can have on your algorithm.

Some people also take time to see how fast the code runs. This is not the right thing to do since not every program or algorithm you key in is completed first by the processor. Since an algorithm does not run in the computer's kernel mode, the processor can get another task to perform. This means the algorithm is put on hold. Therefore, the time you write down is not an accurate representation of how fast the code can run. If you have more than one processor in the system, it is harder to identify which processor is running the algorithm. It is tricky to calculate the speed at which the processor completes running your code.

If you want to optimize or improve the speed at which the program runs, you need to prevent the processor from shifting the code to a different core during the run. You also need to find a way to prevent the counter from switching between tasks since that only increases the time the processor takes to run the code. You may also notice some differences in your code since the computer does not transfer all optimizations into machine code.

Using Input and Output Operators

When you write code, it is best to identify the functions you can use which do not occupy too much space in the memory. Most times, you can improve the speed of the program by using a different function to perform the same task. Printf and scanf are two functions used often in C programming, but you can use the same keywords in C++ if you can manipulate some files. This increases the speed of the program and can save you a lot of time and memory.

Let us understand this better through an example. You have two numbers in a file and need to read those numbers. It is best to use the keywords cin and cout on files in terms of security since you have instructions passed to the compiler from the header library in C++. If you use printf or scanf, you may need to use other functions of keywords to increase the speed of the program. If you want to print strings, you can use the keyword put or use an equivalent from file operations.

Optimizing the Use of Operators

You need to use operators to perform certain functions in C++. Basic operators, such as +=, *= or -= use a lot of space in the memory. This is especially true when it comes to basic data types. Experts recommend you use a postfix decrement or increment along with the prefix operator if you want to improve the functioning of the code. You may also need to use the << or >> operators instead of division and multiplication, but you need to be careful when you use those operators.

This may lead to a huge mistake in the code. It takes some time to identify these mistakes and, to overcome the mistake, you need to add more lines of code. This is only going to reduce the speed and performance of the program.

It is best to use bit operators in your code since these increase the speed of the program. If you are not careful about how you use these operators, you may end up with machine-dependent code, and this is something you need to avoid.

C++ is a hybrid language and allows you to use an assembler's support to improve the functioning of your program. It also allows you to develop solutions to problems using object-oriented programming. If you are adept at coding, you can develop libraries to improve your code's functioning.

Optimization of Conditional Statements

You may need to include numerous conditional statements in your code, depending on the type of code you are writing. Most people choose to use the 'if' conditional statement, but it is advised that you do not do this. It is best to use the switch statement. When you use the former conditional statement, the compiler needs to test every element in the code, and this creates numerous temporary variables to store the code. This reduces the performance of the code.

It is important to note that the 'if' conditional statement has many optimizations built into the statement itself. If you only have a few conditions to test, and if these are connected to the or operator, you can use the 'if' conditional statement to calculate the value. Let us look at this using an example. We have two conditions, and each of these uses the and operator. If you have two variables and want to test if both values are equal to a certain number, you use the and operator. If the compiler notes that one value does not meet the condition, it returns false and does not look at the second value.

When you use conditional statements in your code, it is best to identify the statements which often occur before the other conditional statements. This is the best way to determine if an expression is true or false. If you have too many conditions, you need to sort them and split them into a nested conditional statement. There may be a possibility that the compiler does not look at every branch in the nest you have created. Some lines of code may be useless to the compiler, but they simply occupy memory.

You may also come across instances where you have long expressions with numerous conditions. Most programmers choose to use functions in this instance, but what they forget is that functions take up a lot of memory. They create calls and stacks in memory. It is best to use a macro to prevent the usage of memory. This increases the speed of the program. It is important to remember that negation is also an operation you can use in your code.

Dealing with Functions

If you are not careful when you use functions, you may end up with bad code. Consider the following example. If you have code written in the same format as the statements below, it will lead to a bad code:

for(int i=1; i<=10; ++i) DoSomething(i);

Why do you think this is the case? When you write some code similar to the above, you need to call the function a few times. It is important to remember that the calls the compiler makes to the functions in the code use a lot of memory. If you want to improve the performance of the code, you can write the statement in the following format:

DoSomething(n);

The next thing you need to learn more about is inline functions. The compiler will use an inline function similar to a macro if it is small. This is one way to improve the performance of your code. You can also increase the reusability of the code in this manner. When you pass large objects from one function to another, it is best to use references or pointers. It is better to use a reference since this allows you to write code that is easy to read. Having said that, if you are worried about changing the value of the actual variable being passed to the function, you should avoid using references. If you use a constant object, you should use the keyword const since it will save you some time.

It is important to note that the arguments and parameters passed in the function will change depending on the situation. When you create a temporary object for a function, it will only reduce the speed of the program. We have looked at how you can avoid using or creating temporary variables in the code.

Some programmers use recursive functions depending on the situation. Recursive functions can slow the code down. So, you should avoid the use of recursive functions if you can since these reduce the performance of your code.

Optimizing Loops

Let us assume you have a set of numbers, and you are to check if the value is greater than 5 or less than 0. When you write the code, you need to choose the second option. It is easier for the compiler to check if a value is greater than zero than to check which number is greater than 10. In simple words, the statement written below makes the program slower when compared to the second statement in this section.

```
for( i =0; i<10; i++)
```

As mentioned, it is best to use this loop instead of the above. If you are not well-versed with C++ programming, this line of code may be difficult for you to read.

```
for(i=10; i--; )
```

Similarly, if you find yourself in a situation where you need to pick from <=n or !=0, you should choose the second option since that is faster. For instance, if you want to calculate a factorial, do not try to use a loop since you can use a linear function. If you ever find yourself in a situation where you need to choose between a few loops or one loop with different tasks, you should choose the second option. This method may help you develop a better performing program.

Optimizing Data Structures

Do you think a data structure affects the performance of your code? It is not easy to answer this question. Since data structures are used everywhere in your code, the answer is difficult to formulate and vague. Let us look at the following example to understand this better. If you are tasked with creating permutations (using the pattern below), you may choose to use a linked list or array.

```
1, 2, 3, 4,
2, 3, 4, 1,
3, 4, 1, 2,
4, 1, 2, 3,
```

If you use an array, you can copy the first element in the array and move every other element in the array towards that element. You then need to move the first element in the array to the end of the list. To do this, you need to use multiple operations, and your program will be very slow. If you leave the data in a list, you can develop a program, which will improve the performance of the code. You can also store the data in the form of a tree. This data structure allows you to develop a faster program.

Bear in mind that the type of data structure you use affects the performance of your program. You can solve any problem you have in the code without using arrays or any other data structure.

Sequential or Binary Search?

When you look for a specific object or variable in the code, which method should you opt for – binary or sequential search?

No matter what you do in your code, you always look for some value in a data structure. You may need to look for data in tables, lists, etc.

There are two ways to do this:

The first method is simple. You create an array and assign some values to the array. If you want to look for a specific value in the array, you need to start looking at the start of the array until you find the value in the array. If you do not find the value at the start of the array, the compiler moves to the end of the array. This reduces the speed at which the program is compiled.

In the second strategy, you need to sort the array before you search for an element in the array. If you do not sort the array before you look for the element, you cannot obtain the results on time. When the array is sorted, the compiler will break it into two parts from the middle. It will then look for the value in either part of the array depending on the values in the sections. When you identify the part where the element may be, you need to divide it through the middle again. You continue to do this until you find the value you are looking for. If you do not, then you know the array does not have the value.

What is the difference between these strategies? When you sort the elements in the array, you may lose some time. Having said that, if you give the compiler time to do this, you will benefit faster from the search. When it comes to choosing between a sequential and binary search, you need to understand the problem before you implement the method you want to use.

Optimizing the Use of Arrays

We looked at arrays in the previous book, and this is one of the basic data structures used in C++. An array contains a list of objects of a similar data type. Every object in an array holds a separate location in the memory.

If you want to learn more about optimizing the work or use of an array, you need to understand the structure of this structure. What does this mean? An array is similar to a pointer, and it points to the elements in the array. You can access array methods using arithmetic pointers or any other type of pointer if needed.

Consider the following example:

for(int i=0; i<n; i++) nArray[i]=nSomeValue;

The code below is better than the statement above.

Why do you think this is the case?

for(int* ptrInt = nArray; ptrInt< nArray+n; ptrInt++)
*ptrInt=nSomeValue;

The second line of code is better than the first line of code since the operations rely only on pointers. In the example above, we are using pointers to access the values stored in the integer data type. The pointer takes the address of the variable in the memory. In the case of the example, the pointer points to the variable nArray. When we add the increment operator to the variable, the pointer will move from the first element in the array to the next until it reaches the end of the array. If you use the double data type, the compiler will know how far it should move the address.

It is difficult to interpret and read the code using this method, but this is the only way to increase the speed of the program. In simple words, if you do not use a good algorithm, you can increase compiling speed by writing code using the right syntax.

Consider the following example: You have a matrix with the required elements. A matrix is a type of array, and it will be stored in your memory based on the rows. So, how do you think you should access the elements in the array? You should access every element in the matrix row by row. It does not make sense for you to use any other method because you reduce the speed of the program.

It is best to avoid initializing large sections of the memory for only one element. If you know the size of the element, make sure to stick to that size. Do not allot more memory space. You can use the function memset or other commands to allot some space in the memory to the variables used in the code.

Let us assume you want to create an array of characters or strings. Instead of defining the variables or assigning the array to specific variables, it is best to use pointers. You can assign each element in the array to a string, but this would only reduce the speed of the program. The compiler will run the code faster, even if the file is big. If you use the new keyword to create or declare an array in the code, your program will not do well since it will use a lot of memory the minute you try to run the code. It is for this reason you should use vectors. These objects add some space to your memory, allowing the program to do well.

If you want to move large volumes of data from one section in the memory to another, it is best to use an array of pointers. When you do this, you do not change the original values of the data but only replace the addresses of the objects stored in the memory.

Conclusion: Mastering Data Structures and Algorithms in C++

Data structures and algorithms form the foundation of computer science and software development. They are essential tools for solving complex problems efficiently, optimizing performance, and managing data effectively. In this comprehensive guide, we explored key data structures and algorithms in C++, including linked lists, stacks, queues, trees, graphs, sorting algorithms, and hash tables. By understanding these concepts and their implementations, you can write efficient, scalable, and maintainable code. Let's summarize the key takeaways and reflect on the importance of mastering these topics.

1. The Importance of Data Structures and Algorithms

Data structures and algorithms are the building blocks of software development. They enable programmers to:

- **Organize Data Efficiently**: Data structures like arrays, linked lists, and trees provide ways to store and manage data in a structured manner.

- **Optimize Performance**: Algorithms like sorting and searching ensure that operations are performed efficiently, even with large datasets.

- **Solve Complex Problems**: Techniques like graph traversal and dynamic programming help solve real-world problems, such as route planning and resource allocation.

- **Improve Code Quality**: Well-designed data structures and algorithms lead to cleaner, more modular, and reusable code.

In C++, these concepts are implemented using a combination of object-oriented programming (OOP) and procedural techniques, making the language a powerful tool for building high-performance applications.

2. Key Data Structures and Their Applications

2.1 Linked Lists

Linked lists are dynamic data structures that allow efficient insertion and deletion operations. They are particularly useful when the size of the data is unknown or frequently changing.

- **Singly Linked Lists**: Simple and memory-efficient, but limited to unidirectional traversal.

- **Doubly Linked Lists**: Allow bidirectional traversal, making them more versatile but requiring additional memory.

- **Circular Linked Lists**: Useful for representing circular data, such as round-robin scheduling.

2.2 Stacks and Queues

Stacks and queues are linear data structures that follow specific access patterns.

- **Stacks**: Follow the Last In, First Out (LIFO) principle. They are used in scenarios like function call management, undo operations, and expression evaluation.

- **Queues**: Follow the First In, First Out (FIFO) principle. They are used in task scheduling, print spooling, and breadth-first search (BFS).

2.3 Trees and Binary Search Trees (BST)

Trees are hierarchical data structures that represent relationships between data points.

- **Binary Trees**: Each node has at most two children. They are used in hierarchical data representation and decision-making processes.

- **Binary Search Trees (BST)**: A specialized binary tree where the left subtree contains smaller values and the right subtree contains larger values. BSTs enable efficient searching, insertion, and deletion operations.

2.4 Graphs

Graphs are non-linear data structures that represent relationships between entities.

- **Directed and Undirected Graphs**: Used to model one-way and two-way relationships, respectively.

- **Weighted Graphs**: Assign weights to edges, making them suitable for applications like route planning and network analysis.

- **Graph Traversal**: Techniques like Depth-First Search (DFS) and Breadth-First Search (BFS) are used to explore graphs and solve problems like connectivity and shortest path.

3. Sorting Algorithms: Efficiency and Trade-offs

Sorting algorithms are essential for organizing data in a specific order. Each algorithm has its strengths and weaknesses, making it suitable for different scenarios.

- **QuickSort**: A divide-and-conquer algorithm with an average time complexity of O(n log n). It is efficient for large datasets but has a worst-case complexity of $O(n^2)$.

- **MergeSort**: Another divide-and-conquer algorithm with a consistent time complexity of O(n log n). It is stable and suitable for linked lists but requires additional memory.

- **HeapSort**: Uses a binary heap to sort elements with a time complexity of O(n log n). It is in-place but not stable.

Choosing the right sorting algorithm depends on factors like dataset size, memory constraints, and stability requirements.

4. Hash Tables: Fast Data Retrieval

Hash tables are data structures that enable fast data retrieval using key-value pairs. They use a hash function to map keys to indices in an array, allowing for average-case constant-time operations.

- **Collision Handling**: Techniques like chaining and open addressing ensure that collisions (when two keys map to the same index) are resolved efficiently.

- **Applications**: Hash tables are used in databases, caches, and compilers for fast lookups and data storage.

5. Practical Applications of Data Structures and Algorithms

The concepts covered in this guide have numerous real-world applications:

- **Linked Lists**: Used in memory management, undo functionality, and implementing stacks and queues.

- **Stacks and Queues**: Essential for parsing expressions, managing function calls, and scheduling tasks.

- **Trees**: Used in file systems, database indexing, and decision-making algorithms.

- **Graphs**: Applied in social networks, GPS navigation, and network routing.

- **Sorting Algorithms**: Used in data analysis, search engines, and organizing large datasets.

- **Hash Tables**: Utilized in caching, database indexing, and spell checkers.

6. Best Practices for Implementing Data Structures and Algorithms in C++

To write efficient and maintainable code, follow these best practices:

- **Choose the Right Data Structure**: Select a data structure that aligns with the problem requirements. For example, use a hash table for fast lookups or a tree for hierarchical data.

- **Optimize Algorithms**: Analyze the time and space complexity of algorithms to ensure they meet performance requirements.

- **Use Standard Libraries**: Leverage C++ Standard Library containers like std::vector, std::list, and std::map to simplify implementation.

- **Test Thoroughly**: Validate your implementations with edge cases and large datasets to ensure correctness and efficiency.

- **Document Your Code**: Write clear comments and documentation to make your code understandable and maintainable.

7. The Future of Data Structures and Algorithms

As technology evolves, the importance of data structures and algorithms continues to grow. Emerging trends include:

- **Big Data**: Efficient algorithms are essential for processing and analyzing massive datasets.

- **Machine Learning**: Data structures like graphs and trees are used in decision trees, neural networks, and clustering algorithms.

- **Parallel and Distributed Computing**: Algorithms are being adapted to run on multi-core processors and distributed systems.

- **Quantum Computing**: New data structures and algorithms are being developed to harness the power of quantum computers.

By staying updated with these trends, you can remain at the forefront of software development and innovation.

8. Final Thoughts

Mastering data structures and algorithms is a journey that requires continuous learning and practice. In C++, these concepts are implemented using a combination of OOP and procedural techniques, making the language a powerful tool for building high-performance applications. By understanding the principles and applications of linked lists, stacks, queues, trees, graphs, sorting algorithms, and hash tables, you can solve complex problems efficiently and write scalable code.

As you continue your journey, remember to:

- **Practice Regularly**: Implement data structures and algorithms from scratch to deepen your understanding.

- **Learn from Others**: Study open-source projects and collaborate with peers to gain new insights.

- **Stay Curious**: Explore advanced topics like dynamic programming, greedy algorithms, and graph theory.

- **Apply Your Knowledge**: Use data structures and algorithms to solve real-world problems and build impactful projects.

With dedication and persistence, you can become a proficient programmer and leverage the power of data structures and algorithms to create innovative solutions. Happy coding!

7. Memory Management in C++

1. Introduction

What is Memory Management?

Memory management refers to the process of allocating, using, and deallocating memory in a program. In C++, memory management is primarily manual, meaning the programmer is responsible for allocating and freeing memory. This contrasts with languages like Java or Python, which use automatic garbage collection.

Why is Memory Management Important?

- **Performance**: Efficient memory management ensures optimal use of system resources.

- **Reliability**: Proper memory management prevents crashes and undefined behavior.

- **Security**: Memory-related vulnerabilities, such as buffer overflows, can lead to security breaches.

Memory Layout in C++

A C++ program's memory is typically divided into four segments:

1. **Code Segment**: Stores the compiled program instructions.

2. **Data Segment**: Contains global and static variables.

3. **Heap**: Dynamically allocated memory (managed using new and delete).

4. **Stack**: Stores local variables and function call information.

2. Manual Memory Management

new and delete Operators

C++ provides the new and delete operators for dynamic memory allocation and deallocation.

```
int* ptr = new int;  // Allocate memory for an integer
```

```
*ptr = 42;          // Assign a value
```

```
delete ptr;         // Free the memory
```

For arrays:

```
int* arr = new int[10];  // Allocate memory for an array
```

```
delete[] arr;            // Free the memory
```

Common Pitfalls in Manual Memory Management

- **Memory Leaks**: Forgetting to deallocate memory.

- **Dangling Pointers**: Using pointers to freed memory.

- **Double Deletion**: Attempting to delete the same memory twice.

Best Practices for Manual Memory Management

- Always pair new with delete and new[] with delete[].

- Initialize pointers to nullptr and check for nullptr before deletion.

- Use RAII (Resource Acquisition Is Initialization) to manage resources.

3. Smart Pointers

Smart pointers are a modern C++ feature that automates memory management, reducing the risk of leaks and dangling pointers.

std::unique_ptr

A std::unique_ptr owns the memory it points to and automatically deallocates it when it goes out of scope.

```cpp
#include <memory>

std::unique_ptr<int> ptr = std::make_unique<int>(42);
```

std::shared_ptr

A std::shared_ptr allows multiple pointers to share ownership of the same memory. The memory is deallocated when the last shared_ptr goes out of scope.

```cpp
#include <memory>

std::shared_ptr<int> ptr1 = std::make_shared<int>(42);

std::shared_ptr<int> ptr2 = ptr1;  // Shared ownership
```

std::weak_ptr

A std::weak_ptr is used to break circular references between shared_ptr instances.

```cpp
std::weak_ptr<int> weakPtr = ptr1;

if (auto sharedPtr = weakPtr.lock()) {

    // Use sharedPtr

}
```

Custom Deleters

Smart pointers support custom deleters for specialized cleanup logic.

```cpp
std::unique_ptr<int, void(*)(int*)> ptr(new int, [](int* p) {

    delete p;

});
```

4. Memory Pools and Custom Allocators

What are Memory Pools?

Memory pools are pre-allocated blocks of memory used to manage dynamic memory allocation more efficiently. They reduce fragmentation and improve performance.

Implementing Memory Pools in C++

```cpp
class MemoryPool {

public:

    MemoryPool(size_t size) : poolSize(size), pool(new char[size]) {}

    ~MemoryPool() { delete[] pool; }

    void* allocate(size_t size) {

        if (currentOffset + size > poolSize) return nullptr;

        void* ptr = pool + currentOffset;

        currentOffset += size;

        return ptr;

    }

private:

    size_t poolSize;

    char* pool;

    size_t currentOffset = 0;
```

};

Custom Allocators in STL Containers

C++ allows custom allocators for STL containers.

```cpp
#include <vector>

#include <memory>

template<typename T>

class CustomAllocator {

public:

    using value_type = T;

    T* allocate(size_t n) { return static_cast<T*>(::operator new(n * sizeof(T))); }

    void deallocate(T* p, size_t n) { ::operator delete(p); }

};

std::vector<int, CustomAllocator<int>> vec;
```

5. Garbage Collection in C++

Overview of Garbage Collection

Garbage collection automates memory deallocation by identifying and reclaiming unused memory.

Garbage Collection in C++ (Boehm GC)

The Boehm-Demers-Weiser garbage collector can be used in C++ for automatic memory management.

```
#include <gc/gc.h>
```

```
int* ptr = GC_MALLOC(sizeof(int));
```

Pros and Cons of Garbage Collection

- **Pros**: Simplifies memory management, reduces leaks.

- **Cons**: Overhead, non-deterministic deallocation.

6. Modern Memory Management Features in C++ 2025

std::pmr (Polymorphic Memory Resources)

C++17 introduced std::pmr for flexible memory management.

```
#include <memory_resource>
```

```
std::pmr::monotonic_buffer_resource pool;
```

```
std::pmr::vector<int> vec(&pool);
```

std::allocate_shared and std::make_shared

These functions allow custom allocators for shared_ptr.

```
auto ptr = std::allocate_shared<int>(CustomAllocator<int>(), 42);
```

Memory Safety Features in C++23 and Beyond

C++23 introduces features like std::out_ptr and std::inout_ptr for safer pointer management.

7. Memory Management Best Practices

- Use smart pointers instead of raw pointers.

- Prefer stack allocation over heap allocation when possible.

- Regularly test for memory leaks using tools like Valgrind or AddressSanitizer.

- Minimize dynamic memory allocation in performance-critical code.

Let's begin,

In this chapter, we'll study what memory management is and why it's essential, as well as what memory management operators are and why they're helpful. Furthermore, we will learn what dynamic memory allocation is, how to allocate memory dynamically, and why memory management is essential. What are objects' new and delete operators? In addition, we will learn about memory objects and custom memory.

A logical grouping of statements that execute a given purpose is called a function. You may avoid writing the same code for different input values within the program by introducing a function. To conduct the action, all you have to do is call the function.

- **Return type:** This specifies the type of value that the function will return as an output. Integer, character, and other return types are possible. A function does not always have to return a value. You can define the function with a void return type in this instance.

- **Function name:** The function's name, for instance, foo. This name can be used to invoke the function from anywhere inside the program's scope.

- **Function parameters:** Variables containing the argument values given when the function is invoked are function parameters.

In C++, we may allocate memory for a variable or an array during runtime. Dynamic memory allocation is the term for this. The compiler controls the memory assigned to variables in other programming languages, such as Java and Python. In C++, however, this is not the case.

After we do not need a variable in C++, we must manually deallocate the dynamically created memory. Using the new and delete operators, we may dynamically allocate and subsequently deallocate memory.

What Is the Purpose of Memory Management?

Because arrays contain homogenous data, memory is allocated to the array when it is declared most of the time. When the precise memory is not specified until runtime, a problem might emerge. We declare an array with a limit size to avoid this issue, but some memory will be unused. To prevent memory waste, we utilize the new operator to allocate memory during runtime dynamically.

Operators for Memory Management

In C, the malloc() and calloc() functions are used to allocate memory at runtime, whereas the free () function is used to deallocate dynamically generated memory. These functions are also available in

C++, although unary operators such as new and delete are defined to do the same job, namely allocating and freeing memory.

The New Operator's Benefits

The new operator has the following advantages over the malloc() function:

- It does not need the size of() operator since the size of the data object is calculated automatically.
- It does not necessary to employ typecasting because it delivers the right data type pointer.
- The new and delete operators, like other operators, can be overloaded.
- It also lets you initialize the data object while it's being built in memory.

New Operator in C++

The new operator gives a variable memory. As an example,

```
// declare a reference to an int
int* pointerVar;
// allocate memory dynamically
pointerVar = new int;
// assign a value to the memory that has been allocated
*pointerVar = 55;
```

Using the new operator, we have dynamically allocated memory for an int variable.

We allocated memory dynamically using the reference pntVar. Because the new operator returns the memory location's address, this is the case. When dealing with an array, the new operator returns the address of the array's first element.

The syntax for employing the new operator may be seen in the example above:

```
pointerVar = new dataType;
```

Delete Operator

We can deallocate the memory held by a variable that we have declared dynamically after requiring it. The delete operator is used for this. Memory deallocation refers to the process of returning memory to the operating system.

This operator's syntax is as follows:

```
delete pointerVar;
```

Example:

```
// declare a reference to an int
int* pointVari;
// allocate memory dynamically
pointVari = new int;
// assign value to the variable memory
*pointVari = 55;
// print the value stored in memory
cout << *pointVari;
// deallocate the memory delete
pointVari;
```

Using the pointer pointVari, we have dynamically allocated memory for an int variable.

Is It Permissible for a Member Function to Tell You to Remove Something?

- You must be sure that this object was allocated using new (not new[], placement new, a local object on the stack, a namespace-scope/global, or a member of another object; but just new).

- You must be confident that your member function will be the very last member function called on this object.

- You must be sure that the remainder of your member function (after the delete this line) does not come into contact with any part of this object. This includes code that will execute in destructors for any still-alive objects allocated on the stack.

- You must be very specific that no one touches this pointer after you delete this line. To put it another way, you can't look at it, compare it to another pointer, compare it to nullptr, print it, cast it, or do anything with it.

Allocating Memory in a Dynamic Way

A simple memory architecture utilized by each C++ software is shown below:

- **Code segment:** This is where the compiled program containing executive instructions is saved. It is a read-only document. The code portion is put behind the stack and heap to avoid overwriting them.

- **Data segment:** This is where global variables and static variables are maintained. It isn't just for reading.

- **Stack:** A stack is a type of memory that has been pre-allocated. A LIFO data structure is a stack. The stack is pushed up with each new variable. Memory is released when a variable is no longer in scope. When a stack variable is removed, the memory space it used becomes accessible for other variables. As functions push and pop local variables, the stack expands and contracts. It keeps track of local data, return addresses, arguments provided to functions, and memory status.

- **Heap:** Memory is allocated while the application is running. Memory is allocated using the new operator, whereas memory is dealt with using the delete operator.

Source Code:

```
#include <iostream> using namespace std; int main() {
    // int pointer declaration
    int* pntInt;
    // declare float     float* pntFloat;
    // allocate memory dynamically
    pntInt = new int;     pntFloat = new float;
    // value assigning to the memory     *pntInt = 55;
    *pntFloat = 55.55f;     cout << *pntInt << endl;     cout << *pntFloat << endl;
    // deallocate memory     delete pntInt;     delete pntFloat;     return 0; }
```

Output:

```
55
55.55
```

Arrays' New and Delete Operators Source Code:

```
// GPA of several students is stored and shown in this program where n is the num of students
entered

#include <iostream> using namespace std;

int main() {     int numb;
    cout << "Enter total number of
students: ";     cin >> numb;     float* pntr;

    // memory allocation     pntr = new float[numb];

    cout << "Enter GPA" << endl;     for (int c = 0; c < numb; ++c) {     cout << "Student" <<
c + 1 <<
". ";
        cin >> *(pntr + c);     }

    cout << "\nDisplaying GPA" << endl;     for (int c = 0; c < numb; ++c) {     cout << "Student"
<< c + 1 <<
" :" << *(pntr + c) << endl;     }
    // ptr memory is released     delete[] pntr;

    return 0; }
```

Output:

Enter total number of students: 5
Enter GPA
Student1: 4.4
Student2: 5
Student3: 3
Student4: 7
Student5: 8

Displaying GPA
Student1: 4.4
Student2: 5
Student3: 3
Student4: 7
Student5: 8

In this application, the user enters the number of students and saves it in the numb variable, and then we dynamically allocate memory for the float array using new.

We use pointer notation to insert data into the array (and eventually output it).
We use the code delete[] pntr; to deallocate the array memory when we no longer require it.
Use [] after delete. To indicate that the memory deallocation is for an array, we use square brackets [].

Objects' New and Delete Operators Source Code:

```cpp
#include <iostream> using namespace std;

class Stud {    int age;    public:
    // constructor initializes age
    Stud() : age(10) {}

    void getAge() {
        cout << "Age: " << age << endl;
    }
}; int main() {
    // declare Student object
dynamically    Stud* pntr = new Stud();

    // call getAge()    pntr->getAge();

    // released ptr memory    delete pntr;

    return 0;
```

}

Output:

Age: 10

We've built a Stud class with a private variable age in this application.

In the default function Stud(), we set the age to 10 and use the method getAge to report its result (). In main(), we use the new operator to construct a Student object and the pointer pntr to refer to its address.

The Stud() function sets the age to 10 as soon as the object is created.

In C++, Malloc() Vs New

In C++, both malloc() and new are used for the same thing. At runtime, they are utilized to allocate memory. Malloc() and new, on the other hand, have distinct syntax. The significant distinction between malloc() and new is that new is an operator, whereas malloc() is a predefined standard library function in a stdlib header file.

So, What's New?

The new is a memory allocation operator that is used at runtime to allocate memory. The heap stores the memory allocated by the new operator. It returns the memory's beginning address, which is then assigned to the variable. The new operator in C++ works similarly to the malloc() function in the C programming language. Although the malloc() method is compatible with C++, the new operator is more commonly employed because of its benefits.

Syntax:

type variable = new type(parameter_list);

- **type:** This specifies the datatype of the variable for which the new operator is allocating memory.

- **variable:** The name of the variable that points to the memory is variable.

- **parameter_list:** The parameter list is a list of initialized values for a variable.

The sizeof() operator is not used by the new operator to allocate memory. It also avoids using the resize operator because the new operator creates enough memory for an object. It's a construct that invokes the function to initialize an object at the moment of declaration.

Because the new operator allocates memory in a heap, an exception is thrown if it is not available when the new operator tries to assign it. The application will be terminated unexpectedly if our code is unable to handle the exception.

Example:

```
#include <iostream> using namespace std; int main()
{
int *pntr; // integer pointer  pntr=new int; // allocating memory  std::cout << "Enter number: "
<<
std::endl;  std::cin >>*pntr;
 std::cout << "Entered number"
<<*pntr<< std::endl;
return 0; }
```

Output:
Enter number:
30
Entered number 30

What Exactly Is Malloc()?

A malloc() function is a runtime memory allocation function. This method returns a void pointer, which may be given to any kind of pointer. This void pointer can be typecast to get a pointer that refers to a specific type of memory.

The malloc syntax is as follows:

type vari_name = (type *) malloc(sizeof(type));

Because heap memory is utilized to meet all dynamic memory requirements, the realloc() function might increase the memory if sufficient memory is not available. The malloc() function returns a reference to memory allocated in a heap. The heap memory is restricted, our code detects that it is in use when it starts running. It uses the free() function to release the memory when it has finished its task. After it completes its work, it frees the memory using the free() method. When code attempts to use memory that isn't accessible, the malloc() function returns a NULL pointer.

The free() function can be used to deallocate memory allocated by the malloc() method.

Example:

```
#include <iostream>
#include<stdlib.h> using namespace std;

int main() {

  int ln;  // declaration variable   std::cout << "Enter the count:" <<
std::endl;   std::cin >> ln;
  int *pntr; // pointer variable
declaration
  pntr=(int*) malloc(sizeof(int)*ln);
// allocating memory   for(int c=0;c<ln;c++)
```

```
  {
      std::cout << "Enter num : " <<
std::endl;
      std::cin >> *(pntr+c);
  }
  std::cout << "Entered elements: " <<
std::endl;
   for(int c=0;c<ln;c++)
   {
      std::cout << *(pntr+c) << std::endl;
   } free(pntr);     return 0;
}
```

Output:

Enter the count:
5 Enter num:
12 Enter num:
5 Enter num:
7 Enter num:
9 Enter num:
8 Entered elements:
12 5 7 9 8

Differences Between Malloc() and New()?

- The new operator generates an object by calling the procedure, but the malloc() method does not. The function is called by the new operator, whereas the destructor is called by the delete operator to destroy the object. The most important contrast between malloc() and new is this.

- Malloc() is a predefined function in the stdlib header file, while new is an operator.

- Overloading the new operator is possible, but not with the malloc() function.
- If there isn't enough memory in a heap, the new operator will throw an exception, and the malloc() method will return a NULL pointer.

- We must specify the number of objects to be allocated in the new operator, while we must specify the number of bytes to be allocated in the malloc() function.

- To deallocate memory in the event of a new operator, we must utilize the delete operator. However, in the malloc() method, we must deallocate the memory using the free() function.

Syntax: type reference_vari = new type name;

Example:
int *b; p = (int *) malloc(sizeof(int))

The above line allocates memory on a heap for an integer variable and then saves the address of the reserved memory in the "b" variable.

- The memory allocated using the malloc() method may be freed with the free() function.

- The memory can't be expanded after it's been allocated with the new operator. On the other hand, the memory is allocated using the malloc() method and subsequently reallocated using the realloc() function.

- Because new is a construct and malloc is a function, new takes less time to execute than malloc().

- The address of the newly formed object is returned by the new operator, not the distinct pointer variable. The malloc() method, on the other hand, returns a void pointer that may be typecast into any type.

Process Memory

A process is a runnable program that is loaded into memory. A method is just a running program.

When a program is generated, it is nothing more than a collection of bytes saved on the hard disc as a passive object. When a program is double-clicked on Windows or the name of the executable file is entered on the command line, the program begins loading in memory and becomes an active entity.

Operating System Memory Management

Memory management is a component of the operating system that regulates or maintains primary memory and moves processes from the main memory to the disc during execution. Memory management maintains track of every memory location, whether it's in use or not. It determines how much memory should be allotted to each process. It specifies which methods will be allocated memory and when they will be given memory. It monitors when memory is freed or unallocated and adjusts the state accordingly.

Memory may be defined as a collection of data in a certain format. It's utilized to keep track of instructions and data that have been processed. A vast array or set of words or bytes makes up the memory, each with its place. A computer system's principal goal is to run programs. During execution, these programs and the data they access should reside in the main memory. The CPU retrieves instructions from memory based on the program counter value.

What Is Main Memory?

A modern computer's main memory is critical to its functionality. A vast array of words or bytes, ranging in size from hundreds of thousands to billions, is referred to as main memory. The CPU and I/O devices share main memory, which is a store of quickly accessible information. When the CPU is actively using programs and data, they are stored in the main memory. Because main memory is linked to the CPU, transferring instructions and data in and out of the processor is lightning fast.

RAM stands for random access memory. This memory is a volatile memory, which means it may be erased at any time. When there is a power outage, the data in RAM is last.

What Is Memory Management?

In a multiprogramming computer, the operating system takes up a portion of memory, while other processes rest. The process of assigning memory to various uses is known as memory management. Memory management is a mechanism used by operating systems to coordinate actions between the main memory and the disc while running. The fundamental objective of memory management is to achieve practical usage of memory.

Why Is Memory Management Necessary?

- Before and after the procedure, allocate and de-allocate memory

- To keep track of how much memory is being utilized by processes

- To keep fragmentation to a minimum

- To make the most use of the main memory

- To keep data safe while the procedure is running

Space for Logical and Physical Addresses

- **Space for logical addresses:** The term "logical address" refers to an address created by the CPU. A virtual address is another name for it. The size of the process can be described as the logical address space. It is possible to modify a logical address.

- **Physical Address space:** A "Physical Address" is an address viewed by the memory unit (i.e. one that is loaded into the memory's memory address register). A Real address is the same as a physical address.

Physical address space is the collection of all physical addresses that correspond to these logical addresses. Memory Management Unit (MMU) generates a physical address. A hardware component known as a MMU performs the run-time mapping from virtual to physical locations. The physical address is always the same.

Loading Methods: Static and Dynamic

A loader loads a process into the main memory in two ways: static and dynamic. Loading can be divided into two categories:

- **Static loading:** Static loading is when the complete program is loaded into a single address. It necessitates additional memory.

- **Dynamic loading:** The whole program and its data must be in physical memory for a process to operate. As a result, the size of a function is restricted by the amount of physical memory available. Dynamic loading is utilized to ensure optimal memory use. In dynamic loading, a procedure is not loaded until it is called.

Linking, Both Static and Dynamic

A linker is used to conduct static and dynamic linking tasks. A linker is a software that merges several object files created by a compiler into a single executable file.

- **Static linking:** The linker merges all essential software modules into a single executable program via static linking. As a result, there isn't any runtime dependence. Some operating systems only allow static linking, which treats system language libraries like any other object module.

- **Dynamic linking:** Dynamic linking is comparable to dynamic loading in terms of its core principle. For each suitable library routine reference, "Stub" is included in dynamic linking. A stub is a chunk of code that is only a few lines long. When the stub is run, it checks to see if the required procedure is already present in memory. If the routine is not accessible, the software loads it into memory.

Swapping

A process must have resided in memory when it is run. Swapping temporarily moves a process from main memory to secondary memory, which is faster than secondary memory. More operations may be executed and fit into memory at the same time, thanks to swapping. The transferred time is the most critical aspect of swapping, and the overall time is proportional to the quantity of memory swapped. Because if a higher priority process requests service, the memory manager can swap out the lower priority process and then load and run the higher priority process, swapping is also known as roll-out, roll-in. After completing the higher priority activity, the lower priority process swapped back into memory and resumed the execution process.

Contiguous Memory Allocation

The main memory should be accessible to both the operating system and the numerous client programs. As a result, memory allocation in the operating system becomes an essential activity. Memory is usually partitioned into two parts: the resident operating system and user processes. Many user processes must be retained in memory at the same time in most instances. As a result, we must examine how to assign available memory to the processes waiting to be brought into memory from the input queue. Each process in neighboring memory allotment is housed in a single contiguous memory segment.

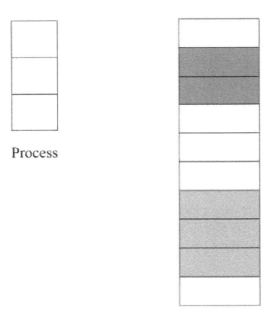

Process

Memory Blocks

Memory Allocation

Memory allocation must be allocated efficiently to achieve optimal memory utilization. Divide memory into numerous fixed-size divisions, each containing precisely one process, is one of the simplest ways for allocating memory. The number of divisions determines the degree of multiprogramming.

Multiple Partition Allocation

A process is chosen from the input queue and loaded into a free partition in this approach. The division becomes accessible for other functions after the process finishes.

Fixed Partition Allocation

In this technique, the operating system keeps track of which sections of memory are free and used up by processes. All memory is initially available for user processes and is treated as a single giant block of memory. The available memory is referred to as a "Hole". When a new process that requires memory, we look for a large enough hole to store it. If the need is met, we allocate RAM to process it; otherwise, the remaining memory is kept accessible for future requests.

When allocating memory, dynamic storage allocation difficulties might arise, such as meeting a request of size n from a list of available holes. There are a few options for dealing with this issue:

First Fit

In this case, the first accessible free slot satisfies the process's criteria.

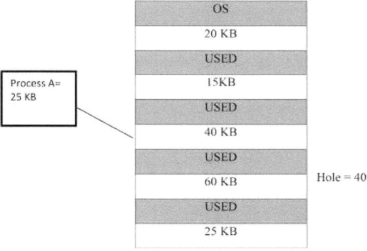

Because the previous two memory blocks did not have enough memory space, the first available free hole in this diagram is a 40 KB memory block that can hold process A (size of 25 KB). Best Fit

Assign the smallest hole that is large enough to process requirements for the optimum fit. Unless the list is sorted by size, we search the entire list for this.

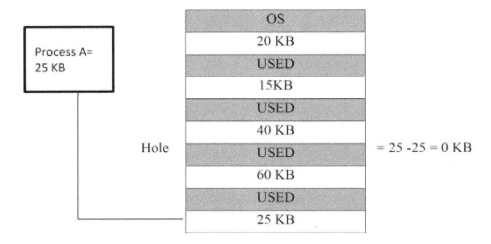

Worst Fit

In the worst-case scenario, process the most enormous available hole. This approach yields the most significant remaining hole.

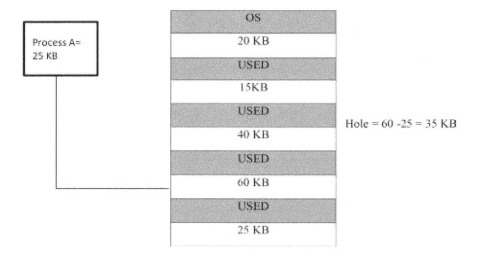

Process A (size 25 KB) is allocated to the most significant available memory block of 60 KB in this case. In the worst-case scenario, inefficient memory use is a big concern.

Fragmentation

A Fragmentation is described as a tiny free hole created when a process is loaded and deleted from memory after execution. These holes can't be allocated to new techniques since they're not merged or don't meet the process's memory requirements. We must decrease memory waste or fragmentation to accomplish a degree of multiprogramming.

There are two forms of fragmentation in operating systems:

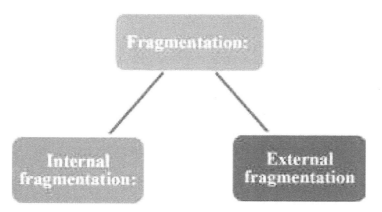

Internal Fragmentation

Internal fragmentation happens when the process is given more memory blocks than requested. As a result, some space remains, resulting in internal fragmentation.

External Fragmentation

We have a free memory block in external fragmentation, but we can't allocate it to process since the blocks aren't contiguous.

Paging

Paging is a memory management method that eliminates the need for physical memory allocation in contiguous blocks. This technique allows a process's physical address space to be non-contiguous.

- **Logical address:** A logical address, sometimes known as a virtual address, is created by the CPU.
- **Logical address space:** The collection of all logical addresses created by a program is the logical address space or virtual address space.
- **Physical address:** An address that can be found on a memory unit.
- **Physical address space:** The collection of all physical addresses that correlate to logical addresses.

What Are Objects in Memory?

Above the bar, programs get storage in-memory objects, which are virtual storage chunks. The system divides a memory object into virtual segments, each one a megabyte in size and starting on a megabyte boundary. A memory object might be as large as your installation's memory limitations or as tiny as one megabyte.

A program specifies a location where the system should return the memory object's low address when it creates a memory object. You may think of the address as the memory object's name. The application can use the storage in the memory object the same way it used storage in the 2-gigabyte address space after generating it; see using a memory object. The software is unable to work with storage regions that span several memory objects.

A program can alert the system to its usage of some physical pages that back ranges of addresses in-memory objects, making them accessible for the system to steal and later return. This helps the system manage the physical pages that back ranges of addresses in-memory objects.

The software can release physical pages that have memory object back ranges and, if desired, clear those ranges to zeros. The software can then request that the system return the physical backup from auxiliary storage. When the software no longer needs the memory item, it completely frees it.

Object in C++

In C++, an object is a physical object such as a chair, automobile, pen, phone, laptop, etc.

An object is a state-and-behavior entity, to put it another way. In this context, the terms "state" and "behaviour" are interchangeable.

A runtime entity is produced during runtime.

A class instance is referred to as an object. The object may be used to access all of the class's members.

Syntax:
Class c1;

Custom Memory Management

When memory blocks are required during runtime, it is necessary. You may have used standard library methods such as malloc and free to dynamically allocate memory from the heap for your application in C and C++. The application then uses this memory for a specific purpose. The goal is usually to add a node to a data structure. To get the memory for a new object in object-oriented languages, dynamic memory allocation is employed.

It's a common misconception that heap will always meet our memory requirements. However, heap has a limit. The physical limit may be evident to most of us, but there is also a subtle "virtual" limit. This constraint becomes more apparent when we use a lot of allocation and deallocation in a long-running application. There is a penalty even while we have complete freedom to return memory to the heap when it is no longer required. Where previously allocated memory has been returned between blocks of memory still in use, the heap may develop "holes".

Our memory allocator would have to seek a new request among the free holes for the suitable "hole" (i.e. large enough to satisfy our demand). Consider a case in which we may not find a large enough hole, but there is plenty of open space. Confused?

Because we want a continuous memory block, none of the holes may be large enough; instead, there may be an excessive number of tiny holes. One of the most significant issues with dynamic memory allocation is memory fragmentation.

A variety of approaches are employed to reduce fragmentation, such as adopting a suitable memory allocation strategy or merging small holes into larger ones. It motivates us to create a bespoke memory manager in which we have total control over the allocation scheme and other ways of dealing with such issues.

But hold on a second. Why can't C and C++'s default memory allocators save us? Let's get into the specifics to address this question.

- The malloc and new are examples of general-purpose memory allocators. Although our code is single threaded, the malloc function to which it is connected may also handle multithreaded paradigms. This added functionality harms the performance of these procedures.

- The malloc and new, in turn, make memory demands to the operating system kernel, whereas free and delete make memory release requests. This implies that the operating system must transition between user-space and kernel code whenever a memory request is caused because of the frequent context switching; programs that make repeated calls to malloc or new ultimately become sluggish.

- Memory allocated in a program but not used is frequently left undeleted accidentally, and C/C++ does not allow for automated garbage collection. The program's memory footprint grows as a result of this. Because accessible memory becomes increasingly scarce and hard-disk operations are time-consuming, performance suffers significantly in extensive programs.

Custom Memory Allocation

Memory leak detection and fast memory allocations can have a significant influence on game speed. The malloc and new are two well-known C++ methods for allocating dynamic (heap) memory; however, because they're general-purpose functions, they're generally sluggish, and some implementations need a context transfer from user mode to kernel mode. These functions also don't come with a built-in memory leak detection mechanism. We can have well-defined use patterns and improve the allocation process using custom allocators. For decades, dynamic memory allocation has been an integral element of most computer systems.

Smart Pointers and Memory Management

- **RAII and Reference Counting:** Reference counting is a notion that should be familiar to programmers who are familiar with Objective-C/Swift/JavaScript. To prevent memory leaks, the reference count is kept track of. The main concept is to count how many dynamically allocated objects there are. The reference count of the referenced object is increased once every time you add a reference to it. The reference count is decremented by one every time a reference is removed. The pointed heap memory is automatically erased when an object's reference count is decreased to zero. It is not necessarily a great practice in conventional C++ to "remember" to manually release resources.

  So, for an object, we usually apply for space when the function is called, and release space when the destructor (called after exiting the scope) is invoked. That example, the RAII resource acquisition is sometimes referred to as the initialization technique.

  Everything has exceptions; therefore we must always assign objects to free storage. To "remember" to release resources in conventional C++, we must utilize new and delete. Smart pointers are introduced in C++11, and they use the notion of reference counting to eliminate the need for programmers to manually release memory. These smart pointers need the header file ory>, and include std::shared ptr/ std::unique ptr/std::weak ptr.

- **std::shared_ptr:** std::shared_ptr is a smart pointer that keeps track of how many shared ptr refers to an object, obviating the need for the call delete, which deletes the object when the reference count reaches zero.

  However, this is insufficient since std::shared_ ptr must still be called with new, resulting in some imbalance in the code.

  To avoid the usage of new, std::make shared can be used instead. std::make shared will allocate the objects in the given arguments. This object type's std::shared_ptr reference is returned.

Example:
```
#include <iostream>
#include <memory>
void foo(std::shared_ptr<int> j)
{
(*j)++;
} int main() {
// auto pointer = new int(20); // illegal, no direct assignment // Constructed a
std::shared_ptr

auto pointer = std::make_ shared<int>(20); foo(pointer); std::cout << *pointer << std::endl;
// before leaving the scope the shared_ptr will be destructed
return 0;
}
```

The get() function of std::shared ptr may be used to obtain the raw pointer, and the reset() method can be used to lower the reference count (). Use count to see an object's reference count ().

Example:

```
auto pointer = std::make_shared<int>(20); auto pointer3 = pointer; auto pointer4 = pointer;

int *g = pointer.get(); // no increase of reference count std::cout << "pointer.use_count() = " << pointer.use_count() <<
std::endl;
std::cout << "pointer3.use_count() = " << pointer3.use_count() <<
std::endl;
std::cout << "pointer4.use_count() = " << pointer4.use_count() << std::endl;

pointer3.reset(); std::cout << "reset pointer3:" <<
std::endl;
std::cout << "pointer.use_count() = " << pointer.use_count() <<
std::endl;
std::cout << "pointer3.use_count() = " << pointer2.use_count() <<
std::endl;
std::cout << "pointer4.use_count() = " << pointer3.use_count() << std::endl;

pointer4.reset(); std::cout << "reset pointer4:" <<
std::endl;
std::cout << "pointer.use_count() = " << pointer.use_count() <<
std::endl;
std::cout << "pointer3.use_count() = " << pointer2.use_count() <<
std::endl;
std::cout << "pointer4.use_count() = " << pointer3.use_count() << std::endl;
```

- **std::unique_ptr:** The exclusive smart pointer std::unique_ptr prevents other smart pointers from sharing the same object, keeping the code safe:

```
std::unique_ptr<int> pointer = std::make_unique<int>(20); std::unique_ptr<int> pointer3 = pointer;
```

It's not difficult to use std::make_unique doesn't exist in C++11. make_unique, which may be used on its own:

```cpp
template<typename D, typename ...Args> std::unique_ptr<D> make_unique( Args&&
...args )
{
return std::unique_ptr<D>( new D( std::forward<Args>(args)... ) );
}
```

It can't be duplicated since it's monopolized, in other words. We may, however, use std::move to relocate it to another unique_ptr, such as:

```cpp
#include <iostream>
#include <memory> struct Foo
{
Foo() { std::cout << "Foo::Foo" << std::endl;
}
~Foo() { std::cout << "Foo::~Foo" << std::endl; } void foo()
{
std::cout << "Foo::foo" << std::endl;
}
};
void f(const Foo &) { std::cout << "f(const Foo&)" <<
std::endl; }

int main() { std::unique_ptr<Foo> p1(std::make_unique<Foo>());

if (c1) c1->foo();
{
std::unique_ptr<Foo> c2(std::move(c1)); f(*c2); if(c2) c2->foo(); if(c1) c1->foo(); c1 =
std::move(c2);
if(c2) c2->foo();
std::cout << "c2 was destroyed" <<
std::endl; } if (c1) c1->foo();
}
```

- **std::weak_ptr:** If you closely consider std::shared_ptr, you will notice that there is still a problem with resources not being released. Consider the following scenario:

```cpp
#include <iostream>
#include <memory>

class C; class D; class C { public: std::shared_ptr<D> pointer;
~C() {
std::cout << "A was destroyed" <<
std::endl;
}
}; class D { public: std::shared_ptr<C> pointer;
~D() {
std::cout << "D was destroyed" <<
```

```
std::endl;
}
}; int main() {
std::shared_ptr<C> c = std::make_ shared<C>(); std::shared_ptr<D> d = std::make_shared<D>();
c->pointer = d; d->pointer = c;
return 0;
}
```

As a result, neither C nor D will be destroyed. Because the pointer within c, d also refers c, d, c, d's reference count reaches 2, and the scope is exited. The reference count of this region may only be decremented by one when the c, d smart pointer is destroyed. This causes the c, d object's memory area reference count to be non-zero, but the external has no method of finding this region, resulting in a memory leak.

Conclusion: Mastering Memory Management in C++

Memory management is one of the most critical aspects of programming in C++. It is the foundation upon which efficient, reliable, and secure applications are built. As we have explored in this guide, C++ provides developers with a wide array of tools and techniques for managing memory, ranging from manual memory management to modern, automated solutions like smart pointers and garbage collection. In this conclusion, we will summarize the key concepts, reflect on the evolution of memory management in C++, and provide actionable insights for mastering memory management in C++ 2025.

The Evolution of Memory Management in C++

C++ has come a long way since its inception in the 1980s. Initially, memory management in C++ was entirely manual, relying on the new and delete operators for dynamic memory allocation and deallocation. While this approach provided developers with fine-grained control over memory, it also introduced significant challenges, such as memory leaks, dangling pointers, and fragmentation. These issues often led to unstable and insecure applications, especially in large-scale projects.

Over the years, the C++ language and its standard library have evolved to address these challenges. The introduction of **RAII (Resource Acquisition Is Initialization)** in the early days of C++ laid the groundwork for safer resource management. RAII ensures that resources, including memory, are automatically released when an object goes out of scope. This principle is the backbone of modern memory management techniques in C++.

The C++11 standard marked a significant milestone in memory management with the introduction of **smart pointers** (std::unique_ptr, std::shared_ptr, and std::weak_ptr). These tools automated memory management, reducing the burden on developers and minimizing the risk of memory-related errors. Subsequent standards, such as C++14, C++17, and C++20, further refined these features and introduced new ones, such as **polymorphic memory resources (std::pmr)** and **custom allocators**.

In C++ 2025, memory management continues to evolve, with a focus on **memory safety**, **performance optimization**, and **ease of use**. Features like std::out_ptr, std::inout_ptr, and improvements to the memory model ensure that C++ remains a powerful and modern language for systems programming and beyond.

Key Concepts in Memory Management

To master memory management in C++ 2025, it is essential to understand and apply the following key concepts:

1. Manual Memory Management

Manual memory management involves explicitly allocating and deallocating memory using new and delete. While this approach provides maximum control, it is error-prone and requires careful attention to detail. Best practices for manual memory management include:

- Always pairing new with delete and new[] with delete[].
- Initializing pointers to nullptr and checking for nullptr before deletion.
- Using RAII to manage resources automatically.

2. Smart Pointers

Smart pointers are a cornerstone of modern C++ memory management. They automate memory deallocation, reducing the risk of leaks and dangling pointers. The three main types of smart pointers are:

- **std::unique_ptr**: Manages exclusive ownership of a resource.
- **std::shared_ptr**: Allows multiple pointers to share ownership of a resource.
- **std::weak_ptr**: Breaks circular references between shared_ptr instances.

3. Memory Pools and Custom Allocators

Memory pools and custom allocators are advanced techniques for optimizing memory allocation and reducing fragmentation. Memory pools pre-allocate a block of memory and manage allocations within that block, while custom allocators allow developers to define their own memory allocation strategies for STL containers.

4. Garbage Collection

Although C++ does not natively support garbage collection, libraries like the Boehm-Demers-Weiser garbage collector can be used to automate memory management. Garbage collection simplifies memory management but introduces overhead and non-deterministic deallocation.

5. Modern Features in C++

C++ 2025 introduces several features to enhance memory management, including:

- **std::pmr**: Provides polymorphic memory resources for flexible memory management.
- **std::allocate_shared and std::make_shared**: Enable custom allocators for shared_ptr.
- **Memory safety features**: Tools like std::out_ptr and std::inout_ptr improve pointer safety.

Best Practices for Memory Management in C++

To write efficient, reliable, and secure C++ code, follow these best practices for memory management:

1. Prefer Smart Pointers Over Raw Pointers

Smart pointers automate memory management and reduce the risk of memory-related errors. Use std::unique_ptr for exclusive ownership and std::shared_ptr for shared ownership. Avoid using raw pointers unless absolutely necessary.

2. Use RAII for Resource Management

RAII ensures that resources are automatically released when an object goes out of scope. This principle applies not only to memory but also to other resources, such as file handles and network connections.

3. Minimize Dynamic Memory Allocation

Dynamic memory allocation is slower than stack allocation and can lead to fragmentation. Whenever possible, use stack allocation or static allocation for small, short-lived objects.

4. Avoid Memory Leaks

Memory leaks occur when allocated memory is not deallocated. To avoid leaks:

- Use smart pointers or RAII.
- Regularly test your code with tools like Valgrind or AddressSanitizer.
- Follow the "rule of three" or "rule of five" for managing resources in classes.

5. Prevent Dangling Pointers

Dangling pointers occur when a pointer points to freed memory. To prevent this:

- Set pointers to nullptr after deallocating memory.
- Avoid returning pointers to local variables.
- Use std::weak_ptr to break circular references.

6. Optimize Memory Usage

Efficient memory usage is critical for performance. Techniques for optimizing memory usage include:

- Using memory pools to reduce fragmentation.
- Allocating memory in large blocks rather than small chunks.
- Reusing memory whenever possible.

7. Debug Memory Issues

Memory-related issues can be challenging to debug. Use tools like Val grind, Address Sanitizer, and GDB to identify and fix memory leaks, buffer overflows, and other issues.

The Future of Memory Management in C++

As C++ continues to evolve, memory management will remain a central focus. The following trends are likely to shape the future of memory management in C++:

1. Increased Emphasis on Memory Safety

Memory safety is a growing concern in software development, particularly in systems programming. C++ 2025 introduces features like std::out_ptr and std::inout_ptr to improve pointer safety. Future standards may include additional tools and language constructs to further enhance memory safety.

2. Integration with Modern Hardware

Modern hardware, such as GPUs and TPUs, requires specialized memory management techniques. C++ is likely to incorporate features for managing memory on heterogeneous hardware, enabling developers to write high-performance code for a wide range of platforms.

3. Simplified Memory Management

While C++ provides powerful tools for memory management, it can be complex and error-prone. Future versions of C++ may introduce higher-level abstractions to simplify memory management without sacrificing performance or control.

4. Concurrency and Memory Management

Concurrency is a key challenge in modern software development. C++ 2025 and beyond will likely include features for managing memory in concurrent and parallel programs, ensuring thread safety and performance.

Final Thoughts

Memory management is both an art and a science. It requires a deep understanding of the language, the hardware, and the application's requirements. In C++ 2025, developers have access to a rich set of tools and techniques for managing memory, from low-level manual management to high-level abstractions like smart pointers and garbage collection.

By mastering these tools and following best practices, you can write C+− code that is efficient, reliable, and secure. Whether you are working on a small project or a large-scale system, effective memory management is essential for success.

As C++ continues to evolve, staying up-to-date with the latest features and trends will be crucial. Embrace the power and flexibility of C++ 2025, and use it to build the next generation of high-performance applications.

8. C++ Web Programming

Introduction

C++ has long been known as a powerful, high-performance programming language, primarily used for system programming, game development, and applications requiring fine-grained control over hardware resources. However, with the evolution of web technologies and the increasing demand for high-performance web applications, C++ has found its way into web programming. By 2025, C++ web programming has matured significantly, offering developers a robust set of tools and frameworks to build scalable, efficient, and secure web applications.

1. Why Use C++ for Web Programming?

Performance

C++ is renowned for its performance. It allows developers to write highly optimized code, making it ideal for web applications that require low latency and high throughput, such as real-time systems, gaming backends, and financial platforms.

Control Over Resources

C++ provides fine-grained control over memory and system resources, enabling developers to build lightweight and efficient web servers that can handle thousands of concurrent connections.

Cross-Platform Compatibility

C++ is a cross-platform language, meaning web applications written in C++ can run on various operating systems, including Linux, Windows, and macOS, without significant modifications.

Integration with Existing Systems

Many legacy systems and high-performance applications are written in C++. Using C++ for web programming allows seamless integration with these systems, reducing the need for complex middleware.

Growing Ecosystem

By 2025, the C++ ecosystem for web development has expanded significantly, with numerous libraries, frameworks, and tools available to simplify web application development.

2. Key Features of C++ for Web Development

Object-Oriented Programming (OOP)

C++ supports OOP principles, enabling developers to create modular, reusable, and maintainable code. This is particularly useful for building complex web applications.

Templates and Generic Programming

C++ templates allow for generic programming, making it easier to write reusable and type-safe code for web applications.

Concurrency and Multithreading

C++ provides robust support for concurrency and multithreading, which is essential for handling multiple client requests simultaneously in web servers.

Standard Library and Boost

The C++ Standard Library and Boost provide a wealth of utilities for web development, including data structures, algorithms, and networking capabilities.

Compatibility with C

C++ is backward-compatible with C, allowing developers to leverage existing C libraries and codebases in their web applications.

3. Popular C++ Web Frameworks in 2025

Crow

Crow is a micro web framework for C++ that is lightweight and easy to use. It is ideal for building RESTful APIs and small web applications.

Pistache

Pistache is a modern C++ web framework designed for building high-performance HTTP servers and REST APIs. It provides a clean and intuitive API for handling HTTP requests and responses.

CppCMS

CppCMS is a full-featured web framework for C++ that supports MVC architecture, templating, and session management. It is suitable for building large-scale web applications.

Wt (Web Toolkit)

Wt is a C++ library for developing web applications with a widget-centric approach. It allows developers to build web UIs using C++ code, similar to desktop application development.

Drogon

Drogon is an asynchronous web framework for C++ that is designed for high-performance applications. It supports HTTP/2, WebSocket, and other modern web technologies.

4. Setting Up a C++ Web Development Environment

Prerequisites

- A C++ compiler (e.g., GCC, Clang, or MSVC)

- CMake for building projects
- A package manager like vcpkg or Conan for managing dependencies

Installing a Web Framework

Most C++ web frameworks can be installed using a package manager or by cloning their repositories from GitHub. For example, to install Crow using vcpkg:

vcpkg install crow

Configuring the Build System

Use CMake to configure and build your C++ web application. Here's an example CMakeLists.txt file for a project using Crow:

cmake_minimum_required(VERSION 3.10)

project(MyWebApp)

set(CMAKE_CXX_STANDARD 17)

find_package(Crow REQUIRED)

add_executable(MyWebApp main.cpp)

target_link_libraries(MyWebApp Crow::Crow)

Running the Application

After building the project, run the executable to start the web server:

./MyWebApp

5. Building a Basic Web Application in C++

Creating a Simple HTTP Server

Here's an example of a basic HTTP server using the Crow framework:

```
#include "crow.h"
int main() {
  crow::SimpleApp app;

  CROW_ROUTE(app, "/")([](){
    return "Hello, World!";
  });

  app.port(8080).multithreaded().run();
```

```
}
```

This code creates a web server that listens on port 8080 and responds with "Hello, World!" when accessed.

Handling HTTP Requests

C++ web frameworks provide APIs for handling different HTTP methods (GET, POST, PUT, DELETE, etc.). For example, to handle a POST request:

```
CROW_ROUTE(app, "/submit").methods("POST"_method)([](const crow::request& req){
    auto data = crow::json::load(req.body);
    if (!data) {
        return crow::response(400, "Invalid JSON");
    }
    return crow::response(200, "Data received");
});
```

Serving Static Files

Most frameworks allow you to serve static files (e.g., HTML, CSS, JavaScript) from a directory. For example, in Crow:

```
CROW_ROUTE(app, "/static/<string>")([](const std::string& filename){

return crow::response(crow::mustache::load_text(filename));

});
```

6. Advanced Topics in C++ Web Programming

Asynchronous Programming

Asynchronous programming is crucial for building high-performance web applications. Frameworks like Drogon provide built-in support for asynchronous I/O operations.

WebSockets

WebSockets enable real-time communication between the client and server. C++ frameworks like Drogon and Pistache support WebSocket protocols.

Database Integration

C++ web applications can integrate with databases using libraries like SQLite, MySQL++, or ODBC. ORM (Object-Relational Mapping) libraries such as ODB simplify database interactions.

Security

Security is a critical aspect of web development. C++ web frameworks provide features for handling authentication, authorization, and encryption. Always validate user input and use secure coding practices to prevent vulnerabilities like SQL injection and XSS.

Deployment

C++ web applications can be deployed using containerization tools like Docker or orchestration platforms like Kubernetes. This ensures scalability and reliability in production environments.

7. Challenges and Best Practices

Challenges

- **Complexity**: C++ is a complex language, and web development adds another layer of complexity.
- **Lack of High-Level Abstractions**: Compared to languages like Python or JavaScript, C++ lacks high-level abstractions for web development.
- **Debugging**: Debugging C++ web applications can be challenging due to low-level errors and memory issues.

Best Practices

- Use modern C++ features (C++17/20) to write clean and efficient code.
- Leverage existing libraries and frameworks to avoid reinventing the wheel.
- Follow secure coding practices to protect your application from vulnerabilities.
- Optimize performance by profiling and benchmarking your code.

8. Future Trends in C++ Web Programming

Increased Adoption of C++20/23 Features

By 2025, C++20 and C++23 features like modules, coroutines, and ranges will be widely adopted in web development, making C++ more expressive and easier to use.

Growth of Asynchronous Frameworks

Asynchronous web frameworks like Drogon will continue to gain popularity, enabling developers to build highly scalable and performant web applications.

Integration with AI and Machine Learning

C++ is a popular choice for AI and machine learning applications. In the future, we can expect tighter integration between C++ web frameworks and AI libraries like TensorFlow and PyTorch.

Cloud-Native Development

C++ web applications will increasingly be designed for cloud-native environments, leveraging technologies like serverless computing and microservices.

What is CGI?

- The Common Gateway Interface, or CGI, is a set of standards that define how information is exchanged between the web server and a custom script.

- The CGI specs are currently maintained by the NCSA and NCSA defines CGI is as follows −

- The Common Gateway Interface, or CGI, is a standard for external gateway programs to interface with information servers such as HTTP servers.

- The current version is CGI/1.1 and CGI/1.2 is under progress.

Web Browsing

To understand the concept of CGI, let's see what happens when we click a hyperlink to browse a particular web page or URL.

- Your browser contacts the HTTP web server and demand for the URL ie. filename.

- Web Server will parse the URL and will look for the filename. If it finds requested file then web server sends that file back to the browser otherwise sends an error message indicating that you have requested a wrong file.

- Web browser takes response from web server and displays either the received file or error message based on the received response.

However, it is possible to set up the HTTP server in such a way that whenever a file in a certain directory is requested, that file is not sent back; instead, it is executed as a program, and produced output from the program is sent back to your browser to display.

The Common Gateway Interface (CGI) is a standard protocol for enabling applications (called CGI programs or CGI scripts) to interact with Web servers and with clients. These CGI programs can be a written in Python, PERL, Shell, C or C++ etc.

CGI Architecture Diagram

The following simple program shows a simple architecture of CGI

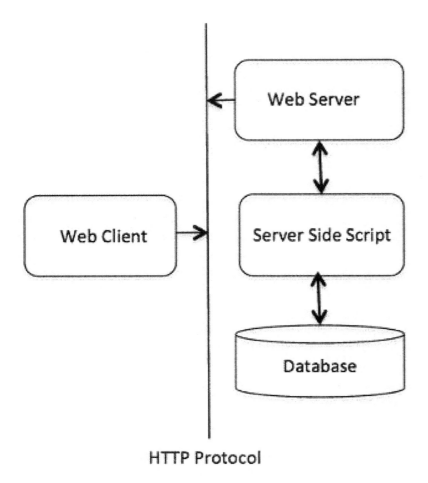

HTTP Protocol

Web Server Configuration

Before you proceed with CGI Programming, make sure that your Web Server supports CGI and it is configured to handle CGI Programs. All the CGI Programs to be executed by the HTTP server are kept in a preconfigured directory. This directory is called CGI directory and by convention it is named as /var/www/cgi-bin. By convention CGI files will have extension as **.cgi**, though they are C++ executable.

By default, Apache Web Server is configured to run CGI programs in /var/www/cgi-bin. If you want to specify any other directory to run your CGI scripts, you can modify the following section in the httpd.conf file

<Directory "/var/www/cgi-bin">

AllowOverride None

Options ExecCGI

Order allow,deny

Allow from all

</Directory>

<Directory "/var/www/cgi-bin">

Options All

</Directory>

Here, I assume that you have Web Server up and running successfully and you are able to run any other CGI program like Perl or Shell etc.

First CGI Program

Consider the following C++ Program
content

```
#include <iostream> using
namespace std;

int main () { cout << "Content-type:text/html\r\n\r\n";
    cout << "<html>\n"; cout << "<head>\n"; cout << "<title>Hello World - First CGI
    Program</title>\n"; cout << "</head>\n"; cout << "<body>\n"; cout << "<h2>Hello
    World! This is my first CGI program</h2>\n"; cout << "</body>\n"; cout <<
    "</html>\n";

    return 0;
}
```

Compile above code and name the executable as cplusplus.cgi. This file is being kept in /var/www/cgi-bin directory and it has following content. Before running your CGI program make sure you have change mode of file using **chmod 755 cplusplus.cgi** UNIX command to make file executable.

My First CGI program

The above C++ program is a simple program which is writing its output on STDOUT file i.e. screen. There is one important and extra feature available which is first line printing **Content-type:text/html\r\n\r\n**. This line is sent back to the browser and specify the content type to be displayed on the browser screen. Now you must have understood the basic concept of CGI and you can write many complicated CGI programs using Python. A C++ CGI program can interact with any other external system, such as RDBMS, to exchange information.

HTTP Header

The line **Content-type:text/html\r\n\r\n** is a part of HTTP header, which is sent to the browser to understand the content. All the HTTP header will be in the following form −
HTTP Field Name: Field Content

For Example,
Content-type: text/html\r\n\r\n
There are few other important HTTP headers, which you will use frequently in your CGI Programming.

Sr.No	Header & Description
1	**Content-type:** A MIME string defining the format of the file being returned. Example is Content-type:text/html.
2	**Expires: Date** The date the information becomes invalid. This should be used by the browser to decide when a page needs to be refreshed. A valid date string should be in the format 01 Jan 1998 12:00:00 GMT.
3	**Location: URL** The URL that should be returned instead of the URL requested. You can use this filed to redirect a request to any file.
4	**Last-modified: Date** The date of last modification of the resource.
5	**Content-length: N** The length, in bytes, of the data being returned. The browser uses this value to report the estimated download time for a file.

6

Set-Cookie: String

Set the cookie passed through the *string*.

CGI Environment Variables

All the CGI program will have access to the following environment variables. These variables play an important role while writing any CGI program.

Sr.No	Variable Name & Description
1	**CONTENT_TYPE** The data type of the content, used when the client is sending attached content to the server. For example file upload etc.
2	**CONTENT_LENGTH** The length of the query information that is available only for POST requests.
3	**HTTP_COOKIE** Returns the set cookies in the form of key & value pair.
4	**HTTP_USER_AGENT** The User-Agent request-header field contains information about the user agent originating the request. It is a name of the web browser.

5

PATH_INFO

The path for the CGI script.

6

QUERY_STRING

The URL-encoded information that is sent with GET method request.

7

REMOTE_ADDR

The IP address of the remote host making the request. This can be useful for logging or for authentication purpose.

8

REMOTE_HOST

The fully qualified name of the host making the request. If this information is not available then REMOTE_ADDR can be used to get IR address.

9

REQUEST_METHOD

The method used to make the request. The most common methods are GET and POST.

10

SCRIPT_FILENAME

The full path to the CGI script.

11

SCRIPT_NAME

The name of the CGI script.

12

SERVER_NAME

The server's hostname or IP Address.

13

SERVER_SOFTWARE

The name and version of the software the server is running.

Here is small CGI program to list out all the CGI variables.

```
#include <iostream> #include <stdlib.h> using namespace std;

const string ENV[ 24 ] = {
"COMSPEC", "DOCUMENT_ROOT", "GATEWAY_INTERFACE",
"HTTP_ACCEPT", "HTTP_ACCEPT_ENCODING",
"HTTP_ACCEPT_LANGUAGE", "HTTP_CONNECTION",
"HTTP_HOST", "HTTP_USER_AGENT", "PATH",
"QUERY_STRING", "REMOTE_ADDR", "REMOTE_PORT",
"REQUEST_METHOD", "REQUEST_URI", "SCRIPT_FILENAME",
"SCRIPT_NAME", "SERVER_ADDR", "SERVER_ADMIN",
"SERVER_NAME","SERVER_PORT","SERVER_PROTOCOL",
"SERVER_SIGNATURE","SERVER_SOFTWARE" };

int main () { cout << "Content-type:text/html\r\n\r\n";
cout << "<html>\n"; cout << "<head>\n"; cout << "<title>CGI Environment Variables</title>\n";
cout << "</head>\n"; cout << "<body>\n";
cout << "<table border = \"0\" cellspacing = \"2\">";

for ( int i = 0; i < 24; i++ ) { cout << "<tr><td>" << ENV[ i ] << "</td><td>";

// attempt to retrieve value of environment variable char *value = getenv( ENV[ i ].c_str() ); if (
value != 0 ) { cout << value;
} else { cout << "Environment variable does not exist.";
}
cout << "</td></tr>\n";
```

```
}
cout << "</table><\n"; cout << "</body>\n"; cout << "</html>\n";

return 0;

}
```

C++ CGI Library

For real examples, you would need to do many operations by your CGI program. There is a CGI library written for C++ program which you can download from ftp://ftp.gnu.org/gnu/cgicc/ and follow the steps to install the library −

```
$tar xzf cgicc-X.X.X.tar.gz
$cd cgicc-X.X.X/
$./configure --prefix=/usr
$make
$make install
```
You can check related documentation available at 'C++ CGI Lib Documentation.

GET and POST Methods

You must have come across many situations when you need to pass some information from your browser to web server and ultimately to your CGI Program. Most frequently browser uses two methods to pass this information to web server. These methods are GET Method and POST Method.

Passing Information Using GET Method

The GET method sends the encoded user information appended to the page request. The page and the encoded information are separated by the ? character as follows −

http://www.test.com/cgi-bin/cpp.cgi?key1=value1&key2=value2

The GET method is the default method to pass information from browser to web server and it produces a long string that appears in your browser's Location:box. Never use the GET method if you have password or other sensitive information to pass to the server. The GET method has size limitation and you can pass upto 1024 characters in a request string.

When using GET method, information is passed using QUERY_STRING http header and will be accessible in your CGI Program through QUERY_STRING environment variable.

You can pass information by simply concatenating key and value pairs alongwith any URL or you can use HTML <FORM> tags to pass information using GET method.

Simple URL Example: Get Method

Here is a simple URL which will pass two values to hello_get.py program using GET method.
/cgi-bin/cpp_get.cgi?first_name=ZARA&last_name=ALI

Below is a program to generate **cpp_get.cgi** CGI program to handle input given by web browser. We are going to use C++ CGI library which makes it very easy to access passed information − Now, compile the above program as follows −

```
#include <iostream>
#include <vector>
#include <string>
#include <stdio.h>
#include <stdlib.h>
#include <cgicc/CgiDefs.h>
#include <cgicc/Cgicc.h>
#include <cgicc/HTTPHTMLHeader.h> #include <cgicc/HTMLClasses.h>
using namespace std; using namespace cgicc;
int main () { Cgicc formData;
cout << "Content-type:text/html\r\n\r\n";
cout << "<html>\n"; cout << "<head>\n"; cout << "<title>Using GET and POST
Methods</title>\n"; cout << "</head>\n"; cout << "<body>\n";
form_iterator fi = formData.getElement("first_name"); if( !fi->isEmpty() && fi !=
(*formData).end()) { cout << "First name: " << **fi << endl;
} else { cout << "No text entered for first name" << endl;
}
cout << "<br/>\n";
fi = formData.getElement("last_name"); if( !fi->isEmpty() &&fi != (*formData).end()) { cout <<
"Last name: " << **fi << endl;
} else { cout << "No text entered for last name" << endl;
}
cout << "<br/>\n"; cout << "</body>\n"; cout << "</html>\n";
return 0;
}
```

$g++ -o cpp_get.cgi cpp_get.cpp -lcgicc

Generate cpp_get.cgi and put it in your CGI directory and try to access using following link −
/cgi-bin/cpp_get.cgi?first_name=ZARA&last_name=ALI

This would generate following result −
First name: ZARA Last name:
ALI

Simple FORM Example: GET Method

Here is a simple example which passes two values using HTML FORM and submit button. We are going to use same CGI script cpp_get.cgi to handle this input.

<form action = "/cgi-bin/cpp_get.cgi" method = "get">

First Name: <input type = "text" name = "first_name">

Last Name: <input type = "text" name = "last_name" />

<input type = "submit" value = "Submit" /> </form>

Here is the actual output of the above form. You enter First and Last Name and then click submit button to see the result.

First Name: [   ]   Last Name: [   ]   Submit

Passing Information Using POST Method

A generally more reliable method of passing information to a CGI program is the POST method. This packages the information in exactly the same way as GET methods, but instead of sending it as a text string after a ? in the URL it sends it as a separate message. This message comes into the CGI script in the form of the standard input.

The same cpp_get.cgi program will handle POST method as well. Let us take same example as above, which passes two values using HTML FORM and submit button but this time with POST method as follows −

<form action = "/cgi-bin/cpp_get.cgi" method = "post">
    First Name: <input type = "text" name = "first_name">
 Last Name: <input type
    = "text" name = "last_name" />

<input type = "submit" value = "Submit" /> </form>

Here is the actual output of the above form. You enter First and Last Name and then click submit button to see the result.

First Name: [   ]   Last Name: [   ]   Submit

Passing Checkbox Data to CGI Program

Checkboxes are used when more than one option is required to be selected.
Here is example HTML code for a form with two checkboxes −

```
<form action = "/cgi-bin/cpp_checkbox.cgi" method = "POST" target = "_blank">
<input type = "checkbox" name = "maths" value = "on" /> Maths
<input type = "checkbox" name = "physics" value = "on" /> Physics
<input type = "submit" value = "Select Subject" />
</form>
```

The result of this code is the following form −

Below is C++ program, which will generate cpp_checkbox.cgi script to handle input given by web browser through checkbox button.

```
#include <iostream>
#include <vector>
#include <string>
#include <stdio.h>
#include <stdlib.h>
#include <cgicc/CgiDefs.h>
#include <cgicc/Cgicc.h>
#include <cgicc/HTTPHTMLHeader.h> #include <cgicc/HTMLClasses.h>
using namespace std; using namespace cgicc;
int main () { Cgicc formData;
bool maths_flag, physics_flag;
cout << "Content-type:text/html\r\n\r\n";
cout << "<html>\n"; cout << "<head>\n"; cout << "<title>Checkbox Data to CGI</title>\n"; cout << "</head>\n"; cout << "<body>\n";
maths_flag = formData.queryCheckbox("maths"); if( maths_flag ) { cout << "Maths Flag: ON " << endl;
} else { cout << "Maths Flag: OFF " << endl;
}
cout << "<br/>\n";
physics_flag = formData.queryCheckbox("physics"); if( physics_flag ) { cout << "Physics Flag: ON " << endl;
} else { cout << "Physics Flag: OFF " << endl;
}
cout << "<br/>\n"; cout << "</body>\n"; cout << "</html>\n";
return 0;
```

}

Passing Radio Button Data to CGI Program

Radio Buttons are used when only one option is required to be selected. Here is example HTML code for a form with two radio buttons −

<form action = "/cgi-bin/cpp_radiobutton.cgi" method = "post" target = "_blank">

<input type = "radio" name = "subject" value = "maths" checked = "checked"/> Maths

<input type = "radio" name = "subject" value = "physics" /> Physics

<input type = "submit" value = "Select Subject" />

</form>

The result of this code is the following form −

Below is C++ program, which will generate cpp_radiobutton.cgi script to handle input given by web browser through radio buttons.

```cpp
#include <iostream>
#include <vector>
#include <string>
#include <stdio.h>
#include <stdlib.h>
#include <cgicc/CgiDefs.h>
#include <cgicc/Cgicc.h>
#include <cgicc/HTTPHTMLHeader.h> #include <cgicc/HTMLClasses.h>
using namespace std; using namespace cgicc;
int main () { Cgicc formData;

cout << "Content-type:text/html\r\n\r\n";

cout << "<html>\n"; cout << "<head>\n"; cout << "<title>Radio Button Data to CGI</title>\n"; cout << "</head>\n"; cout << "<body>\n";

form_iterator fi = formData.getElement("subject"); if( !fi->isEmpty() && fi != (*formData).end()) {
cout << "Radio box selected: " << **fi << endl;
```

```
}
cout << "<br/>\n"; cout << "</body>\n"; cout << "</html>\n";
return 0;
}
```

Passing Text Area Data to CGI Program

TEXTAREA element is used when multiline text has to be passed to the CGI Program.

Here is example HTML code for a form with a TEXTAREA box −

```
<form action = "/cgi-bin/cpp_textarea.cgi" method = "post" target =
"_blank">
    <textarea name = "textcontent" cols = "40" rows = "4"> Type your text here...
    </textarea>
<input type = "submit" value = "Submit" /> </form>
```

The result of this code is the following form −

Below is C++ program, which will generate cpp_textarea.cgi script to handle input given by web browser through text area.

```
#include <iostream>
#include <vector>
#include <string>
#include <stdio.h>
#include <stdlib.h>
#include <cgicc/CgiDefs.h>
#include <cgicc/Cgicc.h>
#include <cgicc/HTTPHTMLHeader.h> #include <cgicc/HTMLClasses.h>
using namespace std; using namespace cgicc;
int main () { Cgicc formData;
cout << "Content-type:text/html\r\n\r\n";
cout << "<html>\n"; cout << "<head>\n";
cout << "<title>Text Area Data to CGI</title>\n"; cout << "</head>\n"; cout << "<body>\n";
```

```
form_iterator fi = formData.getElement("textcontent"); if( !fi->isEmpty() && fi !=
(*formData).end()) { cout << "Text Content: " << **fi << endl;
} else { cout << "No text entered" << endl;
}
cout << "<br/>\n"; cout << "</body>\n"; cout << "</html>\n";
return 0;
}
```

Passing Drop down Box Data to CGI Program

Drop down Box is used when we have many options available but only one or two will be selected.
Here is example HTML code for a form with one drop down box −

```
<form action = "/cgi-bin/cpp_dropdown.cgi" method = "post" target =
"_blank">
    <select name = "dropdown">
        <option value = "Maths" selected>Maths</option>
        <option value = "Physics">Physics</option>
    </select>

<input type = "submit" value = "Submit"/> </form>
```

The result of this code is the following form −

Below is C++ program, which will generate cpp_dropdown.cgi script to handle input given by web
browser through drop down box.

```
#include <iostream>
#include <vector>
#include <string>
#include <stdio.h>
#include <stdlib.h>

#include <cgicc/CgiDefs.h>
#include <cgicc/Cgicc.h>
#include <cgicc/HTTPHTMLHeader.h> #include
<cgicc/HTMLClasses.h>

using namespace std; using namespace
cgicc;
```

```
int main () { Cgicc
    formData;

    cout << "Content-type:text/html\r\n\r\n";
    cout << "<html>\n"; cout << "<head>\n"; cout << "<title>Drop Down Box
    Data to CGI</title>\n"; cout << "</head>\n"; cout << "<body>\n";

    form_iterator fi = formData.getElement("dropdown"); if( !fi->isEmpty()
    && fi != (*formData).end()) { cout << "Value Selected: " << **fi <<
    endl;
    }

    cout << "<br/>\n"; cout <<
    "</body>\n"; cout <<
    "</html>\n";

    return 0;
}
```

Using Cookies in CGI

HTTP protocol is a stateless protocol. But for a commercial website it is required to maintain session information among different pages. For example, one user registration ends after completing many pages. But how to maintain user's session information across all the web pages.

In many situations, using cookies is the most efficient method of remembering and tracking preferences, purchases, commissions, and other information required for better visitor experience or site statistics.

How It Works

Your server sends some data to the visitor's browser in the form of a cookie. The browser may accept the cookie. If it does, it is stored as a plain text record on the visitor's hard drive. Now, when the visitor arrives at another page on your site, the cookie is available for retrieval. Once retrieved, your server knows/remembers what was stored.

Cookies are a plain text data record of 5 variable-length fields −

Expires − This shows date the cookie will expire. If this is blank, the cookie will expire when the visitor quits the browser.

Domain − This shows domain name of your site.

Path − This shows path to the directory or web page that set the cookie. This may be blank if you want to retrieve the cookie from any directory or page.

Secure − If this field contains the word "secure" then the cookie may only be retrieved with a secure server. If this field is blank, no such restriction exists.

Name = Value − Cookies are set and retrieved in the form of key and value pairs.

Setting up Cookies

It is very easy to send cookies to browser. These cookies will be sent along with HTTP Header before the Content-type filed. Assuming you want to set UserID and Password as cookies. So, cookies setting will be done as follows

```
#include <iostream> using namespace std;

int main () { cout << "Set-Cookie:UserID = XYZ;\r\n"; cout << "Set-Cookie:Password = XYZ123;\r\n";

cout << "Set-Cookie:Domain = www.tutorialspoint.com;\r\n"; cout << "Set-Cookie:Path = /perl;\n";
cout << "Content-type:text/html\r\n\r\n";

cout << "<html>\n"; cout << "<head>\n"; cout << "<title>Cookies in CGI</title>\n"; cout << "</head>\n"; cout << "<body>\n"; cout << "Setting cookies" << endl;

cout << "<br/>\n"; cout << "</body>\n"; cout << "</html>\n";

return 0;

}
```

From this example, you must have understood how to set cookies. We use **Set-Cookie** HTTP header to set cookies.

Here, it is optional to set cookies attributes like Expires, Domain, and Path. It is notable that cookies are set before sending magic line **"Contenttype:text/html\r\n\r\n.**

Compile above program to produce setcookies.cgi, and try to set cookies using following link. It will set four cookies at your computer − /cgi-bin/setcookies.cgi

Retrieving Cookies

It is easy to retrieve all the set cookies. Cookies are stored in CGI environment variable HTTP_COOKIE and they will have following form. key1 = value1; key2 = value2; key3 = value3....

Here is an example of how to retrieve cookies.

```
#include <iostream>

#include <vector>

#include <string>

#include <stdio.h>
```

```
#include <stdlib.h>

#include <cgicc/CgiDefs.h>

#include <cgicc/Cgicc.h>

#include <cgicc/HTTPHTMLHeader.h> #include <cgicc/HTMLClasses.h>

using namespace std; using namespace cgicc;

int main () { Cgicc cgi; const_cookie_iterator cci;

cout << "Content-type:text/html\r\n\r\n";

cout << "<html>\n"; cout << "<head>\n"; cout << "<title>Cookies in CGI</title>\n"; cout <<
"</head>\n"; cout << "<body>\n";

cout << "<table border = \"0\" cellspacing = \"2\">";

// get environment variables

const CgiEnvironment& env = cgi.getEnvironment();

for( cci = env.getCookieList().begin(); cci != env.getCookieList().end();

++cci ) { cout << "<tr><td>" << cci->getName() << "</td><td>";

cout << cci->getValue();                     cout << "</td></tr>\n";

}

cout << "</table>\n"; cout << "<br/>\n"; cout << "</body>\n"; cout << "</html>\n"; return 0;

}
```

Now, compile above program to produce getcookies.cgi, and try to get a list of all the cookies
available at your computer − /cgi-bin/getcookies.cgi

This will produce a list of all the four cookies set in previous section and all other cookies set in
your computer −

UserID XYZ
Password XYZ123
Domain www.tutlspoint.com
Path /perl

File Upload Example

To upload a file the HTML form must have the enctype attribute set to **multipart/form-data**. The
input tag with the file type will create a "Browse" button.

```
<html>
   <body>
      <form enctype = "multipart/form-data" action =
"/cgibin/cpp_uploadfile.cgi" method = "post">
```

```
<p>File: <input type = "file" name = "userfile" /></p>
        <p><input type = "submit" value = "Upload" /></p> </form>
   </body>
</html>
```

The result of this code is the following form −

File:

Note − Above example has been disabled intentionally to stop people uploading files on our server. But you can try above code with your server.

Here is the script **cpp_uploadfile.cpp** to handle file upload −

```
#include <iostream>

#include <vector>

#include <string>

#include <stdio.h>

#include <stdlib.h>

#include <cgicc/CgiDefs.h>

#include <cgicc/Cgicc.h>

#include <cgicc/HTTPHTMLHeader.h> #include <cgicc/HTMLClasses.h>

using namespace std; using namespace cgicc;

int main () { Cgicc cgi;

cout << "Content-type:text/html\r\n\r\n";

cout << "<html>\n"; cout << "<head>\n"; cout << "<title>File Upload in CGI</title>\n"; cout << "</head>\n"; cout << "<body>\n";

// get list of files to be uploaded

const_file_iterator file = cgi.getFile("userfile"); if(file != cgi.getFiles().end()) { // send data type at cout. cout << HTTPContentHeader(file->getDataType()); // write content at cout.

file->writeToStream(cout);
```

```
}
cout << "<File uploaded successfully>\n"; cout << "</body>\n"; cout << "</html>\n";
return 0;
}
```

The above example is for writing content at **cout** stream but you can open your file stream and save the content of uploaded file in a file at desired location.

Conclusion: The Future of C++ Web Programming in 2025 and Beyond

As we look ahead to 2025 and beyond, C++ web programming has evolved into a mature and viable option for building high-performance, scalable, and secure web applications. While traditionally not the first choice for web development, C++ has carved out a niche in areas where performance, resource control, and integration with existing systems are critical. This conclusion will summarize the key points discussed in this guide, reflect on the current state of C++ web programming, and explore the future trends and opportunities that lie ahead.

The Evolution of C++ in Web Development

C++ has come a long way since its inception in the 1980s. Originally designed for system programming and performance-critical applications, it has gradually expanded into domains like game development, embedded systems, and, more recently, web development. The rise of modern web frameworks, libraries, and tools has made C++ a compelling choice for developers who need to build high-performance web applications.

By 2025, the C++ ecosystem for web development has matured significantly. Frameworks like Crow, Pistache, CppCMS, Wt, and Drogon have gained widespread adoption, offering developers the tools they need to build everything from simple REST APIs to complex, real-time web applications. Additionally, the introduction of modern C++ standards (C++17, C++20, and C++23) has made the language more expressive, safer, and easier to use, further driving its adoption in web development.

Why C++ is a Strong Contender for Web Programming

Performance and Efficiency

C++ is renowned for its performance, making it an ideal choice for web applications that require low latency and high throughput. Unlike interpreted languages like Python or JavaScript, C++ compiles directly to machine code, allowing developers to fine-tune their applications for maximum efficiency. This is particularly important for real-time systems, gaming backends, and financial platforms, where even milliseconds of latency can have a significant impact.

Fine-Grained Resource Control

One of C++'s greatest strengths is its ability to provide fine-grained control over system resources.

This is crucial for web applications that need to handle thousands of concurrent connections or operate in resource-constrained environments. By managing memory and system resources directly, developers can build lightweight and efficient web servers that outperform those written in higher-level languages.

Cross-Platform Compatibility

C++ is a cross-platform language, meaning web applications written in C++ can run on various operating systems, including Linux, Windows, and macOS, without significant modifications. This makes it an attractive option for developers who need to deploy their applications across multiple platforms.

Integration with Existing Systems

Many legacy systems and high-performance applications are written in C++. Using C++ for web programming allows seamless integration with these systems, reducing the need for complex middleware. This is particularly valuable in industries like finance, healthcare, and telecommunications, where legacy systems are still widely used.

Growing Ecosystem

By 2025, the C++ ecosystem for web development has expanded significantly. Developers now have access to a wide range of libraries, frameworks, and tools that simplify web application development. From HTTP servers and WebSocket libraries to database connectors and templating engines, the C++ ecosystem has everything developers need to build modern web applications.

Key Takeaways from C++ Web Programming in 2025

Modern Frameworks and Libraries

The availability of modern frameworks and libraries has been a game-changer for C++ web programming. Frameworks like Crow, Pistache, and Drogon provide developers with the tools they need to build high-performance web applications quickly and efficiently. These frameworks abstract away much of the complexity of web development, allowing developers to focus on building features rather than worrying about low-level details.

Asynchronous Programming

Asynchronous programming has become a cornerstone of modern web development, and C++ is no exception. Frameworks like Drogon provide built-in support for asynchronous I/O operations, enabling developers to build highly scalable and performant web applications. By leveraging asynchronous programming, developers can handle thousands of concurrent connections without blocking the main thread, resulting in faster response times and better resource utilization.

WebSockets and Real-Time Communication

Real-time communication is becoming increasingly important in web applications, and C++ is well-suited to meet this demand. Frameworks like Drogon and Pistache support WebSocket protocols, enabling developers to build real-time features like chat applications, live notifications, and multiplayer gaming backends. With its low latency and high performance, C++ is an ideal choice for real-time web applications.

Database Integration

Database integration is a critical aspect of web development, and C++ provides a variety of options for working with databases. Libraries like SQLite, MySQL++, and ODBC allow developers to connect to and interact with databases directly, while ORM (Object-Relational Mapping) libraries like ODB simplify database interactions by mapping database tables to C++ objects. This flexibility makes it easy to build data-driven web applications in C++.

Security

Security is a top priority in web development, and C++ web frameworks provide a range of features to help developers build secure applications. From authentication and authorization to encryption and input validation, C++ frameworks offer the tools developers need to protect their applications from common vulnerabilities like SQL injection and cross-site scripting (XSS). By following secure coding practices and leveraging these features, developers can build web applications that are both performant and secure.

Challenges and Best Practices

Challenges

Despite its many strengths, C++ web programming is not without its challenges. The language's complexity and lack of high-level abstractions can make web development more difficult compared to languages like Python or JavaScript. Additionally, debugging C++ web applications can be challenging due to low-level errors and memory issues. However, these challenges can be mitigated by following best practices and leveraging modern tools and frameworks.

Best Practices

To succeed in C++ web programming, developers should adhere to the following best practices:

Use Modern C++ Features: Take advantage of modern C++ standards (C++17, C++20, and C++23) to write clean, efficient, and maintainable code.

Leverage Existing Libraries and Frameworks: Use established libraries and frameworks to avoid reinventing the wheel and reduce development time.

Follow Secure Coding Practices: Validate user input, use encryption, and follow secure coding practices to protect your application from vulnerabilities.

Optimize Performance: Profile and benchmark your code to identify and address performance bottlenecks.

Adopt Asynchronous Programming: Use asynchronous programming techniques to build scalable and performant web applications.

Future Trends in C++ Web Programming

Increased Adoption of C++20/23 Features

By 2025, the adoption of C++20 and C++23 features will be widespread in web development. Features like modules, coroutines, and ranges will make C++ more expressive and easier to use, further driving its adoption in web development. For example, coroutines will simplify asynchronous programming, making it easier to write scalable and performant web applications.

Growth of Asynchronous Frameworks
Asynchronous web frameworks like Drogon will continue to gain popularity, enabling developers to build highly scalable and performant web applications. These frameworks will play a key role in meeting the growing demand for real-time communication and low-latency web applications.

Integration with AI and Machine Learning

C++ is a popular choice for AI and machine learning applications, and we can expect tighter integration between C++ web frameworks and AI libraries like TensorFlow and PyTorch. This will enable developers to build web applications that leverage AI and machine learning for tasks like natural language processing, image recognition, and predictive analytics.

Cloud-Native Development

C++ web applications will increasingly be designed for cloud-native environments, leveraging technologies like serverless computing and microservices. This will enable developers to build scalable, resilient, and cost-effective web applications that can run on cloud platforms like AWS, Azure, and Google Cloud.

Emphasis on Security

As cyber threats continue to evolve, security will remain a top priority in web development. C++ web frameworks will continue to enhance their security features, providing developers with the tools they need to build secure applications. Additionally, the adoption of secure coding practices and the use of encryption will become standard in C++ web development.

Final Thoughts

C++ web programming in 2025 represents a powerful and efficient way to build high-performance web applications. With its unparalleled performance, fine-grained resource control, and growing ecosystem, C++ is well-suited to meet the demands of modern web development. While challenges remain, the availability of modern frameworks, tools, and libraries has made C++ an attractive option for developers who need to build scalable, secure, and cross-platform web applications.

As we look to the future, the adoption of modern C++ standards, the growth of asynchronous frameworks, and the integration of AI and machine learning will continue to drive the evolution of C++ web programming. Whether you're building a real-time system, a gaming backend, or a financial platform, C++ is a language worth considering for your next web project.

In conclusion, C++ web programming in 2025 is not just a niche skill—it's a powerful tool that can help developers build the next generation of high-performance web applications. By embracing the strengths of C++ and staying ahead of emerging trends, developers can unlock new possibilities and create web applications that are faster, more efficient, and more secure than ever before.

9. Networking and Sockets

Introduction

Networking and socket programming are fundamental concepts in computer science, enabling communication between devices over a network. In C++, socket programming provides a powerful way to build networked applications, ranging from simple client-server models to complex distributed systems. This guide will cover the basics of networking and sockets in C++, including client-server architecture, HTTP and TCP/IP communication, and asynchronous programming. By the end of this guide, you will have a solid understanding of how to implement networked applications in C++.

1. Socket Programming Basics

1.1 What is a Socket?

A socket is an endpoint for communication between two machines over a network. It provides a mechanism for sending and receiving data across a network connection. Sockets can be thought of as a combination of an IP address and a port number, which together uniquely identify a communication channel.

1.2 Types of Sockets

There are several types of sockets, but the most commonly used are:

- **Stream Sockets (SOCK_STREAM)**: These sockets use the Transmission Control Protocol (TCP) for communication. They provide a reliable, connection-oriented communication channel where data is delivered in the same order it was sent.

- **Datagram Sockets (SOCK_DGRAM)**: These sockets use the User Datagram Protocol (UDP) for communication. They provide a connectionless, unreliable communication channel where data may arrive out of order or not at all.

- **Raw Sockets (SOCK_RAW)**: These sockets allow direct access to the underlying network protocols, enabling the creation of custom protocols or the manipulation of low-level network data.

1.3 Socket Address Structure

In C++, the sockaddr structure is used to represent a socket address. The most commonly used structure is sockaddr_in, which is specific to IPv4 addresses. It contains the following fields:

- **sin_family:** The address family (e.g., AF_INET for IPv4).

- **sin_port:** The port number in network byte order.

- **sin_addr:** The IP address in network byte order.

For IPv6 addresses, the sockaddr_in6 structure is used.

1.4 Creating a Socket

To create a socket in C++, you use the socket() function, which returns a socket descriptor. The function takes three arguments:

- **domain:** The communication domain (e.g., AF_INET for IPv4).

- **type:** The socket type (e.g., SOCK_STREAM for TCP).

- **protocol:** The protocol to be used (usually 0 for default).

```
#include <sys/types.h>

#include <sys/socket.h>

int sockfd = socket(AF_INET, SOCK_STREAM, 0);

if (sockfd < 0) {

    // Handle error

}
```

1.5 Binding a Socket

After creating a socket, you need to bind it to a specific address and port using the bind() function. This is typically done on the server side.

```
#include <netinet/in.h>

struct sockaddr_in server_addr;

server_addr.sin_family = AF_INET;

server_addr.sin_port = htons(8080);  // Port number

server_addr.sin_addr.s_addr = INADDR_ANY;  // Bind to any available interface

if (bind(sockfd, (struct sockaddr*)&server_addr, sizeof(server_addr)) < 0) {

    // Handle error

}
```

1.6 Listening for Connections

For a server to accept incoming connections, it must first listen on the socket using the listen() function. This function takes two arguments:

- **sockfd:** The socket descriptor.

- **backlog:** The maximum number of pending connections.

```
if (listen(sockfd, 5) < 0) {

    // Handle error

}
```

1.7 Accepting Connections

Once the server is listening, it can accept incoming connections using the accept() function. This function blocks until a client connects and returns a new socket descriptor for the connection.

```
struct sockaddr_in client_addr;

socklen_t client_len = sizeof(client_addr);

int client_sockfd = accept(sockfd, (struct sockaddr*)&client_addr, &client_len);

if (client_sockfd < 0) {

    // Handle error

}
```

1.8 Connecting to a Server

On the client side, you can connect to a server using the connect() function. This function takes the socket descriptor and the server's address as arguments.

```
struct sockaddr_in server_addr;

server_addr.sin_family = AF_INET;

server_addr.sin_port = htons(8080);

inet_pton(AF_INET, "127.0.0.1", &server_addr.sin_addr);

if (connect(sockfd, (struct sockaddr*)&server_addr, sizeof(server_addr)) < 0) {

    // Handle error
```

```
}
```

1.9 Sending and Receiving Data

Once a connection is established, you can send and receive data using the send() and recv() functions.

```
char buffer[1024];

ssize_t bytes_sent = send(client_sockfd, buffer, sizeof(buffer), 0);

if (bytes_sent < 0) {

    // Handle error

}

ssize_t bytes_received = recv(client_sockfd, buffer, sizeof(buffer), 0);

if (bytes_received < 0) {

    // Handle error

}
```

1.10 Closing a Socket

When you're done with a socket, you should close it using the close() function.

```
close(sockfd);
```

2. Client-Server Architecture

2.1 Overview

The client-server architecture is a model where one machine (the server) provides services to other machines (clients). The server listens for incoming connections, processes requests, and sends responses back to the clients.

2.2 Server-Side Implementation

A typical server-side implementation involves the following steps:

1. Create a socket.

2. Bind the socket to an address and port.

3. Listen for incoming connections.

4. Accept a connection.

5. Communicate with the client.

6. Close the connection.

2.3 Client-Side Implementation

A typical client-side implementation involves the following steps:

1. Create a socket.

2. Connect to the server.

3. Communicate with the server.

4. Close the connection.

2.4 Example: Echo Server and Client

Let's implement a simple echo server and client in C++. The echo server receives data from the client and sends it back.

Server Code

```cpp
#include <iostream>

#include <cstring>

#include <unistd.h>

#include <arpa/inet.h>

int main() {

    int sockfd = socket(AF_INET, SOCK_STREAM, 0);

    if (sockfd < 0) {

        std::cerr << "Error creating socket" << std::endl;

        return 1;

    }

    struct sockaddr_in server_addr;

    server_addr.sin_family = AF_INET;
```

```cpp
server_addr.sin_port = htons(8080);

server_addr.sin_addr.s_addr = INADDR_ANY;

if (bind(sockfd, (struct sockaddr*)&server_addr, sizeof(server_addr)) < 0) {

    std::cerr << "Error binding socket" << std::endl;

    return 1;

}

if (listen(sockfd, 5) < 0) {

    std::cerr << "Error listening on socket" << std::endl;

    return 1;

}

std::cout << "Server listening on port 8080..." << std::endl;

struct sockaddr_in client_addr;

socklen_t client_len = sizeof(client_addr);

int client_sockfd = accept(sockfd, (struct sockaddr*)&client_addr, &client_len);

if (client_sockfd < 0) {

    std::cerr << "Error accepting connection" << std::endl;

    return 1;

}

char buffer[1024];

ssize_t bytes_received = recv(client_sockfd, buffer, sizeof(buffer), 0);

if (bytes_received < 0) {

    std::cerr << "Error receiving data" << std::endl;

    return 1;

}

buffer[bytes_received] = '\0';
```

```cpp
        std::cout << "Received: " << buffer << std::endl;
        ssize_t bytes_sent = send(client_sockfd, buffer, bytes_received, 0);
        if (bytes_sent < 0) {
            std::cerr << "Error sending data" << std::endl;
            return 1;
        }
        close(client_sockfd);
        close(sockfd);
        return 0;
}
```

Client Code

```cpp
#include <iostream>
#include <cstring>
#include <unistd.h>
#include <arpa/inet.h>
int main() {
    int sockfd = socket(AF_INET, SOCK_STREAM, 0);
    if (sockfd < 0) {
        std::cerr << "Error creating socket" << std::endl;
        return 1;
    }
    struct sockaddr_in server_addr;
    server_addr.sin_family = AF_INET;
    server_addr.sin_port = htons(8080);
    inet_pton(AF_INET, "127.0.0.1", &server_addr.sin_addr);
```

```cpp
    if (connect(sockfd, (struct sockaddr*)&server_addr, sizeof(server_addr)) < 0) {

        std::cerr << "Error connecting to server" << std::endl;

        return 1;

    }

    const char* message = "Hello, Server!";

    ssize_t bytes_sent = send(sockfd, message, strlen(message), 0);

    if (bytes_sent < 0) {

        std::cerr << "Error sending data" << std::endl;

        return 1;

    }

    char buffer[1024];

    ssize_t bytes_received = recv(sockfd, buffer, sizeof(buffer), 0);

    if (bytes_received < 0) {

        std::cerr << "Error receiving data" << std::endl;

        return 1;

    }

    buffer[bytes_received] = '\0';

    std::cout << "Received: " << buffer << std::endl;

    close(sockfd);

    return 0;

}
```

3. HTTP and TCP/IP Communication

3.1 Overview

HTTP (Hypertext Transfer Protocol) is an application-layer protocol used for transmitting hypermedia documents, such as HTML. It is built on top of TCP/IP, which provides reliable, connection-oriented communication.

3.2 HTTP Request and Response

An HTTP transaction consists of a request from the client and a response from the server. The request includes a method (e.g., GET, POST), a URI, and headers. The response includes a status code, headers, and the response body.

3.3 Implementing an HTTP Server in C++

To implement a simple HTTP server in C++, you need to:

1. Create a TCP socket.

2. Bind the socket to a port (e.g., 80 for HTTP).

3. Listen for incoming connections.

4. Accept a connection.

5. Parse the HTTP request.

6. Generate an HTTP response.

7. Send the response back to the client.

8. Close the connection.

3.4 Example: Simple HTTP Server

```cpp
#include <iostream>

#include <cstring>

#include <unistd.h>

#include <arpa/inet.h>

int main() {

  int sockfd = socket(AF_INET, SOCK_STREAM, 0);

  if (sockfd < 0) {

    std::cerr << "Error creating socket" << std::endl;

    return 1;

  }
```

```cpp
    struct sockaddr_in server_addr;
    server_addr.sin_family = AF_INET;
    server_addr.sin_port = htons(80);
    server_addr.sin_addr.s_addr = INADDR_ANY;
    if (bind(sockfd, (struct sockaddr*)&server_addr, sizeof(server_addr)) < 0) {
        std::cerr << "Error binding socket" << std::endl;
        return 1;
    }
    if (listen(sockfd, 5) < 0) {
        std::cerr << "Error listening on socket" << std::endl;
        return 1;
    }
    std::cout << "HTTP server listening on port 80..." << std::endl;
    while (true) {
        struct sockaddr_in client_addr;
        socklen_t client_len = sizeof(client_addr);
        int client_sockfd = accept(sockfd, (struct sockaddr*)&client_addr, &client_len);
        if (client_sockfd < 0) {
            std::cerr << "Error accepting connection" << std::endl;
            continue;
        }
        char buffer[1024];
        ssize_t bytes_received = recv(client_sockfd, buffer, sizeof(buffer), 0);
        if (bytes_received < 0) {
            std::cerr << "Error receiving data" << std::endl;
```

```cpp
        close(client_sockfd);

        continue;

    }

    buffer[bytes_received] = '\0';

    std::cout << "Received HTTP request:\n" << buffer << std::endl;

    const char* response = "HTTP/1.1 200 OK\r\nContent-Type: text/plain\r\n\r\nHello, World!";

    ssize_t bytes_sent = send(client_sockfd, response, strlen(response), 0);

    if (bytes_sent < 0) {

        std::cerr << "Error sending data" << std::endl;

    }

    close(client_sockfd);

    }

    close(sockfd);

    return 0;

}
```

3.5 Implementing an HTTP Client in C++

To implement a simple HTTP client in C++, you need to:

1. Create a TCP socket.

2. Connect to the server.

3. Send an HTTP request.

4. Receive the HTTP response.

5. Close the connection.

3.6 Example: Simple HTTP Client

```cpp
#include <iostream>
```

```cpp
#include <cstring>
#include <unistd.h>
#include <arpa/inet.h>
int main() {
    int sockfd = socket(AF_INET, SOCK_STREAM, 0);
    if (sockfd < 0) {
        std::cerr << "Error creating socket" << std::endl;
        return 1;
    }
    struct sockaddr_in server_addr;
    server_addr.sin_family = AF_INET;
    server_addr.sin_port = htons(80);
    inet_pton(AF_INET, "127.0.0.1", &server_addr.sin_addr);
    if (connect(sockfd, (struct sockaddr*)&server_addr, sizeof(server_addr)) < 0) {
        std::cerr << "Error connecting to server" << std::endl;
        return 1;
    }
    const char* request = "GET / HTTP/1.1\r\nHost: localhost\r\n\r\n";
    ssize_t bytes_sent = send(sockfd, request, strlen(request), 0);
    if (bytes_sent < 0) {
        std::cerr << "Error sending data" << std::endl;
        return 1;
    }
    char buffer[1024];
    ssize_t bytes_received = recv(sockfd, buffer, sizeof(buffer), 0);
```

```cpp
    if (bytes_received < 0) {

        std::cerr << "Error receiving data" << std::endl;

        return 1;

    }

    buffer[bytes_received] = '\0';

    std::cout << "Received HTTP response:\n" << buffer << std::endl;

    close(sockfd);

    return 0;

}
```

4. Asynchronous Programming

4.1 Overview

Asynchronous programming allows a program to perform multiple tasks concurrently without blocking the execution of other tasks. In the context of networking, asynchronous programming is essential for handling multiple connections simultaneously, such as in a web server.

4.2 Asynchronous I/O in C++

C++ provides several mechanisms for asynchronous programming, including:

- **Threads**: Using the std::thread class to create and manage threads.

- **Futures and Promises**: Using std::future and std::promise to handle asynchronous results.

- **Asynchronous I/O Libraries**: Using libraries like Boost.Asio or the C++20 std::net (proposed) for asynchronous networking.

4.3 Example: Asynchronous TCP Server using Boost.Asio

Boost.Asio is a popular C++ library for asynchronous I/O, including networking. Here's an example of an asynchronous TCP server using Boost.Asio:

```cpp
#include <iostream>

#include <boost/asio.hpp>

using boost::asio::ip::tcp;
```

```cpp
class Session : public std::enable_shared_from_this<Session> {
public:
  Session(tcp::socket socket) : socket_(std::move(socket)) {}
  void start() {
    do_read();
  }
private:
  void do_read() {
    auto self(shared_from_this());
    socket_.async_read_some(boost::asio::buffer(data_, max_length),
      [this, self](boost::system::error_code ec, std::size_t length) {
        if (!ec) {
          do_write(length);
        }
      });
  }
  void do_write(std::size_t length) {
    auto self(shared_from_this());
    boost::asio::async_write(socket_, boost::asio::buffer(data_, length),
      [this, self](boost::system::error_code ec, std::size_t /*length*/) {
        if (!ec) {
          do_read();
        }
      });
  }
```

```cpp
    tcp::socket socket_;
    enum { max_length = 1024 };
    char data_[max_length];
};
class Server {
public:
    Server(boost::asio::io_context& io_context, short port)
        : acceptor_(io_context, tcp::endpoint(tcp::v4(), port)) {
        do_accept();
    }
private:
    void do_accept() {
        acceptor_.async_accept(
            [this](boost::system::error_code ec, tcp::socket socket) {
                if (!ec) {
                    std::make_shared<Session>(std::move(socket))->start();
                }
                do_accept();
            });
    }
    tcp::acceptor acceptor_;
};
int main(int argc, char* argv[]) {
    try {
        if (argc != 2) {
```

```cpp
        std::cerr << "Usage: async_tcp_server <port>\n";

        return 1;

    }

    boost::asio::io_context io_context;

    Server server(io_context, std::atoi(argv[1]));

    io_context.run();

} catch (std::exception& e) {

    std::cerr << "Exception: " << e.what() << "\n";

}

return 0;

}
```

4.4 Example: Asynchronous HTTP Client using Boost.Asio

Here's an example of an asynchronous HTTP client using Boost.Asio:

```cpp
#include <iostream>

#include <boost/asio.hpp>

#include <boost/beast.hpp>

namespace beast = boost::beast;

namespace http = beast::http;

namespace net = boost::asio;

using tcp = net::ip::tcp;

void perform_request(net::io_context& io_context, const std::string& host, const std::string& port)
{

    tcp::resolver resolver(io_context);

    beast::tcp_stream stream(io_context);

    auto const results = resolver.resolve(host, port);

    stream.connect(results);
```

```cpp
    http::request<http::string_body> req{http::verb::get, "/", 11};
    req.set(http::field::host, host);
    req.set(http::field::user_agent, "Boost.Beast");
    http::write(stream, req);
    beast::flat_buffer buffer;
    http::response<http::dynamic_body> res;
    http::read(stream, buffer, res);
    std::cout << res << std::endl;
    beast::error_code ec;
    stream.socket().shutdown(tcp::socket::shutdown_both, ec);
}
int main(int argc, char* argv[]) {
    try {
        if (argc != 3) {
            std::cerr << "Usage: async_http_client <host> <port>\n";
            return 1;
        }
        net::io_context io_context;
        perform_request(io_context, argv[1], argv[2]);
        io_context.run();
    } catch (std::exception& e) {
        std::cerr << "Exception: " << e.what() << "\n";
    }
    return 0;
```

}

Let's begin,

In this chapter, readers will delve into the critical role that network protocols play in enabling seamless communication between devices. By exploring the structure and function of models such as the OSI and TCP/IP, the chapter emphasizes how these protocols govern data exchange across networks. It examines commonly used internet protocols such as HTTP, FTP, and DNS, providing a comprehensive view of their purposes and applications. Additionally, the chapter addresses challenges in protocol implementation, preparing readers for potential issues they might encounter in practical scenarios.

Concept of Network Protocols

The concept of network protocols holds a foundational place in the domain of computer networking. Network protocols dictate the rules and conventions for communication between network devices, ensuring the reliable transmission and reception of data across diverse types of networks. These protocols are akin to languages spoken by computers, allowing them to establish clear and structured communication pathways.

In networking, understanding protocols requires recognizing their pivotal role in harmonizing data exchange processes. Each protocol is specifically designed to perform a distinct function within the network, addressing different aspects of communication such as synchronization, error handling, data packetization, and routing. The specifications of a protocol incorporate a comprehensive set of rules that include syntax, semantics, and timing. Syntax refers to the structure or format of the data, semantics pertains to the meaning of each section of bits, and timing coincides with the coordination of data transmission.

The diversity of network protocols opens up several layers of communication, which can be visualized through structured models such as the OSI and TCP/IP. These models compartmentalize network functions to provide a framework for protocol standardization and interoperability. Despite their layered approaches, the models share the objective of enhancing network communication efficiency and robustness.

Within the operational context, network protocols can be broadly classified into several key categories:

Communication Protocols: These protocols establish the procedures for the transmission of data between network devices. Examples include Transmission Control Protocol (TCP) and User Datagram Protocol (UDP).

Their main function is ensuring that data packets are sent and received reliably.

Routing Protocols: These ensure the proper routing of data across networks, providing pathways for packet delivery. Protocols like Border Gateway Protocol (BGP) and Open Shortest Path First

(OSPF) fall under this category.

Management Protocols: Such protocols are used to manage network devices and troubleshoot network issues.

Simple Network Management Protocol (SNMP) is a common example.

Security Protocols: These protocols ensure the authentication and authorization of users and data encryption. Protocols like Secure Sockets Layer (SSL) and Transport Layer Security (TLS) are typical instances.

Each protocol brings its own set of capabilities that contribute to the efficient function of networks. For instance, TCP provides a reliable, connection-oriented service that sees to the successful delivery of data, with error detection and correction, as well as source and destination node acknowledgment before communication ensues. The simplicity and efficiency of UDP, allowing data to be sent without prior communications to set up special transmission channels or data paths, make it suitable for applications that require time-sensitive data such as streaming.

To further appreciate the importance of network protocols, one could consider a practical coding example illustrating a rudimentary implementation of a TCP client-server communication model. This scenario encapsulates the initiation, data exchange, and termination of a connection between a client and a server.

```python
# Python program for a simple TCP client

import socket
def tcp_client():    host
= '127.0.0.1'    port =
65432

    # Create a TCP/IP socket    with socket.socket(socket.AF_INET,
socket.SOCK_STREAM) as s:

        # Connect to the server        s.connect((host,
port))

        # Send data        message =
"Hello, Server"
        s.sendall(message.encode())

        # Receive response        data
= s.recv(1024)

    print('Received', data.decode())
if __name__ ==
'__main__':    tcp_client()
```

The client script establishes a connection to a TCP server specified by an IP address and port number. After setting up the connection, it demonstrates message delivery with 's.sendall()' and receives the server's reply using 's.recv()', thus completing the basic exchange cycle.

Protocols serve as blueprints for building interoperable networked environments. They enable hardware and software from various vendors to interact, fostering greater innovation in network technologies. The adherence to standard protocols ensures devices can communicate with minimal configuration, promoting a seamless user experience. This aspect is crucial in environments where equipment from multiple sources coexists.

Network protocols also address data congestion through mechanisms that regulate traffic flow. Flow control meticulously manages the rate of data transmission between sender and receiver, ensuring receivers are not overwhelmed by a data influx. Protocols such as TCP employ flow control through windowing techniques to manage buffer resources effectively.

Error detection and correction are integral to network protocols. They employ mechanisms like checksums, cyclic redundancy checks (CRC), and acknowledgments to maintain data integrity. These mechanisms detect corrupted packets and facilitate their retransmission, ascertaining that data arrives at its destination correctly.

Delving further into protocol analysis, it becomes apparent that network security protocols play an essential role in safeguarding communications. Consider the employment of TLS in securing web transactions:

```
# Python code for a simple SSL-enabled server

 import ssl
import socket
def ssl_server():
   context = ssl.create_default_context(ssl.Purpose.CLIENT_AUTH)
context.load_cert_chain(certfile="server.pem", keyfile="server.key")

   bindsocket = socket.socket()    bindsocket.bind(('127.0.0.1',
10023))    bindsocket.listen(5)
    while True:
      newsocket, fromaddr = bindsocket.accept()      conn =
context.wrap_socket(newsocket, server_side=True)      try:
        data = conn.recv(1024)
if data:
         conn.sendall(b"Hello, SSL Client")      finally:
        conn.close()
if __name__ ==
'__main__':    ssl_server()
```

The server utilizes SSL to create a secure connection channel with the client, providing confidentiality and integrity to data transmitted over insecure channels. This level of protection is vital in modern-day applications where data privacy is paramount.

The continuous evolution of networking protocols reflects the adaptability of the technology to meet emerging requirements. From the simple data exchanges of the ARPANET era to today's complex, high-speed internet, protocols have evolved to manage increased traffic loads, more sophisticated attacks, and the unprecedented demand for real-time data processing. This evolution prompts continuous updates in established protocols and the introduction of new ones to address specific challenges.

In summary, the knowledge of network protocols empowers network administrators, engineers, and developers to architect reliable, secure, and efficient communication systems. These protocols encompass the entire spectrum of networking needs, from the fundamental handshakes that establish communication to the sophisticated encryptions that protect it. Understanding their mechanisms and applications allows for a deeper appreciation of the intricacies involved in the interconnectivity of modern devices and systems.

The OSI Model

The Open Systems Interconnection (OSI) model, established by the International Organization for Standardization (ISO), is a conceptual framework that standardizes the functions of a telecommunication or computing system into seven abstract layers. Each layer serves a specific role and communicates with directly adjacent layers to facilitate modular network architecture. Understanding the OSI model is essential for network designers and engineers to diagnose network issues and apply network protocols effectively. The OSI model consists of the following seven layers:

Physical Layer: This layer is the first and lowest layer in the OSI model. It deals with the physical connection between devices and the transmission and reception of raw bit streams over a physical medium. It defines the electrical, optical, and mechanical characteristics of the network's hardware interfaces. Examples of standards at this layer include Ethernet, USB, and RS-232.

Data Link Layer: This layer provides node-to-node data transfer and error correction through mechanisms like checksums and frame synchronization. It is divided into two sublayers: the Logical Link Control (LLC) sublayer that manages Frame Synchronization, error checking, and flow control, and the Media Access Control (MAC) sublayer that determines permission to access the transmission medium. Protocols such as Ethernet for LANs and PPP for point-to-point connections operate at this level.

Network Layer: The primary responsibility of this layer is routing—deciding the physical or logical paths for data transmission from source to destination across multiple networks. It handles packet forwarding, including routing through intermediary routers. The Internet Protocol (IP) is the principal protocol used at this layer, ensuring data packets are transferred across networks.

Transport Layer: Providing end-to-end communication service for applications, the transport layer deals with error recovery, flow control, and ensures complete data transfer. It can provide a reliable connection-oriented service like TCP or a connectionless service like UDP. Error detection and correction, as well as data segmentation and reassembly, are key processes performed by the transport layer.

Session Layer: This layer establishes, manages, and terminates sessions between two communicating hosts. It controls the dialogues (connections) between computers, managing data exchange and providing checkpoint and recovery measures whenever needed. Protocols like RPC and SQL are associated with this layer.

Presentation Layer: Often called the syntax layer, it translates data between the application layer and the network format. It is responsible for data encryption, decryption, compression, and decompression, ensuring the data sent by the application layer of one system is readable by the application layer of another. Encryption protocols like SSL operate within this layer.

Application Layer: The topmost layer of the OSI model deals with the interaction between software applications and lower network services. This layer supports network access, data integrity, and additional security features. Protocols like HTTP, FTP, SMTP, and DNS reside at this layer, serving end-user applications and facilitating data exchange between computers.

The OSI model facilitates an understanding of the complex interactions involved in network communication by separating them into more manageable and distinct functions. Such abstraction allows for the interchangeability and interoperability among products from different manufacturers, as each component only needs to adhere to specific standards relevant to its layer.

To illustrate the practical application of OSI layers in a network communication scenario, consider a simple implementation of a TCP communication that engages multiple layers of the OSI model. This hypothetical example emphasizes the encapsulation process as data moves downward from the application layer to the physical layer, across the network, then back up to the application layer on the receiving end.

Application Layer: The user's action - requesting a web page through a browser initiates communication at this level.

Presentation Layer: If data encryption is required, SSL/TLS encrypts the HTTP request.

Session Layer: The application opens a session for HTTP communication, allowing multiple request/response transactions.

Transport Layer: TCP segments the data and attaches header information for error detection and flow control, establishing a connection-oriented service.

Network Layer: Each segment from TCP is encapsulated into packets, adding IP-specific routing and addressing information.

Data Link Layer: The packets are framed with MAC addresses and prepared for transmission over the physical network.

Physical Layer: The actual binary data is transmitted over physical media using electrical signals, cables, or wireless technologies.

For a further understanding, a Python example simulating a TCP Echo Server can demonstrate how transport-level protocols (such as those implemented through socket programming) manage data transmission reliability and connectivity in accordance with OSI model layers:

```
# Python program simulating a simple TCP Echo Server import socket

 def tcp_echo_server():
host = '127.0.0.1'    port
= 65432

    # Create a TCP/IP socket    with socket.socket(socket.AF_INET,
socket.SOCK_STREAM) as server_socket:
        # Bind the socket to the address        server_socket.bind((host,
port))

        # Enable the server to accept connections, backlog queue size is 5
server_socket.listen(5)
        print("Server listening on", (host, port))

        # Wait for client connection        while
True:
            client_socket, address = server_socket.accept()          with
client_socket:
            print("Connected by", address)
while True:
            data = client_socket.recv(1024)
if not data:                break
            client_socket.sendall(data)
 if __name__ ==
'__main__':
tcp_echo_server()
```

In the example above, the server provides an endpoint for a client through the transport layer, handling the encapsulation of messages through TCP for reliable data transfer. The server indefinitely listens for incoming connections and, upon connection, echoes back any data received from the client. At each layer in the OSI model, data undergoes processing steps that wrap it with necessary control information, enabling reliable, scalable communication.

The OSI model is pivotal in modern network architecture, not only used for theoretical understanding but also as a reference during the troubleshooting of network issues. By providing specific roles for varying communication functions, the OSI model simplifies diagnosing process failures. For instance, a problem in inter-networking could be isolated to the network layer, whereas a data encryption issue could point to the presentation layer.

Understanding the OSI model extends beyond simply grasping the responsibilities of each layer. It involves an appreciation of how these layers interdependently operate to ensure the smooth transfer of data, from source to destination, across complex network infrastructures. With evolving technologies and new communication demands, the principles of the OSI model remain a foundational guide for developing effective and efficient communication systems.

TCP/IP Model and Protocols

The TCP/IP model, also known as the Internet Protocol Suite, is a set of communication protocols that dictate how data should be packaged, transmitted, routed, and received in a network environment. It forms the core architecture of the Internet and many local networks. Unlike the OSI model with its seven layers, the TCP/IP model comprises four layers, each contributing to the seamless transfer of data across heterogeneous systems and networks. These layers are the Link layer, Internet layer, Transport layer, and Application layer.

Link Layer: The Link layer, equivalent to a combination of the OSI's Data Link and Physical layers, handles the intricacies of hardware addressing and the physical transmission of data within the same network. It encompasses protocols and hardware standards that facilitate communication over the network's physical media. Protocols like Ethernet, Wi-Fi (IEEE 802.11), and Point-to-Point Protocol (PPP) are integral to this layer, ensuring that data packets are properly formatted for transmission over the defined medium.

Internet Layer: Operating independently of the underlying network infrastructure, the Internet layer's primary function is to control the routing of packets across different networks, essentially acting as the navigational component that interconnects vast arrays of networks into a cohesive whole known as the internet. The Internet Protocol (IP) serves as a cornerstone at this layer, tasked with addressing and forwarding packets without establishing end-to-end connections. IP operates in two versions: IPv4 and IPv6. The availability of IPv6 addresses the limitations of IPv4 in terms of address scarcity and enhanced routing performance. Other protocols in this layer include the Internet Control Message Protocol (ICMP) for diagnostics and error reporting, and the Address Resolution Protocol (ARP) which facilitates IP addressing within local networks.

Transport Layer: Comparable to the Transport layer in the OSI model, it ensures the reliable delivery of messages across networks. Transport layer protocols standardize communication endpoints called ports, distinguishing multiple applications hosted on a single device. Transmission Control Protocol (TCP) and User Datagram Protocol (UDP) are the primary protocols. TCP offers a reliable, connection-oriented delivery mechanism, using methods like three-way handshakes, acknowledgments, and retransmissions for dependable packet delivery. Conversely, UDP provides a connectionless service suitable for applications where speed outweighs reliability, such as video streaming.

Application Layer: This topmost layer amalgamates functionalities of the OSI's Session, Presentation, and Application layers, addressing interaction with software applications involved in communication processes. Protocols operating at this layer include HTTP for web traffic, FTP for file transfers, SMTP for sending emails, and DNS for resolving domain names to IP addresses. Its vast array of protocols enables diverse applications to operate over the network seamlessly, ensuring data is presented correctly to the end-user.

Examining Key Protocols

Transmission Control Protocol (TCP): TCP ensures secure connections and reliable data transfer between devices. By implementing flow control, error detection, and correction, TCP maintains data integrity and delivery accuracy.

Simple illustration of a TCP client using Python

```python
import socket
def tcp_client():
    server_address = ('localhost', 8080)
    client_socket = socket.socket(socket.AF_INET, socket.SOCK_STREAM)
client_socket.connect(server_address)
    try:
        message = 'Hello, TCP Server!'
client_socket.sendall(message.encode())          response =
client_socket.recv(1024)          print('Received:',
response.decode())
    finally:
        client_socket.close()
    if __name__ == "__main__":
tcp_client()
```

This Python code demonstrates a simple TCP client connecting to a server, sending and receiving data while utilizing TCP's promise of reliable communication through established connections and acknowledgments.

User Datagram Protocol (UDP): UDP is optimized for lower overhead communication where speed is prioritized over reliability. It does not require establishing or maintaining a connection, suitable for real-time applications like online gaming or VoIP.

Simple illustration of a UDP sender using Python

```python
import socket
def udp_sender():
    server_address = ('localhost', 6789)
    udp_socket = socket.socket(socket.AF_INET, socket.SOCK_DGRAM)
    try:
        message = 'Hello, UDP Server!'
        udp_socket.sendto(message.encode(), server_address)
print('Message sent to', server_address)
    finally:
        udp_socket.close()
```

```python
if __name__ == "__main__":
udp_sender()
```

This demonstrates sending a simple message to a server using UDP, showcasing the speed and simplicity of connectionless communication.

Internet Protocol (IP): IP provides navigational assistance across networks, managing addresses and data packet routing, essential for internet communication. Its two versions, IPv4 and IPv6, differ primarily in the address length, with IPv6 offering a larger address space necessary for modern network demands.

Contrast and Integration with the OSI Model While the OSI model provides a comprehensive theoretical foundation for network communications, the TCP/IP model is practical and tailored to the designs and implementations used for internet technologies. The TCP/IP model's layers are less abstract, detailing specific protocol suites utilized in everyday networking tasks. Understanding the relationships between OSI and TCP/IP facilitates seamless troubleshooting and network analysis, with each offering separate insights into how data traverses networked systems.

The TCP/IP model substantially informs the design of network infrastructure, hosting modern, distributed applications by linking computing domains, enabling expansive connectivity, and supporting scalable architectures. Through its well-defined layers, network designers leverage TCP/IP for efficient and extensible systems, accommodating diverse protocols and legacy systems under a single, cohesive framework.

Implementing TCP/IP Protocols Consider a simplified client-server interaction where both TCP and UDP are implemented to understand their contrast in operation.

TCP vs. UDP Server Implementation:

```python
# Python code illustrating TCP vs. UDP server-side setup

import socket
def tcp_server():
    server_socket = socket.socket(socket.AF_INET, socket.SOCK_STREAM)
server_socket.bind(('localhost', 8090))        server_socket.listen()

    print('TCP server listening...')        while True:
        conn, addr = server_socket.accept()            with
conn:
            print('Connected by', addr)                while
True:
                data = conn.recv(1024)
if not data:                    break
            conn.sendall(data.upper())
    def udp_server():
        udp_socket = socket.socket(socket.AF_INET, socket.SOCK_DGRAM)
udp_socket.bind(('localhost', 8091))
```

```python
        print('UDP server ready...')          while
True:
            data, addr = udp_socket.recvfrom(1024)          print('Connection
from', addr)          udp_socket.sendto(data.upper(), addr)

    # Uncomment to run either server function
    # if __name__ == "__main__":
    #    tcp_server()
    #    udp_server()
```

The TCP server establishes a persistent connection, ensuring comprehensive data transmission integrity. In contrast, the UDP server offers immediate data transmission without the need for a connection handshake, focusing on efficiency and low-latency feedback.

The TCP/IP suite's famed versatility and robust application engagement ensure it remains the backbone of modern networking, incorporating key protocol developments and reflecting evolving technologies that ensure prompt, reliable data exchange across the vast expanse of the internet. By grasping its operational paradigms, professionals in the field are better equipped to design and maintain robust network systems tailored for diverse and dynamic environments.

Common Internet Protocols

In the landscape of digital communication, common internet protocols facilitate the robust exchange of data among devices over the vast network infrastructure known as the internet. These protocols help establish connections, transfer information, and maintain reliability and security across diverse network environments. Among these, Hypertext Transfer Protocol (HTTP), File Transfer Protocol (FTP), Simple Mail Transfer Protocol (SMTP), and Domain Name System (DNS) stand out due to their critical roles in web services, file transfers, email communication, and domain resolution, respectively.

Hypertext Transfer Protocol (HTTP) HTTP is a foundational protocol in the World Wide Web, employed for transferring hypertext documents between clients and servers. Operating primarily over TCP, HTTP dictates the transmission of data across the web, encapsulating requests and responses into comprehensible formats for seamless user interaction with web resources. It resides at the Application layer of the TCP/IP model and leverages methods such as GET, POST, PUT, DELETE, among others, to perform various operations on web resources.

HTTP Methods:

GET: Used to request data from a specified resource, usually without causing any state change on the server.

POST: Submits data to be processed to a specified resource, often resulting in state changes on the server.

PUT: Updates an existing resource or creates a new resource with provided data.
DELETE: Removes a specified resource.

The evolution of HTTP to HTTP/2 has introduced advancements such as multiplexing, header compression, and improved flow control, enhancing speed and efficiency. HTTP/3 is emerging with new transport mechanisms leveraging Quick UDP Internet Connections (QUIC).

A Python example of a simple HTTP client using the http.client module demonstrates basic HTTP operations:

Python HTTP client example using http.client

```
import http.client
  def fetch_website():
    connection = http.client.HTTPConnection("www.example.com")
connection.request("GET", "/")         response =
connection.getresponse()

    print("Status:", response.status)       print("Headers:",
response.getheaders())        print("Content:",
response.read().decode())
    if __name__ == "__main__":
fetch_website()
```

This script establishes a connection to www.example.com, sends a GET request, and prints the status, headers, and content of the response.

File Transfer Protocol (FTP) FTP is designed for the seamless transfer of files over the internet, providing mechanisms for uploading and downloading files between computers. Utilizing separate data and control channels, FTP offers command execution and data exchange independently, often under the transport secured connection. FTP clients can interact with servers using user credentials, allowing authenticated and anonymous access modes.

Active vs. Passive FTP:

Active Mode: The client opens a random port and communicates to the server's command port (21), providing the IP and port to which the server connects back to establish the data transfer.

Passive Mode: The server opens a random port and communicates that port to the client, allowing the client to initiate the data connection.

To highlight FTP operations, Python's ftplib library can demonstrate list retrieval and file download functionalities:

Python FTP client example using ftplib

```
from ftplib import FTP
```

```python
def download_file():
    ftp = FTP('ftp.example.com')          ftp.login()  #
Anonymous Login          ftp.cwd('some_directory')

    # List Files          files =
ftp.nlst()
    print("Files in directory:", files)

    # Download File          with open('downloaded_file.txt', 'wb') as
local_file:          ftp.retrbinary('RETR example.txt', local_file.write)

    ftp.quit()
if __name__ == "__main__":
download_file()
```

This example logs into an FTP server, lists files in a directory, and downloads a specified file.

Simple Mail Transfer Protocol (SMTP) SMTP is the de facto standard for email transmission across the internet, delineating the rules for sending, receiving, and routing email messages. SMTP typically operates over TCP. While SMTP is employed for sending emails, protocols like Post Office Protocol (POP3) and Internet Message Access Protocol (IMAP) are used for retrieving messages. SMTP uses commands like HELO, MAIL FROM, RCPT TO, DATA, and QUIT to coordinate message transactions between mail servers.

With the advent of security requirements, SMTP supports extensions like STARTTLS for encrypted mail transfer:

Python SMTP client example using smtplib

```python
    import smtplib
    def send_mail():
        smtp_server = 'smtp.example.com'
sender = 'example@example.com'
recipient = 'friend@example.com'
message = """\          Subject: Test Email

    This is a test email sent from Python."""
        with smtplib.SMTP(smtp_server, 587) as server:
server.starttls()  # Secure connection
server.login(sender, 'password')
server.sendmail(sender, recipient, message)
print("Email sent successfully")
    if __name__ == "__main__":
send_mail()
```

This script establishes an SMTP connection, encrypts it with TLS, and dispatches an email message.

Domain Name System (DNS) DNS translates human-readable domain names (e.g., www.example.com) into machine-understandable IP addresses required for locating and identifying computer services and devices with the underlying network protocols. Functionally analogous to a massive distributed database, DNS resolves queries through a hierarchy of name servers, including root, top-level domain (TLD), and authoritative name servers.

DNS records categorially include A, AAAA, CNAME, MX, TXT, and more, serving various resolving functions:

A Record: Maps a domain to an IPv4 address.
AAAA Record: Maps a domain to an IPv6 address.
CNAME Record: Maps an alias name to the canonical domain name.
MX Record: Directs email to mail servers for a domain.

The Python library socket provides methods to resolve DNS queries programmatically:

```python
# Python DNS query example using the socket library
import socket
    def resolve_domain(domain):
ip_address =
socket.gethostbyname(domain)
    print(f'The IP address of {domain} is {ip_address}')
    if __name__ == "__main__":
resolve_domain('www.example.com')
```

This example resolves a domain into its associated IP address via DNS lookup.

Analyzing Protocol Security and Evolution

Network protocol security encompasses strategies to protect data integrity and privacies, such as Transport Layer Security (TLS) and Secure Socket Layer (SSL), which adjoin secure extensions to protocols like HTTP (resulting in HTTPS) and SMTP. Security measures such as encryption, authentication, integrity, and non-repudiation underpin protocols to counter threats in data communication.

With the internet's continued growth, protocols have adapted to encompass performance enhancements, accommodating the exponential rise in network users and data consumption demands. Protocols mature with iterative refinements aimed at latency reduction, data compression, adaptive congestion control, and fortified security postures.

In the contemporary digital era, these internet protocols serve invaluable roles, seamlessly enabling communication and interaction on an unprecedented scale. They form the backbone of e-commerce, online services, cloud computing, and an ever-expanding array of internet-dependent functionalities. Mastery of these protocols empowers developers, network engineers, and IT professionals to optimize and secure the modern internet infrastructure, ensuring efficient and secure data exchanges.

Protocol Implementation Challenges

Implementing network protocols involves an intricate balance of software engineering, network programming, and system design to ensure efficient and performant communication across digital environments. Protocol implementation challenges arise from the diverse considerations needed to maintain compatibility, scalability, security, and reliability. As networks expand and evolve, addressing these challenges becomes pivotal for developers and engineers who aim to provide robust network solutions.

Compatibility and Interoperability

Ensuring that new and existing protocols can coexist and communicate effectively across a broad range of systems and devices is a primary challenge. Different systems may use heterogeneous hardware, operating environments, and software stacks, necessitating protocols that can adapt while maintaining compatibility. This challenge is often addressed through adherence to open standards and specifications that facilitate interoperability. Nevertheless, real world implementations may encounter deviations in protocol interpretation and execution, leading to network incompatibilities.

To alleviate such disparities, thorough testing using diverse test suites and environments is essential to verify adherence to protocol standards. Simulators and network emulators can play critical roles in modeling network conditions and identifying interoperability issues.

Security Threats and Vulnerabilities

Security remains one of the leading challenges in protocol implementation, primarily due to evolving threat landscapes and sophisticated cyberattacks targeting vulnerabilities. Implementing secure network protocols entails ensuring confidentiality, authentication, integrity, and non-repudiation.

Protocols must implement encryption mechanisms appropriately while balancing performance and security overheads. For example, introducing cryptographic handshakes, as in the Transport Layer Security (TLS), adds latency but provides significant security benefits. A practical challenge lies in designing protocols to minimize these performance impacts without compromising security features.

```python
# Example of TLS-encrypted communication in Python using ssl module

import socket import
ssl  def
secure_client():
    hostname = 'www.example.com'
context = ssl.create_default_context()
    with socket.create_connection((hostname, 443)) as sock:        with
context.wrap_socket(sock, server_hostname=hostname) as secure_sock:
secure_sock.sendall(b"GET / HTTP/1.1\r\nHost: www.example.com\r\n\r\n")
```

```
response = secure_sock.recv(4096)
print(response.decode('utf-8'))
 if __name__ ==
"__main__":
secure_client()
```

This example illustrates secure communication over TLS, integral to maintaining confidentiality and integrity for HTTP transactions.

Scalability

A protocol must handle increased loads without degradation in performance, which presents a significant implementation challenge. Scalability encompasses aspects such as breadth (handling more clients) and depth (handling complex transactions). As networks grow and extend, protocols must anticipate these changes to accommodate growth in user base, data volumes, and transaction complexities.

Implementing efficient data handling, load balancing mechanisms, and distributed systems are key strategies for scaling protocols. Network Load Balancers (NLBs) and Content Delivery Networks (CDNs) are examples of technologies that ameliorate scaling issues by distributing loads efficiently across multiple servers.

Latency and Throughput

The opposing needs to minimize latency and maximize throughput present a technical conundrum. While high throughput ensures large volumes of data transfer efficiently, low latency requirements demand minimal delay in transmission and reception of information. Protocol designers must craft algorithmic optimizations and network behaviors to balance these factors effectively.

TCP's congestion control mechanisms, such as Slow Start and Fast Retransmit, exemplify protocol features aimed at maintaining high throughput with acceptable latency. These components must be meticulously implemented and tested to ensure they adapt dynamically to network conditions.

Packet Loss and Error Handling

Protocols must remain resilient in the face of packet loss and transmission errors, ensuring data integrity and seamless user experiences. Implementing error detection and correction algorithms forms a cornerstone of reliable protocol design. Techniques such as checksums, cyclic redundancy checks (CRCs), and Automatic Repeat reQuest (ARQ) mechanisms are commonly employed to detect and correct errors.

UDP, despite its connectionless nature, often integrates with higher layer protocols to manage disorderly packets and data corruption, facilitating error handling without the extensive overhead of TCP.

```python
# Python code using UDP with basic acknowledgement to demonstrate error handling
import socket
 def udp_server_with_ack():
host = '127.0.0.1'     port =
65432
    udp_socket = socket.socket(socket.AF_INET, socket.SOCK_DGRAM)
udp_socket.bind((host, port))
    while True:
data, addr =
udp_socket.recvfr
om(1024)
        print(f"Received message from {addr}: {data.decode()}")

        # Send Acknowledgment         ack =
f"ACK for {data.decode()}"
udp_socket.sendto(ack.encode(), addr)
 if __name__ ==
"__main__":
udp_server_with_ack()
```

This example demonstrates UDP communication with a simple acknowledgment mechanism, offering an alternative to mitigate dropped packets.

Resource Constraints

Resource-limited environments, such as embedded systems and IoT devices, present another layer of difficulty in protocol implementation. These devices must communicate efficiently, often with limited memory, processing power, and energy resources. Protocols need to be optimized for low overhead while retaining core functionality, an area where lightweight protocols like MQTT and CoAP excel.

Designers must strategically trim resource-intensive features, emphasizing compressed message formats, streamlined operation sequences, and the use of lightweight encryption when necessary.

Network Topologies and Dynamics

Protocols must adapt to various network topologies and dynamic conditions, such as mobility and environmental changes. Mobile ad-hoc networks (MANETs) and vehicular networks introduce further challenges, as protocols must accommodate frequent topology changes and varying signal strengths.

Routing protocols like AODV (Ad hoc On-Demand Distance Vector Routing) have emerged to cater to such dynamics by providing self-starting, loop-free, and multihop routing for ad-hoc networks.

Socket Programming in C++

This topic provides an in-depth exploration of socket programming with C++, a fundamental aspect of network communication development. It begins by defining the concept of sockets and their critical role in creating networked applications. Through detailed, step-by-step guidance, readers learn how to create and manage sockets, including binding, listening, and accepting connections to facilitate client-server interactions. The chapter further covers essential techniques for sending and receiving data, alongside effective error handling practices, equipping readers with the skills to implement robust network applications using sockets.

What are Sockets

In computer science, a socket is a fundamental and binding interface for network communications that connects software applications over a network. Sockets play an essential role in enabling communication between different processes and systems, permitting them to exchange data efficiently through standardized interfaces. To understand sockets, one must grasp both their theoretical underpinning and practical applications.

The concept of a socket originated with the Berkeley Software Distribution (BSD) UNIX operating systems. A socket represents an endpoint for sending and receiving data across a computer network. In a Unix-like environment, it is treated like a file descriptor employed by programs to establish a communication channel to other processes, either locally on the same machine or on a remote system. This concept is extended in most other operating systems, making socket programming a universally applicable skill.

Sockets can be understood as an abstraction layer that separates the specifics of the physical network from the application layers, enabling developers to focus on higher-level concerns of data transmission without delving into the intricacies of the medium itself. Technically, a socket is defined by an IP address and a port number, forming a unique identifier for communications over Internet Protocol (IP)-based networks.

The types of sockets can broadly be categorized into several types, each catering to specific communication models and used semi-transparently to differentiate between various architectures:

Stream Sockets (SOCK_STREAM): These provide two-way, reliable, and sequenced communication channels that operate over Transmission Control Protocol (TCP). Stream sockets ensure data integrity and order, making them suitable for applications where delivery order and data integrity are paramount, such as HTTP, FTP, and SMTP. Due to TCP's connection-oriented nature, a socket connection must be established and maintained, which involves an overhead of managing connection states and handshakes.

Datagram Sockets (SOCK_DGRAM): These facilitate communication using User Datagram Protocol (UDP), enabling connectionless messaging where each message is an independent packet. Unlike stream sockets, datagram sockets do not guarantee order or reliability of messages, which can be advantageous for applications that require speed and efficiency over reliability, such as streaming services, online gaming, and VoIP.

Raw Sockets: These afford direct access to lower-layer protocols, allowing applications to manipulate headers for fields like IP. Raw sockets serve specialized purposes, such as testing new protocol implementations, network monitoring, or conducting security assessments.

Sequenced Packet Sockets (SOCK_SEQPACKET): Combining features from both SOCK_STREAM and SOCK_DGRAM, they provide a neutral ground offering reliable packet sequencing through a connection-oriented service.

The lifecycle of a socket entails a series of well-defined operations performed in sequence. Understanding this lifecycle is crucial for implementing socket-based communications correctly:

**Socket Creation: ** The initial step involves creating a socket using the |socket| system call, which requires defining the protocol family (usually AF_INET for IPv4 or AF_INET6 for IPv6), the socket type, and the protocol. For instance, creating a TCP stream socket in C++ for IPv4 might look like:

```
int socket_fd = socket(AF_INET, SOCK_STREAM, 0);
if (socket_fd < 0) {
perror("Error creating socket");     }
```

**Binding: ** Associating a socket with a specific port and IP address on the local machine is achieved through the |bind| call. This process assigns a specific communication endpoint to the socket within the local network interface, making it recognizable when data arrives.

```
struct sockaddr_in server_address;    server_address.sin_family =
AF_INET;    server_address.sin_port = htons(8080);
server_address.sin_addr.s_addr = INADDR_ANY;

if (bind(socket_fd, (struct sockaddr*)&server_address, sizeof(server_address)) < 0) {
perror("Binding failed");     }
```

**Listening: ** Primarily relevant for server-side applications, the socket is set to accept incoming connections. The |listen| function sets the maximum number of queued connections:

```
if (listen(socket_fd, 5) < 0) {
perror("Error on listen");     }
```

**Accepting Connections: ** Specifically for server implementations, a socket is instantiated for each client connection, created as a result of the |accept| system call. This provides a dedicated communication channel:

```
int client_socket = accept(socket_fd, (struct sockaddr*)&client_address, &client_length);    if
(client_socket < 0) {        perror("Accept failed");     }
```

Data Transmission: The core function where data packets are sent and received via established sockets, using |send| and |recv|:

```
int n = send(client_socket, buffer, sizeof(buffer), 0);    if (n < 0) {
perror("Error sending data");
    }
n = recv(client_socket, buffer, sizeof(buffer), 0);    if (n < 0) {
perror("Error receiving data");    }
```

**Termination: ** The socket is closed once communication is complete, freeing resources:

```
close(socket_fd);
close(client_socket);
```

Sockets also incorporate a set of parameters that dictate their behavior during communications, such as socket options that can be configured using the |setsockopt| function, including options like TCP_NODELAY, SO_REUSEADDR, and SO_LINGER. These options alter how data is buffered, how connections are reused, and the handling of unfinished communications.

Understanding socket communication further involves grasping several critical considerations:

**Concurrency Control: ** Because sockets are a shared resource and communications occur asynchronously, concurrent connections may lead to complex intertwining of communications unless managed appropriately. This often necessitates concurrent programming mechanisms, such as multithreading or asynchronous input/output operations.

**Network Byte Order: ** Networks sometimes require consistency in data representation. To facilitate this, conversion functions like |htonl| (host to network long), |ntohl| (network to host long) ensure correct byte order across different architectures. This is particularly important when exchanging binary data between heterogeneous systems.

**Non-blocking and Blocking IO: ** By default, sockets operate in blocking mode, which can pause process execution until operations complete. Non-blocking IO allows for function calls to return immediately, preventing the program from stalling and enabling efficient event-driven programming.

Advanced socket operations encompass integrating with technologies such as Secure Sockets Layer (SSL) to encrypt communications, critical for secure data exchange over public networks. Libraries like OpenSSL provide APIs that abstract these complexities, allowing developers to secure their socket communications without delving into cryptographic detail.

Sockets' versatility and ubiquity have made them a foundation for numerous network applications, not only limited to web servers but also in database communications, multimedia applications, and distributed systems. Whether through a simple local communication between processes or an extensive multi-tiered network, sockets simplify the programmer's task.

Developing a robust understanding of sockets aids markedly in designing systems that are efficient, scalable, and adaptable to future networking protocols and standards. Mastering both the syntactic foundations and conceptual intricacies of socket programming opens a pathway for creating intricate and highly responsive networked applications.

Creating a Socket in C++

Creating a socket in C++ marks the initial step toward enabling network communication between different programs or devices across a network. The socket serves as a cornerstone of networked application development, providing a communication endpoint for sending and receiving data. This section delivers a comprehensive guide to creating sockets in C++ using relevant libraries, with an emphasis on practicality and detailed explanations of underlying processes.

Sockets in C++ are facilitated via system calls wrapped in the POSIX (Portable Operating System Interface) API, which encompasses a suite of standardized operating system interfaces. This makes socket programming highly portable across various Unix-like systems. Windows environments, though similar, require slight deviations due to variations in system libraries and header files.

The implementation of sockets in C++ usually revolves around the inclusion of certain essential libraries, specifically the header <sys/socket.h> for socket calls, and <netinet/in.h> for handling internet addresses. To support these, additional headers like <arpa/inet.h> and <unistd.h> might be necessary for IP address functions and system calls, respectively.

A socket in C++ is essentially initialized using the socket system call, creating an unbound socket in a specified communication domain: int socket(int domain, int type, int protocol);

Domain: Specifies the family of protocols to be used with the socket. Typically, AF_INET is employed for IPv4 networks and AF_INET6 for IPv6 networks. This parameter defines the address format and protocol family for the socket. Other domains include AF_UNIX for local socket communication.

Type: Dictates the communication semantics of the socket. Common values include:

SOCK_STREAM: For a reliable, connection-oriented TCP transportation.
SOCK_DGRAM: Supports connectionless UDP communication.
SOCK_RAW: Ensures raw socket implementation for direct network layer access.

Protocol: Usually set to 0, allowing the operating system to select the appropriate protocol based on the domain and type provided. This parameter can facilitate specification when multiple protocols exist under a single domain.

Socket Creation Example

To create a socket utilizing TCP with IPv4, the invocation of the socket function looks as follows:

```
#include <sys/socket.h>
#include <netinet/in.h>
#include <arpa/inet.h>
#include <unistd.h>
```

```cpp
#include <iostream>
#include <cstring>

using namespace std;
 int main() {
int sockfd;
    sockfd = socket(AF_INET, SOCK_STREAM,
0);    if (sockfd < 0) {
        cerr << "Error opening socket" << endl;        return
1;
    }
    cout << "Socket created successfully" << endl;

    close(sockfd);
return 0;
}
```

The code above:

Includes necessary header files for standard input/output and socket-related functions.

Declares an integer variable sockfd to store the socket descriptor returned by the socket function. This descriptor is analogous to a file handle used when engaging with files.

Initializes the socket using AF_INET, SOCK_STREAM, and protocol 0.

Implements basic error handling that checks if the socket descriptor is negative, signaling socket creation failure.

Closes the socket using the close system call. Closing a socket is essential for releasing allocated resources.

Detailed Error Handling

Robust error handling is paramount in socket operations. Functions like perror or strerror(errno) can be used to obtain human-readable error messages:

```cpp
#include <cerrno>
#include <cstdio>

sockfd = socket(AF_INET,
SOCK_STREAM, 0); if (sockfd < 0) {
perror("socket failed");    return 1; }
```

The use of perror provides insights into errors relating to insufficient resources, permission issues, or unsupported configurations, helping distinguish between transient and persistent issues.

IPv4 vs. IPv6 Sockets

Modern networks often necessitate support for both IPv4 and IPv6 addressing schemes. Sockets tailored for IPv6 employ AF_INET6:

```
int sockfd = socket(AF_INET6,
SOCK_STREAM, 0); if (sockfd < 0) {
perror("socket failed");    return 1; }
```

An IPv6 socket can typically handle an IPv4-mapped IPv6 address, bridging compatibility gaps. This harmonization streamlines applications that must operate across both addressing paradigms without extensive refactoring.

Socket Options and Optimization

Socket performance and behavior can be subtly adjusted using socket options manipulated via setsockopt. These options might include:

Address Reusability: SO_REUSEADDR allows binding a socket to an address that may be presently in use, avoiding common startup delays.

Linger Options: SO_LINGER determines the socket's closing behavior, specifying how long the socket remains in an active state as it finishes sending pending data.

Non-blocking Mode: fcntl can toggle the socket into non-blocking mode, beneficial for asynchronous event driven models.

Example setting a socket into non-blocking mode:

```
#include <fcntl.h>
int flags = fcntl(sockfd, F_GETFL, 0); fcntl(sockfd, F_SETFL, flags | O_NONBLOCK);
```

Blocking vs. Non-blocking Sockets and IO Multiplexing

The blocking nature of sockets implies that certain operations pause progress until data is fully sent or received. While straightforward, blocking sockets inhibit responsive design in high-concurrency environments, leading to potential inefficiencies as threads wait idle. Non-blocking sockets ameliorate this by allowing an operation's continuation, even if data remains in transit.

To effectively manage multiple socket requests, IO multiplexing approaches like select, poll, or epoll help respond dynamically to varying network demands. These methods allow a single thread to monitor numerous sockets, adapting as data read or write requirements evolve.

Windows Variations

While POSIX API dominantly features in Unix-like operating systems, Windows employs Winsock for socket operations, leading to minor deviations involving header files, library linking, and initialization requirements. A Windows-centric example involves initializing the Winsock library:

```
#include <winsock2.h>
```

```cpp
#include <ws2tcpip.h>

WSADATA wsaData;
int iResult = WSAStartup(MAKEWORD(2,2),
&wsaData); if (iResult != 0) {
    cout << "WSAStartup failed: " << iResult << endl;    return
1;
}

SOCKET sockfd = socket(AF_INET, SOCK_STREAM,
IPPROTO_TCP); if (sockfd == INVALID_SOCKET) {
    cout << "Socket creation failed" << endl;    return
1;
}
closesocket(sockfd);
WSACleanup();
```

Here, WSAStartup and WSACleanup manage Winsock's lifecycle, and the inclusion of <winsock2.h> adapts socket-based code to the Windows environment.

Binding, Listening, and Accepting Connections

In socket programming, the transition from socket creation to actively handling communication demands a sequence of steps that include binding, listening, and accepting connections. These steps prepare a socket to receive incoming requests, effectively setting the stage for robust client-server interactions. This section meticulously explores each of these processes in a C++ programming context, offering insight into implementation nuances and best practices.

The workflow for binding, listening, and accepting connections revolves around a server socket, which acts as the initial point of contact in client-server architecture. By effectively managing these processes, a server becomes capable of managing multiple clients, delivering efficient communication handling, and ensuring system stability under varying load conditions.

Binding a Socket

Binding a socket is the process of associating it with a specific IP address and port number on the local machine. This association defines a unique endpoint through which data can be transmitted and received.

The bind function accomplishes this task, taking three primary arguments: the socket descriptor, a pointer to the address structure (such as struct sockaddr_in for IPv4), and the size of the address structure. A typical binding operation with error checking:

```cpp
#include <sys/socket.h>
#include <netinet/in.h>
#include <arpa/inet.h>
```

```cpp
#include <iostream>
#include <cstring>

using namespace std;
 int main() {
int sockfd;
    struct sockaddr_in server_addr;

    sockfd = socket(AF_INET, SOCK_STREAM,
0);    if (sockfd < 0) {
        cerr << "Error opening socket" << endl;        return
1;
    }
    memset(&server_addr, 0, sizeof(server_addr));
server_addr.sin_family = AF_INET;
    server_addr.sin_addr.s_addr = INADDR_ANY;  // Bind to any available network interface
server_addr.sin_port = htons(8080);  // Convert port number to network byte order

    if (bind(sockfd, (struct sockaddr*)&server_addr, sizeof(server_addr)) < 0) {
perror("Bind failed");        close(sockfd);        return 1;
    }
    cout << "Socket successfully bound to port 8080" << endl;
close(sockfd);    return 0; }
```

Key concepts:

Port Number and IP Address: The bind function associates a socket with a port and IP address. A port number is crucial, serving as an access point for incoming messages, while the IP address confirms the network interface on which the server listens. The use of INADDR_ANY allows the server to listen on all available interfaces.

Address Family: The AF_INET constant indicates IPv4 usage. Extended implementations might involve struct sockaddr_in6 for IPv6.

Network Byte Order: Utilizing htons ensures correct byte ordering of the port number, essential for cross platform interaction given the differences in endianness across systems.

Listening for Connections

Once a socket is bound, it must be put into listening mode to prepare it for incoming connections. This is done using the listen system call, which designates the socket's role as a passive listener and establishes a backlog queue to hold pending connections:

```cpp
if (listen(sockfd, SOMAXCONN) < 0)
{    perror("Listen failed");
close(sockfd);    return 1; }
```

Breakdown:

Backlog Queue: The second parameter to listen defines the number of active, unaccepted connections that can be queued, waiting for service. The SOMAXCONN constant allows the system to manage the queue size dynamically.

Passive Role: Listen mode transforms the socket into a passive one, incapable of initiating data exchange until a connection is accepted. This is crucial for handling incoming client-server dialogues effectively, preventing premature shutdowns or excessive resource utilization.

Accepting Connections

The final step in preparing a server to handle active connections involves accepting client requests through the accept function. This function creates a new, dedicated socket for the connection with each client, thereby isolating communications:

```
struct sockaddr_in client_addr; socklen_t
client_len = sizeof(client_addr);
int client_sockfd = accept(sockfd, (struct sockaddr*)&client_addr, &client_len); if
(client_sockfd < 0) {    perror("Accept failed");    close(sockfd);    return 1;
} cout << "Connection established with client" << endl;
```

Highlights:

Connection Acquiescence: The accept blocks until a connection request occurs, creating a new socket for client-server communication. This establishes a unique channel, enabling concurrent communication across multiple sockets created for different clients.

Client Address Storage: The client_addr structure collects the respective properties of connected clients. With each accepted connection, client identifiers—such as IP address and port number—are obtainable, adding a layer of control and readability for server administration.

Concurrency Management: By handling each client request with a distinct socket, the architecture fosters efficient multi-client scenarios using strategies such as forked processes or threads. Accepting non-blocking communication through select or poll enhances responsiveness and throughput.

Concurrent Server: Multi-client Handling

Addressing simultaneous client connections necessitates leveraging concurrent processing strategies. A fork/multithreaded server example:

```
#include <pthread.h>
```

```
void* handle_client(void* arg) {    int
client_sockfd = *((int*)arg);    char
buffer[1024];

    // Communicate with the client
    recv(client_sockfd, buffer, sizeof(buffer), 0);    cout <<
"Client message: " << buffer << endl;

    // Echo message back to the client
    send(client_sockfd, buffer, sizeof(buffer), 0);

    // Client connection ending
close(client_sockfd);    return
NULL;
}
pthread_t client_thread; // Inside
the main accept loop
int client_sockfd = accept(sockfd, (struct sockaddr*)&client_addr, &client_len); if
(pthread_create(&client_thread, NULL, handle_client, (void*)&client_sockfd) != 0) {
cerr << "Failed to spawn thread" << endl;    close(client_sockfd);
}
pthread_detach(client_thread);
```

With threading:

Thread Creation and Management: Each connection spawns a new thread that manages client-specific interactions, thereby decoupling connection logic from the main thread and augmenting scalability through parallel processing.

Thread Detachment: The pthread_detach ensures that resources are properly freed once threads have completed execution, preventing memory leaks or undue resource accumulation.

An alternative approach utilizing the fork mechanism is particularly applicable when protocol separation or improved security is required, albeit at the cost of higher overhead compared to threading:

```
#include <unistd.h>

pid_t pid = fork(); if (pid
< 0) {
    perror("fork failed");
} else if (pid == 0) {
    // In child process to handle client    close(sockfd);
    handle_client(client_sockfd);    exit(0);
} else {
```

```
    // In parent process, close client socket
close(client_sockfd);
}
```

Lessons and Best Practices:

Resource Management: Ensuring that sockets and resources are released and utilized judiciously avoids lingering resource allocation and server degradation.

Security Considerations: Implementing authentication mechanisms or firewalls restrict unauthorized access, thus thickening defense against vulnerabilities exploited over open networks.

Load Balancing: Employ load balancers to distribute incoming requests across multiple servers, improving response rates and system reliability.

In binding, listening, and accepting connections, mastery of these foundational networking concepts provides the framework needed to build responsive and robust network applications, each capable of handling high demand and dynamic requests seamlessly. A pragmatic understanding of these processes fueled by insightful code and best practices leads to superior application agility, allowing developers to innovate and provision concurrent network solutions adapted to evolving technological landscapes.

Establishing Client-Server Communication

The essence of socket programming lies in the successful establishment of client-server communication, an architecture that forms the backbone of numerous networking applications. This section outlines the steps and considerations involved in crafting a reliable client-server communication model in C++. Through detailed code examples and analysis, we explore how two distinct entities—a client and a server—exchange data seamlessly over a network.

Client-Server Model Overview

The client-server architecture operates on a fundamental principle where the server provides resources, services, or data, and the client consumes these services. This separation of concerns allows clients to make requests to the server and the server to respond accordingly. Such a model is not only pivotal for web services but also for applications like email, file transfer, and database access.

In a typical client-server communication lifecycle:

Server Initialization: The server starts by creating a socket, binding it to a port, and listening for incoming client connections.

Client Connection: The client initiates contact with the server by creating a socket and attempting to connect to the server's IP address and port.

Data Exchange: Once the connection is established, data is exchanged through send and receive operations.

Connection Termination: Both client and server terminate the connection gracefully once data exchange is complete.

Server Implementation

The server's responsibility is to be available for communication with any incoming client connections. Below is a detailed server-side implementation that encompasses socket creation, binding, listening, accepting connections, and handling client-server communication within a thread to maintain simultaneous interactions.

```cpp
#include <sys/socket.h>
#include <netinet/in.h>
#include <arpa/inet.h>
#include <unistd.h>
#include <iostream>
#include <cstring>
#include <pthread.h>

using namespace std;

const int PORT = 8080;

void *handle_client(void *client_socket) {
int client_fd = *(int *)client_socket;    char
buffer[1024];    int bytes_received;

  // Receive data
  bytes_received = recv(client_fd, buffer, sizeof(buffer), 0);    if
(bytes_received < 0) {
     cerr << "Error in receiving data" << endl;
  } else {
buffer[bytes_received] = '\0';
cout << "Client message: " << buffer << endl;

    // Send response
    const char *response = "Message received";
send(client_fd, response, strlen(response), 0);
  }
  close(client_fd);    pthread_exit(NULL);
} int main() {
  int server_fd, client_fd;
  struct sockaddr_in server_addr, client_addr;    socklen_t
client_len = sizeof(client_addr);
```

```cpp
    server_fd = socket(AF_INET,
SOCK_STREAM, 0);    if (server_fd < 0) {
perror("socket failed");        return -1;
    }
    memset(&server_addr, 0, sizeof(server_addr));
server_addr.sin_family = AF_INET;    server_addr.sin_addr.s_addr
= INADDR_ANY;    server_addr.sin_port = htons(PORT);

    if (bind(server_fd, (struct sockaddr *) &server_addr, sizeof(server_addr)) < 0) {
perror("bind failed");        close(server_fd);        return -1;
    }
    if (listen(server_fd, 10) < 0) {
perror("listen failed");
close(server_fd);        return -1;
    }
    cout << "Server is listening on port " << PORT << endl;

    while (true) {
        client_fd = accept(server_fd, (struct sockaddr *) &client_addr, &client_len);
if (client_fd < 0) {            perror("accept failed");            continue;
        }
        cout << "Accepted connection from client" << endl;

        pthread_t client_thread;
        pthread_create(&client_thread, NULL, handle_client, &client_fd);
pthread_detach(client_thread);
    }
    close(server_fd);
return 0;

}
```

Client
Implementation

The client's task is to connect to the server and initiate data exchange. Below is a typical client-side implementation in C++ that establishes a connection to the server, sends messages, and receives responses.

```cpp
#include <sys/socket.h>
#include <netinet/in.h>
#include <arpa/inet.h>
#include <unistd.h>
#include <iostream>
#include <cstring>
```

```cpp
using namespace std;

const int PORT = 8080;
const char *SERVER_IP = "127.0.0.1";
 int main() {
int sockfd;
    struct sockaddr_in server_addr;    char
buffer[1024] = "Hello, Server!";

    sockfd = socket(AF_INET, SOCK_STREAM,
0);    if (sockfd < 0) {
        perror("Socket creation failed");        return -
1;
    }
    memset(&server_addr, 0, sizeof(server_addr));
server_addr.sin_family = AF_INET;    server_addr.sin_port
= htons(PORT);

    if (inet_pton(AF_INET, SERVER_IP, &server_addr.sin_addr) <=
0) {        cerr << "Invalid server address" << endl;        close(sockfd);
return -1;
    }
    if (connect(sockfd, (struct sockaddr *) &server_addr, sizeof(server_addr)) < 0) {
perror("Connection to server failed");        close(sockfd);        return -1;
    }
    cout << "Connected to the server" << endl;

    // Send a message to the server    send(sockfd,
buffer, strlen(buffer), 0);

    // Receive a response from the server
    int bytes_received = recv(sockfd, buffer, sizeof(buffer)-1, 0);    if
(bytes_received > 0) {        buffer[bytes_received] = '\0';
        cout << "Server reply: " << buffer << endl;
    } else {
        cerr << "Server response failed" << endl;
    }
    close(sockfd);
return 0;
}
```

Key Components and Considerations

Socket Creation: Both client and server create a socket with the socket function, choosing IPv4 (AF_INET) and TCP (SOCK_STREAM) as the protocol. The error handling ensures that any problems in socket creation are promptly identified and addressed.

IP Address and Port Handling: The server binds to a port specified by htons(PORT). The client specifies the server's address using inet_pton, which converts the textual IP address to the appropriate form. Such conversions are critical for ensuring compatibility across different platforms and network architectures.

Connection Management: The server's use of the accept function creates a dedicated socket for each client connection, maintaining isolation of communication streams. The client establishes a connection using the connect function, effectively initiating the communication pathway.

Data Transmission and Reception: The send and recv functions facilitate data exchange between client and server. Proper buffer management—including setting null terminators for strings— ensures data integrity and meaningful communication.

Concurrency and Threading: Server-side threading permits multiple client connections to be managed concurrently, crucial for responsive and scalable systems. This threading model is versatile, supporting high request environments effectively with minimal performance degradation.

Error Handling and Resource Management: Comprehensive error checking across socket operations, binding, listening, and accepting connections safeguards against operational failures. Closing socket descriptors ensures released resources and prevents leaks, maintaining server and client stability over time.

Advanced Considerations

Security Enhancements: To safeguard communication, integrating TLS (Transport Layer Security) via libraries like OpenSSL offers encryption. Securing transmitted data guards against interception and spoofing.

Non-blocking Sockets: Leveraging non-blocking I/O operations or using asynchronous patterns (e.g., select, poll) can further enhance performance in high-load scenarios by allowing other operations to execute while waiting for I/O completion.

Load Balancing and Fault Tolerance: Employing load balancers distributes client requests across multiple servers, optimizing response times and providing resilience against individual server failure. Architectural considerations such as stateless server design aid in scaling and failover operations.

Protocol Design: Designing the data exchange protocol for client-server interaction requires careful consideration, including serialization methods (e.g., JSON, XML) and error-checking mechanisms for data consistency and transaction reliability.

Successfully establishing client-server communication isn't a mere exchange of data; it involves crafting robust, efficient, and secure pathways that accommodate the needs of varying application domains.

Mastering these techniques enables the creation of sophisticated network services, placing developers at the forefront of distributed system innovations. The knowledge gained through adept management of client-server interactions serves as a foundational element for building complex systems that underpin modern computational tasks and services.

Sending and Receiving Data

Sending and receiving data are fundamental procedures in socket programming, forming the essence of network communication. Once a connection is established between a client and a server, the exchange of data becomes the primary mode of interaction. This section provides an in-depth exploration of the techniques and nuances involved in sending and receiving data over networks using sockets in C++. Through extensive examples, we delineate various data transfer methods and address both theoretical and practical aspects.

Understanding Data Transmission

At the core of data transmission is the reliable exchange of bytes, achieved using functions like send and recv for stream-based (TCP) sockets, or sendto and recvfrom for datagram-based (UDP) sockets. These functions form the building blocks that enable the flow of information across networked systems.

Basic Usage of Send and Receive

The send function transmits data across a connected socket. For a stream socket, it accepts parameters including the socket descriptor, a data buffer, the length of the data to be sent, and flags to modify the behavior of the function.

```cpp
#include <sys/socket.h>
#include <unistd.h> #include
<cstring>
#include <iostream>

using namespace std;

int sendData(int socket_fd, const char* message) {
int total_sent = 0;    int bytes_left = strlen(message);
int bytes_sent;

    while (total_sent < bytes_left) {
        bytes_sent = send(socket_fd, message + total_sent, bytes_left, 0);
if (bytes_sent == -1) {          perror("send failed");          return -1;
        }
```

```
        total_sent += bytes_sent;        bytes_left -
= bytes_sent;
    }
    return total_sent;
}
```

Reliability and Completeness: Due to potential network variability, the loop continues until all bytes are sent. This ensures message integrity and completeness by handling partial sends—a common occurrence with the send function where fewer bytes are sent than requested.

Flags: The MSG_DONTWAIT flag, for instance, allows for non-blocking operations, which is vital in high performance situations where waiting for I/O hampers responsiveness.

On the receiving end, the recv function corresponds to reading data from the socket, with similar parameters— socket descriptor, buffer, buffer length, and flags.

```
int receiveData(int socket_fd, char* buffer, int size) {    int
bytes_received = recv(socket_fd, buffer, size - 1, 0);    if
(bytes_received < 0) {        perror("receive failed");        return
-1;
    } else if (bytes_received == 0) {
        cout << "Connection closed by peer" << endl;
return 0;
    }
    buffer[bytes_received] = '\0'; // Null-terminate string    return
bytes_received;
}
```

Connection State Awareness: A return of 0 indicates a gracefully closed connection from the peer, which is essential information when ensuring proper shutdown procedures and resource management.

Advanced Techniques and Considerations

While the basic usage of these functions provides a framework for data exchange, several advanced considerations must be addressed to achieve a robust communication model.

Buffer Management and Size Considerations

Efficient buffer management mitigates memory-related issues and optimizes throughput. Buffer size should be adjusted based on message size expectations and available network bandwidth. Larger buffers can reduce the number of send and receive calls, enhancing efficiency.

```
const int BUFFER_SIZE = 4096; // Example buffer size
```

```
void processData() {    char
buffer[BUFFER_SIZE];    //
Receiving and processing data
}
```

Dynamic Buffering: Adapting buffer allocation based on runtime data size analysis ensures that applications remain agile across varied workload conditions.

Handling Large Data Transfers

Transferring large datasets demands segmentation into manageable chunks, ensuring each is transmitted and received correctly.

```
void sendLargeData(int socket_fd, const char* large_data, size_t size) {
size_t bytes_sent = 0;    while (bytes_sent < size) {
    size_t segment_size = min(size - bytes_sent, BUFFER_SIZE);        int
sent = send(socket_fd, large_data + bytes_sent, segment_size, 0);        if (sent
< 0) {
        perror("Error in sending large data");
break;        }
    bytes_sent += sent;
  }
}
```

Message Framing and Protocol Design

Implementing a framing protocol is vital when designing network applications to delimit pieces of data clearly. This aids in the correct interpretation and reconstruction of messages.

Fixed-Length Framing: Each frame has a predefined size, reducing complexity at the cost of potential overhead.

Delimiter-based Framing: Using character sequences (e.g., newlines) to signify frame boundaries.

Length-Field Framing: Incorporates a header indicating the size of the subsequent data payload.

```
// Length-field framing example

void sendFramedMessage(int socket_fd, const char* message)
{    uint32_t length = htonl(strlen(message));
send(socket_fd, &length, sizeof(length), 0);    send(socket_fd,
message, strlen(message), 0); }
```

Here, the header encodes the message length, ensuring that the receiver extracts exactly the intended bytes.

Event-Driven Data Transfer

Using event-driven or asynchronous I/O improves responsiveness by allowing application processing to continue while waiting for data operations to complete.

Select, Poll, and Epoll

Using select, poll, or epoll, developers can monitor multiple file descriptors to determine when I/O is possible without blocking.

```
#include <sys/select.h>

void handleIOSelect(int server_fd) {
fd_set read_fds;    struct timeval
timeout;
   FD_ZERO(&read_fds);
   FD_SET(server_fd, &read_fds);

   timeout.tv_sec = 5;    timeout.tv_usec
= 0;

   if (select(server_fd + 1, &read_fds, NULL, NULL, &timeout) < 0) {
perror("Select error");
   } else if (FD_ISSET(server_fd, &read_fds)) {
// Ready to accept connections or read data
   }
}
```

The select function allows checking readiness across multiple sockets, facilitating simultaneous client management and improving performance by reducing latency in request handling.

Protocol-Specific Considerations

For applications dependent on specific protocols beyond basic TCP/IP, additional considerations are essential:

Binary Data Handling: Consider systems with varying endianness—e.g., converting multibyte integers with htonl or ntohl.

Data Encryption: Integrating encryption libraries such as OpenSSL secures data transfers, protecting content from unauthorized access.

Compression: Applying compression (e.g., Zlib) lessens bandwidth impacts by reducing message size.

```
// Example encryption using OpenSSL
#include <openssl/ssl.h>
```

```
// Assume ssl is an initialized SSL* pointer void
encryptedSend(SSL *ssl, const char *message) {
    SSL_write(ssl, message, strlen(message));
}
```

Error Handling in Socket Programming

Error handling in socket programming is a crucial aspect in ensuring the robustness and reliability of network applications. Network environments can be unpredictable, with various factors contributing to potential points of failure. These can range from resource limitations and network interruptions to software bugs. Effective error management involves detecting errors, responding appropriately, and implementing strategies to mitigate repeated issues.

Importance of Error Handling

Error handling provides a safety net, allowing programs to fail gracefully without losing data or becoming unresponsive. It facilitates debugging, enhances user experience, and ensures system stability. By anticipating possible failures and implementing robust handling routines, developers can design applications that are resilient to the unpredictability's of network environments.

Common Sources of Errors

Errors in socket programming can be broadly categorized into three main areas:

System Resource Constraints: Limitations in memory, file descriptors, or other resources can impede socket operations.

Network Issues: Packet loss, latency, or disconnection can disrupt communication channels.

Code and Logic Errors: Bugs or incorrect logic in code may lead to unexpected behavior or crashes.

Implementing Error Handling

Error handling in socket programming typically involves the use of return values, examination of the global errno variable, and application-specific logging or notification systems.

Standard Error Reporting Mechanism

Most socket functions return a negative value or -1 upon encountering an error, commonly accompanied by setting errno to a specific error code. For instance:

```
int sockfd = socket(AF_INET, SOCK_STREAM,
0); if (sockfd == -1) {
    perror("Error opening socket");
return -1; }
```

In this example, perror maps errno to a descriptive text string, providing immediate feedback on the nature of the failure.

Common err no Values

EACCES: Permission denied.
EADDRINUSE: Address already in use.
EAFNOSUPPORT: Address family not supported.
ECONNRESET: Connection reset by peer.
ENOMEM: Insufficient memory available.
ETIMEDOUT: Connection timed out.

Handling Specific Error Scenarios

Each stage of socket communication involves potential errors that require tailored handling strategies.

Socket Creation Errors

Creating a socket might fail due to lack of resources, requiring fallback mechanisms or user notifications to address the failure.

```
int sockfd = socket(AF_INET, SOCK_STREAM, 0); if (sockfd
== -1) {    switch(errno) {       case EACCES:         cerr <<
"Permission denied" << endl;          break;       case EMFILE:
cerr << "Too many file descriptors in use" << endl;          break;
default:
         cerr << "Socket creation failed: " << strerror(errno) << endl;
   }
return -1;
}
```

Connection Errors

Establishing a connection, particularly in client-side applications, is prone to timeouts or unreachable network paths.

```
int status = connect(sockfd, (struct sockaddr *)&server_addr, sizeof(server_addr)); if (status == -1)
{    if (errno == ECONNREFUSED) {

    cerr << "Connection refused by server" << endl;
  } else if (errno == ETIMEDOUT) {
    cerr << "Connection timed out" << endl;
  } else {
    cerr << "Unknown connection error: " << strerror(errno) << endl;
  }
```

```
    close(sockfd);
}
```

Data Transmission Errors

Even during established connections, sending and receiving data can face issues due to network anomalies, requiring retries or alternative actions.

```
int bytes_sent = send(sockfd, message, message_length, 0);
if (bytes_sent == -1) {    if (errno == EINTR) {
    cerr << "Operation interrupted, retrying" << endl;
    // Retry logic here
  } else {
    cerr << "Data send error: " << strerror(errno) << endl;
  }
  close(sockfd);
}
```

Enhancing Error Handling

Use of Exceptions: While C++ exceptions are less common in socket programming due to the traditionally Cbased APIs, they can encapsulate errors and streamline complex error propagation.

```
class SocketException : public std::runtime_error {    public:
    explicit SocketException(const std::string &message)
      : std::runtime_error(message) {}
};
void sendData(int socket_fd, const char* message) {        if
(send(socket_fd, message, strlen(message), 0) == -1) {            throw
SocketException(strerror(errno));
    }
}
```

Logging and Monitoring: Implement robust logging systems to capture detailed error information, providing critical insights during development and operations.

```
#include <fstream>

void logError(const std::string &error_message) {
    std::ofstream log_file("socket_errors.log", std::ios_base::app);
log_file << error_message << std::endl;    }
```

Using Back-off Strategies: Particularly for network operations, applying exponential back-off strategies in retries helps in managing transient network issues without overwhelming the system.

```
int retry_count = 0;
while (retry_count < MAX_RETRIES) {
```

```
    int result = connect(sockfd, (struct sockaddr *)&server_addr, sizeof(server_addr));       if
(result == 0) {          break;       }
    int backoff_time = pow(2, retry_count);
sleep(backoff_time);        retry_count++;
  }
  if (retry_count == MAX_RETRIES) {
    cerr << "Max retries reached, connection failed" << endl;
close(sockfd);      }
```

Graceful Degradation: Design interfaces and services to handle failures gracefully, notifying users of issues without application or service crashes.

Distributed and Advanced Network Environments

For applications in distributed systems or utilizing advanced technologies such as cloud services and IoT, error handling requires adaptability and coordination between multiple components.

Failover and Redundancy: Implementing system redundancy ensures continued operation despite individual component failures, crucial in cloud-based applications.

Fault Tolerance: Design systems with fault-tolerant protocols that can dynamically reroute communications or manage partial failures without total collapse.

Alert Systems: Integrate alerting mechanisms that inform administrators of critical errors in real-time, allowing for rapid response to mitigate adverse effects.

TCP/IP Protocol Suite

This chapter examines the TCP/IP protocol suite, the foundational architecture for modern internet communication. It explores the structural layers of the TCP/IP model, detailing the functionalities and interactions of critical protocols such as IP, TCP, and UDP. Emphasizing their distinct roles, the chapter also addresses application layer protocols like HTTP and FTP, highlighting their integration within the suite. Additionally, it discusses networking tools and utilities essential for analyzing and troubleshooting TCP/IPbased networks, providing a comprehensive understanding of these vital communication protocols.

Structure of the TCP/IP Model

The TCP/IP model, or the Internet Protocol Suite, is a conceptual framework used to understand and configure network protocols. It draws its roots from the Department of Defense's ARPANET project, leading to a robust model for large-scale network protocol design. Unlike the OSI model, which contains seven layers, the TCP/IP model is traditionally composed of four layers: the Link Layer, the Internet Layer, the Transport Layer, and the Application Layer. This structure guides how data is transmitted across diverse networks and encompasses all processes involved in networking, from hardware to application software.

The core philosophy of the TCP/IP model is to divide the network functions into a set of layers, with each layer focusing on specific tasks. This separation allows engineers to modify one layer without affecting the others, facilitating scalable, flexible development. Furthermore, the TCP/IP model operates with a 'bottom-up' approach, starting from physical network operations (in the Link Layer) up to user applications (in the Application Layer). Below, we discuss each of these layers in greater detail, elucidating their roles and the protocols operating within them.

Link Layer

The Link Layer is the foundation of the TCP/IP model; it is responsible for the physical transmission of data packets. Operating on the boundary between tangible, physical hardware and abstract networking layers, it governs how data is physically sent over various types of media. Specific tasks include framing, addressing, and managing the Medium Access Control (MAC) layer protocols.

Protocols such as Ethernet, Wi-Fi (IEEE 802.11), and others fall under this category. These protocols define how devices within the same network segment communicate. They handle error correction of data, synchronize devices and media, and ensure collision-free transmission through various techniques like Carrier Sense Multiple Access with Collision Detection (CSMA/CD) or Carrier Sense Multiple Access with Collision Avoidance (CSMA/CA).

Essential control components such as network interface cards (NICs) operate within the Link Layer to control and interface with the physical transmission medium of a network (e.g., optics or copper cabling).

An illustration of Access Control in Ethernet using CSMA/CD while transmitting:
if channel is quiet: transmit frame wait for acknowledgment elif collision occurs: stop transmission wait a random time interval # Retry

Internet Layer

Situated above the Link Layer, the Internet Layer is pivotal for laying out the communication path across networks by handling the logical addressing of hosts and managing data packet routing through interconnected networks. It is primarily focused on forming the Internet's backbone structure, interlinking multiple networks together on the global scale.

The most prominent protocol in this layer is the Internet Protocol (IP), with its two versions: IPv4 and IPv6. IP handles both addressing and fragmenting data packets to traverse different networks and reassemble them appropriately.

IP addresses are unique identifiers for network devices, allowing packets to find their destination. Routing protocols such as the Routing Information Protocol (RIP), and more advanced methods like Open Shortest Path First (OSPF) and Border Gateway Protocol (BGP), work in the Internet Layer to determine the most efficient routing path for packets through networks.

```
# Simple Python script demonstrating conversion of IPv4 address import
socket

hostname = 'www.example.com'
ip_address = socket.gethostbyname(hostname)
print(f'The IP address of {hostname} is {ip_address}')
```

The Internet Layer also accommodates the Internet Control Message Protocol (ICMP), whose primary uses involve error reporting and diagnostics such as in the widely used 'ping' command.

```
> ping www.example.com
Pinging example.com [93.184.216.34] with 32 bytes of data:
Reply from 93.184.216.34: bytes=32 time=56ms TTL=56
```

Transport Layer

The Transport Layer, crucial for maintaining robust end-to-end communication, is responsible for the reliability and control of message transmission between hosts. It establishes, maintains, and terminates communication sessions. Two key protocols dominate this layer: the Transmission Control Protocol (TCP) and the User Datagram Protocol (UDP).

TCP provides a connection-oriented service, ensuring reliable data transmission with error detection, packet ordering, and flow control. It is suitable for applications where data integrity and order are vital (e.g., web browsing using HTTP, email via SMTP).

```
# Pseudocode for a simple TCP Client def tcp_client(): create socket connect to server send data
```
receive response close connection UDP, on the other hand, offers a connectionless service with low overhead by forgoing reliability guarantees; it is used for applications requiring fast data transmission without error correction, such as video streaming or online gaming.

```
# Pseudocode for a UDP Client def udp_client(): create socket bind to address send data to
destination    receive response close socket
```

The choice between TCP and UDP depends on the application's requirements regarding speed, reliability, and overhead.

Application Layer

The Application Layer sits at the apex of the TCP/IP model and integrates all protocols and technologies developed for specific communication tasks, providing necessary interfaces for network services. Protocols include Hypertext Transfer Protocol (HTTP), File Transfer Protocol (FTP), Simple Mail Transfer Protocol (SMTP), Domain Name System (DNS), among others.

HTTP, a foundational protocol in web communications, facilitates the retrieval of web resources and operates on a client-server principle. A typical HTTP transaction involves a client sending a request for resources and a server responding with the desired resource, often alongside an HTTP status code.

```
# Example of HTTP GET request using Python's requests library
import requests

response = requests.get('https://www.example.com') print(response.content)
```

Similarly, FTP offers a protocol for transferring files over networks, while SMTP is crucial for the transmission of email messages. DNS translates human-readable domain names into machine-readable IP addresses, essential for locating and addressing devices on an IP network.

The Application Layer protocols inherently depend on the layers beneath them, illustrating intricate interrelationships between all layers of the TCP/IP model to facilitate comprehensive network communication.

Throughout the TCP/IP model, data encapsulation plays a critical role. As data travels from the upper layers down to the Link Layer, each layer encapsulates the data from the previous layer, adding its header information. Conversely, each layer on the receiving end interprets the incoming data, removing the header attached by its counterpart. This process is fundamental to understanding how network communications successfully traverse diverse network infrastructures.

Through its layered architecture, the TCP/IP model offers a resilient, adaptive framework that has stood the test of time, effectively meeting the demands of modern internet communications while allowing for innovations and advancements without necessitating a complete overhaul of each component part.

Internet Protocol (IP)

The Internet Protocol (IP) serves as a core protocol in the Internet Layer of the TCP/IP model, facilitating the routing of packets across network boundaries. It is the principal communications protocol responsible for delivering packets from the source host to the destination host based solely on their IP addresses. The protocol ensures that messages, known as datagrams, traverse various networks efficiently and arrive at the correct destination. IP is the linchpin of the Internet, allowing computers connected over diverse networks to communicate seamlessly. This section delves into the fundamental aspects of IP, including its architecture, addressing mechanisms, and routing functions, as well as the distinctions between IP versions.

IP addressing is central to the functionality of the Internet Protocol, serving as a unique identifier for each device connected to a network. An IP address performs two primary roles: identifying the host or network interface and providing a location of the host in the network, thus facilitating the routing of traffic.

An IP address is typically a numerical label, intricately structured, to imbue distinct characteristics that aid in both network identification and routing. There are two principal types of IP addresses based on the version of the Internet Protocol: IPv4 and IPv6.

IPv4 Addresses IPv4, the first version of IP to be widely deployed, uses a 32-bit address scheme, yielding over 4 billion unique addresses. These addresses are conventionally expressed in dot-decimal notation, comprising four octets separated by periods, such as 192.168.1.1.

IPv4 addresses are categorized into classes (A, B, C, D, E) to accommodate networks of different sizes and purposes. Classful networking has largely become obsolete with the advent of Classless Inter-Domain Routing (CIDR), which allows more flexible allocation of IP addresses.

```python
# Python demonstration for converting an IPv4 address to binary
ip = "192.168.1.1"
ip_as_binary = '.'.join([f"{int(octet):08b}" for octet in ip.split('.')]) print(f"The
binary representation of {ip} is {ip_as_binary}")
```

CIDR notation, such as 192.168.100.0/24, specifies the number of bits in the address used for the network portion, enhancing address allocation efficiency and improving routing performance.

IPv6 Addresses The limitations of IPv4, particularly in address exhaustion, led to the development of IPv6, which uses a 128-bit address space, vastly expanding the available IP address pool to accommodate the growing number of internet-connected devices. An IPv6 address is typically represented in hexadecimal, separated by colons, like 2001:0db8:85a3:0000:0000:8a2e:0370:7334.

IPv6 introduces several enhancements, such as simplified address headers, improved support for extension headers, and native support for IPsec. The adoption of IPv6 is gradually increasing as organizations prepare for inevitable IPv4 depletion.

```python
# Python code to demonstrate IPv6 address manipulation
import ipaddress

# Create an IPv6 address object
ip = ipaddress.IPv6Address('2001:0db8:85a3:0000:0000:8a2e:0370:7334')
print(f"The compressed form of the IPv6 address is {ip.compressed}")
```

IP routing is a crucial function of the Internet Protocol, responsible for deciding the path that data packets take from their source to their destination. This process involves directing packets through intermediary nodes, known as routers, which forward packets towards their eventual endpoints based on a pre-determined set of rules and routing protocols.

Routers build and maintain routing tables, using these to efficiently forward packets through networks. Routing protocols can be divided into two primary types: interior gateway protocols (IGPs) and exterior gateway protocols (EGPs). IGPs, such as RIP and OSPF, are used within a single administrative domain, while EGPs, particularly BGP, are used between domains.

```
# Pseudocode illustrating basic IP packet forwarding logic while receiving packet:

determine destination address lookup routing table for next hop if route found:
send packet to next hop else:
send ICMP destination unreachable message
```

Internet Control Message Protocol (ICMP) is an integral component of the IP protocol suite, primarily used for network diagnostics and error-reporting purposes. Routers and hosts use ICMP to communicate issues with IP packet processing. For instance, if a host is unreachable, ICMP might be employed to inform the sending host of the difficulty.

Common ICMP message types include echo request and echo reply (used by the 'ping' utility) and destination unreachable messages. ICMP messages serve as an essential network administrator tool, enabling troubleshooting and problem resolution.

```
> ping -6 www.google.com
Pinging www.google.com [2a00:1450:4009:802::200e] with 32 bytes of data:
Reply from 2a00:1450:4009:802::200e: time=30ms
```

Fragmentation occurs when IP packets exceed the maximum transmission unit (MTU) of the network path. IP handles fragmentation by breaking large packets into smaller units, or fragments, which are reassembled into the original packet at their destination.
This process happens transparently to higher-layer protocols, but its significance becomes apparent when ensuring data arrives intact across networks with varying MTUs.

```
# Pseudocode for basic packet fragmentation if packet size > MTU:
divide packet into fragments attach required header information for each fragment:
send fragment else: send packet
```

The Address Resolution Protocol (ARP) functions within the Internet Layer, helping resolve the IP addresses to MAC (Media Access Control) addresses. This capability is essential for communication within Ethernet networks. When a device wishes to communicate with another device on the same local network, it broadcasts an ARP request to retrieve the MAC address corresponding to the destination IP address.

ARP operates within the confines of the local network and ensures that devices can reliably establish direct communication lines essential for packet delivery.

```
# Example ARP request packet created using Scapy (Python library)
from scapy.all import ARP, send

arp_pkt = ARP(op=1, pdst='192.168.1.1')
send(arp_pkt)
```

Despite IP's critical role, the protocol faces several challenges. The eventual exhaustion of IPv4 addresses necessitated the transition to IPv6, requiring significant infrastructure overhaul and compatibility considerations. Security is another concern, as IP inherently lacks robust mechanisms to ensure data integrity and authenticity. This shortcoming makes it vulnerable to various attacks, such as IP spoofing.

Network professionals leverage IPsec, an additional suite of protocols that adds security to IP communications, providing authentication, integrity, and confidentiality.

Network Address Translation (NAT) is another adaptation to IP shortcomings, particularly the scarcity of public IP addresses. NAT allows multiple devices on a local network to share a single public IP address. However, NAT can complicate direct peer-to-peer communication and may interfere with certain applications.

Pseudocode for a simple NAT translation table lookup for incoming packet:
retrieve source and destination IP if match exists in NAT table:
translate IPs as per header information forward packet else: drop packet or initiate new NAT entry
Internet Protocol stands as the backbone of modern networking, exhibiting a high degree of adaptability demonstrated by the transition from IPv4 to IPv6, the enhancement in routing efficiencies, and constant troubleshooting advancements through ICMP and related technologies. This expertise forms a foundation to explore further progress in computer networking, heralding seamlessly interconnected digital ecosystems.

Transmission Control Protocol (TCP)

The Transmission Control Protocol (TCP) is a core protocol of the Internet Protocol suite, vital for facilitating reliable communication over packet-switched networks. Positioned in the Transport Layer of the TCP/IP model, TCP offers a connection-oriented, error-checked, and retransmission-capable data delivery service. TCP empowers datagram transmission with the capability to reconstruct data streams reliably, making it indispensable for applications where data integrity and order are crucial. This section provides an exhaustive examination of TCP, elucidating its mechanisms, internal architecture, and significance in a practical networking context.

TCP distinguishes itself through several key features:

Connection-Oriented: TCP establishes a connection between two endpoints prior to data transfer, known as a TCP session, ensuring readiness before communication begins.

Reliable Data Transfer: Reliability is achieved through sequence numbers, acknowledgments, and retransmissions, ensuring data packets reach destinations error-free and in order.

Flow Control: TCP manages data flow between sender and receiver to prevent overwhelming slower devices. Congestion Control: Techniques like slow start, congestion avoidance, and fast recovery optimize network performance by managing data flow during varying network conditions.

Stream-Oriented: TCP views data as a continuous stream, contrasting UDP's discrete datagrams. The coupling of these features empowers TCP to support varied applications, from web browsers to email clients, where orderly and reliable data delivery is non-negotiable.

Data is encapsulated into TCP segments, each comprising a header and payload. The TCP header, typically 20 bytes in standard form, includes fields vital for segment management and reliability assurance.

Source and Destination Ports (16 bits each): Mark communication endpoints, allowing multiplexing of applications.

Sequence Number (32 bits): Identifies the segment's ordinal range in the data stream, ensuring ordered assembly at the receiver.

Acknowledgment Number (32 bits): Confirms received data range, prompting further data flow.

Offset (4 bits): Indicates the start of data in the segment, indicating header length.

Flags (9 bits): Control indicators, including SYN, ACK, FIN, RST, URG, to manage connection lifecycle and urgent data.

Window (16 bits): Defines buffer size for flow control, indicating receiver readiness for additional data.

Checksum (16 bits): Validates segment integrity, computed over both header and payload.

Urgent Pointer (16 bits, optional): Offsets location of urgent data within the segment.

```
# Pseudocode to construct a basic TCP header struct TCPHeader {    unsigned short source_port;
unsigned short dest_port;    unsigned int sequence;    unsigned int acknowledgment;    unsigned
short offset_and_flags;    unsigned short window;    unsigned short checksum;    unsigned short
urgent_pointer; };
```

This structural foundation supports TCP's core reliability mechanisms, making it indispensable for many crucial network applications.

TCP's connection-oriented nature is embodied in the three-way handshake process, a critical protocol mechanism establishing a reliable session between two network hosts.

SYN: The client initiates a connection by sending a SYN (synchronize) packet, encapsulating its initial sequence number.

SYN-ACK: The server responds with a SYN-ACK (synchronize-acknowledge) segment, which acknowledges the client's SYN and announces its initial sequence number.

ACK: The client sends an ACK (acknowledge) packet, acknowledging the server's sequence number, finalizing the connection setup.

```python
# Python example using the Scapy library to simulate TCP SYN packet
from scapy.all import IP, TCP, send

src_ip = "192.168.1.2"
dst_ip = "192.168.1.1"
src_port = 1234 dst_port =
80

ip_packet = IP(src=src_ip, dst=dst_ip)
tcp_packet = TCP(sport=src_port, dport=dst_port, flags='S', seq=1000)
```

packet = ip_packet / tcp_packet send(packet)

The three-way handshake establishes a full-duplex connection, ensuring both parties are synchronized for data exchange.

Data transmission within an established TCP connection relies on sequence numbers and acknowledgments to maintain reliability. TCP ensures data integrity and order through dependable mechanisms:

Sliding Window Protocol: This dynamic window size dictates the number of bytes sent without waiting for acknowledgments, balancing sender pace with receiver readiness. The window size adjusts based on network conditions and receiver capability.

Cumulative Acknowledgments: TCP sends cumulative ACKs, indicating all data up to a certain sequence number has been received correctly.

Selective Acknowledgment (SACK): An optional extension allowing acknowledgment of specific data segments; particularly effective in high-latency connections or during packet loss.

Retransmission Timers: TCP employs timers to detect lost packets, triggering retransmission if ACKs are not received within a specified timeframe.

Example of TCP segment retransmission using pseudocode set timer send segment while waiting for ACK: if timer expires: retransmit segment reset timer if ACK received: send next segment update sliding window

These features bolster TCP against network unreliability, maintaining data coherence across complex, potentially fickle environments.

TCP connection termination involves a controlled four-step process to safely release resources:

FIN from Sender: The sender requests connection termination, sending a FIN (finish) packet.
ACK from Receiver: The receiver confirms the FIN packet.
FIN from Receiver: Upon transmitting remaining data, the receiver sends its FIN packet.
ACK from Sender: The sender sends an ACK, allowing both parties to close the connection.

# Python example to close a TCP connection using Scapy
from scapy.all import TCP, IP, send

fin_packet = TCP(flags='FA', seq=1020, ack=1025)
ip_packet = IP(src="192.168.1.2", dst="192.168.1.1")
full_packet = ip_packet / fin_packet
 send(full_packet)

Graceful connection termination prevents data loss and ensures proper resource deallocation, achieving completeness in communication.

Congestion control is imperative to TCP's reliability, aiming to optimize data flow across the network. Notable algorithms include:

Slow Start: Initially increases the congestion window size exponentially to probe network capacity.
Congestion Avoidance: Upon reaching a threshold, it shifts to linear growth, cautiously expanding the window.
Fast Retransmit and Fast Recovery: Designed to respond swiftly to segment loss, executing accelerated retransmissions without entering slow start, stabilizing window size.

```
# Pseudocode for TCP congestion control in slow start initialize congestion_window = 1 threshold =
predefined_value while data to send: if network condition is favorable:
congestion_window *= 2    else:
threshold = congestion_window / 2  congestion_window = 1 enter congestion avoidance
```

TCP's congestion control mechanisms allow scalability, ensuring fair resource sharing and avoiding packet loss.

TCP's robust characteristics render it suitable for a variety of applications requiring reliability:

Web Browsing (HTTP/HTTPS): Ensures HTML data integrity for consistent browsing experiences.

Email (SMTP/IMAP/POP3): Supports error-free transmission of electronic mail, maintaining message completeness.

File Transfer (FTP): Invokes orderly file exchange across networks, crucial for sensitive data transport.
Its integrated mechanisms provide a framework through which data-intense applications maintain functionality and reliability across volatile networks.

While TCP offers reliable data exchange, it inherently lacks security features, exposing it to vulnerabilities including:

TCP Spoofing: Unauthorized data injection by impersonating legitimate packets.
Man-in-the-Middle Attacks: Eavesdropping and potential alteration of communication.
Denial-of-Service (DoS) and Distributed Denial-of-Service (DDoS) Attacks: Overwhelming a system through excessive traffic targeting.

To combat these, Internet Protocol Security (IPsec) or Transport Layer Security (TLS) can be overlaid to provide encryption, authentication, and integrity checks without altering the original framework from which TCP operates.

Through the comprehensive strength of its design, TCP represents a foundational element of Internet communications, accommodating diverse needs while maintaining robustness and flexibility. Its evolution represents efforts to adapt to new challenges while preserving its core principles of reliable, sequenced, and error checked data transport.

User Datagram Protocol (UDP)

The User Datagram Protocol (UDP) is a fundamental communication protocol in the Internet Protocol suite, delivering a connectionless transport mechanism in the Transport Layer. Unlike the Transmission Control Protocol (TCP), UDP prioritizes simplicity and speed over reliability and order, making it a quintessential choice for applications where delay sensitivity is valued over data accuracy. This section delves into the structure, functionality, and applications of UDP, illustrating its strategic role in facilitating rapid communication across diverse networks.

UDP is defined by several distinct characteristics that differentiate it from TCP:

Connectionless Communication: UDP does not establish a persistent session or connection between two endpoints; instead, it transmits data as discrete packets known as datagrams.

Minimal Overhead: The absence of connection setup, sequencing, and acknowledgment phases results in low protocol overhead, enabling faster data transfer.

Best-Effort Delivery: UDP does not guarantee delivery, order preservation, or error checking in the communication process, relying on higher-level applications to manage these concerns if necessary.

Broadcast and Multicast Support: Unlike TCP, UDP supports broadcast and multicast transmissions, making it suitable for applications such as streaming media and gaming.

These characteristics render UDP advantageous in scenarios where rapid data transmission is vital and occasional data loss is tolerable.

UDP encapsulates data in units called datagrams. Each UDP datagram consists of a header and a payload. The simplicity of its header contributes to UDP's efficiency and performance.

Source Port (16 bits): Indicates the port number at the sender's end, assisting in application-specific communication.

Destination Port (16 bits): Specifies the recipient's port number, directing the datagram to the appropriate application.

Length (16 bits): Describes the total length of the datagram, including both header and payload, useful for determining message boundaries.

Checksum (16 bits): Provides a basic validation for data integrity; optional in IPv4 but mandatory for IPv6.

The UDP header's minimal complexity is vital for efficient processing, particularly in environments where computational resources or bandwidth are constrained.

```
# Pseudocode to create a basic UDP header
struct UDPHeader {
unsigned short source_port;     unsigned short destination_port;
unsigned short length;
unsigned short checksum;
};
```

The elegance of UDP's format facilitates expeditious handling of data, aligning with its design philosophy of simplicity and speed.

UDP's connectionless nature supports various communication models:

Unicast: One-to-one communication between a single sender and receiver.
Broadcast: Sending a message to all potential nodes within a network segment.
Multicast: Targeted communication with multiple specific receivers, optimizing bandwidth by reducing redundant data packets.

These methodologies underpin UDP's utility in applications like DHCP (Dynamic Host Configuration Protocol), where initial device configuration can reach multiple clients simultaneously.

```
# Python code using socket library to send a UDP broadcast import
socket

broadcast_address = ('<broadcast>', 12345) message = b'Hello, network!'

sock = socket.socket(socket.AF_INET, socket.SOCK_DGRAM)
sock.setsockopt(socket.SOL_SOCKET, socket.SO_BROADCAST, 1)
sock.sendto(message, broadcast_address)
```

UDP's flexibility grants developers the ability to tailor transmissions for specific network demands effectively.

UDP shines in scenarios where speed and efficiency are paramount, and minor packet loss is permissible:

Streaming Applications: Video and audio streams use UDP to minimize latency. Protocols such as RTP (Real-time Transport Protocol) are layered over UDP to accommodate real-time media delivery.

Online Gaming: Fast-paced games leverage UDP to reduce input lag and enhance responsiveness, conditions crucial for competitive play.

VoIP (Voice over IP): Real-time audio communication across networks benefits from UDP's low latency, enhancing call quality despite occasional audio packet loss.

DNS (Domain Name System): UDP supports rapid query-response cycles, essential for the quick resolution of domain names into IP addresses.

These applications illustrate UDP's versatility, addressing the need for immediacy in data transmission across global networks.

Despite its advantages, UDP has inherent limitations:

Lack of Reliability: There are no assurances of packet delivery integrity; applications must implement their own error-checking mechanisms.

No Congestion Control: UDP does not address network congestion issues, potentially leading to packet loss in heavily loaded networks.

Packet Duplication: Due to its stateless nature, UDP does not inherently prevent duplicate datagrams.
Applications using UDP must integrate additional strategies to compensate for these shortcomings if correctness is imperative.

Socket programming offers a gateway for implementing network applications using UDP. Through the 'socket' library, developers can construct lightweight client-server models over UDP, capitalizing on its rapid, efficient protocol stack.

Here is an example of a basic UDP client-server communication schema:

```
# UDP Server using Python's socket library import
socket
server_address = ('localhost', 65432) buffer_size =
1024
# Create a UDP server socket
server_socket = socket.socket(socket.AF_INET,
socket.SOCK_DGRAM) server_socket.bind(server_address)
print("UDP server up and listening")

while True:
data, client_addr = server_socket.recvfrom(buffer_size)    print(f"Received
message: {data} from {client_addr}")    server_socket.sendto(b"ACK",
client_addr)

# UDP Client using Python's socket library import
socket

server_address = ('localhost', 65432) message
= b'Hello, UDP server!'

# Create a UDP client socket
client_socket = socket.socket(socket.AF_INET, socket.SOCK_DGRAM)
```

```
try:
    client_socket.sendto(message, server_address)    data,
server = client_socket.recvfrom(4096)
print(f"Received message: {data}")
finally:
client_socket.close()
```

This example demonstrates a simple UDP echo server, capturing data from clients and sending an acknowledgment, 'ACK', back. The intrinsic simplicity of UDP simplifies the application design, focusing purely on data exchange without connection management overhead.

UDP's lack of intrinsic security features poses challenges:

Packet Spoofing and Injection: Attackers can insert malicious packets into a communication stream. **Amplification Attacks**: UDP's connectionless nature is exploited in reflection attacks, generating excessive response traffic to a target.

To mitigate such threats, developers often employ additional security protocols, like Datagram Transport Layer Security (DTLS), which provides data integrity, authentication, and confidentiality through encryption.

By incorporating these methods, applications can balance the speed and simplicity benefits of UDP with necessary security mechanisms to safeguard user data.

UDP's foundational simplicity offers significant benefits for applications prioritizing latency and simplicity over reliability and order assurance. Its operation forms the backbone of many mission-critical, latency-sensitive applications, empowering real-time data streaming, dynamic communications, and swift transactions across the vast expanse of the Internet. Despite inherent challenges concerning data reliability and security, UDP persists as an invaluable component of the modern networking tableau, sustaining innovations that revolutionize connectivity and interaction.

Application Layer Protocols

The Application Layer resides at the top of the TCP/IP model and is responsible for interacting directly with end user software applications. It provides numerous protocols that define how applications communicate over a network. These protocols manage data exchange directly tied to particular application needs and functionalities, offering services such as file transfers, email delivery, and web browsing. This section explores key Application Layer protocols such as HTTP, HTTPS, FTP, SMTP, and DNS, explaining their functions, use cases, and impact on network communications.

Hypertext Transfer Protocol (HTTP) HTTP is integral to the World Wide Web, facilitating the exchange of hypertext documents between web servers and clients (web browsers). Operating as a stateless protocol, HTTP functions upon request-response paradigms, where a client sends an HTTP request for a specific resource and the server responds with that resource, typically in the form of an HTML document.

HTTP Methods HTTP defines a set of request methods which indicate the desired action:

GET: Retrieves data from a specified resource.
POST: Sends data to a server to create or update resources.
PUT: Updates a resource with the provided data.
DELETE: Removes the specified resource.

Request and response headers further encapsulate metadata, including content type, encoding, and cache control, guiding data interchange specifics.

```
# Python example to perform an HTTP GET request using requests library
import requests

url = 'http://www.example.com' response
= requests.get(url)
print(f"Response status: {response.status_code}") print(response.content)
```

HTTP/2 and HTTP/3 introduce enhancements in multiplexing requests, reducing latency, and improving performance, addressing the protocol's historical limitations concerning performance efficiency.

Security - HTTPS HTTPS, or HTTP Secure, elevates traditional HTTP by incorporating encryption using TLS (Transport Layer Security). HTTPS ensures confidentiality, integrity, and authentication of data between clients and servers, protecting communication against eavesdropping, man-in-the-middle attacks, and data integrity violations.

The secure transport provided by HTTPS is essential for sensitive transactions such as online banking, confidential communications, and secure commercial operations.

```
# Simple HTTPS request example using Python's requests
library url = 'https://www.secureexample.com' response =
requests.get(url)
print(f"Response secure status: {response.status_code}") if
response.ok:    print(response.content)
```

File Transfer Protocol (FTP) FTP offers a standard method to transfer files between systems over a network, enabling both file upload and download capabilities. Operating on a client-server model, FTP uses two separate connections: a control connection for transmitting commands and a data connection for actual file transfers.

FTP Commands Core FTP commands offer control functionalities:

USER: Provides a username for authentication.
PASS: Supplies the password to complete login.
LIST: Lists files in a directory.

RETR: Downloads a file.
STOR: Uploads a file.

FTP supports active and passive modes. Active mode uses server-initiated data connections, while passive mode, beneficial for firewall traversal, uses client-initiated connections.

```
# Python FTP example using ftplib to download a file from
ftplib import FTP

ftp = FTP('ftp.example.com')
ftp.login() ftp.cwd('pub') filename =
'example.txt' with open(filename,
'wb') as file: ftp.retrbinary(f'RETR
{filename}', file.write) ftp.quit()
```
Security - FTPS and SFTP FTP, inherently insecure due to plain text data transmission, can be augmented with security enhancements:

FTPS: Extends FTP with SSL/TLS for encrypted channels.
SFTP: Employs Secure Shell (SSH) for both secure file transfer and control, offering robust security compared to its counterparts.

Simple Mail Transfer Protocol (SMTP) SMTP governs the transmission of emails across the Internet, facilitating communication between mail servers. It defines the process through which email messages are sent from a client to a recipient's mail server, subsequently delivering these to the appropriate mailboxes.

SMTP Commands SMTP communication utilizes text commands for message transfer:

HELO: Identifies the client to the server.
MAIL FROM: Identifies the sender's email address.
RCPT TO: Specifies recipient addresses.
DATA: Initiates the transfer of the email contents.

Compatibility with MIME (Multipurpose Internet Mail Extensions) allows SMTP to handle diverse formats beyond plain text, including attachments, images, and multimedia.

```
# Python example to send an email using smtplib import
smtplib
from email.mime.text import MIMEText

msg = MIMEText('This is the body of the email.')
msg['Subject'] = 'Test Email' msg['From'] =
'sender@example.com' msg['To'] =
'recipient@example.com'
 with smtplib.SMTP('smtp.example.com') as
server:
```

```
server.login('username', 'password')
server.sendmail(msg['From'], [msg['To']], msg.as_string())
```

Security Enhancements SMTP's vulnerability to unauthorized access and eavesdropping can be mitigated using encryption protocols such as STARTTLS, providing both confidentiality and integrity.

Domain Name System (DNS) DNS plays a crucial role in Internet functioning by translating human-readable domain names into IP addresses, essential for locating and routing data to web servers.

Components and Operation DNS operates through hierarchical databases, consisting of domain names mapped to IP addresses. Its core components, including Domain Name Servers and resolvers, interact to fulfill queries and return corresponding IP addresses:

Root Nameservers: Serve as the initial step in DNS resolution, directing queries to appropriate top-level domain (TLD) nameservers.

TLD Nameservers: Direct requests to authoritative nameservers for specific domain hierarchies (e.g., com, org, net).

Authoritative Nameservers: Provide direct IP address mappings for domain queries.

The DNS resolution process exemplifies distributed computing where cache mechanisms significantly enhance query performance by storing previous responses locally, reducing latency.

```
# DNS query example using Python's socket module
import socket

domain = 'www.example.com' ip =
socket.gethostbyname(domain) print(f'The IP
address for {domain} is {ip}')
```

Security - DNSSEC DNS, initially designed without built-in security, is susceptible to spoofing attacks. DNS Security Extensions (DNSSEC) mitigate security vulnerabilities by employing digital signatures to ensure data integrity and authenticity.

Additional Application Layer Protocols Beyond the heavily utilized protocols, the application layer embraces diverse protocols serving specific communication needs:

Telnet: Allows remote command-line interface access to systems but lacks inherent security.

SSH (Secure Shell): Grants secure command-line administration over networks, replacing Telnet with robust encryption.

SIP (Session Initiation Protocol): Fundamental to real-time communication such as VoIP, enabling signaling and control over multimedia sessions.

LDAP (Lightweight Directory Access Protocol): Facilitates accessing and maintaining distributed directory databases over an IP network.

Each protocol carries features tailored to its operations, enhancing network functionality and enriching user experiences.

Security Challenges and Considerations Despite inherent challenges, application layer protocols contribute significantly to the vibrant ecosystem of interactive communications. Security remains a primary concern, demanding careful analysis and enhancements:

Data Encryption: Ensures confidentiality and integrity of data exchanged between clients and servers.
Authentication Measures: Verifies user identities before granting access to sensitive data or services. **Regular Updates**: Ensures protocol implementations address vulnerabilities, benefiting from the latest security research.

In integrating these protocols, network architects and developers strive to balance efficient data exchange against security imperatives, creating resilient systems poised to meet evolving demands. The constellation of protocols residing in the application layer forms the foundation upon which the Internet's wide-ranging services build, driving innovation and connectivity across the digital landscape.

Networking Tools and Utilities

In the domain of computer networks, tools and utilities play a crucial role in both the analysis and maintenance of networking environments. These tools assist network administrators and engineers in monitoring, diagnosing, and optimizing network performance and security. This section elaborates on the most significant networking tools and utilities, covering their functionalities, practical applications, and illustrating how they facilitate efficient network management.

Ping The tool ping is a fundamental network utility employed for testing connectivity between devices through ICMP (Internet Control Message Protocol) echo request and reply messages. It gauges whether a host is reachable over an IP network and measures round-trip time for messages sent to the destination.

Functionality and Use

Reachability Test: Determines if a host is active on a network.
Latency Measurement: Assesses the responsiveness and round-trip time to a remote host.
Packet Loss Detection: Identifies any loss in data transmission, aiding in diagnosing network reliability.

```
# Example use of ping command in terminal
ping google.com
```

PING google.com (142.250.190.78): 56 data bytes

64 bytes from 142.250.190.78: icmp_seq=0 ttl=118 time=29.9 ms

Limitations While ping can confirm connectivity and delay metrics, it cannot diagnose nuanced network pathology or packet integrity. Firewalls might also obstruct ICMP packets, rendering the tool non-operational in such guarded environments.

Traceroute and Tracert Traceroute (on UNIX-like systems) and tracert (on Windows) illustrate the pathway that packets take across a network. By revealing each hop's IP address, these utilities provide insights into the network's routing topology.

Functional Details

Path Discovery: Identifies each router traversed along the path to a destination.
Latency Analysis: Provides time data per hop, indicating where delays occur.
Network Troubleshooting: Discerns where packets may be dropped or misrouted.

```
# Example use of traceroute command
traceroute example.com
```

```
traceroute to example.com (93.184.216.34), 30 hops max
    192.168.1.1 (192.168.1.1)  1.123 ms  1.211 ms  1.304 ms
    10.0.0.1 (10.0.0.1)  9.654 ms  10.332 ms  10.789 ms
```

Variability Across Networks Results from traceroute can vary due to dynamic routing algorithms, network congestion, and timeouts at different network hops. These variations necessitate multiple runs for reliable data collection.

Netstat The netstat utility provides comprehensive insights into the network connections and sockets on a device. It is indispensable in assessing network activity and diagnosing connectivity issues.

Capabilities and Usage

Active Connection Listing: Displays both incoming and outgoing connections on a system, including protocol, local and foreign addresses, and connection state.
Routing Tables: Outputs kernel routing tables, offering a glimpse into how packets are routed. **Interface Statistics**: Provides data traffic statistics for each network interface.

```
# Example use of netstat to display active connections netstat -
tuln
```

```
Active Internet connections (only servers)
Proto Recv-Q Send-Q Local Address      Foreign Address    State tcp
0    0 0.0.0.0:80          0.0.0.0:*        LISTEN udp    0    0 0.0.0.0:53
0.0.0.0:*
```

Diagnostic Benefits Through its detailed output, netstat assists in identifying suspicious activities that may indicate security breaches, such as unexpected open ports or foreign addresses.

NSLookup The nslookup tool queries the Domain Name System to obtain domain names or IP address mappings, facilitating domain diagnostics and resolution verification.

Functional Advantages

Domain Resolution: Verifies that domain names correctly resolve to their respective IP addresses.
Server Query: Directs queries to specific DNS servers, useful for troubleshooting DNS issues.
Mail Exchange Server Check: Examines MX records to validate email server configuration.

```
# Example use of nslookup to query a domain
nslookup www.example.com
```

```
Server:        8.8.8.8
Address:       8.8.8.8#53
```

```
Non-authoritative answer:
Name:  www.example.com
Address: 93.184.216.34
```

Limitations and Considerations nslookup commands rely on the response of the DNS servers involved and might be influenced by caching, leading to variations in output over successive queries.

Wireshark Wireshark is a powerful network protocol analyzer that captures and decodes network packets, providing a microscopic view of network traffic.

Core Features

Real-Time Packet Capture: Monitors live network data traffic across multiple interfaces.
Protocol Analysis: Supports deep inspection of hundreds of protocols, aiding diagnostics of complex network issues.
Reassembly and Filtering: Ability to reassemble fragmented traffic and apply packet filters to focus analysis.

```
# Basic command line invocation of Wireshark's command-line tool, 'tshark'
tshark -i eth0 -c 10
```

```
Capturing on 'eth0'
1   0.000000 192.168.1.2 -> 192.168.1.1 TCP 74 44350 > 80 [SYN] Seq=0 Win=65535 Len=0
```

Precautions and Ethical Usage Wireshark's ability to capture sensitive data mandates ethical use, with permissions secured prior to deployment, to avoid privacy violations and legal repercussions.

Curl curl is a versatile command-line tool that interacts with network protocols, primarily used to transfer data to or from a server using a broad range of supported protocols, including HTTP, HTTPS, FTP, and more.

Functional Scope

Data Transfer: Moves data; supports file transfer with FTP, HTTP POST requests, and custom headers. **API Testing**: Verifies RESTful API endpoints, allowing for the execution of GET, PUT, DELETE actions directly from the console.

Automation Potential: Supports scripting and automation of web interactions.

```
# Example of using curl to fetch data from a URL curl -
I http://www.example.com
```

```
HTTP/1.1 200 OK
Date: Mon, 01 Jan 2022 12:00:00 GMT
Server: ExampleServer/0.1
```

Advanced Scripting Capabilities Beyond manual operations, curl can be integrated into scripts for dynamic data processing, offering customizable options for headers, authentication, and more.

Nmap The nmap utility (Network Mapper) is renowned for its network discovery and security auditing capabilities, often employed to map networks and reveal security vulnerabilities.

Key Abilities

Network Discovery: Efficiently scans large networks, providing insights into available hosts and services.
Port Scanning: Identifies open ports and associated services on a system.
Vulnerability Assessment: Offers extensions through nmap scripts to detect vulnerabilities within systems.

```
# Example nmap command to perform a comprehensible scan
nmap -A -T4 scanme.example.com
```

```
Starting Nmap 7.80 ( https://nmap.org ) at 2022-01-01 12:00 UTC
Nmap scan report for scanme.example.com (93.184.216.34)
Host is up (0.045s latency).
Not shown: 998 closed ports
PORT   STATE SERVICE VERSION
80/tcp  open  http   Apache httpd 2.4.1
```

Responsible Use and Regulatory Compliance As with any robust network analysis tool, nmap should be utilized responsibly, ensuring compliance with network policies and regulations to mitigate unauthorized scans.

Implications and Strategic Use The array of networking tools and utilities discussed enhances network management, troubleshooting, and security. The strategic deployment of these tools enables sophisticated insight into network behavior, facilitating informed decision-making in both operational and security contexts. Observing ethical guidelines and legal constraints is imperative to leverage their capacity effectively, ensuring networks are robust, responsive, and resilient against evolving challenges.

These utilities provide the backbone for dynamic network oversight, empowering administrators to achieve balanced, secure, and high-performance networking environments.

Asynchronous and Synchronous Communication

This topic explores the fundamental differences between asynchronous and synchronous communication methods in network programming. It defines each communication type, highlighting their unique characteristics, advantages, and typical use cases. The chapter provides practical guidance on implementing both methods in C++ applications, along with a comparative analysis to assist in selecting the appropriate approach based on specific requirements. It also examines real-world scenarios and performance considerations, offering insights into the strategic application of these communication techniques in network software development.

Defining Synchronous Communication

Synchronous communication in computer science refers to a communication method where operations are executed in a predetermined sequence, with each operation waiting for the previous one to complete before initiating. This is particularly relevant in scenarios where immediate response is crucial, and it is necessary to ensure that data integrity or the order of operations is maintained.

A defining characteristic of synchronous communication is its reliance on time constraints for each interaction. Unlike asynchronous communication methods, which allow processes to operate independently and may lead to a state where operations continue without waiting for a response, synchronous communication entails a strict adherence to the operation order. This sequential handling makes it incredibly suited for tasks that require precision and certainty of response.

Blocking Nature: Synchronous communications are blocking. A process that is in communication mode will not proceed to the next step until it has received a response. This blocking can simplify the logic of a program since the programmer does not have to manage complex states or check if an operation is complete.

Predictable Timing: Since each operation must wait for the completion of the previous one, the timing in synchronous communication is predictable, a desirable feature in systems demanding high assurance levels, such as avionics or industrial systems.

Ease of Debugging: Because operations proceed in a set order, debugging synchronous communication systems is generally simpler than their asynchronous counterparts. Each step can be traced sequentially, which makes identifying the source of a problem more straightforward.

Resource Utilization: Synchronous communication can be resource-intensive, especially when network conditions are suboptimal since any delays affect the entire pipeline of operations.

In network communications, synchronous communication methods are implemented in protocols where direct and fast exchange of information is mandatory, such as HTTP/1.x where a request must receive a response before another request can be sent on the same connection.

Implementation in Real-World Systems

In real-world systems, synchronous communication is evident in many client-server models where operations proceed in a request-response fashion. Consider a traditional web browser communicating with a web server using the HTTP protocol. For each request, the client waits for an explicit response before sending another request.

```cpp
#include <iostream>
#include <cstring>
#include <sys/socket.h>
#include <arpa/inet.h>
#include <unistd.h>
 int main() {    int socket_desc;    struct
sockaddr_in server;    char *message,
server_reply[2000];    // Create socket
   socket_desc = socket(AF_INET, SOCK_STREAM,
0);   if (socket_desc == -1) {
     std::cout << "Could not create socket";
   }
   server.sin_addr.s_addr = inet_addr("74.125.235.20");
server.sin_family = AF_INET;    server.sin_port =
htons(80);

   // Connect to remote server
   if (connect(socket_desc, (struct sockaddr *)&server, sizeof(server)) < 0) {
std::cout << "connect error";    return 1;
   }

   // Send some data
   message = "GET / HTTP/1.1\r\n\r\n";
   if (send(socket_desc, message, strlen(message), 0) < 0) {
std::cout << "Send failed";    return 1;
   }
```

```cpp
    // Receive a reply from the server
    if (recv(socket_desc, server_reply, 2000, 0) < 0) {          std::cout
<< "recv failed";
    }
    std::cout << "Reply received: " << server_reply;

    close(socket_desc);
return 0;
}
```

This example demonstrates a simple synchronous communication model using sockets in C++. Here, the client establishes a connection to a server and waits for the server's response before proceeding further. The blocking nature of the 'recv' function ensures that the subsequent actions are only taken once a message is received from the server.

Advantages and Drawbacks

The advantages of synchronous communication mainly derive from its straightforwardness and predictability. In environments where it is crucial to have operations executed in a precise order and ensuring that feedback is immediately available from each operation, synchronous systems provide an excellent solution.

However, the blocking nature of synchronous communication can be inefficient, particularly in distributed systems where network latency can introduce significant delays. Additionally, because each operation must complete before the next can start, it can lead to increased waiting times and can be less scalable when the number of concurrent interactions grows.

Despite these drawbacks, synchronous communication remains a valuable approach in specific scenarios. Critical systems or those interacting with physical devices where precise timing is paramount often employ synchronous methods to maintain control flow integrity and reliability.

Application Domains

Synchronous communication is applied across a variety of domains where immediate acknowledgment and order maintenance are priority. Some notable applications include:

Telecommunications: Traditional telephony systems where talk-spurt alternates between speaker and listener necessitating strict order.

Embedded Systems: Such as industrial automation systems, which require precise control and feedback on each operation to ensure safety compliance.

Financial Transactions: Especially in stock exchanges and banking transactions, where the flow of information is critically dependent on synchronous operations.

Command and Control Systems: In military applications, where the response and the timing of command execution need to be predictable and reliable.

Synchronous Models in Application Development

In application development, synchronous methods are typically easier to implement when the transaction volume is manageable, and the structure of the communications follows a predictable pattern. This provides clear scalability limits and encourages disciplined coding practices.

```cpp
std::string synchronousRequest(const std::string& url) {
    // Set up the request    std::string
response;    CURL *curl =
curl_easy_init();
    if(curl) {
        curl_easy_setopt(curl, CURLOPT_URL, url.c_str());
curl_easy_setopt(curl, CURLOPT_WRITEFUNCTION, WriteCallback);
curl_easy_setopt(curl, CURLOPT_WRITEDATA, &response);

        // Perform the request, res will get the return code
        CURLcode res = curl_easy_perform(curl);
if(res != CURLE_OK) {
            std::cerr << "curl_easy_perform() failed: " << curl_easy_strerror(res) << std::endl;
        }

        // Cleanup
        curl_easy_cleanup(curl);
    }
    return response;
}
```

In this C++ example, a synchronous HTTP request is made using the libcurl library. The simplicity of such an implementation is one of the main draws towards synchronous communication: setup, execution, and error handling are all neatly contained within a straightforward and easily monitorable pipeline.

Considerations for Synchronous Communication Design

When designing a system that employs synchronous communication, several factors must be considered:

Throughput Requirements: Synchronous systems can restrict throughput, as operations are inherently serialized. In systems with high throughput requirements, alternative asynchronous or multi-threaded approaches may be recommended.

Fault Tolerance: Since operations are closely coupled, a failure in one component can halt the process chain, making fault tolerance and error recovery critical design elements.

Latency Sensitivity: The system must be capable of tolerating network-induced latencies without significant performance degradation or blocked processes.

Network Reliability: The communication channel's reliability directly impacts the effectiveness of synchronous communication. High packet loss or erratic transmission speeds can introduce inefficiencies.

By understanding these factors, developers can effectively weigh synchronous communication's merits against its limitations, ensuring a well-informed decision tailored to the specific application context. Ultimately, synchronous communication remains a pivotal technique in the vast landscape of networked systems, its disciplined and linear approach indispensable in certain scenarios demanding an absolute order and clarity of operations.

Defining Asynchronous Communication

Asynchronous communication is a method that allows operations to occur independently from one another, enabling processes to progress without waiting for a response or completion of prior commands. This decoupling makes asynchronous communication a powerful technique, particularly in networked systems where latency and variable response times are inherent challenges.

A defining aspect of asynchronous communication is its ability to initiate multiple operations simultaneously, thereby optimizing resource utilization and enhancing system responsiveness. Unlike its synchronous counterpart, asynchronous communication does not follow a strict order of operations completion, offering flexibility in how tasks are managed and scheduled.

Characteristics of Asynchronous Communication

Asynchronous communication is marked by several distinguishing attributes:

Non-blocking Operations: Operations in asynchronous communication are initiated without waiting for the prior operation to finish, allowing the system to continue its processes and manage other tasks simultaneously.

Concurrency: Asynchronous communication supports concurrent operations, where multiple tasks are engaged in processing at the same time, improving the system's overall throughput and capabilities.

Scalability: Asynchronous systems are inherently more scalable. They can handle a larger volume of operations simultaneously due to their non-blocking nature.

Complexity in Implementation: Coding asynchronous systems requires more sophisticated constructs such as callbacks, promises, and future objects, which can add complexity to application development.

These features make asynchronous communication particularly well-suited for modern applications, including web services, where client expectations for speed and responsiveness are high.

Implementation in Real-World Systems

In practical applications, asynchronous communication is evident across various domains where independent task processing enhances efficiency. One clear use case is in the development of non-blocking server architectures, such as Node.js, which ensures high throughput and efficient resource utilization.

```cpp
#include <iostream>
#include <future>
#include <chrono>

int performAsyncTask(int duration) {
    std::this_thread::sleep_for(std::chrono::seconds(duration));    return
duration;
} int main() {
    std::future<int> result = std::async(std::launch::async, performAsyncTask, 5);

    std::cout << "Processing other tasks while waiting for asynchronous task." << std::endl;
    // Simulate doing other work here
    std::this_thread::sleep_for(std::chrono::seconds(2));

    int value = result.get(); // This will block if the task is not done yet    std::cout
<< "Async task completed with duration: " << value << std::endl;

    return 0;
}
```

This example demonstrates the use of asynchronous operations using C++'s 'std::async'. Here, the 'performAsyncTask' function runs independently of the main thread, allowing other processes to execute concurrently. This ability to manage tasks concurrently without impeding the execution flow is a significant advantage of asynchronous communication models.

Advantages and Drawbacks

The advantages of asynchronous communication lie primarily in its ability to enhance responsiveness and maximize the efficiency of system resource utilization. Systems employing asynchronous techniques can handle more operations simultaneously, reducing wait times and increasing throughput.

However, the complexity associated with implementing asynchronous communication can pose significant challenges.

Developers must manage concurrency-related issues such as race conditions and deadlocks, which requires a solid understanding of concurrency primitives and careful design planning.

The decoupled nature of asynchronous communication can also lead to challenges in maintaining data integrity and ensuring transactions complete successfully without interference, often necessitating additional mechanisms for handling failures and retries.

Application Domains

Asynchronous communication is highly applicable in environments where efficiency, speed, and scalability are critical. Prominent domains utilizing asynchronous methods include:

Web Development: JavaScript and Node.js heavily rely on asynchronous calls to handle high volumes of requests efficiently without blocking the main execution thread.

Cloud Computing: Cloud platforms frequently use asynchronous communication for operations that require rapid processing and high scalability potential.

Machine Learning Pipelines: Distributing tasks and computations asynchronously maximizes computational resources and speeds up data processing pipelines.

Distributed Systems: Distributed architectures often employ asynchronous protocols to communicate effectively over networks of independent nodes.

Asynchronous Models in Application Development

Developers use various models and structures to achieve asynchronous communication. Common patterns involve using callbacks, promises, and reactive programming paradigms that allow seamless integration of asynchronous tasks. Frameworks and languages offer diverse support for these models, enabling efficient, non-blocking application design.

```
#include <iostream>
#include <future>

void doTask(std::promise<int>&& p) {
    std::this_thread::sleep_for(std::chrono::seconds(1));
    p.set_value(42); // Task completed
} int main() {
    std::promise<int> promise;
    std::future<int> future = promise.get_future();

    std::thread taskThread(doTask, std::move(promise));

    std::cout << "Performing other operations while waiting for task result." << std::endl;

    auto status = future.wait_for(std::chrono::seconds(2));    if
(status == std::future_status::ready) {
        std::cout << "Received result: " << future.get() << std::endl;
    } else {
```

```
        std::cout << "Task is taking longer than expected." << std::endl;
    }
    taskThread.join();
    return 0;
}
```

This example uses 'std::promise' and 'std::future' to manage asynchronous operations, representing typical building blocks for asynchronous communication in C++. It illustrates how these constructs enable responses from asynchronous tasks to be awaited flexibly and provides a mechanism for determining task completion or ongoing status.

Considerations for Asynchronous Communication Design

Designing systems around asynchronous communication requires careful consideration of several factors:

Concurrency Control: Proper use of synchronization mechanisms to manage operation overlap and resource contention should be considered.

Error Handling: Asynchronous operations often require robust error handling strategies that can recover from partial failures naturally.

Performance Tuning: Asynchronous systems should be designed with performance metrics in mind, ensuring that the benefits of concurrent processing outweigh overhead costs.

Scalability Arrangements: The system should scale appropriately with the operation load, ensuring that system resources are adequately managed to sustain high concurrency levels.

As developers design asynchronous systems, they must understand the implications of breaking tasks into smaller, independently executable units and provide appropriate strategies for coordinating completed results. By acknowledging the inherent complexities yet substantial advantages, asynchronous communication remains a formidable tool in the arsenal for crafting advanced, responsive, and scalable networked systems.

Comparative Analysis of Communication Methods

Understanding the principles behind synchronous and asynchronous communication is crucial for the effective design and deployment of networked systems. These communication methods have unique attributes and serve different requirements based on system needs. An in-depth comparative analysis helps in choosing the most fitting approach for specific application scenarios, ensuring optimized performance, reliability, and scalability.

Operation Control: Synchronous communication demands that each operation wait for the completion of the preceding one before proceeding. This is contrasted with the non-blocking structure of asynchronous communication, where operations can be initiated independently and executed out-of-order. This operational divergence significantly affects how systems are designed and optimized for task management and processing.

Response Manageability: Synchronous systems are usually simpler to manage due to their predictable and linear control flow, where each step must be completed before the next one begins. In asynchronous systems, multiple operations run concurrently, complicating the tracking and synchronization of responses but enabling greater system throughput and efficiency.

Performance Considerations: Performance is a critical evaluation criterion when comparing communication methods. The blocking nature of synchronous communication can introduce latency into a system, particularly evident in networked environments where delays are common due to transmission time. In contrast, asynchronous communication thrives in environments where the system can continue processing other tasks while waiting for operations to complete, reducing idle time and improving overall system throughput.

```cpp
#include <iostream>
#include <thread>
#include <chrono>

// Simulate a blocking synchronous task void
synchronousTask() {
    std::this_thread::sleep_for(std::chrono::seconds(2)); // Simulate delay
std::cout << "Synchronous task completed." << std::endl;
}

// Simulate an asynchronous task void
asynchronousTask() {
    std::this_thread::sleep_for(std::chrono::seconds(2)); // Simulate delay
std::cout << "Asynchronous task completed." << std::endl;
} int main() {
    std::cout << "Starting synchronous task..." << std::endl;    synchronousTask();

    std::cout << "Starting asynchronous task..." << std::endl;
std::thread taskThread(asynchronousTask);    taskThread.detach();

    std::cout << "Main thread is free to perform other tasks." << std::endl;    //
Simulate doing other work
    std::this_thread::sleep_for(std::chrono::seconds(1));    std::cout <<
"Main thread work completed." << std::endl;

    return 0;
}
```

In this C++ example, a comparison is drawn between synchronous and asynchronous tasks. The synchronous function blocks the main thread until completed, leading to potential inefficiencies. Conversely, the asynchronous task runs on a separate thread, allowing the main thread to execute other tasks concurrently, thus demonstrating enhanced parallelism and resource utilization.

Synchronous Communication: Typically finds its place in systems where operation order integrity and immediate response are critical, such as legacy systems and tightly coupled transactional systems in finance where atomic transactions need assured sequential completion.

Asynchronous Communication: Excels in environments where parallelism and scalability are paramount, such as modern web servers and cloud-based applications, which must efficiently handle numerous concurrent requests without bottlenecks.

```python
import asyncio
 async def handle_request(reader, writer):
    data = await reader.read(100)     message
= data.decode()
    addr = writer.get_extra_info('peername')

    print(f"Received {message} from {addr}")

    print("Send: %s" % message)
writer.write(data)     await
writer.drain()

    print("Closing the connection")     writer.close()
async def main():
    server = await asyncio.start_server(
handle_request, '127.0.0.1', 8888)
    async with server:
      await server.serve_forever()
asyncio.run(main())
```

Asynchronous communication technologies like Python's 'asyncio' are commonly used in web servers to handle many connections concurrently without the need for multi-threading, showcasing how asynchronous communication can enable efficient, scalable service architectures.

Ease of Debugging and Maintainability: Synchronous communication offers an easier debugging experience due to its straightforward, linear execution model. Tracking the execution path and identifying points of failure is substantially more amenable in a predictable, step-by-step process flow.

Asynchronous systems, due to their non-linear and often concurrent nature, require more sophisticated debugging strategies, potentially involving logging and performance profiling tools capable of managing concurrency issues such as deadlocks and race conditions. Nevertheless, though challenging, frameworks and libraries provide constructs to improve both traceability and maintainability in asynchronous applications.

Resource Management and Scalability: Scaling synchronous systems often requires significant resource allocations because of the blocking operations that tie up resources, waiting for replies before moving forward. In contrast, asynchronous systems can efficiently manage resources by continuing operations while waiting, thus enabling better scalability in distributed and heavily loaded environments.

For network protocols, implementing an asynchronous communication scheme can greatly reduce latencies and increase throughput, particularly where the network round trip time (RTT) is variable. By allowing other operations to progress while waiting for network responses, systems can maintain high responsiveness to user requests.

Security Implications: Security considerations also play a role in the choice between synchronous and asynchronous communications. Synchronous systems, with their sequential operation, naturally limit the concurrency-related security issues but must handle blocking-related vulnerabilities, such as denial of service (DoS) attacks where processes are lodged indefinitely waiting for network responses.

Asynchronous systems require more careful consideration of security issues related to concurrency, such as resource access violations arising from unprotected shared data and ensuring the integrity and confidentiality of data that may linger in transit or in-memory caches between asynchronous executions.

Summary of Comparative Implications: Having explored synchronous and asynchronous communication's core attributes, it is essential for engineers and developers to consider specific use-cases and balance the advantages. The choice between these methods should be driven by the application's requirements regarding process synchronization, resource allocation, and performance objectives.

Aspect	Synchronous Communication
Operation	Mode Blocking and sequential execution.
Scalability	Limited by blocking operations' resource holding.
Responsiveness	Predictable timing but can delay other tasks.
Debugging	Easier due to linear control flow.
Security	Fewer concurrency-related issues but susceptible to DoS vulnerabilities.

Aspect	Asynchronous Communication
Operation Mode	Non-blocking and concurrent execution.
Scalability	Superior with efficient resource utilization.
Responsiveness	Maximized throughput but potentially complex to manage.
Debugging	Complex due to non-linear events and concurrency issues.

Security Requires handling data integrity during concurrency operations.

Both synchronous and asynchronous communication techniques possess distinct benefits and trade-offs; careful consideration is necessary to determine their suitability in specific contexts requiring different levels of transaction control, response time, and cost-efficiency tuning. This careful analysis serves as a guide for professionals when architecting systems designed to achieve both reliability and scalability in various domains.

Implementing Synchronous Communication in C++

The implementation of synchronous communication in C++ is crucial in a multitude of use cases where operation order integrity and immediacy are imperative. This section delves into various techniques and constructs within C++ that facilitate synchronous communication, adhering to the language's standard libraries and capabilities. In C++, synchronous communication is typically characterized by blocking operations that follow a sequential execution flow.

One of the fundamental applications of synchronous communication is in network programming, particularly using sockets. TCP/IP socket programming is inherently a synchronous operation, providing guarantees on message ordering and delivery acknowledgment.

To establish a synchronous TCP connection using C++, the standard socket API is the primary gateway. The following C++ example establishes a simple synchronous connection to a server using sockets.

```cpp
#include <iostream>
#include <cstring>
#include <sys/socket.h>
#include <arpa/inet.h>
#include <unistd.h>
 int main() {
int sock;
    struct sockaddr_in server;
    char message[1000], server_reply[2000];

    // Create socket
    sock = socket(AF_INET, SOCK_STREAM,
0);    if (sock == -1) {
        std::cerr << "Could not create socket" << std::endl;          return
1;
    }
    std::cout << "Socket created" << std::endl;

    server.sin_addr.s_addr = inet_addr("192.168.1.1");
server.sin_family = AF_INET;    server.sin_port =
htons(8888);

    // Connect to remote server
    if (connect(sock, (struct sockaddr *)&server, sizeof(server)) < 0) {
std::cerr << "Connection failed" << std::endl;          return 1;
    }
    std::cout << "Connected" << std::endl;

    // Send some data
```

```cpp
    strcpy(message, "GET / HTTP/1.1\r\n\r\n");    if
(send(sock, message, strlen(message), 0) < 0) {
std::cerr << "Send failed" << std::endl;        return 1;
    }
    std::cout << "Data sent" << std::endl;

    // Receive a reply from the server    if (recv(sock,
server_reply, 2000, 0) < 0) {        std::cerr <<
"Receive failed" << std::endl;        return 1;
    }
    std::cout << "Reply received:\n" << server_reply << std::endl;

    close(sock);
    return 0;
}
```

In the example above, a socket is created using the POSIX socket API, which blocks the client application until a connection is successfully established with the server. The program waits for a response to each block, achieving the critical sequential execution characteristic of synchronous communication.

In C++, synchronous communication is not limited to network programming but extends to various other areas such as file I/O operations, where data is read or written in a blocking manner. The standard C++ I/O library provides classes like fstream for such operations.

```cpp
#include <iostream>
#include <fstream>
 int main() {
    std::ofstream outfile("example.txt");

    if (!outfile.is_open()) {
        std::cerr << "Error opening file for writing" << std::endl;        return 1;
    }
    outfile << "This is a line.\n";    outfile <<
"This is another line.\n";

    outfile.close();
    std::cout << "File written successfully" << std::endl;

    std::ifstream infile("example.txt");    if
(!infile.is_open()) {
        std::cerr << "Error opening file for reading" << std::endl;        return 1;
    }
    std::string line;
    while (std::getline(infile, line)) {        std::cout <<
line << std::endl;
```

```
    }
    infile.close();
return 0;
}
```

This example illustrates synchronous file handling, where fstream operations ensure that writing to and reading from a file occur sequentially and completely before proceeding to the next statement. The synchronous sequences guarantee that data consistency and temporal ordering are appropriately preserved.

Synchronous communication also plays a vital role in IPC, where processes communicate through mechanisms such as pipes or shared memory. In such settings, data is typically exchanged in a blocking manner to maintain coordination.

```cpp
#include <iostream> #include
<fcntl.h>
#include <unistd.h> #include
<sys/stat.h>
 int main() {
    const char* pipeName = "/tmp/testpipe";
mkfifo(pipeName, 0666);

    pid_t pid = fork();     if (pid == 0) { // Child
process        int readFd = open(pipeName,
O_RDONLY);        char buffer[100];
        read(readFd, buffer, sizeof(buffer));
        std::cout << "Child process received: " << buffer << std::endl;
close(readFd);     } else { // Parent process
        int writeFd = open(pipeName, O_WRONLY);
char message[] = "Hello from parent!";
write(writeFd, message, sizeof(message));
close(writeFd);
    }

    // Remove the named pipe after use
unlink(pipeName);
return 0;
}
```

In this code, both parent and child processes engage in a synchronous exchange over a named pipe (/tmp/testpipe). The read and write operations are blocking, requiring each party to wait for the respective operation to complete, typifying synchronous communication within IPC.

In environments with concurrent threads, synchronization primitives are necessary to ensure ordered execution through mutual exclusion and condition variables. These primitives help maintain the systematic exchange between threads to avoid race conditions.

```cpp
#include <iostream>
#include <thread>
#include <mutex>
#include <condition_variable>

std::mutex mtx;
std::condition_variable cv; bool
ready = false;

void print_id(int id) {
    std::unique_lock<std::mutex> lock(mtx);
cv.wait(lock, []{ return ready; });    std::cout <<
"Thread " << id << std::endl;
}
void set_ready() {
    {
        std::lock_guard<std::mutex> lock(mtx);
ready = true;
    }
    cv.notify_all();
} int main() {
    std::thread threads[10];    for (int
i = 0; i < 10; ++i) {
        threads[i] = std::thread(print_id, i);
    }
    std::this_thread::sleep_for(std::chrono::seconds(1));    std::cout
<< "Setting ready state." << std::endl;    set_ready();

    for (auto &t: threads) {
        t.join();    }
return 0;
}
```

In this example, the std::mutex and std::condition_variable work together to synchronize threads, ensuring that all threads wait for the ready condition. This synchronization enforces a specific order of operations, critical in applications requiring controlled access to shared resources in synchronous communication schemes.

Implementing synchronous communication in C++ requires careful consideration of potential pitfalls such as deadlocks in multi-threaded environments and the impact of blocking operations on application responsiveness. The design of synchronous systems should consider factors such as:

Deadlock Avoidance: Ensuring that resources are acquired and released in a consistent order can prevent deadlock scenarios.

Timeouts: Introducing time limitations on blocking operations can mitigate adverse effects such as liveness issues or long wait times.

Error Handling: Robust error handling mechanisms are crucial, especially in network communications where latency and transmission errors might affect synchronous operations.

Performance Impacts: Awareness of the performance trade-offs involved in blocking operations is necessary to select appropriate techniques based on application needs.

Synchronous communication in C++ provides a reliable means for order-dependent communication tasks, offering simplicity in coding logic best suited for applications where predictability and process simplicity are prerequisites. Through careful implementation and consideration of the pros and cons of synchronous models, developers can effectively exploit C++ capabilities to design solutions tailored to specific operational demands that adhere to the synchronous approach.

Implementing Asynchronous Communication in C++

Asynchronous communication is integral to the design of modern software systems, allowing for efficient resource use through concurrent operation execution. In C++, implementing asynchronous communication leverages a range of features and libraries allowing developers to design systems that are responsive and capable of handling large volumes of tasks in parallel.

C++11 introduced several features that provide native support for asynchronous programming. These include threads, futures, promises, and the standard asynchronous library, providing a foundation for constructing complex, non-blocking communications.

Threads are the building blocks of concurrent applications where multiple paths of execution occur simultaneously. The std::thread library in C++ enables developers to manage asynchronous tasks and improve application performance through parallel processing.

```cpp
#include <iostream>
#include <thread>

void computeTask(int duration) {
    std::this_thread::sleep_for(std::chrono::seconds(duration));
    std::cout << "Task duration: " << duration << " seconds completed." << std::endl;
} int main() {
    std::thread t1(computeTask, 3);    std::thread
t2(computeTask, 5);

    std::cout << "Main thread continues execution..." << std::endl;
    t1.join();
t2.join();

    std::cout << "All tasks completed." << std::endl;
return 0; }
```

In this example, two asynchronous tasks are spawned using threads, allowing the main program to continue its execution while waiting for these tasks to finish. This approach ensures optimal use of multiple processors.

Futures and promises provide a mechanism to work with deferred computations and handle the results once tasks complete. They allow initiating asynchronous operations and later retrieving their results without blocking the main execution flow.

```cpp
#include <iostream>
#include <thread>
#include <future>

int asyncComputation(int value) {
    std::this_thread::sleep_for(std::chrono::seconds(value));    return
value * 2;
}  int main() {
    std::promise<int> prom;
    std::future<int> fut = prom.get_future();

    std::thread t([&prom]() {
        prom.set_value(asyncComputation(5));
    });
    std::cout << "Waiting for the result..." << std::endl;    std::cout <<
"Result: " << fut.get() << std::endl;

    t.join();
return 0;
}
```

Using a promise, we encapsulate a long-running computation. A future is used to obtain the result when it becomes available. This approach abstracts the asynchrony and provides a straightforward way to wait for computations without locking the main thread.

The std::async function template is part of the C++ standard library used to asynchronously run a function.

std::async manages thread creation and workload distribution, offering the benefit of launching tasks asynchronously or synchronously based on the launch policy.

```cpp
#include <iostream>
#include <future>

int performCalculation(int x) {
    std::this_thread::sleep_for(std::chrono::seconds(3));    return x
* x;
}  int main() {
    std::future<int> result = std::async(std::launch::async, performCalculation, 10);
```

```
    std::cout << "Main continues, waiting for the result..." << std::endl;    std::cout
<< "Calculation result: " << result.get() << std::endl;

    return 0; }
```

The std::async facilitates the operation of performCalculation in a non-blocking manner, where the main program can perform other tasks while waiting for the result. The result is retrieved through a future, allowing the result to be processed once ready.

In addition to standard threading and concurrency utilities, specialized libraries provide enhanced capabilities for asynchronous network programming. Libraries such as Boost.Asio enable developers to structure nonblocking communication applications efficiently.

Boost.Asio is a cross-platform C++ library for network and low-level I/O programming that emphasizes asynchronous operations. Manifesting through a strong async model, Boost.Asio allows sophisticated asynchronous system designs.

```
#include <iostream>
#include <boost/asio.hpp> #include
<boost/bind/bind.hpp>

using boost::asio::ip::tcp;

void connectHandler(const boost::system::error_code& ec) {
if (!ec) {
    std::cout << "Connection established successfully." << std::endl;
  } else {
    std::cerr << "Failed to connect: " << ec.message() << std::endl;
  }
}  int main() {
  boost::asio::io_context io_context;

  tcp::socket socket(io_context);

  tcp::resolver resolver(io_context);
  auto endpoints = resolver.resolve("example.com", "80");

  boost::asio::async_connect(socket, endpoints, connectHandler);

  io_context.run();
return 0;
}
```

Here, the connection process is initiated asynchronously using async_connect, providing a connect Handler callback to handle the completion signal. The io_context.run() executes the operations associated with the io_context until the work is done.

Successfully building asynchronous applications requires understanding design patterns and best practices that govern this non-linear execution model.

The event-driven model is foundational to creating asynchronous systems. It enables applications to react to events or messages and execute corresponding callbacks without blocking operations.

```cpp
#include <iostream>
#include <functional>

void asyncOperation(std::function<void(int)> callback) {
std::cout << "Performing some operation..." << std::endl;
std::this_thread::sleep_for(std::chrono::seconds(2));    callback(42);
// Trigger callback with result
}
void resultCallback(int result) {
    std::cout << "Operation completed with result: " << result << std::endl;
} int main() {
    asyncOperation(resultCallback);
    std::cout << "Main function continues execution." << std::endl;
    std::this_thread::sleep_for(std::chrono::seconds(3)); // Keep the main thread alive for asynch
return 0;
}
```

This example demonstrates an asynchronous operation that invokes a callback function once the task completes. The main function continues execution during this asynchronous operation, illustrating effective decoupling.

Asynchronous systems require thoughtful error handling methods. Whether using try-catch blocks within task threads or leveraging features like exceptions in futures, robust error management is critical to maintaining system stability.

```cpp
#include <iostream>
#include <future>

int riskyComputation() {
    std::this_thread::sleep_for(std::chrono::seconds(3));    throw
std::runtime_error("An error occurred in computation!");
} int main() {
    std::future<int> result = std::async(std::launch::async, riskyComputation);
    try {
      int value = result.get();
      std::cout << "Computation result: " << value << std::endl;
    } catch (const std::exception &e) {
      std::cerr << "Caught exception: " << e.what() << std::endl;
    }
    return 0;
}
```

In this code, std::async is used to manage a risky calculation, where exceptions are anticipated and caught when retrieving the result from the future, preventing the application from terminating unexpectedly.

Implementing asynchronous communication in C++ extends beyond mere multithreading. It envelops the complete asynchronous paradigms, ranging from task parallelism to network I/O and event-driven patterns. C++ provides a robust toolset to create non-blocking applications, ensuring high responsiveness and throughput. Proper application design to adhere to asynchronous strategies, coupled with judicious use of C++ features and libraries like std::async and Boost.Asio, results in systems that are both scalable and efficient.

Understanding the intricacies, pitfalls, and best practices of asynchronous programming equips developers to create sophisticated, high-performance applications suited to the demands of modern software infrastructure.

Use Cases and Performance Considerations

The decision to employ synchronous or asynchronous communication models in software systems is heavily influenced by specific use cases and the performance objectives to be achieved. Each model's characteristics render them more suitable for certain applications based on network conditions, resource availability, scalability requirements, and user expectations. It is essential to perform a thorough analysis of these aspects to create systems capable of meeting both operational and performance standards.

Real-world Use Cases

Synchronous Communication Use Cases

Transaction Processing Systems: In financial services, transaction processing demands high integrity and sequential consistency. Systems such as online banking, stock trading platforms, and payment gateways often rely on synchronous communication to ensure that operations like fund transfers and order placements occur in a well-defined sequence, avoiding anomalies like double spending.

```
#include <iostream>
#include <mutex>

int accountBalance = 1000;        std::mutex
balanceMutex;

    void performTransaction(int withdrawalAmount) {
std::lock_guard<std::mutex> lock(balanceMutex);              if
(accountBalance >= withdrawalAmount) {              accountBalance -=
withdrawalAmount;
        std::cout << "Transaction successful, new balance: " << accountBalance <<
        } else {
```

```
            std::cout << "Insufficient balance for transaction." << std::endl;
        }
    }
    int main() {
        performTransaction(200);
performTransaction(500);
return 0;
}
```

In the code above, mutexes enforce synchronous access to shared resources, ensuring transaction integrity.

Command and Control Systems: In military or critical infrastructure applications, operations rely on
precise control of commands executed in a strict order. Such applications prioritize immediate processing and confirmation before executing subsequent commands, emphasizing reliability and predictability.

Collaborative Software and Interactive Applications: Applications that feature real-time collaboration, for example, multiplayer games and virtual meetings, often utilize synchronous communication to maintain a consistent state across all participants, reducing latency in response to user actions.

Asynchronous Communication Use Cases

Web and Network Servers: Modern web servers such as Nginx and Node.js leverage asynchronous communication to handle a multitude of client connections simultaneously, optimizing performance and resource utilization without the need for multithreading.

```
const http = require('http');
const server = http.createServer((req, res) => {
res.writeHead(200, {'Content-Type': 'text/plain'});
res.end('Hello, World!\n');
});
server.listen(3000, '127.0.0.1');
console.log('Server running at http://127.0.0.1:3000/');
```

The non-blocking model allows the server to continue accepting new connections while handling active requests.

Background Processing and Tasks: Applications like email servers, web crawlers, or data pipelines often offload intensive computations or I/O-bound tasks to asynchronous processes, enabling continued system responsiveness without waiting for task completion.

Microservices: Asynchronous communication is prevalent in microservice architectures, where services are loosely coupled, and communication often occurs through message brokers or event-driven patterns. This enhances fault tolerance and scalability, as services can operate independently and asynchronously handle failures or latency.

Performance Considerations

Latency and Throughput

Synchronous Communication: Latency in synchronous systems is typically determined by the round-trip time required for each operation to complete. The sequential execution process commonly accumulates delays, impacting throughput and overall system responsiveness if unforeseen network latencies arise.

Processing Order:
[Request 1] -> [Response 1]
[Request 2] -> [Response 2]
(increased latency with dependency on prior completion)

Asynchronous Communication: Asynchronous systems excel in environments where latency is variable, as tasks can be processed concurrently without the need for preliminary completion. This architecture results in higher throughput and resource efficiency as tasks complete independently.

Processing Order:

[Request 1] -------\
[Request 2] ----> (processes complete independently)

Resource Utilization

Synchronous Systems: The blocking nature of synchronous communication often results in inefficient resource use, as active resources are held indefinitely while waiting for operations to complete.

Asynchronous Systems: Resources are utilized more efficiently due to non-blocking operations. Systems can serve multiple requests simultaneously without the fixed overhead of waiting for results, optimizing CPU and I/O resources.

Complexity and Maintenance

Synchronous Communication: Offers a straightforward implementation with linear control flow, simplifying maintenance and reducing potential points of failure. The lack of concurrency-related complexity facilitates easier debugging and issue resolution.

Asynchronous Communication: Demands a more intricate implementation due to concurrency and potential race conditions. Designing non-blocking architectures introduces additional complexity but enhances adaptiveness to diverse performance criteria.

Design Considerations

Choosing the Right Model: The determination between synchronous and asynchronous designs must consider application requirements, such as data integrity, response time expectations, and processing volume. Applications demanding real-time interactions and immediacy might favor synchronous models, whereas those demanding scalability and high throughput might prefer asynchronous.

Error Handling and Reliability: Asynchronous systems necessitate robust error-handling mechanisms, including retries, message logging, and compensatory transactions to address incomplete or failed operations.

System Scalability: Asynchronous systems are inherently more scalable due to their capacity to independently handle tasks without the need for sequential dependencies.

Development Complexity: The complexity of managing concurrent operations in asynchronous systems must be weighed against the benefits of enhanced performance and responsiveness.

Conclusion: Networking and Sockets in C++

Networking and socket programming are foundational concepts in modern software development, enabling communication between devices over a network. In C++, these concepts are implemented using low-level system calls and libraries, providing developers with the flexibility to build efficient, scalable, and high-performance networked applications. This guide has explored the core aspects of networking and sockets in C++, including socket programming basics, client-server architecture, HTTP and TCP/IP communication, and asynchronous programming.

In this conclusion, we will synthesize the key takeaways, discuss the importance of these concepts in modern software development, and explore future trends in networking and C++.

1. Recap of Key Concepts

1.1 Socket Programming Basics

Sockets are the building blocks of networked applications. They provide an endpoint for communication between two machines over a network. In C++, sockets are created using the socket() system call, which returns a socket descriptor. The two most common types of sockets are:

- **Stream Sockets (SOCK_STREAM)**: These use the Transmission Control Protocol (TCP) and provide reliable, connection-oriented communication.

- **Datagram Sockets (SOCK_DGRAM)**: These use the User Datagram Protocol (UDP) and provide connectionless, unreliable communication.

The sockaddr_in structure is used to represent socket addresses, including the IP address and port number. Key functions like bind(), listen(), accept(), connect(), send(), and recv() are used to establish and manage communication between clients and servers.

1.2 Client-Server Architecture

The client-server model is a fundamental architecture for networked applications. In this model:

- The **server** listens for incoming connections, processes requests, and sends responses.

- The **client** initiates connections, sends requests, and receives responses.

This architecture is widely used in applications such as web servers, databases, and online gaming. Implementing a client-server system in C++ involves creating sockets, binding them to addresses, and managing communication between the client and server.

1.3 HTTP and TCP/IP Communication

HTTP (Hypertext Transfer Protocol) is an application-layer protocol built on top of TCP/IP. It is the backbone of the World Wide Web, enabling communication between web browsers and servers. HTTP transactions consist of requests (from the client) and responses (from the server). Implementing an HTTP server in C++ involves parsing HTTP requests, generating appropriate responses, and sending them back to the client.

TCP/IP (Transmission Control Protocol/Internet Protocol) is the suite of protocols that underlies the internet. TCP provides reliable, connection-oriented communication, while IP handles addressing and routing. Understanding TCP/IP is essential for building networked applications that operate over the internet.

1.4 Asynchronous Programming

Asynchronous programming is critical for building scalable and efficient networked applications. It allows a program to handle multiple tasks concurrently without blocking the execution of other tasks.

In C++, asynchronous programming can be achieved using:

- **Threads**: The std::thread class allows developers to create and manage threads.

- **Futures and Promises**: The std::future and std::promise classes provide a mechanism for handling asynchronous results.

- **Asynchronous I/O Libraries**: Libraries like Boost.Asio simplify asynchronous networking by providing high-level abstractions for I/O operations.

Asynchronous programming is particularly important for servers that need to handle multiple clients simultaneously, such as web servers or chat applications.

2. Importance of Networking and Sockets in Modern Software Development

2.1 Enabling Distributed Systems

Networking and sockets are the foundation of distributed systems, which are systems composed of multiple independent components that communicate over a network. Examples of distributed systems include cloud computing platforms, microservices architectures, and peer-to-peer networks. By mastering socket programming, developers can build systems that scale across multiple machines and handle large volumes of traffic.

2.2 Building Real-Time Applications

Real-time applications, such as online gaming, video conferencing, and financial trading platforms, require low-latency communication between clients and servers. Socket programming enables developers to implement custom protocols and optimize communication for real-time performance.

2.3 Supporting the Internet of Things (IoT)

The Internet of Things (IoT) refers to the network of interconnected devices that communicate with each other over the internet. IoT devices, such as smart home appliances and industrial sensors, rely on networking protocols to send and receive data. Socket programming in C++ allows developers to build lightweight, efficient applications for IoT devices.

2.4 Facilitating Cross-Platform Communication

Sockets provide a universal interface for communication between devices running different operating systems. For example, a C++ application running on a Linux server can communicate with a Python application running on a Windows client using sockets. This cross-platform compatibility makes sockets a versatile tool for building networked applications.

3. Challenges in Networking and Socket Programming

3.1 Complexity of Low-Level Programming

Socket programming in C++ involves working with low-level system calls and data structures, which can be complex and error-prone. Developers must handle issues such as memory management, error handling, and protocol implementation manually.

3.2 Concurrency and Synchronization

Handling multiple clients simultaneously requires careful management of concurrency and synchronization. Threads, mutexes, and condition variables are commonly used to manage concurrent access to shared resources. However, improper use of these tools can lead to race conditions, deadlocks, and other concurrency issues.

3.3 Security Concerns

Networked applications are vulnerable to security threats such as eavesdropping, man-in-the-middle attacks, and denial-of-service (DoS) attacks. Developers must implement security measures such as encryption, authentication, and input validation to protect their applications.

3.4 Performance Optimization

Optimizing the performance of networked applications requires careful consideration of factors such as latency, bandwidth, and resource utilization. Techniques such as connection pooling, load balancing, and asynchronous I/O can help improve performance.

4. Future Trends in Networking and C++

4.1 Adoption of C++20 and Beyond

The C++20 standard introduced several features that simplify networking and asynchronous programming, such as coroutines and the <net> library (proposed). These features provide higher-level abstractions for networking, reducing the complexity of socket programming and making it more accessible to developers.

4.2 Integration with Modern Protocols

As new networking protocols emerge, C++ libraries and frameworks are evolving to support them. For example, libraries like Boost.Asio are adding support for protocols such as HTTP/2, WebSocket, and QUIC. These protocols enable faster, more efficient communication and are increasingly being used in modern applications.

4.3 Increased Use of Asynchronous Programming

Asynchronous programming is becoming the standard for building scalable, high-performance networked applications. The adoption of asynchronous I/O libraries and frameworks is expected to grow, enabling developers to build applications that handle thousands or even millions of concurrent connections.

4.4 Focus on Security

With the increasing prevalence of cyber threats, security is becoming a top priority in networked applications. Future developments in C++ networking are likely to focus on providing built-in support for encryption, authentication, and other security measures.

4.5 Cloud-Native and Edge Computing

The rise of cloud-native and edge computing is driving demand for networked applications that can operate in distributed environments. C++ is well-suited for building high-performance applications for these environments, and future developments in networking are likely to focus on supporting cloud-native and edge computing use cases.

5. Best Practices for Networking and Socket Programming in C++

5.1 Use High-Level Libraries

While low-level socket programming provides flexibility, it can be complex and error-prone. Using high-level libraries like Boost.Asio or the proposed C++20 <net> library can simplify networking and reduce the likelihood of errors.

5.2 Handle Errors Gracefully

Networked applications are prone to errors such as connection failures, timeouts, and data corruption. Developers should implement robust error handling to ensure that their applications can recover from errors and continue operating.

5.3 Optimize for Performance

Performance is critical in networked applications. Developers should use techniques such as connection pooling, load balancing, and asynchronous I/O to optimize performance and ensure that their applications can handle high volumes of traffic.

5.4 Prioritize Security

Security should be a top priority in networked applications. Developers should implement encryption, authentication, and input validation to protect their applications from security threats.

5.5 Test Thoroughly

Networked applications are complex and can be difficult to debug. Thorough testing, including unit tests, integration tests, and stress tests, is essential to ensure that applications are reliable and performant.

6. Final Thoughts

Networking and socket programming in C++ are powerful tools for building networked applications. By understanding the basics of sockets, client-server architecture, HTTP and TCP/IP communication, and asynchronous programming, developers can create efficient, scalable, and high-performance systems. While socket programming can be complex, the use of high-level libraries and frameworks can simplify the process and reduce the likelihood of errors.

As the demand for networked applications continues to grow, mastering these concepts will become increasingly important for developers. Whether you're building a simple echo server or a complex distributed system, the knowledge and skills gained from this guide will serve as a solid foundation for your work in C++ networking.

In the future, advancements in C++ standards, networking protocols, and asynchronous programming will continue to shape the landscape of networked applications. By staying up-to-date with these developments and adopting best practices, developers can build applications that meet the demands of modern software development and deliver exceptional performance, scalability, and security.

10. Concurrency, Synchronization, and Performance Optimization

Introduction

In the ever-evolving world of software development, performance optimization and efficient resource management remain critical challenges. As hardware architectures continue to advance, with multi-core processors becoming the norm, leveraging concurrency and synchronization has become essential for writing high-performance applications. C++, with its low-level capabilities and high-level abstractions, is a powerful language for building performant systems. However, writing efficient, concurrent, and synchronized code in C++ requires a deep understanding of both the language and modern hardware architectures.

This guide provides a comprehensive introduction to concurrency, synchronization, and performance optimization in C++ as of 2025. We will explore the latest features, best practices, and tools available in C++ to help you write scalable, efficient, and maintainable code.

Concurrency in C++

What is Concurrency?

Concurrency is the ability of a program to manage multiple tasks simultaneously. In a multi-core processor, concurrency allows different threads to execute independently, potentially improving performance by utilizing all available cores. C++ provides robust support for concurrency through the C++ Standard Library, which includes threading, asynchronous tasks, and synchronization primitives.

Threads in C++

Threads are the fundamental building blocks of concurrent programming. A thread represents an independent sequence of instructions that can be executed concurrently with other threads. In C++, threads are managed using the <thread> library.

Creating Threads

```cpp
#include <iostream>

#include <thread>

void printMessage(const std::string& message) {

    std::cout << message << std::endl;

}

int main() {
```

```
    std::thread t1(printMessage, "Hello from Thread 1!");

    std::thread t2(printMessage, "Hello from Thread 2!");

    t1.join();

    t2.join();

    return 0;

}
```

In this example, two threads (t1 and t2) are created to execute the printMessage function concurrently.

Thread Management

- **Joinable Threads**: A thread is joinable if it represents an active thread of execution. Use join() to wait for the thread to finish.

- **Detached Threads**: A thread can be detached using detach(), allowing it to run independently. Detached threads cannot be joined.

Asynchronous Tasks

C++ provides the <future> and <async> libraries for asynchronous programming. These allow you to execute tasks concurrently and retrieve their results at a later time.

Using std::async

```
#include <iostream>

#include <future>

int computeSum(int a, int b) {

    return a + b;

}

int main() {

    auto futureResult = std::async(std::launch::async, computeSum, 10, 20);

    int result = futureResult.get();

    std::cout << "Result: " << result << std::endl;

    return 0;

}
```

Here, std::async launches the computeSum function asynchronously, and futureResult.get() retrieves the result.

Thread Pools

Thread pools are a common pattern for managing a group of threads that execute tasks concurrently. In 2025, C++ continues to lack a built-in thread pool implementation in the standard library, but third-party libraries like **Intel TBB** or **Boost.Asio** provide robust solutions.

Synchronization in C++

Why Synchronization?

When multiple threads access shared resources concurrently, race conditions can occur, leading to undefined behavior. Synchronization ensures that only one thread accesses a shared resource at a time, maintaining data integrity.

Mutexes

A mutex (mutual exclusion) is a synchronization primitive that prevents multiple threads from accessing a shared resource simultaneously.

Using std::mutex

```cpp
#include <iostream>

#include <thread>

#include <mutex>

std::mutex mtx;

void printMessage(const std::string& message) {

    mtx.lock();

    std::cout << message << std::endl;

    mtx.unlock();

}

int main() {

    std::thread t1(printMessage, "Hello from Thread 1!");

    std::thread t2(printMessage, "Hello from Thread 2!");

    t1.join();

    t2.join();
```

```
    return 0;
}
```

In this example, std::mutex ensures that only one thread can execute the printMessage function at a time.

Lock Guards

To avoid manual locking and unlocking, use std::lock_guard or std::unique_lock.

```
void printMessage(const std::string& message) {
    std::lock_guard<std::mutex> lock(mtx);
    std::cout << message << std::endl;
}
```

Condition Variables

Condition variables allow threads to wait for certain conditions to be met before proceeding. They are often used in producer-consumer scenarios.

Example

```
#include <iostream>
#include <thread>
#include <mutex>
#include <condition_variable>
#include <queue>
std::mutex mtx;
std::condition_variable cv;
std::queue<int> queue;
void producer() {
    for (int i = 0; i < 10; ++i) {
        std::unique_lock<std::mutex> lock(mtx);
        queue.push(i);
        cv.notify_one();
    }
```

```cpp
}
void consumer() {
    while (true) {
        std::unique_lock<std::mutex> lock(mtx);
        cv.wait(lock, [] { return !queue.empty(); });
        int value = queue.front();
        queue.pop();
        std::cout << "Consumed: " << value << std::endl;
    }
}
int main() {
    std::thread t1(producer);
    std::thread t2(consumer);
    t1.join();
    t2.join();
    return 0;
}
```

Atomic Operations

Atomic operations ensure that certain operations on shared variables are performed without interruption. The <atomic> library provides atomic types like std::atomic<int>.

Example

```cpp
#include <iostream>
#include <thread>
#include <atomic>
std::atomic<int> counter(0);
void increment() {
    for (int i = 0; i < 1000; ++i) {
        counter++;
```

```
    }
}
int main() {
    std::thread t1(increment);
    std::thread t2(increment);
    t1.join();
    t2.join();
    std::cout << "Counter: " << counter << std::endl;
    return 0;
}
```

Optimizing Your Code for Performance

Profiling and Benchmarking

Before optimizing, identify performance bottlenecks using profiling tools like **Valgrind, gprof,** or **Intel VTune**. Benchmarking tools like **Google Benchmark** can help measure the performance of specific code sections.

Memory Management

Efficient memory management is crucial for performance. Use smart pointers (std::unique_ptr, std::shared_ptr) to avoid memory leaks and manage object lifetimes.

Example

```
#include <memory>
void processData() {
    auto data = std::make_unique<int[]>(1000);
    // Use data
}
```

Cache Optimization

Modern CPUs rely heavily on caches. Optimize your code for cache locality by:

- Using contiguous memory (e.g., std::vector instead of std::list).
- Minimizing cache misses by accessing data sequentially.

Parallel Algorithms

C++17 introduced parallel algorithms in the <algorithm> library. Use std::execution::par to parallelize operations like sorting and searching.

Example

```
#include <algorithm>

#include <vector>

#include <execution>

int main() {

    std::vector<int> data = {5, 3, 1, 4, 2};

    std::sort(std::execution::par, data.begin(), data.end());

    return 0;

}
```

Compiler Optimizations

Enable compiler optimizations using flags like -O2 or -O3 in GCC/Clang. Use link-time optimization (LTO) for additional performance gains.

Advanced Topics

Coroutines

C++20 introduced coroutines, which enable asynchronous programming with synchronous-looking code. Coroutines are particularly useful for I/O-bound tasks.

Example

```
#include <iostream>

#include <coroutine>

struct Task {

  struct promise_type {

    Task get_return_object() { return {}; }

    std::suspend_never initial_suspend() { return {}; }

    std::suspend_never final_suspend() noexcept { return {}; }

    void return_void() {}
```

```cpp
        void unhandled_exception() {}
    };
};

Task myCoroutine() {
    std::cout << "Hello from Coroutine!" << std::endl;
    co_return;
}

int main() {
    myCoroutine();
    return 0;
}
```

SIMD (Single Instruction, Multiple Data)

SIMD instructions allow parallel processing of multiple data points. Libraries like **Intel's SIMD** or compiler intrinsics can be used to leverage SIMD.

Example

```cpp
#include <immintrin.h>

void addVectors(float* a, float* b, float* result, int size) {
    for (int i = 0; i < size; i += 8) {
        __m256 va = _mm256_load_ps(&a[i]);
        __m256 vb = _mm256_load_ps(&b[i]);
        __m256 vresult = _mm256_add_ps(va, vb);
        _mm256_store_ps(&result[i], vresult);
    }
}
```

In this chapter, we will learn how to properly handle concurrency, synchronization, and parallelism in C++. Here, it is essential that you have a general knowledge of C++ and C++ threads. This chapter is important because working with C++ typically requires the use of shared resources, which can easily become corrupt if thread-safety is not implemented properly. We will start with an extensive overview of std::mutexes, which provides a means to synchronizing C++ threads. We will then look at atomic data types, which provide another mechanism for handling parallelism safely.

This chapter has recipes that demonstrate how to handle different scenarios while working with C++ threads, including handling const &, thread-safety wrapping, blocking versus asynchronous programming, and C++ promises and futures. This is important, as this knowledge is critical when working with multiple threads of execution.

Technical requirements

To compile and run the examples in this chapter, you must have administrative access to a computer running Ubuntu 18.04 with a functional internet connection. Prior to running these examples, you must install the following:

sudo apt-get install build-essential git cmake

If this is installed on any operating system other than Ubuntu 18.04, then GCC 7.4 or higher and CMake 3.6 or higher will be required.

Working with mutexes

In this recipe, we will learn why and how to use a mutex in C++. When working with multiple threads in C++, it is common to establish resources that are shared between threads. As we will demonstrate in this recipe, attempting to use these shared resources simultaneously leads to race conditions that are capable of corrupting the resource.

A mutex (in C++, this is written as std::mutex) is an object that is used to guard a shared resource, ensuring that more than one thread can access a shared resource in a controlled manner. This prevents it from becoming corrupt.

Before we begin, please ensure that all of the technical requirements are met, including installing Ubuntu 18.04 or higher and running the following in a terminal window:

sudo apt-get install build-essential git

This will ensure your operating system has the proper tools to compile and execute the examples in this recipe. Once this is complete, open a new terminal. We will use this terminal to download, compile, and run our examples.

You need to perform the following steps to try this recipe:

1. From a new terminal, run the following to download the source code:

```
> cd ~/
> git clone https://github.com/PacktPublishing/Advanced-CPP-
CookBook.git
> cd Advanced-CPP-CookBook/chapter10
```

2. To compile the source code, run the following:

```
> cmake .
```

> make recipe01_examples

3. Once the source code is compiled, you can execute each example in this recipe by running the following commands:

> ./recipe01_example01
The answer is: 42
The answer is: 42
The answer is: 42 The
answer is: 42
The answer is: 42 ...

> ./recipe01_example02
The answer is: 42
The answer is: 42
The answer is: 42
The answer is: 42
The answer is: 42 ...

> ./recipe01_example03 ...

> ./recipe01_example04
The answer is: 42

> ./recipe01_example05
The answer is: 42
The answer is: 42
The answer is: 42
The answer is: 42
The answer is: 42 ...

> ./recipe01_example06
The answer is: 42
The answer is: 42

> ./recipe01_example07

> ./recipe01_example08

lock acquired lock failed

In the next section, we will step through each of these examples and explain what each example program does and how it relates to the lessons being taught in this recipe.

In this recipe, we will learn how to use std::mutex to protect a shared resource from becoming corrupt. To start, let's first review how a resource could become corrupt when more than one thread is accessing it at the same time:

#include <thread>

```cpp
#include <string>
#include <iostream>

void foo() {
static std::string msg{"The answer is:
42\n"};    while(true) {       for (const
auto &c : msg) {          std::clog << c;
}
} }

int main(void)
{
std::thread t1{foo};
std::thread t2{foo};

t1.join();    t2.join();
// Never reached
return 0;
}
```

When executed, we get the following output:

```
user@localhost: ~/book/chapter05/build          —    □    ×

[~/book/chapter05/build]: ./recipe01_example01
TThe answer is: 42
The answer is: he answer is: 42
The answer is: 42
Th42
The answer is: 42
The answere answer is: 42
The answer is: 42
The answer is: 42
The answer is: 42
The answer is: 42
The answer is: 42
The answer is: is: 42
The answer is: 42
The answer is: 42
The answer is: 42
T 42
The answer is: 42
The answer is: 42
The answer is: 42
The answer is: 42
The answer is: 42
The answer is: 42
The answer is: 42
The answer is:he answer is: 42
The 42
The answer is: 42
The answer is: 42
The answer is: 42
The answer is: 42
```

In the preceding example, we create a function that outputs to stdout in an endless loop. We then create two threads, with each thread executing the previously defined function. As you can see, when both threads execute, the resulting output becomes corrupt. This is because while one thread is in the middle of outputting its text to stdout, the other thread outputs to stdout at the same time, resulting in the output from one thread being mixed with the output of the other thread.

To deal with this issue, we must ensure that, once one of the threads attempts to output its text to stdout, it should be allowed to finish its output before the other thread is able to output. In other words, each thread must take turns outputting to stdout. While one thread is outputting, the other thread must wait its turn. To do this, we will leverage an std::mutex object.

std::mutex

A mutex is an object that is used to guard a shared resource to ensure the use of the shared resource does not result in corruption. To accomplish this, std::mutex has a lock() function and an unlock() function. The lock function acquires access to a shared resource (sometimes referred to as a critical section). unlock() releases this previously acquired access. Any attempt to execute the lock() function after another thread has already executed lock() will result in the thread having to wait until the unlock() function is executed.

How std::mutex is implemented depends on the CPU's architecture and the operating system; however, in general, a mutex can be implemented with a simple integer. If the integer is 0, the lock() function will set the integer to 1 and return, which tells the mutex that it is acquired. If the integer is 1, meaning the mutex is already acquired, the lock() function will wait (that is, block) until the integer becomes 0, and then it will set the integer to 1 and return. How this wait is implemented depends on the operating system.

For example, the wait() function can loop forever until the integer becomes 0, which is called a **spinlock**, or it can execute a sleep() function and wait for a period of time, allowing other threads and processes to execute while the mutex is locked. The release function always sets the integer to 0, meaning the mutex is no longer acquired. The trick to ensuring the mutex works properly is to ensure the integer is read/written using atomic operations. If non-atomic operations are used, the integer itself would suffer the same shared resource corruption the mutex is trying to prevent.

For example, consider the following:

```cpp
#include <mutex>
#include <thread>
#include <string>
#include <iostream>
std::mutex m{};

void foo() {
static std::string msg{"The answer is: 42\n"};    while(true) {        m.lock();
for (const auto &c : msg) {
std::clog << c;
}
m.unlock();
} }

int main(void)
{
std::thread t1{foo};
std::thread t2{foo};

t1.join();    t2.join();

// Never reached
return 0;
}
```

This example, when run, outputs the following:

```
[~/book/chapter05/build]: ./recipe01_example02
The answer is: 42
The answer is: 42
The answer is: 42
The answer is: 42
The answer is: 42
The answer is: 42
The answer is: 42
The answer is: 42
The answer is: 42
The answer is: 42
The answer is: 42
The answer is: 42
The answer is: 42
The answer is: 42
The answer is: 42
The answer is: 42
The answer is: 42
The answer is: 42
The answer is: 42
The answer is: 42
The answer is: 42
The answer is: 42
The answer is: 42
The answer is: 42
The answer is: 42
The answer is: 42
The answer is: 42
The answer is: 42
```

In the preceding example, we create the same function that outputs to stdout. The difference is, before we output to stdout, we acquire std::mutex by executing the lock() function. Once we are done outputting to stdout, we release the mutex by executing the unlock() function. The code in between the lock() and unlock() functions is called the **critical region**. Any code in the critical region can only be executed by one thread at any given time, ensuring our use of stdout does not become corrupt.

Ensuring shared resources do not become corrupt by controlling access to the shared resource (for example, using a mutex) is called **synchronization**. Although the majority of scenarios where thread synchronization is needed are not complicated, some scenarios can result in thread synchronization schemes that require an entire college course to cover. For this reason, thread synchronization is considered an extremely difficult paradigm in computer science to program correctly.

In this recipe, we will cover some of these scenarios. To start, let's discuss something called a **deadlock**. A deadlock occurs when a thread enters an endless wait state when calling the lock() function. A deadlock is often extremely difficult to debug and is the result of several reasons, including the following:

A thread never calling unlock() due to programmer error or the thread that acquired the mutex crashing.
The same thread calling the lock() function more than once before it calls unlock() Each thread locking more than one mutex in a different order.

To demonstrate this, let's look at the following example:

```
#include <mutex>
#include <thread>
std::mutex m{};
void foo()
{
m.lock(); } int
main(void) {
std::thread t1{foo};
std::thread t2{foo};

t1.join();    t2.join();

// Never reached
return 0;
}
```

In the preceding example, we create two threads, both of which attempt to lock the mutex but never call unlock(). As a result, the first thread acquires the mutex and then returns without releasing it. When the second thread attempts to acquire the mutex, it is forced to wait for the first thread to execute unlock(), which it never does, resulting in a deadlock (that is, the program never returns).

Deadlock, in this example, is simple to identify and correct; however, in real-world scenarios, identifying deadlock is a lot more complicated.

Let's look at the following example:

```
#include <array>
#include <mutex>
#include <thread>
#include <string>
#include <iostream>

std::mutex m{};
std::array<int,6> numbers{4,8,15,16,23,42};

int foo(int index)
{
m.lock();    auto element =
numbers.at(index);
m.unlock();

return element;
}

int main(void)
{
```

```
std::cout << "The answer is: " << foo(5) <<
'\n';    return 0;
}
```

In the preceding example, we wrote a function that returns an element in an array, given an index. In addition, we acquire a mutex that guards the array and releases the mutex just before returning. The challenge here is that we have to unlock() the mutex where the function can return, which includes not only every possible branch that returns from the function, but all possible scenarios where an exception could be thrown. In the preceding example, if the index that is provided is larger than the array, the std::array object will throw an exception, resulting in the function returning before the function has a chance to call unlock(), which would result in deadlock if another thread is sharing this array.

std::lock_guard

Instead of littering your code with try/catch blocks to prevent deadlock, which assumes the programmer is even capable of determining every possible scenario where this could occur without making a mistake, C++ provides an std::lock_guard object to simplify the use of the std::mutex object.

For example, consider the following code:

```cpp
#include <mutex>
#include <thread>
#include <iostream>
std::mutex m{};
void foo() {
static std::string msg{"The answer is: 42\n"};

while(true) {
std::lock_guard lock(m);
for (const auto &c : msg) {
std::clog << c;
}
} }
int main(void)
{
std::thread t1{foo};
std::thread t2{foo};

t1.join();    t2.join();

// Never reached
return 0;
}
```

When executed, we see the following:

As shown in the preceding example, std::lock_guard is used when we would normally call lock() on the mutex. std::lock_guard calls the lock() function on the mutex when it is created and then calls unlock() on the mutex when it is destroyed (an idiom called **Resource Acquisition Is Initialization** or **RAII**). No matter how the function returns (either from a normal return or an exception), the mutex will always be released, ensuring deadlock is not possible, preventing the programmer from having to accurately determine every possible scenario where the function could return.

Although std::lock_guard is capable of preventing deadlock in cases where unlock() is never called, it is not capable of preventing deadlock from occurring in cases where lock() is called by the same thread more than once prior to unlock() being called. To handle this scenario, C++ provides std::recursive_mutex.

std::recursive_mutex

A recursive mutex increments the integer stored inside the mutex each time the same thread calls the lock() function without causing the lock() function to wait. For example, if the mutex is released (that is, the integer in the mutex is 0), when thread #1 calls the lock() function, the integer in the mutex is set to 1. Normally, if thread #1 calls the lock() function again, the lock() function would see that the integer is 1 and enter a wait state until the integer is set to 0. Instead, a recursive mutex will determine which thread is calling the lock() function, and, if the thread that acquired the mutex is the same thread calling the lock() function, the integer in the mutex is incremented again (now resulting in 2) using an atomic operation. For the mutex to be released, the thread must call unlock(), which decrements the integer using an atomic operation, until the integer in the mutex is 0.

The recursive mutex allows the same thread to call the lock() function as many times as it wants, preventing multiple calls to the lock() function and resulting in deadlock at the expense that the lock() and unlock() functions must include an added function call to get the thread's id() instance, so that the mutex can determine which thread is calling lock() and unlock().

For example, consider the following code snippet:

```
#include <mutex>
#include <thread>
#include <string>
#include <iostream>
std::recursive_mutex
m{};
void foo()
{
m.lock();
m.lock();    std::cout << "The
answer is: 42\n";
m.unlock();
m.unlock(); }

int main(void)
{
std::thread t1 {foo};
std::thread t2 {foo};

t1.join();    t2.join();

return 0;
}
```

The preceding example results in the following:

In the preceding example, we define a function that calls the lock() function for a recursive mutex twice, outputs to stdout, and then calls the unlock() function twice. We then create two threads that execute this function, resulting in no corruption to stdout and no deadlock.

std::shared_mutex

Up until this point, our synchronization primitives have serialized access to our shared resource. That is, each thread must execute one at a time when accessing the critical region. Although this ensures corruption is not possible, it is inefficient for certain types of scenarios. To better understand this, we must examine what causes corruption in the first place.

Let's consider an integer variable that is incremented by two threads simultaneously. The process for incrementing an integer variable is as follows: $i = i + 1$.

Let's write this as follows:

```
int i = 0;
```

```
auto tmp = i;
tmp++; i = tmp; //
i == 1
```

To prevent corruption, we use a mutex to ensure that if two threads increment the integer, they do so synchronously:

```
auto tmp_thread1 = i;
tmp_thread1++; i =
tmp_thread1; // i == 1
```

```
auto tmp_thread2 = i;
tmp_thread2++; i =
tmp_thread2; // i == 2
```

Corruption occurs when these operations mix (that is, when both operations execute simultaneously in different threads). For example, consider this code:

```
auto tmp_thread1 = i; //
0 auto tmp_thread2 = i;
// 0 tmp_thread1++; // 1
tmp_thread2++; // 1 i =
tmp_thread1; // i == 1 i
= tmp_thread2; // i == 1
```

Instead of the integer being 2, it is 1, because the integer is read before the first increment is allowed to finish. This scenario is possible because both threads are attempting to write to the same shared resource. We call these types of threads **producers**.

What if, however, we create a million threads that read the shared resource simultaneously. Since the integer never changes, no matter what order the threads execute in, they will all read the same value, and therefore corruption is not possible. We call these threads **consumers**. If we only ever have consumers, we do not need thread synchronization as corruption is not possible.

Finally, what happens if we have the same 1 million consumers, but we add a single producer to the mix? Now, we must use thread synchronization because it is possible that while the producer is in the middle of attempting to write a value to the integer that a consumer attempts to read, it will result in a corrupt result. To prevent this, we must use a mutex to guard the integer. If we use std::mutex, however, all 1 million consumers would have to wait on each other, even though the consumers themselves can safely execute simultaneously without the fear of corruption. It is only when the producer attempts to execute that we must be worried.

To handle this obvious performance problem, C++ provides the std::shared_mutex object. For example, consider this code:

```cpp
#include <mutex>
#include <shared_mutex>
#include <thread>
#include <iostream>

int count_rw{}; const auto
&count_ro = count_rw;
std::shared_mutex m{};

void reader()
{
while(true) {
std::shared_lock lock(m);
if (count_ro >= 42) {
return;
}
} }

void writer()
{
while(true) {
std::unique_lock lock(m);
if (++count_rw == 100) {
return;
}
} }

int main(void)
{
std::thread t1{reader};
std::thread t2{reader};
std::thread t3{reader};
```

```cpp
std::thread t4{reader};
std::thread t5{writer};

t1.join();    t2.join();
t3.join();    t4.join();
t5.join();

return 0;
}
```

In the preceding example, we create a producer function (called the reader function) and a consumer function (called the writer function). The producer locks the mutex using std::unique_lock(), while the consumer locks the mutex using std::shared_lock(). Whenever the mutex is locked using std::unique_lock(), all other threads must wait (producer and consumer alike). If, however, the mutex is locked using std::shared_lock(), additional attempts to lock the mutex using std::shared_lock() do not result in the thread waiting.

It's only when std::unique_lock() is called that a wait must occur. This allows the consumers to execute without waiting on each other. It's only when the producer attempts to execute that the consumers must wait, preventing the consumers from serializing each other, ultimately resulting in better performance (especially if the number of consumers is 1 million).

It should be noted that we use the const keyword to ensure that a consumer is not a producer. This simple trick ensures that the programmer doesn't accidentally think they have programmed a consumer when, in fact, they have created a producer, as the compiler would warn the programmer if this occurred.

std::timed_mutex

Finally, we have not dealt with the scenario where a thread that acquired a mutex crashed. In this scenario, any thread that attempts to acquire the same mutex would enter a deadlock state as the thread that crashed never gets a chance to call unlock(). One way to prevent this issue is to use std::timed_mutex.

For example, consider the following code:

```cpp
#include <mutex>
#include <thread>
#include <iostream>
std::timed_mutex m{};

void foo() {
using namespace std::chrono;

if (m.try_lock_for(seconds(1))) {
std::cout << "lock acquired\n";
}    else {        std::cout <<
"lock failed\n";
} }
```

```cpp
int main(void)
{
std::thread t1{foo};
std::thread t2{foo};

t1.join();    t2.join();

return 0;
}
```

When this is executed, we get the following:

In the preceding example, we tell C++ that the thread is only allowed to wait for 1 second. If the mutex is already acquired and it is not released after 1 second, the try_lock_for() function will exit and return false, allowing the thread to gracefully exit and handle the error without entering a deadlock.

Using atomic data types

In this recipe, we will learn how to use atomic data types in C++. Atomic data types provide the ability to read and write simple data types (that is, a Boolean or integer) without the need for thread synchronization (that is, the use of std::mutex and friends). To accomplish this, atomic data types are implemented using special CPU instructions that ensure when an operation is executed, it is done so as a single, atomic operation.

For example, incrementing an integer can be written as follows:

```cpp
int i = 0;

auto tmp = i;
tmp++; i = tmp; //
i == 1
```

An atomic data type ensures that this increment is executed such that no other attempts to increment the integer simultaneously can interleave, and therefore result in corruption. How this is done by the CPU is out of the scope of this book. That's because this is extremely complicated in modern, super-scalar, pipelined CPUs that support the execution of instructions in parallel, out-of-order, and speculatively on multiple cores and sockets.

Before we begin, please ensure that all of the technical requirements are met, including installing Ubuntu 18.04 or higher and running the following in a terminal window:

sudo apt-get install build-essential git

This will ensure your operating system has the proper tools to compile and execute the examples in this recipe. Once this is complete, open a new terminal. We will use this terminal to download, compile, and run our examples.

You need to perform the following steps to try this recipe:

1. From a new terminal, run the following to download the source code:

> cd ~/
> git clone https://github.com/PacktPublishing/Advanced-CPP-
CookBook.git
> cd Advanced-CPP-CookBook/chapter10

2. To compile the source code, run the following:

> cmake .
> make recipe02_examples

3. Once the source code is compiled, you can execute each example in this recipe by running the following commands:

> ./recipe02_example01
count: 711 atomic count:
1000

In the next section, we will step through each of these examples and explain what each example program does and how it relates to the lessons being taught in this recipe.

In this recipe, we will learn how to use C++'s atomic data types. Atomic data types are limited to simple data types such as integers, and since these data types are extremely complicated to implement, the only operations that are supported are simple operations such as add, subtract, increment, and decrement.

Let's take a look at a simple example that not only demonstrates how to use an atomic data type in C++, but also demonstrates why atomic data types are so important:

```cpp
#include <atomic>
#include <thread>
#include <iostream>

int count{};
std::atomic<int> atomic_count{};

void foo() {    do {
count++;
atomic_count++;
}
while (atomic_count < 99999);
```

```
}
int main(void)
{
std::thread t1{foo};
std::thread t2{foo};

t1.join();    t2.join();

std::cout << "count: " << count << '\n';
std::cout << "atomic count: " << atomic_count
<< '\n';

return 0;
}
```

When this code is executed, we get the following:

In the preceding example, we have two integers. The first integer is a normal C/C++ integer type, while the second is an atomic data type (of type integer). We then define a function that loops until the atomic data type is 1000. Finally, we execute this function from two threads, which means our global integers are incremented by two threads simultaneously.

As you can see, the output of this simple test shows that the simple C/C++ integer data type is not the same value as the atomic data type, yet both are incremented the same number of times. The reason for this can be seen in the assembly of this function (on an Intel CPU), as follows:

To increment an integer (without optimizations enabled), the compiler must move the contents of memory into a register, add 1 to the register, and then write the results of the register back to memory. Since this code is executing simultaneously in two different threads, this code interleaves, resulting in corruption. The atomic data type does not suffer this same problem. This is because the process of incrementing the atomic data type occurs in a single, special instruction that the CPU ensures to execute, without interleaving its internal state with the same internal state of other instructions, on other CPUs.

Atomic data types are typically used to implement synchronization primitives such as std::mutex (although, in practice, std::mutex is implemented using test and set instructions, which use a similar principle but oftentimes execute faster than atomic instructions). These data types can also be used to implement special data structures called lock-free data structures, which are capable of operating in multithreaded environments without the need for std::mutex.

The benefit of lockless data structures is that there are no wait states when dealing with thread synchronization at the expense of more complicated CPU hardware and other types of performance penalties (most CPU optimizations provided by the hardware have to be temporarily disabled when the CPU encounters an atomic instruction). So, like anything in computer science, they have their time and place.

Understanding what const & mutable mean in the context of multiple threads

In this recipe, we will learn how to deal with objects that are labeled const, but contain std::mutex that must be used to ensure thread synchronization. This recipe is important because it is useful to store std::mutex as a private member of a class, but, as soon as you do this, passing an instance of this object as a constant reference (that is, const &) will result in a compiler error. In this recipe, we will demonstrate why this occurs and how to overcome it.

Before we begin, please ensure that all of the technical requirements are met, including installing Ubuntu 18.04 or higher and running the following in a terminal window:

sudo apt-get install build-essential git

This will ensure your operating system has the proper tools to compile and execute the examples in this recipe. Once this is complete, open a new terminal. We will use this terminal to download, compile, and run our examples.

You need to perform the following steps to try this recipe:

1. From a new terminal, run the following to download the source code:

```
> cd ~/
> git clone https://github.com/PacktPublishing/Advanced-CPP-
CookBook.git
> cd Advanced-CPP-CookBook/chapter
```

2. To compile the source code, run the following:

```
> cmake .
> make recipe03_examples
```

3. Once the source code is compiled, you can execute each example in this recipe by running the following commands:

```
> ./recipe03_example01
The answer is: 42

> ./recipe03_example03
The answer is: 42
```

In the next section, we will step through each of these examples and explain what each example program does and how it relates to the lessons being taught in this recipe.

In this recipe, we will learn how to add std::mutex to a class's private members while still being able to handle const scenarios. Generally speaking, there are two ways to ensure an object is thread-safe. The first method is to place std::mutex at the global level. Doing this ensures an object can be passed as a constant reference or the object itself can have a function marked as const.

For this, consider the following code example:

```cpp
#include <mutex>
#include <thread>
#include <iostream>
std::mutex m{};

class the_answer
{ public:    void
print() const
{
std::lock_guard lock(m);
std::cout << "The answer is: 42\n";
} };

int main(void)
{
the_answer is;
is.print();

return 0;
}
```

In the preceding example, we create an object that outputs to stdout when the print() function is executed. The print() function is labeled as const, which tells the compiler that the print() function will not modify any class members (that is, the function is read-only). Since std::mutex is global, the const-qualifier of the object is maintained and the code compiles and executes without an issue.

The problem with a global std::mutex object is that every instance of the object must use the same std::mutex object. This is fine if the user intends this, but what if you want each instance of the object to have its own std::mutex object (for example, when the same instance of the object might be executed by more than one thread)?

For this, let's take a look at how that happens using the following example:

```
#include <mutex>
#include <thread>
#include <iostream>

class the_answer
{
std::mutex m{};

public:     void print()
const
{
std::lock_guard lock(m);
std::cout << "The answer is: 42\n";
} };

int main(void)
{
the_answer is;
is.print();

return 0;
}
```

If we attempt to compile this, we get the following:

In the preceding example, all we did was take the previous example and move std::mutex inside the class as a private member. As a result, when we attempt to compile the class, we get a compiler error. This is because the print() function is marked as const, which tells the compiler that the print() function will not modify any of the class's members. The problem is that when you attempt to lock std::mutex, you must modify it, resulting in a compiler error.

To overcome this, we must tell the compiler to ignore this error by marking std::mutex as mutable. Marking a member as mutable tells the compiler that the member is allowed to be modified, even when the object is passed as a constant reference or when the object defines a constant function.

For example, this is how the code appears on const marked as mutable:

```
#include <mutex>
```

```
#include <thread>
#include <iostream>

class the_answer
{
mutable std::mutex m{};

public:    void print()
const
{
std::lock_guard lock(m);
std::cout << "The answer is: 42\n";
} };

int main(void)
{
the_answer is;
is.print();

return 0;
}
```

As you can see in the preceding example, once we mark std::mutex as mutable, the code compiles and executes as we would expect. It should be noted that std::mutex is one of the few examples for which the use of mutable is acceptable. The mutable keyword can easily be abused, resulting in code that doesn't compile or operate as expected.

Making a class thread-safe

In this recipe, we will learn how to make a class thread-safe (that is, how to ensure a class's public member functions can be called at any time, by any number of threads simultaneously). Most classes, especially those provided by the C++ standard library are not thread-safe and, instead, assume the user will add thread-synchronization primitives such as an std::mutex object as needed. The problem with this approach is that every object has two instances that must be tracked in code: the class itself and its std::mutex. The user must also wrap each of the object's functions with custom versions that protect the class using std::mutex, resulting in not only two objects that must be managed, but also a bunch of C-style wrapper functions.

This recipe is important because it will demonstrate how to address these issues in your code by making a thread safe class, which combines everything into a single class.

Before we begin, please ensure that all of the technical requirements are met, including installing Ubuntu 18.04 or higher and running the following in a terminal window:

sudo apt-get install build-essential git

This will ensure your operating system has the proper tools to compile and execute the examples in this recipe. Once this is complete, open a new terminal. We will use this terminal to download, compile, and run our examples.

You need to perform the following steps to try this recipe:

1. From a new terminal, run the following to download the source code:

```
> cd ~/
> git clone https://github.com/PacktPublishing/Advanced-CPP-
CookBook.git
> cd Advanced-CPP-CookBook/chapter
```

2. To compile the source code, run the following:

```
> cmake .
> make recipe04_examples
```

3. Once the source code is compiled, you can execute each example in this recipe by running the following commands:

```
./recipe04_example01
```

In the next section, we will step through each of these examples and explain what each example program does and how it relates to the lessons being taught in this recipe.

In this recipe, we will learn how to make a thread-safe class by implementing our own thread-safe stack. The C++ standard library does not provide thread-safe data structures, and, as a result, if you wish to use a data structure as a global resource across multiple threads, you add thread-safety manually. This can be done by implementing wrapper functions, or by creating a wrapper class.

The advantage of creating wrapper functions is that, for global objects, the amount of code that is needed is oftentimes smaller and easier to understand, while the advantage of a thread-safe class is that you can create multiple instances of the class, as std::mutex is self-contained.

This can be tried with the following code example:

```cpp
#include <mutex>
#include <stack>
#include <iostream>

template<typename T>
class my_stack
{
std::stack<T> m_stack;
mutable std::mutex m{};
public:

template<typename ARG>
void push(ARG &&arg)
{
```

```
std::lock_guard lock(m);
m_stack.push(std::forward<ARG>(arg));
}

void pop()
{
std::lock_guard lock(m);
m_stack.pop();
}

auto empty() const
{
std::lock_guard lock(m);
return m_stack.empty();
}
};
```

In the preceding example, we implement our own stack. This stack has std::stack and std::mutex as member variables. We then reimplement some of the functions the std::stack provides. Each of these functions first attempts to acquire std::mutex and then calls the associated function in std::stack. In the case of the push() function, we leverage std::forward to ensure the arguments passed to the push() function are preserved.

Finally, we can use our custom stack the same way we would use std::stack. For example, take a look at the following code:

```
int main(void)
{
my_stack<int> s;

s.push(4);
s.push(8);
s.push(15);
s.push(16);
s.push(23);
s.push(42);

while(s.empty()) {
s.pop();    }

return 0;
}
```

As you can see, the only difference between std::stack and our custom stack is that our stack is thread-safe.

Synchronization wrappers and how to implement them

In this recipe, we will learn how to make thread-safe synchronization wrappers. By default, the C++ standard library is not thread-safe as not all applications will need this functionality. One mechanism to ensure the C++ standard library is thread-safe is to create a thread-safe class, which adds the data structure you wish to use as well as std::mutex to the class as private members, and then reimplements the data structure's functions to first acquire std::mutex and then forward the function call to the data structure. The problem with this approach is there is a lot of extra code that is added to your program if the data structure is a global resource, making the resulting code hard to read and maintain.

This recipe is important because it will demonstrate how to address these issues in your code by making thread-safe synchronization wrappers.

Before we begin, please ensure that all of the technical requirements are met, including installing Ubuntu 18.04 or higher and running the following in a terminal window:

sudo apt-get install build-essential git

This will ensure your operating system has the proper tools to compile and execute the examples in this recipe. Once this is complete, open a new terminal. We will use this terminal to download, compile, and run our examples.

You need to perform the following steps to try this recipe:

1. From a new terminal, run the following to download the source code:

> cd ~/
> git clone https://github.com/PacktPublishing/Advanced-CPP-CookBook.git
> cd Advanced-CPP-CookBook/chapter10

2. To compile the source code, run the following:

> cmake.
> make recipe05_examples

3. Once the source code is compiled, you can execute each example in this recipe by running the following command:

./recipe05_example01

In the next section, we will step through each of these examples and explain what each example program does and how it relates to the lessons being taught in this recipe.

In this recipe, we will learn how to create thread-safe synchronization wrappers, which allow us to add thread-safety to the C++ standard library data structures, which, by default, are not thread-safe.

To do this, we will create wrapper functions for each function in the C++ standard library that we intend to use. These wrapper functions will first attempt to acquire std::mutex, before forwarding the same function call to the C++ standard library data structure.

To do this, consider the following code example:

```cpp
#include <mutex>
#include <stack>
#include <iostream>
std::mutex m{};

template<typename S,
typename T> void push(S &s,
T &&t)
{
std::lock_guard lock(m);
s.push(std::forward<T>(t));
}

template<typename
S> void pop(S &s)
{
std::lock_guard lock(m);
s.pop(); }

template<typename
S> auto empty(S &s)
{
std::lock_guard lock(m);
return s.empty();
}
```

In the preceding example, we have created a wrapper function for the push(), pop(), and empty() functions. These functions attempt to acquire our global std::mutex object before calling the data structure, which, in this case, is a template. The use of a template creates what is called a concept. Our wrapper functions can be used by any data structure that implements push(), pop(), and empty(). Also, note that we use std::forward in our push() function to ensure the l-valueness and CV qualifiers of the argument being pushed remain unchanged.

Finally, we can use our wrappers the same way we would use the data structure's functions, with the slight difference being that the data structure is passed as the first argument. For example, take a look at the following code block:

```cpp
int main(void)
{
std::stack<int> mystack;

push(mystack, 4);
push(mystack, 8);
push(mystack, 15);
push(mystack, 16);
```

```
push(mystack, 23);
push(mystack, 42);

while(empty(mystack)) {
pop(mystack);
}

return 0;
}
```

As you can see in the preceding example, the use of our synchronization wrappers is simple, while ensuring the stack that we created is now thread-safe.

Blocking operations versus asynchronous programming

In this recipe, we will learn the difference between a blocking operation and an asynchronous operation. This recipe is important because blocking operations serialize the execution of each operation on a single CPU. This is typically fine if the execution of each operation must be executed in serial order; however, if these operations can be executed in parallel, asynchronous programming can be a useful optimization, ensuring that, while an operation is waiting, others can still execute on the same CPU.

Before we begin, please ensure that all of the technical requirements are met, including installing Ubuntu 18.04 or higher and running the following in a terminal window:

sudo apt-get install build-essential git

This will ensure that your operating system has the proper tools to compile and execute the examples in this recipe.

Once this is complete, open a new terminal. We will use this terminal to download, compile, and run our examples.

You need to perform the following steps to try this recipe:

1. From a new terminal, run the following to download the source code:

```
> cd ~/
> git clone https://github.com/PacktPublishing/Advanced-CPP-
CookBook.git
> cd Advanced-CPP-CookBook/chapter
```

2. To compile the source code, run the following:

```
> cmake .
> make recipe06_examples
```

3. Once the source code is compiled, you can execute each example in this recipe by running the following commands:

```
> time ./recipe06_example01
999999
999999
999999 999999

real 0m1.477s ...
```

```
> time ./recipe06_example02
999999
999999
999999 999999

real 0m1.058s ...
```

```
> time ./recipe06_example03
999999
999999
999998 999999

real 0m1.140s ...
```

In the next section, we will step through each of these examples and explain what each example program does and how it relates to the lessons being taught in this recipe.

A blocking operation is an operation that must be completed before the next operation can take place. Most programs are written serially, meaning each instruction must execute before the next instruction. The problem, however, is that some operations can be executed in parallel (that is, either concurrently or asynchronously). Serializing these operations can, in the best case, lead to poor performance and, in some cases, can actually lead to deadlock (the program entering an endless wait state) if the operation that is blocking is waiting on another operation that is never given a chance to execute.

To demonstrate a blocking operation, let's examine the following:

```
#include <vector>
#include <iostream>
#include <algorithm>
constexpr auto size =
1000000;

int main(void)
{
std::vector<int> numbers1(size);
std::vector<int> numbers2(size);
std::vector<int> numbers3(size);
std::vector<int> numbers4(size);
```

The preceding code creates a main function with four std::vector objects of the int type. In the following steps, we will use these vectors to demonstrate a blocking operation:

1. First, we create four vectors that we can store integers in:

```
std::generate(numbers1.begin(), numbers1.end(), []() {
return rand() % size;
});
std::generate(numbers2.begin(), numbers2.end(), []() {
return rand() % size;
});
std::generate(numbers3.begin(), numbers3.end(), []() {
return rand() % size;
});
std::generate(numbers4.begin(), numbers4.end(), []()
{     return rand() % size;     });
```

2. Next, we fill each array with random numbers using std::generate, which results in an array with numbers and a random order:

```
std::sort(numbers1.begin(), numbers1.end());
std::sort(numbers2.begin(), numbers2.end());
std::sort(numbers3.begin(), numbers3.end());
std::sort(numbers4.begin(), numbers4.end());
```

3. Next, we sort the array of integers, which is the main goal of this example, as this operation takes a while to execute:

```
std::cout << numbers1.back() << '\n';
std::cout << numbers2.back() << '\n';
std::cout << numbers3.back() << '\n';
std::cout << numbers4.back() << '\n';

return 0;
}
```

4. Finally, we output the last entry in each array, which will usually be 999999 (but doesn't have to be since the numbers were generated using a random number generator).

The problem with the preceding example is that the operations could be executed in parallel because each array is independent. To address this, we can execute these operations asynchronously, meaning the arrays will be created, filled, sorted, and outputted in parallel. For example, consider the following code:

```
#include <future>
#include <thread>
#include <vector>
#include <iostream>
#include <algorithm>
```

```cpp
constexpr auto size =
1000000;
int foo() {
std::vector<int> numbers(size);
std::generate(numbers.begin(), numbers.end(), []()
{       return rand() % size;
});
std::sort(numbers.begin(),
numbers.end());     return
numbers.back(); }
```

The first thing we do is implement a function called foo() that creates our vector, fills it with random numbers, sorts the list, and returns the last entry in the array (which is identical to the preceding example with the exception that we only work with one array at a time and not 4):

```cpp
int main(void)
{
auto a1 = std::async(std::launch::async, foo);
auto a2 = std::async(std::launch::async, foo);
auto a3 = std::async(std::launch::async, foo);
auto a4 = std::async(std::launch::async, foo);

std::cout << a1.get() << '\n';
std::cout << a2.get() << '\n';
std::cout << a3.get() << '\n';
std::cout << a4.get() << '\n';

return 0;
}
```

We then use std::async to execute this foo() function four times, resulting in the same four arrays, just like our previous example. The std::async() function in this example does the same thing as executing four threads manually.

The result of std::aync() is a std::future object, which stores the result of the function once it has finished executing. The last thing we do in this example is use the get() function to return the value of the function once it is ready.

If we time the results of these functions, we can see that the asynchronous version is faster than the blocking version. The following code shows this (the real time is the time to look for):

```
user@localhost:~/book/chapter05/build
[~/book/chapter05/build]: time ./recipe06_example02
999999
999999
999997
999999

real    0m0.608s
user    0m2.153s
sys     0m0.156s
[~/book/chapter05/build]:
```

The std::async() function can also be used to execute our array function asynchronously in the same thread. For example, consider the following code:

```
int main(void)
{
auto a1 = std::async(std::launch::deferred, foo);
auto a2 = std::async(std::launch::deferred, foo);
auto a3 = std::async(std::launch::deferred, foo);
auto a4 = std::async(std::launch::deferred, foo);

std::cout << a1.get() << '\n';
std::cout << a2.get() << '\n';
std::cout << a3.get() << '\n';
std::cout << a4.get() << '\n';

return 0;
}
```

As you can see in the preceding example, we changed the operation from std::launch::async to std::launch::deferred, which results in each function executing once the result of the function is needed (that is, when the get() function is called). This is useful if you are not sure whether the function needs to execute in the first place (that is, only execute the function when needed), with the downside being that the execution of the program is slower, as threads are not typically used as an optimization method.

Working with promises and futures

In this recipe, we will learn how to use C++ promises and futures. C++ promise is an argument to a C++ thread, while C++ future is the return value of the thread, and can be used to manually implement the same functionality of an std::async call. This recipe is important because a call to std::aync requires that each thread stops execution to get its result, while manually implementing a C++ promise and future allows the user to get the return value of a thread while the thread is still executing.

Before we begin, please ensure that all of the technical requirements are met, including installing Ubuntu 18.04 or higher and running the following in a terminal window:

sudo apt-get install build-essential git

This will ensure your operating system has the proper tools to compile and execute the examples in this recipe. Once this is complete, open a new terminal. We will use this terminal to download, compile, and run our examples.

You need to perform the following steps to try this recipe:

1. From a new terminal, run the following to download the source code:

    > cd ~/
    > git clone https://github.com/PacktPublishing/Advanced-CPP-CookBook.git
    > cd Advanced-CPP-CookBook/chapter10

2. To compile the source code, run the following:

    > cmake .
    > make recipe07_examples

3. Once the source code is compiled, you can execute each example in this recipe by running the following commands:

    > ./recipe07_example01
    The answer is: 42

    > ./recipe07_example02
    The answer is: 42

In the next section, we will step through each of these examples and explain what each example program does and how it relates to the lessons being taught in this recipe.

In this recipe, we will learn how to manually use a C++ promise and future to provide a function that is executed in parallel with an argument, as well as get the function's return value. To start, let's demonstrate how this is done in its most simplistic form, with the following code:

```
#include <thread>
#include <iostream>
#include <future>

void foo(std::promise<int> promise)
{
promise.set_value(42);
}

int main(void)
{
```

```cpp
std::promise<int> promise;
auto future =
promise.get_future();

std::thread t{foo, std::move(promise)};
t.join();    std::cout << "The answer is: " <<
future.get() << '\n';
return 0;
}
```

The preceding example results in the following when executed:

As you can see in the preceding code, the C++ promise is an argument to the function that is threaded. The thread returns its value by setting the promise argument, which, in turn, sets a C++ future that the user can get from the promise argument it provides to the thread. It should be noted that we use std::move() to prevent the promise argument from being copied (which the compiler will prohibit as the C++ promise is a move-only class). Finally, we use the get() function to get the result of the thread, the same way you would get the result of a thread executed using std::async.

One of the benefits of using promise and future manually is that you can get the result of the thread before it completes, allowing the thread to continue to do work. For example, take a look at the following:

```cpp
#include <thread>
#include <iostream>
#include <future>

void foo(std::promise<int> promise)
{
promise.set_value(42);
while (true);
}

int main(void)
{
std::promise<int> promise;    auto
future = promise.get_future();
std::thread t{foo,
std::move(promise)};

future.wait();
std::cout << "The answer is: " << future.get() << '\n';

t.join();
```

```
// Never reached
return 0;
}
```

This results in the following when executed:

In the preceding example, we created the same thread, but we looped forever in the thread, meaning the thread will never return. We then created the thread the same way, but outputted the result of the C++ future as soon as it was ready, which we can determine using the wait() function.

Optimizing Your Code for Performance

Optimizing your code for performance ensures your code is getting the most out of what C++ can offer. Unlike other high-level languages, C++ is capable of providing high-level syntactical freedom without sacrificing performance, although admittedly at the expense of a higher learning curve.

This topic is important because it will demonstrate more advanced methods for optimizing your code, including how to benchmark your software at the unit level, how to examine the resulting assembly code your compiler produces for potential optimizations, how to reduce the number of memory resources your application is using, and why compiler hints such as no except are important. After reading this chapter, you will have the skills to write more efficient C++.

Technical requirements

To compile and run the examples in this chapter, you must have administrative access to a computer running Ubuntu 18.04 with a functional internet connection. Prior to running these examples, you must install the following:

sudo apt-get install build-essential git cmake valgrind

If this is installed on any operating system other than Ubuntu 18.04, then GCC 7.4 or higher and CMake 3.6 or higher will be required.

Benchmarking your code

In this recipe, you will learn how to benchmark and optimize your source code. Optimizing source code will result in more efficient C++, which increases battery life, improves performance, and so on. This recipe is important as the process of optimizing source code starts with determining which resource you plan to optimize, which could include speed, memory, and even power. Without benchmarking tools, it is extremely difficult to compare different approaches to the same problem.

There are countless benchmarking tools (anything that measures a single property of your program) available to C++ programmers, including C++ APIs such as Boost, Folly, and Abseil, and CPU-specific tools such as Intel's vTune. There are also several profiling tools (anything the helps you understand the behavior of your program) such as valgrind and gprof. In this recipe, we will focus on two of these: Hayai and Valgrind. Hayai provides a simple example of a micro-benchmarking, while Valgrind provides an example of a more complete, though more complicated, dynamic analysis/profiling tool.

Before beginning, please ensure that all of the technical requirements have been met, including installing Ubuntu 18.04 or higher and running the following in a Terminal window:

sudo apt-get install build-essential git valgrind cmake

This will ensure your operating system has the proper tools to compile and execute the examples in this recipe. Once you've done this, open a new Terminal. We will use this Terminal to download, compile, and run our examples.

Perform the following steps to complete this recipe:

1. From a new Terminal, run the following to download the source code:

    > cd ~/
    > git clone https://github.com/PacktPublishing/Advanced-CPP-
    CookBook.git
    > cd Advanced-CPP-CookBook/chapter10

2. To compile the source code, run the following command:

    > cmake -DCMAKE_BUILD_TYPE=Debug .
    > make recipe01_examples

3. Once the source code has been compiled, you can execute each example in this recipe by running the following commands:

    > ./recipe01_example01
    [==========] Running 2 benchmarks.
    [RUN] vector.push_back (10 runs, 100 iterations
    per run) [DONE] vector.push_back (0.200741 ms)
    ...
    [RUN] vector.emplace_back (10 runs, 100 iterations
    per run) [DONE] vector.emplace_back (0.166699
    ms) ...

    > ./recipe01_example02

In the next section, we will step through each of these examples and explain what each example program does and how it relates to the lessons being taught in this recipe.

The most common optimization that's applied to C++ is the speed of execution. To optimize C++ for speed, we must start by developing different approaches to the same problem and then benchmark each solution to determine which solution executes the fastest. Benchmarking tools such as Hayai, a C++ based benchmarking library on GitHub, aid in making this determination. To explain this, let's look at a simple example:

```cpp
#include <string>
#include <vector> #include
<hayai.hpp>
std::vector<std::string>
data;
BENCHMARK(vector, push_back, 10, 100)
{
data.push_back("The answer is:
42"); }

BENCHMARK(vector, emplace_back, 10, 100)
{
data.emplace_back("The answer is:
42"); }
```

When we execute the preceding code, we get the following output:

In the preceding example, we use the Hayai library to benchmark the performance difference between adding a string to a vector using push_back() versus emplace_back(). The difference between push_back() and emplace_back() is that push_back() creates the object and then copies or moves it into the vector, while emplace_back() creates the object in the vector itself without the need for the temporary object and subsequent copy/move. That is to say, if you use push_back(), an object must be constructed and then either copied or moved into the vector. If you use emplace_back(), the object is simply constructed. As expected, emplace_back() outperforms push_back(), which is why tools such as Clang-Tidy recommend the use of emplace_back() over push_back() whenever possible.

Benchmark libraries such as Hayai are simple to use and extremely effective at aiding the programmer with optimizing source code and are capable of not only benchmarking speed but also resource usage as well. The problem with these libraries is they are better leveraged at the unit level and not at the integration and system level; that is, to test an entire executable, these libraries are not well suited to aid the programmer as they do not scale well as the size of the test increases.

To analyze an entire executable and not a single function, tools such as Valgrind exist, which help you profile which functions need the most attention with respect to optimizations. From there, a benchmarking tool can be used to analyze the functions that need the most attention.

Valgrind is a dynamic analysis tool that's capable of detecting memory leaks and tracing the execution of a program. To see this in action, let's look at the following example:

```
volatile int data = 0;

void foo() {
data++; }

int main(void)
{
for (auto i = 0; i < 100000; i++) {
foo();
}
}
```

In the preceding example, we increment a global variable (marked volatile to ensure the compiler does not optimize away the variable) from a function named foo() and then execute this function 100,000 times. To analyze this example, run the following (which uses callgrind to output how many times each function is called in your program):

```
> valgrind --tool=callgrind ./recipe01_example02
> callgrind_annotate callgrind.out.*
```

This results in the following output:

```
user@localhost:~/book/chapter06/build
Thresholds:              99
Include dirs:
User annotated:
Auto-annotation:  off

--------------------------------------------------------------------
Ir
--------------------------------------------------------------------
3,639,158   PROGRAM TOTALS


--------------------------------------------------------------------
Ir          file:function
--------------------------------------------------------------------
928,796    ???:_dl_lookup_symbol_x [/usr/lib64/ld-2.30.so]
800,000    ???:foo() [/home/user/book/chapter06/build/recipe01_example02]
687,907    ???:do_lookup_x [/usr/lib64/ld-2.30.so]
500,009    ???:main [/home/user/book/chapter06/build/recipe01_example02]
367,484    ???:_dl_relocate_object [/usr/lib64/ld-2.30.so]
118,759    ???:check_match [/usr/lib64/ld-2.30.so]
 92,113    ???:strcmp [/usr/lib64/libc-2.30.so]
 66,761    ???:_dl_addr [/usr/lib64/libc-2.30.so]
 12,781    ???:__GI___tunables_init [/usr/lib64/ld-2.30.so]
  8,936    ???:_dl_check_map_versions [/usr/lib64/ld-2.30.so]
  7,136    ???:_dl_map_object_from_fd [/usr/lib64/ld-2.30.so]
  4,521    ???:_dl_name_match_p [/usr/lib64/ld-2.30.so]
  4,131    ???:_dl_cache_libcmp [/usr/lib64/ld-2.30.so]
  3,168    ???:_dl_map_object [/usr/lib64/ld-2.30.so]
  2,720    ???:_dl_map_object_deps [/usr/lib64/ld-2.30.so]

[~/book/chapter06/build]:
```

As we can see, the foo() function is listed near the top of the preceding output (with the dynamic linker's dl_lookup_symbol_x() function called the most, which is used to link the program prior to execution). It should be noted that the program lists (on the left-hand side) the total number of instructions for the foo() function as 800,000. This is due to the foo() function being 8 assembly instructions long and being executed 100,000 times. For example, let's look at the assembly of the foo() function using objdump (a tool capable of outputting the compiled assembly of an executable), as follows:

```
user@localhost:~/book/chapter06/build
[~/book/chapter06/build]: objdump -d recipe01_example02 | grep "<_Z3foov>:" -A9
0000000000401106 <_Z3foov>:
  401106:    55                   push   %rbp
  401107:    48 89 e5             mov    %rsp,%rbp
  40110a:    8b 05 10 2f 00 00    mov    0x2f10(%rip),%eax    # 404020 <__TMC_END__>
  401110:    83 c0 01             add    $0x1,%eax
  401113:    89 05 07 2f 00 00    mov    %eax,0x2f07(%rip)    # 404020 <__TMC_END__>
  401119:    90                   nop
  40111a:    5d                   pop    %rbp
  40111b:    c3                   retq

[~/book/chapter06/build]:
```

Using Valgrind, it is possible to profile an executable to determine which functions take the longest to execute. For example, let's look at ls:

> valgrind --tool=callgrind ls
> callgrind_annotate callgrind.out.*

This results in the following output:

```
user@localhost:~/book/chapter06/build                    —    □    ×

------------------------------------------------------------------
Ir
------------------------------------------------------------------
1,234,765  PROGRAM TOTALS

------------------------------------------------------------------
Ir        file:function
------------------------------------------------------------------
217,117   ???:do_lookup_x [/usr/lib64/ld-2.30.so]
147,512   ???:strcoll_l [/usr/lib64/libc-2.30.so]
120,290   ???:_dl_lookup_symbol_x [/usr/lib64/ld-2.30.so]
 85,379   ???:_dl_relocate_object [/usr/lib64/ld-2.30.so]
 66,761   ???:_dl_addr [/usr/lib64/libc-2.30.so]
 51,564   ???:strcmp [/usr/lib64/libc-2.30.so]
 50,640   ???:_nl_make_l10nflist'2 [/usr/lib64/libc-2.30.so]
 40,839   ???:_int_malloc [/usr/lib64/libc-2.30.so]
 37,408   ???:__strlen_avx2 [/usr/lib64/libc-2.30.so]
 35,557   ???:check_match [/usr/lib64/ld-2.30.so]
 31,867   ???:__strcmp_avx2 [/usr/lib64/libc-2.30.so]
 28,030   ???:0x0000000000013d40 [/usr/bin/ls]
 21,623   ???:malloc [/usr/lib64/libc-2.30.so]
 16,016   ???:__stpcpy_avx2 [/usr/lib64/libc-2.30.so]
 14,615   ???:0x000000000000a030 [/usr/bin/ls]
 13,420   ???:read_alias_file [/usr/lib64/libc-2.30.so]
 12,781   ???:__GI___tunables_init [/usr/lib64/ld-2.30.so]
 11,495   ???:_int_free [/usr/lib64/libc-2.30.so]
 11,112   ???:__strcasecmp_l_avx [/usr/lib64/libc-2.30.so]
 10,712   ???:0x00000000000011ba0 [/usr/bin/ls]
 10,058   ???:__memcpy_avx_unaligned_erms [/usr/lib64/libc-2.30.so]
  8,964   ???:getenv [/usr/lib64/libc-2.30.so]
```

As we can see, the strcmp function is called a lot. This information can be combined with benchmarking APIs at the unit level to determine whether a faster version of strcmp can be written (for example, using handwritten assembly and special CPU instructions). Using tools such as Hayai and Valgrind, it is possible to isolate which functions in your program are consuming the most CPU, memory, and even power, and rewrite them to provide better performance while focusing your efforts on the optimizations that will provide the best return of investment.

Looking at assembly code

In this recipe, we will take a look at the resulting assembly from two different optimizations: loop unrolling and pass-by-reference parameters. This recipe is important because it will teach you how to dive deeper into how the compiler converts C++ into executable code. This information will shed light on why C++ specifications such as the C++ Core Guidelines make the recommendations it does with respect to optimizations and performance. This is often critical when you're attempting to write better C++ code, especially when you want to optimize it.

Before beginning, please ensure that all of the technical requirements have been met, including installing Ubuntu 18.04 or higher and running the following in a Terminal window:

sudo apt-get install build-essential git cmake

This will ensure your operating system has the proper tools to compile and execute the examples in this recipe. Once you've done this, open a new Terminal. We will use this Terminal to download, compile, and run our examples.

Perform the following steps to complete this recipe:

1. From a new Terminal, run the following to download the source code:

```
> cd ~/
> git clone https://github.com/PacktPublishing/Advanced-CPP-
CookBook.git
> cd Advanced-CPP-CookBook/chapter10
```

2. To compile the source code, run the following command:

```
> cmake -DCMAKE_BUILD_TYPE=Debug .
> make recipe02_examples
```

3. Once the source code has been compiled, you can execute each example in this recipe by running the following commands:

```
> ./recipe02_example01
```

```
> ./recipe02_example02
```

```
> ./recipe02_example03
```

```
> ./recipe02_example04
```

```
> ./recipe02_example05
```

In the next section, we will step through each of these examples and explain what each example program does and how it relates to the lessons being taught in this recipe.

One of the best ways to learn how to optimize your C++ code is to learn how to analyze the resulting assembly code that the compiler generates after compilation. In this recipe, we will learn how this analysis is done by looking at two different examples: loop unrolling and pass-by-reference parameters.

Before we look at these examples, let's look at a simple example:

int main(void)
{ }

In the preceding example, we have nothing more than a main() function. We haven't included any C or C++ libraries and the main() function itself is empty. If we compile this example, we will see that the resulting binary is still pretty large:

In this case, the example is 22kb in size. To show the resulting assembly that the compiler generated for this code, we can do the following:

objdump -d recipe02_example01

The resulting output of the preceding command should be surprising as there is a lot of code for an application that does absolutely nothing.

To get a better feel for how much code there really is, we can refine the output by using grep, a tool that lets us filter text from any command. Let's look at all of the functions in the code:

```
user@localhost:~/book/chapter06/build
[~/book/chapter06/build]: objdump -d ./recipe02_example01 | grep ">:"
0000000000401000 <_init>:
0000000000401020 <_start>:
000000000040104f <.annobin_init.c>:
0000000000401050 <_dl_relocate_static_pie>:
0000000000401055 <.annobin__dl_relocate_static_pie.end>:
0000000000401060 <deregister_tm_clones>:
0000000000401090 <register_tm_clones>:
00000000004010d0 <__do_global_dtors_aux>:
0000000000401100 <frame_dummy>:
0000000000401106 <main>:
0000000000401120 <__libc_csu_init>:
0000000000401190 <__libc_csu_fini>:
0000000000401198 <_fini>:
[~/book/chapter06/build]:
```

As we can see, there are several functions the compiler automatically adds to the code for you. This includes the _init(), _fini(), and _start() functions. We can also look at a specific function, such as our main function, as follows:

```
user@localhost:~/book/chapter06/build
[~/book/chapter06/build]: objdump -d ./recipe02_example01 | awk '/main>:/,/retq/'
0000000000401106 <main>:
  401106:       55                      push    %rbp
  401107:       48 89 e5                mov     %rsp,%rbp
  40110a:       b8 00 00 00 00          mov     $0x0,%eax
  40110f:       5d                      pop     %rbp
  401110:       c3                      retq
[~/book/chapter06/build]:
```

In the preceding example, we search the output of objdump for main>: and RETQ. All the function names end with >: and the last instruction (typically) for each function is RETQ on an Intel 64-bit system.

The following is the resulting assembly:

401106: push %rbp
401107: mov %rsp,%rbp

First, it stores the current stack frame pointer (rbp) to the stack and loads the stack frame pointer with the current address of the stack (rsp) for the main() function.

This can be seen in every function and is called the function's prolog. The only code that main() executes is return 0, which was added to the code automatically by the compiler:

40110a: mov $0x0,%eax

Finally, the last assembly in this function contains the function's epilog, which restores the stack frame pointer and returns:

40110f: pop %rbp
401110: retq

Now that we have a better understanding of how to get and read the resulting assembly for compiled C++, let's look at an example of loop unrolling, which is the process of replacing a loop of instructions with its equivalent version of the instructions without a loop. To do this, ensure that the examples are compiled in release mode (that is, with compiler optimizations enabled) by configuring them using the following command:

> cmake -DCMAKE_BUILD_TYPE=Release.
> make

To understand loop unrolling, let's look at the following code:

volatile int data[1000];

int main(void)
{
for (auto i = 0U; i < 1000; i++) {
data[i] = 42;
}
}

When the compiler encounters a loop, the resulting assembly it generates contains the following code:

```
user@localhost:~/book/chapter06/build                                    —   □   ×
[~/book/chapter06/build]: objdump -d ./recipe02_example02 | awk '/main>:/,/ret/'
0000000000401020 <main>:
  401020:       31 c0                   xor     %eax,%eax
  401022:       66 0f 1f 44 00 00       nopw    0x0(%rax,%rax,1)
  401028:       89 c2                   mov     %eax,%edx
  40102a:       83 c0 01                add     $0x1,%eax
  40102d:       c7 04 95 40 40 40 00    movl    $0x2a,0x404040(,%rdx,4)
  401034:       2a 00 00 00
  401038:       3d e8 03 00 00          cmp     $0x3e8,%eax
  40103d:       75 e9                   jne     401028  <main+0x8>
  40103f:       31 c0                   xor     %eax,%eax
  401041:       c3                      retq
[~/book/chapter06/build]:
```

Let's break this down:

401020: xor %eax,%eax
401022: nopw 0x0(%rax,%rax,1)

The first two instructions belong to the for (auto i = 0U; portion of the code. In this case, the i variable is stored in the EAX register and is set to 0 using the XOR instruction (the XOR instruction is faster on Intel for setting a register to 0 than a MOV instruction). The NOPW instruction can be safely ignored.

The next couple of instructions are interleaved, as follows:

```
401028: mov %eax,%edx
40102a: add $0x1,%eax
40102d: movl $0x2a,0x404040(,%rdx,4)
```

These instructions represent the i++; and data[i] = 42; code. The first instruction stores the current value of the i variable and then increments it by one before storing 42 into the memory address indexed by i. Conveniently, this resulting assembly demonstrates a possible opportunity for optimization as the compiler could have achieved the same functionality using the following:

```
movl
$0x2a,0x404040(,%rax,4)
add $0x1,%eax
```

The preceding code stores the value 42 before executing i++, thus removing the need for the following:

```
mov %eax,%edx
```

A number of methods exist to realize this potential optimization, including using a different compiler or handwriting the assembly. The next set of instructions execute the i < 1000; portion of us for loop:

```
401038: cmp $0x3e8,%eax
40103d: jne 401028 <main+0x8>
```

The CMP instruction checks to see if the i variable is 1000 and, if not, uses the JNE instruction to jump to the top of the function to continue the loop. Otherwise, the remaining code executes:
```
40103f: xor %eax,%eax
401041: retq
```

To see how loop unrolling works, let's change the number of iterations the loop takes from 1000 to 4, as follows:

```
volatile int data[4];

int main(void)
{
for (auto i = 0U; i < 4; i++) {
data[i] = 42;
}
}
```

As we can see, the code is identical except for the number of iterations the loop takes. The resulting assembly is as follows:

As we can see, the CMP and JNE instructions are missing. Now, the following code is compiled (but there's more!):

```
for (auto i = 0U; i < 4; i++) {
data[i] = 42;
}
```

The compiled code is converted into the following code:

```
data[0] = 42;       data[1]
= 42;       data[2] = 42;
data[3] = 42;
```

return 0; shows up in the assembly in-between the assignments. This is allowed because the return value of the function is independent of the assignment (since the assignment instructions never touch RAX), which provides the CPU with an additional optimization (as it can execute return 0; in parallel, though this is a topic that is out of the scope of this book). It should be noted that loop unrolling doesn't require a small number of loop iterations to be used. Some compilers will partially unroll a loop to achieve optimizations (for example, executing the loop in groups of 4 instead of 1 at a time).

Our last example will look at pass-by-reference instead of pass-by-value. To start, recompile the code in debug mode:

```
> cmake -DCMAKE_BUILD_TYPE=Debug.
> make
```

Let's look at the following example:

```
struct mydata {
int data[100];
};

void foo(mydata d)
{
```

```
(void) d;
}
int main(void)
{   mydata d;
foo(d);
}
```

In this example, we've created a large structure and passed it by-value to a function named foo() in our main function. The resulting assembly for the main function is as follows:

The important instructions from the preceding example are as follows:

```
401137: rep movsq %ds:(%rsi),%es:(%rdi)
40113a: callq 401106 <_Z3foo6mydata>
```

The preceding instructions copy the large structure to the stack and then call our foo() function. The copy occurs because the structure is passed by value, which means the compiler must perform a copy. As a side note, if you would like to see the output in a readable format and not a mangled format, add a C to the options, as follows:

Finally, let's pass-by-reference to see the resulting improvement:

```
struct mydata {
int data[100];
};
void foo(mydata &d)
{
(void) d;
}
int main(void)
{    mydata d;
foo(d);
}
```

As we can see, we pass the structure by-reference instead of by-value. The resulting assembly is as follows:

```
[~/book/chapter06/build]: objdump -d ./recipe02_example05 | awk '/main>:/,/ret/'
0000000000401111 <main>:
  401111:       55                      push    %rbp
  401112:       48 89 e5                mov     %rsp,%rbp
  401115:       48 81 ec 90 01 00 00    sub     $0x190,%rsp
  40111c:       48 8d 85 70 fe ff ff    lea     -0x190(%rbp),%rax
  401123:       48 89 c7                mov     %rax,%rdi
  401126:       e8 db ff ff ff          callq   401106 <_Z3fooR6mydata>
  40112b:       b8 00 00 00 00          mov     $0x0,%eax
  401130:       c9                      leaveq
  401131:       c3                      retq
[~/book/chapter06/build]:
```

Here, there is far less code, resulting in a faster executable. As we have learned, examining what the compiler produces can be effective if we wish to understand what the compiler is producing as this provides more information about potential changes you can make to write more efficient C++ code.

Reducing the number of memory allocations

Hidden memory allocations are produced by C++ all the time when an application runs. This recipe will teach you how to determine when memory is allocated by C++ and how to remove these allocations when possible.

Understanding how to remove memory allocations is important because functions such as new(), delete(), malloc(), and free() are not only slow, but the memory they provide is also finite. Removing unneeded allocations not only improves the overall performance of your application, but it also helps to reduce its overall memory requirements.

Before beginning, please ensure that all of the technical requirements have been met, including installing Ubuntu 18.04 or higher and running the following in a Terminal window:

sudo apt-get install build-essential git valgrind cmake

This will ensure your operating system has the proper tools to compile and execute the examples in this recipe. Once you've done this, open a new Terminal. We will use this Terminal to download, compile, and run our examples.

Perform the following steps to complete this recipe:

1. From a new Terminal, run the following to download the source code:

> cd ~/
> git clone https://github.com/PacktPublishing/Advanced-CPP-
CookBook.git
> cd Advanced-CPP-CookBook/chapter10

2. To compile the source code, run the following command:

> cmake .
> make recipe03_examples

3. Once the source code has been compiled, you can execute each example in this recipe by running the following commands:

> ./recipe03_example01

> ./recipe03_example02

> ./recipe03_example03

> ./recipe03_example04

> ./recipe03_example05

> ./recipe03_example06

> ./recipe03_example07

In the next section, we will step through each of these examples and explain what each example program does and how it relates to the lessons being taught in this recipe.

In this recipe, we will learn how to monitor how much memory an application is consuming, as well as the different ways that C++ can allocate memory behind the scenes. To start, let's look at a simple application that does nothing:

```
int main(void)
{
}
```

As we can see, this application does nothing. To see how much memory the application has used, we will use Valgrind, a dynamic analysis tool, as follows:

As shown in the preceding example, our application has allocated heap memory (that is, memory allocated using new()/delete() or malloc()/free()). To determine where this allocation occurred, let's use Valgrind again, but this time, we will enable a tool called **Massif**, which will trace where the memory allocation came from:

To see the output of the preceding example, we must output a file that was created for us automatically:

cat massif.out.*

This results in us retrieving the following output:

As we can see, the dynamic linker's init() function is performing the allocation, which is 72,704 bytes in size. To further demonstrate how to use Valgrind, let's take a look at this simple example, where we perform our own allocation:

```
int main(void)
{
auto ptr = new int;
delete ptr;
}
```

To see the memory allocation of the preceding source, we need to run Valgrind again:

```
[~/book/chapter06/build]: valgrind ./recipe03_example02
==256915== Memcheck, a memory error detector
==256915== Copyright (C) 2002-2017, and GNU GPL'd, by Julian Seward et al.
==256915== Using Valgrind-3.15.0 and LibVEX; rerun with -h for copyright info
==256915== Command: ./recipe03_example02
==256915==
==256915==
==256915== HEAP SUMMARY:
==256915==     in use at exit: 0 bytes in 0 blocks
==256915==   total heap usage: 2 allocs, 2 frees, 72,708 bytes allocated
==256915==
==256915== All heap blocks were freed -- no leaks are possible
==256915==
==256915== For lists of detected and suppressed errors, rerun with: -s
==256915== ERROR SUMMARY: 0 errors from 0 contexts (suppressed: 0 from 0)
[~/book/chapter06/build]:
```

As we can see, we have allocated 72,708 bytes. Since we know that the application will allocate 72,704 bytes for us automatically, we can see that Valgrind has successfully detected the 4 bytes we allocated (the size of an integer on Intel 64-bit systems running Linux). To see where this allocation occurred, let's use Massif again:

```
[~/book/chapter06/build]: valgrind --tool=massif --threshold=0.1 ./recipe03_example02
==256939== Massif, a heap profiler
==256939== Copyright (C) 2003-2017, and GNU GPL'd, by Nicholas Nethercote
==256939== Using Valgrind-3.15.0 and LibVEX; rerun with -h for copyright info
==256939== Command: ./recipe03_example02
==256939==
==256939==
[~/book/chapter06/build]:
```

As we can see, we've added the --threshold=0.1 to the command-line options as this tells Valgrind that any allocation that makes up .1% of the allocations should be logged. Let's cat the results (the cat program simply echoes the contents of a file to the console):

cat massif.out.*

By doing this, we get the following output:

```
user@localhost:~/book/chapter06/build
snapshot=3
#-----------
time=2376770
mem_heap_B=72708
mem_heap_extra_B=28
mem_stacks_B=0
heap_tree=peak
n2: 72708 (heap allocation functions) malloc/new/new[], --alloc-fns, etc.
 n1: 72704 0x49150A9: ??? (in /usr/lib64/libstdc++.so.6.0.27)
  n1: 72704 0x400FD59: call_init.part.0 (in /usr/lib64/ld-2.30.so)
   n1: 72704 0x400FE60: _dl_init (in /usr/lib64/ld-2.30.so)
    n0: 72704 0x4001149: ??? (in /usr/lib64/ld-2.30.so)
 n0: 4 in 1 place, below massif's threshold (0.10%)
#-----------
snapshot=4
#-----------
time=2376770
mem_heap_B=72704
mem_heap_extra_B=8
mem_stacks_B=0
heap_tree=empty
#-----------
snapshot=5
#-----------
time=2387637
mem_heap_B=0
mem_heap_extra_B=0
mem_stacks_B=0
heap_tree=empty
[~/book/chapter06/build]:
```

As we can see, Valgrind has detected the memory allocations from the init() function, as well as from our main() function.

Now that we know how to analyze the memory allocations our application makes, let's look at some different C++ APIs to see what types of memory allocations they make behind the scenes. To start, let's look at an std::vector, as follows:

```
#include <vector>
std::vector<int> data; int
main(void)
{
for (auto i = 0; i < 10000; i++) {
data.push_back(i);
}
}
```

Here, we've created a global vector of integers and then added 10,000 integers to the vector. Using Valgrind, we get the following output:

```
user@localhost:~/book/chapter06/build                          —    □    ×

[~/book/chapter06/build]: valgrind ./recipe03_example03
==257040== Memcheck, a memory error detector
==257040== Copyright (C) 2002-2017, and GNU GPL'd, by Julian Seward et al.
==257040== Using Valgrind-3.15.0 and LibVEX; rerun with -h for copyright info
==257040== Command: ./recipe03_example03
==257040==
==257040==
==257040== HEAP SUMMARY:
==257040==     in use at exit: 0 bytes in 0 blocks
==257040==   total heap usage: 16 allocs, 16 frees, 203,772 bytes allocated
==257040==
==257040== All heap blocks were freed -- no leaks are possible
==257040==
==257040== For lists of detected and suppressed errors, rerun with: -s
==257040== ERROR SUMMARY: 0 errors from 0 contexts (suppressed: 0 from 0)
[~/book/chapter06/build]:
```

Here, we can see 16 allocations, with a total of 203,772 bytes. We know that the application will allocate 72,704 bytes for us, so we must remove this from our total, leaving us with 131,068 bytes of memory. We also know that we allocated 10,000 integers, which is 40,000 bytes in total. So, the question is, where did the other 91,068 bytes come from?

The answer is in how std::vector works under the hood. std::vector must ensure a continuous view of memory at all times, which means that when an insertion occurs and the std::vector is out of space, it must allocate a new, larger buffer and then copy the contents of the old buffer into the new buffer. The problem is that std::vector doesn't know what the total size of the buffer will be when all of the insertions are complete, so when the first insertion is performed, it creates a small buffer to ensure memory is not wasted and then proceeds to increase the size of the std::vector in small increments as the vector grows, resulting in several memory allocations and memory copies.

To prevent such allocation from happening, C++ provides the reserve() function, which provides the user of a std::vector to estimate how much memory the user thinks they will need. For example, consider the following code:

```
#include <vector>
std::vector<int> data;

int main(void)
{
data.reserve(10000);  // <--- added optimization

for (auto i = 0; i < 10000; i++) {
data.push_back(i);
}
}
```

The code in the preceding example is the same as it is in the previous example, with the difference being that we added a call to the reserve() function, which tells the std::vector how large we think the vector will be. Valgrind's output is as follows:

As we can see, the application allocated 112,704 bytes. If we remove our 72,704 bytes that the application creates by default, we are left with 40,000 bytes, which is the exact size we expected (since we are adding 10,000 integers to the vector, with each integer being 4 bytes in size).

Data structures are not the only type of C++ Standard Library API that performs hidden allocations. Let's look at an std::any, as follows:

```
#include <any>
#include <string>
std::any data;

int main(void)
{    data = 42;    data =
std::string{"The answer is: 42"};
}
```

In this example, we created an std::any and assigned it an integer and an std::string. Let's look at the output of Valgrind:

As we can see, 3 allocations occurred. The first allocation occurs by default, while the second allocation is produced by the std::string. The last allocation is produced by the std::any. This occurs because std::any has to adjust its internal storage to account for any new random data type that it sees. In other words, to handle a generic data type, C++ has to perform an allocation. This is made worse if we keep changing the data type. For example, consider the following code:

```
#include <any>
```

```cpp
#include <string>
std::any data;
int main(void)
{   data = 42;    data = std::string{"The answer is:
42"};    data = 42;                          // <--- keep
swapping    data = std::string{"The answer is: 42"};   //
<--- keep swapping    data = 42;                        //
<--- keep swapping    data = std::string{"The answer
is: 42"};   // ...
data = 42;    data = std::string{"The
answer is: 42"};
}
```

The preceding code is identical to the previous example, with the only difference being that we swap between data types. Valgrind produces the following output:

As we can see, 9 allocations occurred instead of 3. To solve this problem, we need to use an std::variant instead of std::any, as follows:

```cpp
#include <variant> #include
<string> std::variant<int,
std::string> data;

int main(void)
{   data = 42;    data =
std::string{"The answer is: 42"};
}
```

The difference between std::any and std::variant is that std::variant requires that the user states which types the variant must support, removing the need for dynamic memory allocation on assignment. Valgrind's output is as follows:

```
user@localhost:~/book/chapter06/build
[~/book/chapter06/build]: valgrind ./recipe03_example07
==257176== Memcheck, a memory error detector
==257176== Copyright (C) 2002-2017, and GNU GPL'd, by Julian Seward et al.
==257176== Using Valgrind-3.15.0 and LibVEX; rerun with -h for copyright info
==257176== Command: ./recipe03_example07
==257176==
==257176==
==257176== HEAP SUMMARY:
==257176==     in use at exit: 0 bytes in 0 blocks
==257176==   total heap usage: 2 allocs, 2 frees, 72,722 bytes allocated
==257176==
==257176== All heap blocks were freed -- no leaks are possible
==257176==
==257176== For lists of detected and suppressed errors, rerun with: -s
==257176== ERROR SUMMARY: 0 errors from 0 contexts (suppressed: 0 from 0)
[~/book/chapter06/build]:
```

Now, we only have 2 allocations, as expected (the default allocation and the allocation from std::string). As shown in this recipe, libraries, including the C++ Standard Library, can hide memory allocations, potentially slowing down your code and using more memory resources than you intended. Tools such as Valgrind can be used to identify these types of problems, allowing you to create more efficient C++ code.

Declaring noexcept

C++11 introduced the noexcept keyword, which, besides simplifying how exceptions were used in general, also included a better implementation of C++ exceptions that removed some of their performance hits. However, this doesn't mean that exceptions do not include overhead (that is, performance penalties). In this recipe, we will explore how exceptions add overhead to an application and how the noexcept keyword can help reduce these penalties (depending on the compiler).

This recipe is important because it will demonstrate that if a function doesn't throw an exception, then it should be marked as such to prevent the additional overhead regarding the total size of the application, resulting in an application that loads faster.

Before beginning, please ensure that all of the technical requirements have been met, including installing Ubuntu 18.04 or higher and running the following in a Terminal window:

sudo apt-get install build-essential git cmake

This will ensure your operating system has the proper tools to compile and execute the examples in this recipe. Once you've done this, open a new Terminal. We will use this Terminal to download, compile, and run our examples.

Perform the following steps to complete this recipe:

1. From a new Terminal, run the following to download the source code:

> cd ~/
> git clone https://github.com/PacktPublishing/Advanced-CPP-CookBook.git
> cd Advanced-CPP-CookBook/chapter

2. To compile the source code, run the following command:

```
> cmake .
> make recipe04_examples
```

3. Once the source code has been compiled, you can execute each example in this recipe by running the following commands:

```
> ./recipe04_example01
```

```
> ./recipe04_example02
```

In the next section, we will step through each of these examples and explain what each example program does and how it relates to the lessons being taught in this recipe.

In this recipe, we will learn why it is so important to mark a function as no except if it shouldn't throw an exception. This is because it removes the added overhead to the application for exception support, which can improve execution time, application size, and even load time (this depends on the compiler, which Standard Library you are using, and so on). To show this, let's create a simple example:

```
class myclass
{    int answer;

public:
~myclass()    {
answer = 42;
}
};
```

The first thing we need to do is create a class that sets a private member variable when it is destructed, as follows:

```
void foo() {
throw 42;
}
int main(void)
{    myclass c;

try {        foo();
}
catch (...) {
}
}
```

Now, we can create two functions. The first function throws an exception, while the second function is our main function. This function creates an instance of our class and calls the foo() function inside a try/catch block. In other words, at no time will the main() function throw an exception. If we look at the assembly for the main function, we'll see the following:

```
[~/book/chapter06/build]: objdump -d ./recipe04_example01 | awk '/main>:/,/ret/'
000000000040119c <main>:
  40119c:       55                      push   %rbp
  40119d:       48 89 e5                mov    %rsp,%rbp
  4011a0:       53                      push   %rbx
  4011a1:       48 83 ec 18             sub    $0x18,%rsp
  4011a5:       e8 cc ff ff ff          callq  401176 <_Z3foov>
  4011aa:       48 8d 45 ec             lea    -0x14(%rbp),%rax
  4011ae:       48 89 c7                mov    %rax,%rdi
  4011b1:       e8 38 00 00 00          callq  4011ee <_ZN7myclassD1Ev>
  4011b6:       b8 00 00 00 00          mov    $0x0,%eax
  4011bb:       eb 29                   jmp    4011e6 <main+0x4a>
  4011bd:       48 89 c7                mov    %rax,%rdi
  4011c0:       e8 6b fe ff ff          callq  401030 <__cxa_begin_catch@plt>
  4011c5:       e8 86 fe ff ff          callq  401050 <__cxa_end_catch@plt>
  4011ca:       eb de                   jmp    4011aa <main+0xe>
  4011cc:       48 89 c3                mov    %rax,%rbx
  4011cf:       48 8d 45 ec             lea    -0x14(%rbp),%rax
  4011d3:       48 89 c7                mov    %rax,%rdi
  4011d6:       e8 13 00 00 00          callq  4011ee <_ZN7myclassD1Ev>
  4011db:       48 89 d8                mov    %rbx,%rax
  4011de:       48 89 c7                mov    %rax,%rdi
  4011e1:       e8 9a fe ff ff          callq  401080 <_Unwind_Resume@plt>
  4011e6:       48 83 c4 18             add    $0x18,%rsp
  4011ea:       5b                      pop    %rbx
  4011eb:       5d                      pop    %rbp
  4011ec:       c3                      retq
[~/book/chapter06/build]:
```

As we can see, our main function makes a call to _Unwind_Resume, which is used by the exception unwinder. This extra logic is due to the fact that C++ has to add additional exception logic to the end of the function. To remove this extra logic, tell the compiler that the main() function isn't thrown:

```cpp
int main(void) noexcept
{    myclass c;

try {        foo();
}
catch (...) {
}
}
```

Adding no except tells the compiler that an exception cannot be thrown. As a result, the function no longer contains the extra logic for handling an exception, as follows:

```
[~/book/chapter06/build]: objdump -d ./recipe04_example02 | awk '/main>:/,/ret/'
000000000040118c <main>:
  40118c:       55                      push   %rbp
  40118d:       48 89 e5                mov    %rsp,%rbp
  401190:       48 83 ec 10             sub    $0x10,%rsp
  401194:       e8 cd ff ff ff          callq  401166 <_Z3foov>
  401199:       48 8d 45 fc             lea    -0x4(%rbp),%rax
  40119d:       48 89 c7                mov    %rax,%rdi
  4011a0:       e8 19 00 00 00          callq  4011be <_ZN7myclassD1Ev>
  4011a5:       b8 00 00 00 00          mov    $0x0,%eax
  4011aa:       eb 0f                   jmp    4011bb <main+0x2f>
  4011ac:       48 89 c7                mov    %rax,%rdi
  4011af:       e8 7c fe ff ff          callq  401030 <__cxa_begin_catch@plt>
  4011b4:       e8 97 fe ff ff          callq  401050 <__cxa_end_catch@plt>
  4011b9:       eb de                   jmp    401199 <main+0xd>
  4011bb:       c9                      leaveq
  4011bc:       c3                      retq
[~/book/chapter06/build]:
```

As we can see, the unwind function is no longer present. It should be noted that there are calls to catch functions, which are due to the try/catch block and not the overhead of an exception.

Conclusion: Mastering Concurrency, Synchronization, and Performance Optimization in C++

As we conclude this comprehensive exploration of concurrency, synchronization, and performance optimization in C++, it is evident that these topics are not just optional skills but essential pillars of modern software development. The rapid evolution of hardware architectures, with multi-core processors and advanced parallelism, has fundamentally changed how we design and implement software. C++, with its rich feature set and low-level control, remains one of the most powerful languages for building high-performance systems. However, harnessing its full potential requires a deep understanding of concurrency models, synchronization mechanisms, and optimization techniques.

In this guide, we have covered the foundational concepts, advanced techniques, and best practices for writing efficient, scalable, and maintainable C++ code in 2025. Let us now reflect on the key takeaways and their significance in the broader context of software development.

The Importance of Concurrency in Modern Computing

Concurrency is no longer a niche concept; it is a necessity. With the proliferation of multi-core processors, the ability to execute multiple tasks simultaneously has become a cornerstone of performance optimization. C++ provides robust support for concurrency through its Standard Library, which includes threading, asynchronous tasks, and parallel algorithms. By leveraging these tools, developers can unlock the full potential of modern hardware.

Key Takeaways on Concurrency:

1. **Threads Are Fundamental**: Threads are the building blocks of concurrent programming. C++'s <thread> library makes it easy to create and manage threads, enabling developers to execute tasks concurrently.

2. **Asynchronous Programming**: The <future> and <async> libraries provide high-level abstractions for asynchronous programming, allowing developers to execute tasks in the background and retrieve results when needed.

3. **Thread Pools**: While C++ does not yet include a built-in thread pool, third-party libraries like Intel TBB and Boost.Asio offer efficient solutions for managing groups of threads.

Concurrency is not just about performance; it is also about responsiveness. By offloading tasks to separate threads, applications can remain responsive to user input while performing computationally intensive operations in the background. This is particularly important in applications like graphical user interfaces (GUIs), real-time systems, and server-side software.

Synchronization: Ensuring Data Integrity in Concurrent Systems

While concurrency offers significant performance benefits, it also introduces challenges, particularly when multiple threads access shared resources. Race conditions, deadlocks, and data corruption are common pitfalls in concurrent programming. Synchronization mechanisms like mutexes, condition variables, and atomic operations are essential for ensuring data integrity and preventing these issues.

Key Takeaways on Synchronization:

1. **Mutexes**: Mutexes are the most basic synchronization primitive, allowing only one thread to access a shared resource at a time. C++'s std::mutex and std::lock_guard simplify the process of locking and unlocking resources.

2. **Condition Variables**: Condition variables enable threads to wait for specific conditions to be met before proceeding. They are particularly useful in producer-consumer scenarios, where one thread produces data and another consumes it.

3. **Atomic Operations**: Atomic operations ensure that certain operations on shared variables are performed without interruption. The <atomic> library provides atomic types like std::atomic<int>, which are essential for lock-free programming.

Synchronization is not just about preventing race conditions; it is also about designing systems that are predictable and reliable. By carefully managing access to shared resources, developers can build concurrent systems that are both efficient and correct.

Performance Optimization: Beyond Concurrency and Synchronization

While concurrency and synchronization are critical for performance, they are only part of the story. Writing high-performance C++ code requires a holistic approach that includes memory management, cache optimization, and algorithmic efficiency.

Key Takeaways on Performance Optimization:

1. **Profiling and Benchmarking**: Before optimizing, it is essential to identify performance bottlenecks using profiling tools like Valgrind, gprof, or Intel VTune. Benchmarking tools like Google Benchmark can help measure the performance of specific code sections.

2. **Memory Management**: Efficient memory management is crucial for performance. Smart pointers (std::unique_ptr, std::shared_ptr) help avoid memory leaks and manage object lifetimes, while custom allocators can optimize memory usage for specific use cases.

3. **Cache Optimization**: Modern CPUs rely heavily on caches. Optimizing for cache locality—by using contiguous memory and minimizing cache misses—can significantly improve performance.

4. **Parallel Algorithms**: C++17 introduced parallel algorithms in the <algorithm> library, enabling developers to parallelize operations like sorting and searching with minimal effort.

5. **Compiler Optimizations**: Enabling compiler optimizations (e.g., -O2 or -O3 in GCC/Clang) and using link-time optimization (LTO) can provide additional performance gains.

Performance optimization is not just about writing faster code; it is about writing smarter code. By understanding the underlying hardware and leveraging the tools and techniques available in C++, developers can build systems that are not only fast but also efficient and scalable.

Advanced Topics: Coroutines and SIMD

As C++ continues to evolve, new features and techniques are emerging that further enhance its capabilities for concurrent and high-performance programming. Two of the most exciting advancements in 2025 are coroutines and SIMD.

Coroutines

Coroutines, introduced in C++20, enable asynchronous programming with synchronous-looking code. They are particularly useful for I/O-bound tasks, where waiting for external resources (e.g., network requests or file I/O) can block the execution of a program. By using coroutines, developers can write asynchronous code that is easier to read and maintain.

Example Use Case:

```
#include <iostream>
#include <coroutine>
struct Task {
    struct promise_type {
        Task get_return_object() { return {}; }
        std::suspend_never initial_suspend() { return {}; }
        std::suspend_never final_suspend() noexcept { return {}; }
        void return_void() {}
        void unhandled_exception() {}
    };
};

Task myCoroutine() {
    std::cout << "Hello from Coroutine!" << std::endl;
    co_return;
}

int main() {
    myCoroutine();
    return 0;
```

}

Coroutines represent a paradigm shift in asynchronous programming, offering a more intuitive and expressive way to handle concurrency.

SIMD (Single Instruction, Multiple Data)

SIMD instructions allow parallel processing of multiple data points, making them ideal for computationally intensive tasks like image processing, scientific simulations, and machine learning. Libraries like Intel's SIMD and compiler intrinsics enable developers to leverage SIMD in their C++ code.

Example Use Case:

```
#include <immintrin.h>

void addVectors(float* a, float* b, float* result, int size) {
    for (int i = 0; i < size; i += 8) {
        __m256 va = _mm256_load_ps(&a[i]);
        __m256 vb = _mm256_load_ps(&b[i]);
        __m256 vresult = _mm256_add_ps(va, vb);
        _mm256_store_ps(&result[i], vresult);
    }
}
```

SIMD is a powerful tool for optimizing performance, but it requires a deep understanding of both the hardware and the problem domain.

The Future of C++: What Lies Ahead?

As we look to the future, it is clear that C++ will continue to evolve to meet the demands of modern software development. The C++ Standards Committee is actively working on new features and improvements, with a focus on concurrency, performance, and ease of use. Some of the areas to watch in the coming years include:

1. **Standardized Thread Pools**: While third-party libraries currently fill the gap, there is growing demand for a standardized thread pool implementation in the C++ Standard Library.

2. **Enhanced Coroutines**: Coroutines are still a relatively new feature, and future versions of C++ are likely to introduce additional abstractions and utilities to make them even more powerful and easy to use.

3. **Improved SIMD Support**: As SIMD becomes increasingly important for performance optimization, we can expect better support for SIMD in the C++ Standard Library and compilers.

4. **Concurrency Models**: New concurrency models, such as task-based parallelism and dataflow programming, may be introduced to simplify the development of concurrent systems.

Final Thoughts

Concurrency, synchronization, and performance optimization are not just technical challenges; they are opportunities to push the boundaries of what is possible with software. By mastering these concepts, developers can build systems that are faster, more efficient, and more responsive to the needs of users.
In 2025, the landscape of software development is more complex and demanding than ever before.

However, with the right tools, techniques, and mindset, developers can rise to the challenge and create software that is not only functional but also exceptional. C++, with its unparalleled combination of performance and flexibility, remains one of the most powerful languages for achieving this goal.

As you continue your journey in C++ development, remember that learning is a continuous process. Stay curious, experiment with new features, and always strive to write code that is not only correct but also elegant and efficient. The future of software development is in your hands, and with the knowledge and skills you have gained, you are well-equipped to shape it.

11. Real-World Applications, Future and Emerging Technologies with C++

Introduction

C++ has been a cornerstone of software development since its inception in the 1980s. Known for its performance, flexibility, and efficiency, C++ has been widely adopted in various domains, including systems programming, game development, real-time simulations, and high-performance computing. As we approach 2025, C++ continues to evolve, adapting to the demands of modern technology and emerging trends. This article explores the real-world applications of C++ in 2025, its role in future technologies, and the emerging trends that are shaping its future.

Real-World Applications of C++

1. Systems Programming and Operating Systems

C++ remains a dominant language in systems programming, where performance and low-level hardware access are critical. In 2025, C++ is still the language of choice for developing operating systems, device drivers, and embedded systems. Its ability to manage memory efficiently and interact directly with hardware makes it indispensable in this domain.

- **Operating Systems**: Major operating systems like Windows, Linux, and macOS continue to rely on C++ for their core components. The development of new operating systems, especially those designed for specialized hardware (e.g., quantum computers), also leverages C++ for its performance and control.

- **Embedded Systems**: With the proliferation of IoT devices, C++ is extensively used in embedded systems programming. Its efficiency in resource-constrained environments makes it ideal for developing firmware and real-time operating systems (RTOS) for smart devices, wearables, and industrial automation systems.

2. Game Development

The gaming industry has always been a stronghold for C++, and this trend continues into 2025. C++ is the backbone of many game engines, including Unreal Engine and CryEngine, which power some of the most popular games in the world.

- **Game Engines**: C++ is used to develop high-performance game engines that require real-time rendering, physics simulations, and AI. The language's ability to handle complex computations and manage memory efficiently makes it ideal for creating immersive gaming experiences.

- **Virtual Reality (VR) and Augmented Reality (AR)**: As VR and AR technologies advance, C++ is increasingly used to develop the underlying software that powers these experiences. The need for low-latency, high-performance rendering in VR/AR applications makes C++ a natural choice.

3. High-Performance Computing (HPC)

C++ is a key player in the field of high-performance computing, where it is used to develop software for scientific simulations, data analysis, and machine learning. In 2025, C++ continues to be a preferred language for HPC applications due to its ability to optimize performance and handle large-scale computations.

- **Scientific Simulations**: C++ is used to develop simulations for various scientific domains, including physics, chemistry, and biology. These simulations often require complex mathematical computations and the ability to process large datasets, making C++ an ideal choice.

- **Machine Learning and AI**: While Python is often associated with machine learning, C++ is increasingly used for developing high-performance machine learning frameworks and libraries. Libraries like TensorFlow and PyTorch have C++ backends that handle the heavy lifting, ensuring efficient execution of machine learning algorithms.

4. Financial Systems and Trading

The financial industry relies heavily on C++ for developing high-frequency trading systems, risk management software, and financial modeling tools. In 2025, C++ remains a critical language in this domain due to its performance and ability to handle complex calculations in real-time.

- **High-Frequency Trading (HFT)**: C++ is used to develop low-latency trading systems that can execute trades in microseconds. The language's ability to optimize performance and manage memory efficiently is crucial in this highly competitive field.

- **Risk Management and Financial Modeling**: C++ is used to develop software for risk assessment, portfolio management, and financial modeling. These applications require complex mathematical computations and the ability to process large datasets, making C++ a natural fit.

5. Aerospace and Defense

C++ is widely used in the aerospace and defense industries for developing software for flight control systems, radar systems, and simulation environments. In 2025, C++ continues to play a critical role in these domains due to its performance and reliability.

- **Flight Control Systems**: C++ is used to develop software for controlling aircraft, drones, and spacecraft. These systems require real-time processing and high reliability, making C++ an ideal choice.

- **Simulation and Training**: C++ is used to develop simulation environments for training pilots and military personnel. These simulations require realistic physics and graphics, which C++ can handle efficiently.

6. Automotive Industry

The automotive industry has seen a significant increase in the use of C++ for developing software for autonomous vehicles, advanced driver-assistance systems (ADAS), and in-vehicle infotainment systems. In 2025, C++ continues to be a key language in this domain.

- **Autonomous Vehicles**: C++ is used to develop the software that powers autonomous vehicles, including perception, planning, and control systems. These systems require real-time processing and high reliability, making C++ an ideal choice.

- **ADAS and Infotainment Systems**: C++ is used to develop software for ADAS features like lane-keeping assistance, adaptive cruise control, and collision avoidance. It is also used for developing in-vehicle infotainment systems that provide navigation, entertainment, and connectivity features.

7. Healthcare and Medical Devices

C++ is increasingly being used in the healthcare industry for developing software for medical devices, imaging systems, and patient monitoring systems. In 2025, C++ continues to play a critical role in this domain due to its performance and reliability.

- **Medical Imaging**: C++ is used to develop software for medical imaging systems like MRI, CT, and ultrasound. These systems require complex image processing algorithms and real-time performance, making C++ an ideal choice.

- **Patient Monitoring Systems**: C++ is used to develop software for patient monitoring systems that track vital signs like heart rate, blood pressure, and oxygen levels. These systems require high reliability and real-time processing, making C++ a natural fit.

Future and Emerging Technologies with/in C++

1. Quantum Computing

Quantum computing is one of the most exciting emerging technologies, and C++ is playing a significant role in its development. In 2025, C++ is used to develop quantum algorithms, simulators, and programming frameworks.

- **Quantum Algorithms**: C++ is used to implement quantum algorithms that solve complex problems in cryptography, optimization, and material science. These algorithms require high-performance computing and efficient memory management, making C++ an ideal choice.

- **Quantum Simulators**: C++ is used to develop quantum simulators that emulate the behavior of quantum computers on classical hardware. These simulators are essential for testing and validating quantum algorithms before they are run on actual quantum hardware.

- **Quantum Programming Frameworks**: C++ is used to develop programming frameworks like Qiskit and Cirq, which provide tools for writing and executing quantum programs. These frameworks often have C++ backends that handle the heavy lifting, ensuring efficient execution of quantum algorithms.

2. Edge Computing and IoT

As the Internet of Things (IoT) continues to grow, edge computing is becoming increasingly important. In 2025, C++ is used to develop software for edge devices that process data locally, reducing latency and bandwidth usage.

- **Edge AI**: C++ is used to develop AI models that run on edge devices, enabling real-time decision-making without the need for cloud connectivity. These models require efficient memory management and high performance, making C++ an ideal choice.

- **IoT Device Firmware**: C++ is used to develop firmware for IoT devices that require real-time processing and low power consumption. Its ability to interact directly with hardware and manage resources efficiently makes it a natural fit for IoT applications.

3. Blockchain and Decentralized Applications

Blockchain technology is transforming industries by enabling decentralized applications (dApps) and smart contracts. In 2025, C++ is used to develop blockchain protocols, consensus algorithms, and dApps.

- **Blockchain Protocols**: C++ is used to develop blockchain protocols like Bitcoin and Ethereum. These protocols require high performance and security, making C++ an ideal choice.

- **Consensus Algorithms**: C++ is used to implement consensus algorithms like Proof of Work (PoW) and Proof of Stake (PoS). These algorithms require complex computations and efficient memory management, making C++ a natural fit.

- **Decentralized Applications**: C++ is used to develop dApps that run on blockchain platforms. These applications require high performance and security, making C++ an ideal choice.

4. 5G and beyond

The rollout of 5G networks is transforming communication and enabling new applications like autonomous vehicles, smart cities, and remote surgery. In 2025, C++ is used to develop software for 5G infrastructure, network protocols, and applications.

- **5G Infrastructure**: C++ is used to develop software for 5G base stations, routers, and switches. These systems require high performance and low latency, making C++ an ideal choice.

- **Network Protocols**: C++ is used to implement network protocols like TCP/IP, HTTP/3, and QUIC. These protocols require efficient memory management and high performance, making C++ a natural fit.

- **5G Applications**: C++ is used to develop applications that leverage 5G connectivity, such as augmented reality, virtual reality, and remote surgery. These applications require real-time processing and high reliability, making C++ an ideal choice.

5. Artificial Intelligence and Machine Learning

AI and machine learning are transforming industries by enabling automation, predictive analytics, and intelligent decision-making. In 2025, C++ continues to play a critical role in the development of AI and machine learning frameworks, libraries, and applications.

- **AI Frameworks**: C++ is used to develop AI frameworks like TensorFlow, PyTorch, and Caffe. These frameworks often have C++ backends that handle the heavy lifting, ensuring efficient execution of AI algorithms.

- **Machine Learning Libraries**: C++ is used to develop machine learning libraries like MLpack and Shark. These libraries provide tools for implementing machine learning algorithms, making it easier for developers to build AI applications.

- **AI Applications**: C++ is used to develop AI applications like natural language processing, computer vision, and robotics. These applications require high performance and efficient memory management, making C++ an ideal choice.

6. Cybersecurity

As cyber threats continue to evolve, cybersecurity is becoming increasingly important. In 2025, C++ is used to develop software for threat detection, encryption, and secure communication.

- **Threat Detection**: C++ is used to develop software that detects and mitigates cyber threats like malware, ransomware, and phishing attacks. These systems require high performance and efficient memory management, making C++ an ideal choice.

- **Encryption**: C++ is used to implement encryption algorithms like AES, RSA, and ECC. These algorithms require complex computations and efficient memory management, making C++ a natural fit.

- **Secure Communication**: C++ is used to develop software for secure communication protocols like TLS and VPNs. These protocols require high performance and security, making C++ an ideal choice.

7. Robotics and Automation

Robotics and automation are transforming industries by enabling autonomous systems, smart factories, and intelligent machines. In 2025, C++ is used to develop software for robotics control systems, automation frameworks, and AI-driven robots.

- **Robotics Control Systems**: C++ is used to develop software for controlling robots in manufacturing, healthcare, and logistics. These systems require real-time processing and high reliability, making C++ an ideal choice.

- **Automation Frameworks**: C++ is used to develop automation frameworks that enable smart factories and industrial automation. These frameworks require high performance and efficient memory management, making C++ a natural fit.

- **AI-Driven Robots**: C++ is used to develop AI-driven robots that can perform complex tasks like object recognition, navigation, and decision-making. These robots require high performance and efficient memory management, making C++ an ideal choice.

C++ in Game Development

C++ has a significant presence in the field of game development due to its performance, versatility, and ability to work close to the hardware. Game developers often choose C++ for creating high-performance and resource intensive games. In this section, we'll explore why C++ is a popular choice for game development and how it is used in this context.

Why Choose C++ for Game Development?

1. **Performance:** Games demand high performance to deliver smooth graphics and responsive gameplay. C++ allows developers to write code that runs close to the hardware, optimizing CPU and memory usage.

2. **Portability:** C++ code can be compiled and run on various platforms, making it easier to develop games for multiple operating systems and gaming consoles.

3. **Access to Hardware:** C++ provides low-level access to hardware resources, which is essential for tasks like rendering, physics simulation, and audio processing.

4. **Game Engines:** Many popular game engines, such as Unreal Engine and Unity, use C++ as a primary or scripting language, making it a valuable skill for game developers.

5. **Community and Libraries:** C++ has a vibrant game development community, and numerous libraries and frameworks are available to streamline game development.

C++ in Game Engines

Game engines are complex software frameworks that provide essential tools and components for building games.

C++ is commonly used in game engines for the following purposes:

• **Rendering:** C++ is used to create efficient rendering pipelines that generate 2D and 3D graphics on the screen.

• **Physics Simulation:** Physics engines, responsible for realistic object interactions, often rely on C++ for high performance simulations.

• **Audio Processing:** Real-time audio processing requires low-level control over hardware, which C++ provides.

• **AI and Gameplay Logic:** C++ is used to implement game AI and logic systems to control character behavior, enemy AI, and game events.

Game Development Workflow

The typical game development workflow in C++ involves the following steps:

Concept and Design: Game designers create a concept, and artists design characters, environments, and assets.

Engine Selection: Developers choose a game engine based on the project's requirements.

Coding: Programmers write C++ code to implement game mechanics, graphics, and logic.

Testing and Debugging: Extensive testing and debugging are crucial to ensure the game functions correctly and has no critical bugs.

Optimization: Performance optimization is an ongoing process to ensure the game runs smoothly on target platforms.

Deployment: The final game is packaged and deployed to various platforms, including PC, consoles, and mobile devices.

Popular C++ Game Engines

1. **Unreal Engine:** Unreal Engine uses C++ extensively and offers Blueprints, a visual scripting language, to simplify game development.

2.   **Unity:** Unity allows C# scripting but also provides a C++ interface for performance-critical tasks.

3.   **Godot:** While primarily using its scripting language (GDScript), Godot offers a C++ API for developers seeking high performance.

4.   **CryEngine:** Known for its graphical capabilities, CryEngine allows developers to use C++ for gameplay and customization.

C++ in System Programming

System programming involves developing software that interacts closely with the underlying hardware and operating system. C++ is a popular choice for system programming due to its performance, control over memory and resources, and the ability to create efficient and low-level code. In this section, we'll explore how C++ is used in system programming and its advantages in this domain.

Advantages of Using C++ in System Programming

1.   **Performance:** System software often needs to perform tasks with minimal overhead. C++'s ability to write high-performance code and optimize resource utilization is a significant advantage.

2.   **Control Over Memory:** C++ allows precise control over memory management, which is crucial for system programs where resource efficiency is paramount.

3.   **Direct Hardware Interaction:** C++ provides mechanisms like pointers and memory addresses, allowing developers to interact directly with hardware components and write device drivers.

4.   **Compatibility:** C++ code is highly portable and can run on various platforms, making it suitable for developing system software for different operating systems.

5.   **Existing Libraries:** C++ has a rich set of libraries that are useful for system programming tasks, such as file I/O, networking, and multithreading.

Use Cases for C++ in System Programming

1. **Device Drivers:** C++ is commonly used for writing device drivers that enable hardware components to communicate with the operating system.

2. **Operating Systems:** Parts of operating systems, including the kernel, are often implemented in C++ for performance and control reasons.

3. **File Systems:** File systems require low-level access to storage devices, making C++ a suitable choice for their development.

4. **Embedded Systems:** C++ is used in embedded systems programming where memory constraints and performance optimization are critical.

5. **Network Protocols:** Implementing network protocols and socket programming benefits from C++'s efficiency.

Memory Management in System Programming

Memory management is a crucial aspect of system programming. C++ provides mechanisms like pointers, manual memory allocation, and deallocation. While these features offer fine-grained control, they also require careful handling to avoid memory leaks and undefined behavior. System programmers must be skilled in memory management techniques to ensure the reliability of their software.

Multithreading and Concurrency

System software often needs to handle multiple tasks concurrently, such as managing processes and threads. C++ provides robust support for multithreading and concurrency through features like the C++ Standard Library's threading facilities. Proper synchronization mechanisms are essential to prevent data races and ensure the correct operation of concurrent programs.

Debugging and Testing

Debugging system software can be challenging due to its low-level nature. C++ offers various debugging tools and techniques to identify and fix issues. Additionally, thorough testing, including unit testing and integration testing, is crucial to ensure the stability and reliability of system programs.

C++ in Scientific Computing

Scientific computing involves using computer algorithms and simulations to solve complex scientific and engineering problems. C++ is a preferred choice for scientific computing due to its performance, flexibility, and extensive libraries. In this section, we will delve into how C++ is applied in the field of scientific computing.

Performance Advantage

Performance is critical in scientific computing because simulations often involve processing large datasets and performing complex mathematical computations. C++ offers low-level control over memory and CPU resources, allowing developers to optimize code for maximum efficiency. This is particularly important in computational physics, chemistry, biology, and engineering, where milliseconds can make a significant difference.

Libraries and Frameworks

C++ has a rich ecosystem of libraries and frameworks designed for scientific computing:

- **Eigen:** Eigen is a C++ template library for linear algebra. It provides a wide range of matrix operations and is often used for numerical simulations.

- **Boost:** The Boost C++ Libraries include various components useful for scientific computing, such as Boost.MultiArray for multidimensional arrays and Boost.odeint for solving ordinary differential equations.

- **Armadillo:** Armadillo is a C++ linear algebra library that is simple to use and provides high-performance matrix operations.

- **OpenMP and MPI:** C++ supports parallel and distributed computing through OpenMP (shared-memory parallelism) and MPI (message-passing parallelism), which are essential for scientific simulations running on multicore processors and clusters.

High-Level Languages vs. C++

While high-level languages like Python and Julia are gaining popularity in scientific computing for their ease of use, C++ remains a top choice for performance-critical components of simulations. Many scientific computing frameworks and libraries have C++ interfaces to leverage its performance advantages while providing a high-level interface for scientists and engineers.

Numerical Accuracy and Precision

Scientific computing often deals with problems that require high numerical accuracy and precision. C++ allows developers to control data types and perform operations with minimal loss of precision, making it suitable for applications such as climate modeling, molecular dynamics simulations, and finite element analysis.

Optimization Techniques

Optimizing C++ code for scientific computing involves techniques like loop unrolling, vectorization, and using compiler flags to enable optimizations. Profiling tools are essential for identifying performance bottlenecks and improving code efficiency.

Interoperability with Other Languages

In some cases, scientists and engineers use C++ alongside other languages like Python or MATLAB. C++ provides mechanisms like the Python C API and MATLAB Engine API to facilitate interoperability, allowing scientists to leverage C++'s performance while benefiting from the extensive libraries available in other languages.

C++ in Embedded Systems

Embedded systems are specialized computing systems designed to perform specific functions within a larger system. C++ is commonly used in embedded systems development due to its efficiency, control, and versatility. In this section, we will explore the role of C++ in embedded systems.

Efficiency and Resource Constraints

Embedded systems often have strict resource constraints, including limited memory and processing power. C++'s ability to control memory and hardware directly makes it a suitable choice for optimizing code to meet these constraints. Developers can fine-tune memory usage, minimize code size, and optimize performance, ensuring that the embedded system operates efficiently.

Real-Time Capabilities

Many embedded systems require real-time capabilities, where tasks must be executed within specific time constraints. C++ supports real-time programming through techniques like prioritized threads, interrupt handling, and deterministic execution. This is crucial for applications such as automotive control systems, robotics, and industrial automation.

Hardware Abstraction

C++ enables developers to create hardware-abstraction layers (HALs) that allow software to interact with hardware components without needing detailed knowledge of the underlying hardware. This abstraction simplifies development and portability across different hardware platforms.

Cross-Platform Development

Embedded systems often target various microcontrollers and processors. C++ provides the ability to write portable code that can be compiled for different architectures, reducing development time and effort. Tools like cross compilers and embedded development frameworks support this process.

Safety-Critical Systems

In safety-critical applications like medical devices, aerospace systems, and automotive safety systems, C++ is employed with strict adherence to safety standards such as ISO 26262 and DO-178C. Developers use methodologies like static analysis, formal verification, and code reviews to ensure code correctness and reliability.

Embedded Libraries and Tools

C++ has a range of libraries and tools designed for embedded systems development:

• **CMSIS (Cortex Microcontroller Software Interface Standard):** Developed by ARM, CMSIS provides a common interface for Cortex-M microcontrollers and includes hardware abstraction, peripheral drivers, and Realtime operating system (RTOS) support.

• **RTOSs:** Real-time operating systems like FreeRTOS, RTLinux, and µC/OS-II provide task scheduling and management for embedded applications, allowing developers to create responsive and deterministic systems.

- **Embedded IDEs:** Integrated development environments (IDEs) like Keil, IAR Embedded Workbench, and PlatformIO offer specialized tools for embedded C++ development, including code debugging and hardware simulation.

C++ in Software Engineering

C++ is a powerful and versatile programming language that finds extensive use in various domains of software engineering. In this section, we will explore the role of C++ in software engineering practices and how it contributes to building robust, efficient, and maintainable software systems.

1. Systems Software Development

C++ is a preferred choice for developing systems software, including operating systems, device drivers, and middleware. Its low-level capabilities, performance optimization features, and direct memory control make it suitable for tasks that require interaction with hardware and low-level system components.

```cpp
#include <iostream> int main() { std::cout
<< "Hello, Systems World!" << std::endl;
return 0;
}
```

2. Performance-Critical Applications

For performance-critical applications like high-frequency trading systems, scientific simulations, and video game engines, C++ offers the control and performance needed. Features like manual memory management and inline assembly allow developers to fine-tune code for maximum speed.

```cpp
// High-performance matrix multiplication in C++ void
matrixMultiply(const double* A, const double* B, double* C, int
size) { // Implementation for matrix multiplication
// ...

}
```

3. Large-Scale Software Projects

C++'s support for modular programming, encapsulation, and object-oriented design principles makes it suitable for managing large-scale software projects. Features like classes, namespaces, and templates aid in structuring code and managing complexity.

```cpp
// C++ class for representing a bank
account class BankAccount { public:

BankAccount(const std::string& name, double balance) : owner(name),
balance(balance) {} void deposit(double amount) { balance += amount;
```

```
} double getBalance()
const { return balance;
} private:
std::string owner;
double balance;
};
```

4.   Cross-Platform Development

C++ supports cross-platform development, allowing software engineers to write code that can be compiled for different operating systems and architectures. This cross-platform compatibility is valuable for developing software that runs on multiple devices and environments.

5.   Code Reusability

C++ promotes code reusability through object-oriented programming (OOP) and the use of libraries and frameworks. Developers can create reusable classes and components, reducing redundancy and accelerating development.

```
// Example of code reuse with C++
classes class Rectangle { public:
Rectangle(double width, double height) : width(width),
height(height) {} double area() const { return width * height;
} private:
double
width;
double
height;
};
// Reusing the Rectangle class
Rectangle room(5.0, 4.0);
double roomArea = room.area();
```

6.   Software Testing and Debugging

C++ provides tools and frameworks for software testing and debugging, including unit testing libraries and debugging tools like GDB. These aid in verifying software correctness and identifying and resolving issues efficiently.

7.   Collaboration and Teamwork

In software engineering projects involving teams of developers, C++ code can be modularized, documented, and version-controlled using tools like Git. This facilitates collaboration and ensures that the codebase remains maintainable and well-organized.

The Future of C++ Programming

Emerging Trends in C++ Development

C++ has a rich history and a bright future, as it continues to evolve to meet the demands of modern software development. In this section, we'll explore some of the emerging trends and developments in C++ programming, highlighting how the language is adapting to new challenges and opportunities.

1. **C++ Standards Evolution:** The C++ language has been evolving with regular releases of new standards. The C++ Standardization Committee (ISO/IEC JTC1/SC22/WG21) continues to refine the language, adding new features, improving performance, and enhancing safety. Developers can expect continued updates and improvements to the language.

2. **Modern C++ Practices:** C++ developers are increasingly adopting modern coding practices and features. Concepts, modules, and ranges are some of the features introduced in recent standards (C++20 and beyond) that promote cleaner, safer, and more expressive code.

```cpp
// Example of using C++20 concepts
template <typename T> concept Numeric
= std::is_arithmetic<T>::value;
template <Numeric T>
T add(T a, T b) {
return a + b;
}
```

1. **Cross-Platform Development:** With the growth of cross-platform applications, C++ is gaining popularity as a language of choice. Tools like CMake and libraries like Qt make it easier to develop applications that run on various platforms, including Windows, macOS, Linux, and mobile devices.

2. **Concurrency and Parallelism:** C++ provides features like the Standard Library's <thread> and <future> components, as well as support for parallelism through the <execution> library. As multi-core processors become more prevalent, C++ developers are leveraging these features for efficient parallel programming. // Example of C++17 parallelism with std::for_each

```cpp
#include <algorithm>
#include <vector>
int main() { std::vector<int> numbers
= {1, 2, 3, 4, 5};
std::for_each(std::execution::par,
numbers.begin(), numbers.end(),

[](int& n) { n *= 2; });
return 0;
}
```

1. **Embedded Systems and IoT:** C++ is well-suited for embedded systems and Internet of Things (IoT) development due to its performance and portability. Developers are using C++ to create software for devices ranging from microcontrollers to edge computing devices.

2. **AI and Machine Learning:** C++ is gaining traction in the field of AI and machine learning. Libraries like TensorFlow and PyTorch offer C++ APIs, enabling developers to harness the power of machine learning while benefiting from C++'s performance and integration capabilities.

3. **Community and Education:** The C++ community remains strong, with forums, conferences, and online resources for learning and collaboration. Educational institutions continue to teach C++ as part of computer science and engineering curricula, ensuring a new generation of C++ programmers.

4. **Safety and Security:** As software security becomes increasingly critical, C++ standards incorporate features like the C++ Core Guidelines and contract programming to improve code safety and reliability.

```
// Example of C++20 contracts int
divide(int a, int b) [[expects: b != 0]] {
return a / b;
}
```

Ecosystem and Libraries: The C++ ecosystem boasts a wide range of libraries and frameworks for various domains, from game development to scientific computing. The availability of these resources contributes to C++'s continued relevance.

C++ in Emerging Technologies

C++ has a rich history and a long-standing presence in the world of software development. While it is renowned for its use in various domains, it also plays a vital role in emerging technologies that shape our future. In this section, we'll explore how C++ is making its mark in cutting-edge fields like the Internet of Things (IoT), Artificial Intelligence (AI), and more.

C++ and IoT (Internet of Things)

The Internet of Things refers to the network of interconnected physical devices, vehicles, appliances, and other objects that communicate and exchange data with each other. C++ is well-suited for IoT development due to its efficiency, low-level capabilities, and portability across different hardware platforms.

Embedded Systems

C++ is often used in embedded systems programming, which is at the heart of IoT. Microcontrollers and small computing devices powering IoT devices can benefit from C++'s ability to manage hardware resources efficiently.

Libraries like the Arduino C++ libraries enable developers to create firmware for various IoT applications.

```
// Example of Arduino C++ code for an IoT device

#include <Arduino.h>
void setup() {
pinMode(LED_BUILTIN, OUTPUT);
} void loop() {
digitalWrite(LED_BUILTIN,
HIGH); delay(1000);
digitalWrite(LED_BUILTIN,
LOW); delay(1000);
}
```

C++ and AI (Artificial Intelligence)

Artificial Intelligence is another field where C++ finds its application. While Python is popular for AI development due to its libraries and ease of use, C++ offers performance advantages in AI applications that require high computational power.

Machine Learning Frameworks

C++ is used in the development of machine learning and deep learning libraries like TensorFlow and Caffe. These libraries provide C++ APIs that allow developers to build AI models, perform data analysis, and deploy AI solutions with high performance.

```
// Example of using TensorFlow C++
API #include <tensorflow/c/c_api.h>
int main() {
// Create a TensorFlow session and load a pre-trained model

TF_Session* session = nullptr;
TF_Graph* graph = nullptr;
TF_Status* status = TF_NewStatus();
// Perform inference and process AI results

// Clean up resources

TF_CloseSession(session, status);
TF_DeleteSession(session, status);
TF_DeleteGraph(graph);
TF_DeleteStatus(status);
return 0;
```

}

C++ and Emerging Technologies

C++ continues to influence and contribute to emerging technologies like blockchain, quantum computing, and autonomous systems. Its ability to provide low-level control, optimize performance, and ensure code reliability makes it a valuable choice in these cutting-edge fields.

In blockchain development, C++ is used to build and optimize blockchain node software. In quantum computing, C++ helps in developing control systems and simulations for quantum hardware. In autonomous systems like self-driving cars and drones, C++ enables real-time control and processing.

In conclusion, C++ remains a versatile and adaptable language that finds its place in emerging technologies, ensuring that it remains a relevant and valuable skill for developers seeking to contribute to the future of technology and innovation. Developers proficient in C++ can leverage its power to solve complex problems and drive progress in various domains.

Conclusion: The Enduring Legacy and Future of C++ in 2025 and beyond

As we reflect on the role of C++ in 2025, it is clear that this programming language, which has been a cornerstone of software development for over four decades, continues to thrive and adapt to the ever-evolving technological landscape. C++ has proven its resilience and versatility, remaining a critical tool in a wide range of industries and applications. Its ability to deliver high performance, efficiency, and low-level control has made it indispensable in domains where these attributes are paramount. Moreover, C++ is not just maintaining its relevance—it is actively shaping the future of technology, playing a pivotal role in emerging fields such as quantum computing, artificial intelligence, edge computing, and blockchain.

In this conclusion, we will explore the enduring legacy of C++, its continued relevance in 2025, and the factors that ensure its place as a foundational language in the world of software development. We will also discuss the challenges and opportunities that lie ahead for C++ as it continues to evolve in response to the demands of modern technology.

The Enduring Legacy of C++

C++ was born out of the need for a language that could combine the low-level control of C with the abstraction and organizational capabilities of object-oriented programming. Since its inception in the 1980s, it has become one of the most widely used programming languages in the world. Its legacy is built on several key strengths:

1. **Performance and Efficiency**: C++ is renowned for its ability to deliver high performance and efficient memory management. This makes it ideal for applications where speed and resource utilization are critical, such as game development, high-frequency trading, and real-time systems.

2. **Flexibility and Control**: C++ provides developers with fine-grained control over hardware and memory, enabling them to optimize their code for specific use cases. This level of control is unmatched by higher-level languages, making C++ a go-to choice for systems programming and embedded systems.

3. **Cross-Platform Compatibility**: C++ is a portable language, meaning that code written in C++ can be compiled and run on a wide range of platforms, from embedded devices to supercomputers. This cross-platform capability has contributed to its widespread adoption across industries.

4. **Rich Ecosystem**: Over the years, C++ has developed a rich ecosystem of libraries, frameworks, and tools that support a wide range of applications. From game engines like Unreal Engine to machine learning frameworks like TensorFlow, the C++ ecosystem continues to grow and evolve.

5. **Community and Standards**: The C++ community is one of the most active and dedicated in the software development world. The language is governed by the ISO C++ Standard Committee, which regularly updates the language to meet the needs of modern developers. The introduction of C++11, C++14, C++17, and C++20 has brought significant improvements, making the language more expressive, safer, and easier to use.

C++: Continued Relevance

As we look ahead to 2025, C++ remains a critical language in several key areas:

1. Systems Programming and Operating Systems

C++ continues to be the language of choice for developing operating systems, device drivers, and embedded systems. Its ability to interact directly with hardware and manage memory efficiently makes it indispensable in this domain. In 2025, as new hardware architectures emerge (e.g., quantum computers and specialized AI processors), C++ will play a crucial role in developing the software that powers these systems.

2. Game Development and Real-Time Simulations

The gaming industry has always been a stronghold for C++, and this trend shows no signs of slowing down. Game engines like Unreal Engine and CryEngine rely heavily on C++ for their performance and flexibility. In 2025, as virtual reality (VR) and augmented reality (AR) technologies become more mainstream, C++ will be at the forefront of creating immersive and realistic experiences.

3. High-Performance Computing (HPC)

C++ is a key player in high-performance computing, where it is used for scientific simulations, data analysis, and machine learning. In 2025, as the demand for HPC grows in fields like climate modeling, genomics, and AI, C++ will continue to be a preferred language for developing efficient and scalable solutions.

4. Financial Systems and Trading

The financial industry relies on C++ for developing high-frequency trading systems, risk management software, and financial modeling tools. In 2025, as financial markets become more complex and data-driven, C++ will remain a critical tool for building high-performance and reliable systems.

5. Emerging Technologies

C++ is playing a significant role in shaping the future of technology. In 2025, it is at the heart of several emerging fields:

- **Quantum Computing**: C++ is used to develop quantum algorithms, simulators, and programming frameworks, enabling researchers to explore the potential of quantum computing.

- **Edge Computing and IoT**: C++ is used to develop software for edge devices that process data locally, reducing latency and bandwidth usage in IoT applications.

- **Blockchain and Decentralized Applications**: C++ is used to develop blockchain protocols, consensus algorithms, and decentralized applications, enabling secure and transparent transactions.

- **5G and Beyond**: C++ is used to develop software for 5G infrastructure, network protocols, and applications, enabling faster and more reliable communication.

Challenges and Opportunities for C++

While C++ remains a powerful and versatile language, it is not without its challenges. As we move into 2025, the following challenges and opportunities will shape the future of C++:

1. Competition from Modern Languages

C++ faces competition from newer languages like Rust, Go, and Swift, which offer modern features, improved safety, and easier syntax. These languages are gaining traction in domains traditionally dominated by C++, such as systems programming and game development. To remain competitive, C++ must continue to evolve and address the pain points of developers, such as memory safety and ease of use.

2. Memory Safety and Security

Memory safety is a longstanding issue in C++, as manual memory management can lead to vulnerabilities like buffer overflows and memory leaks. In 2025, as cybersecurity threats become more sophisticated, addressing these issues will be critical. The C++ community is already working on solutions, such as smart pointers and static analysis tools, to improve memory safety and security.

3. Adapting to New Hardware Architectures

As new hardware architectures emerge, such as quantum computers and specialized AI processors, C++ must adapt to take full advantage of these technologies. This will require updates to the language standard and the development of new libraries and tools.

4. Simplifying Development

C++ has a reputation for being complex and difficult to learn, which can deter new developers. In 2025, efforts to simplify the language and improve developer productivity will be crucial. Features like modules (introduced in C++20) and improved tooling can help make C++ more accessible to a broader audience.

5. Embracing Modern Programming Paradigms

C++ must continue to embrace modern programming paradigms, such as functional programming and concurrency, to remain relevant in a rapidly changing technological landscape. The introduction of features like lambda expressions, coroutines, and parallel algorithms in recent standards is a step in the right direction.

The Future of C++

The future of C++ is bright, as it continues to evolve and adapt to the demands of modern technology. Several trends will shape the future of C++ in 2025 and beyond:

1. Continued Evolution of the Language

The ISO C++ Standard Committee is committed to regularly updating the language to meet the needs of developers. Future standards (e.g., C++23 and beyond) will likely introduce new features and improvements that enhance performance, safety, and usability.

2. Integration with Emerging Technologies

C++ will continue to play a key role in emerging technologies like quantum computing, AI, and blockchain. Its performance and flexibility make it an ideal choice for developing the software that powers these technologies.

3. Focus on Developer Experience

Improving the developer experience will be a key focus for the C++ community. This includes simplifying the language, improving tooling, and providing better documentation and resources for developers.

4. Collaboration with Other Languages

C++ will increasingly be used in conjunction with other languages, such as Python and Rust, to leverage the strengths of each language. For example, C++ can be used for performance-critical components, while Python can be used for scripting and prototyping.

5. Growing Community and Ecosystem

The C++ community is one of the most active and dedicated in the software development world. As the language continues to evolve, the community will play a crucial role in driving its growth and adoption.

Final Thoughts

C++ has come a long way since its inception, and its journey is far from over. In 2025, it remains a vital language in the world of software development, powering everything from operating systems and game engines to quantum algorithms and AI-driven robots. Its performance, flexibility, and efficiency make it indispensable in domains where these attributes are critical.

As we look to the future, C++ will continue to evolve and adapt to the demands of modern technology. While challenges remain, the C++ community is committed to addressing these issues and ensuring that the language remains relevant in a rapidly changing world. Whether you're a seasoned developer or just starting out, C++ offers a powerful and versatile toolset that can help you bring your ideas to life.

In conclusion, C++ is not just a language—it is a legacy, a community, and a foundation for the future of technology. As we move into 2025 and beyond, C++ will continue to shape the world of software development, enabling us to build faster, smarter, and more efficient systems that push the boundaries of what is possible.

12. Final Thoughts

Thank you for embarking on this journey through C++ Explorer's Handbook: A Beginner's Guide to Mastery. Your dedication to learning C++ and honing your programming skills is truly commendable. Whether you're taking your first steps into coding or sharpening your expertise, I hope this book has provided the clarity and confidence to move forward.

But the journey doesn't end here. If you enjoyed exploring C++, you might find yourself asking:

- How can I take my programming skills to the next level?
- What are the best ways to optimize databases for efficiency?
- How do modern languages like Rust, Python, or Go shape the future of software development?

If these questions intrigue you, I invite you to explore my other works, including The Rust Alchemist, The Python Alchemist, Golang Pro Whisperer, and SQL Mastery: Unlocking the Power of Databases. Each book is designed to deepen your understanding and help you master new technologies with a hands-on approach.

Stay curious, keep coding, and never stop exploring the possibilities of programming.

Until next time happy coding!

Mike Zephalon